T0342107

DEEPLY RESPONSIBLE BUSINESS

DEEPLY RESPONSIBLE BUSINESS

A GLOBAL HISTORY OF VALUES-DRIVEN LEADERSHIP

GEOFFREY JONES

HARVARD UNIVERSITY PRESS

Cambridge, Massachusetts

London, England

2023

Cataloging-in-Publication Data available from the Library of Congress

ISBN: 978-0-674-91653-1 (alk. paper)

CONTENTS

DEEPLY RESPONSIBLE BUSINESS

INTRODUCTION

PROFIT OR PURPOSE?

On June 4, 1927, a crowd of four thousand gathered for a large ceremony to inaugurate a new campus for the Harvard Business School set apart from the historical Harvard campus in Cambridge across the Charles River in Boston. This was the "Roaring Twenties," a prosperous time for the United States, and the campus was financed by a $5 million gift ($75 million in 2021 dollars) from George F. Baker, the former president of the First National Bank of New York, later known as Citibank. The market value of the New York Stock Exchange had risen 20 percent per annum since 1922, and concentration of wealth was approaching a level not seen again until the 2000s.[1]

At some point in the proceedings, the dean of the Business School, Wallace B. Donham, gave a short address that was more of a warning than a celebration. Scientific advances may have opened up "new opportunities for happiness," he observed, but these would not be secured without "a higher degree of responsibility." Business leaders, he went on, needed to develop "social consciousness," accompanied by "competently equipped intelligence and wide vision."[2]

In a longer article published in the *Harvard Business School Alumni Bulletin* eight months later, Donham further clarified his vision of what he called "the social significance of business." He wrote:

> Unless more of our business leaders learn to exercise their powers and responsibilities with a definitively increased sense of responsibility towards other groups in the community . . . our civilization

1

may well head for one of its periods of decline. . . . Political leadership is on the wane while national and international problems assume more vital significance. The stake of the ordinary man in the material developments of the time is large, but these material things have apparently not produced a higher degree of happiness. . . . On all sides, complicated social, political and international questions press for solution, while the leaders who are competent to solve these problems are strangely missing. These conditions are transforming the world simultaneously for better and for worse. They compel a complete reappraisal of the significance of business in the scheme of things.[3]

The warning of a threat to "civilization" at the height of an economic boom might have seemed eccentric to the crowd gathered to celebrate the opening of the Allston campus, and to readers of the *Alumni Bulletin* at the time. In retrospect, his words were prophetic. Twenty months later, the Wall Street crash would set off a massive economic depression that spread across the globe, with profound consequences, including the rise of the Nazi Party in Germany.

Donham's injunction to business leaders was bold. He was not asking them to donate more money to charity to help the less fortunate. Instead, he called for business to fill a perceived leadership void and assume responsibility for saving "civilization." His admonition appears to have had limited effect. The Wall Street crash prompted some amount of self-reflection among business leaders, but there were no radical changes in business practices. It was President Franklin D. Roosevelt's New Deal that aspired to change how the American economy worked through public spending and new social policies such as the introduction of social security. These policies were opposed by all but a handful of the leaders of large corporations. Over the years influential voices, some of them members of the faculty of the Harvard Business School, others farther afield in the windy city of Chicago, would insist that a business's first responsibility was to its shareholders and that it was a mistake to suggest that business leaders should seek to play a part in righting society's wrongs. For several decades, from the 1980s until recently, these voices became the dominant ones.

Donham was neither the first nor the last person to call for business leaders to exercise a positive social impact beyond making profits. Almost one hundred years later, in the aftermath of another shock to the global economy, identical calls are frequently raised in the context of the looming ecological crisis, societal inequalities, and discussions of how best to shore up our faltering democracy. Dominic Barton, the global managing director of McKinsey, denounced short-term thinking by companies obsessed with quarterly reporting.[4] "Companies must benefit all of their stakeholders," Larry Fink, the chief executive of BlackRock, the world's largest asset manager, starkly declared in his annual letter to CEOs in 2018, "including shareholders, employees, customers, and the communities in which they operate."[5] In 2019, 181 chief executives from the Business Roundtable, an association of leaders of the largest US corporations, signed a statement pledging to run their companies "for the benefit of all stakeholders—customers, employees, suppliers, communities, and shareholders."[6]

There is reason to be skeptical whether these recent calls for enhanced responsibility will be answered any more than were Donham's. Global business today is by and large not only relentlessly profit seeking but also well skilled in warping institutions of government and law to serve corporate interests. The opening decades of the twenty-first century saw an extraordinary series of big-name corporate scandals in the United States and many other countries, and there is plenty of evidence of repeated ethical lapses across business systems. But an alternative movement is also gaining steam, supported by younger entrepreneurs committed to engaging with environmental and social inequities, that places purpose and social responsibility at the heart of their business model.

A wide range of critics have asserted that the problems of contemporary capitalism are systems-wide and pose major threats to society, the environment, and democracy.[7] The giant philanthropic foundations created by multibillionaire tech entrepreneurs in the

United States have been lambasted as a charade for rich business elites to dodge taxes and extend their control.[8] Withering criticisms of contemporary capitalism have been joined by wide-ranging technocratic proposals to fix the entire economic system. *Re-imagining Capitalism: Building a Responsible Long-Term Model,* a collection published in 2016 whose editors include Dominic Barton, made the case for introducing major changes ranging from the institution of policy measures to reduce income and educational inequality to the elimination of quarterly reporting, the creation of a bigger role for long-term institutional investors like pension funds, and the establishment of incentives for company boards to act more like owners pursuing long-term value creation rather than short-term gains.[9] Five years later, Harvard Business School professor Rebecca Henderson argued in *Reimagining Capitalism in a World on Fire* that management needs to become more purpose-driven and to pursue stakeholder approaches. She also called, among other things, for the financial system to be "rewired" to permit longer time horizons and for the wholesale renewal of civil society and government.[10]

In contrast to studies that seek to rewrite the rules of the game, including changing individual behavior—Henderson implores individuals to step outside their routines by eating less red meat, driving less, and becoming active in forcing corporations and politicians to be better citizens—this book argues that the best starting point for reimagining capitalism as a system is to reimagine business, as well as its social purpose. I have approached this ambitious task by looking at the history of business leaders who, since the nineteenth century and around the world, have pursued a broader social purpose than simply making profits and who have seen business as a way of improving society, and even solving the world's problems. This may seem hopelessly naïve. But many of these businesses were successful, though financial success was not their only metric of achievement. These stories invite us to learn from history by asking certain key questions. What does a responsible business serving a social purpose really look like? What distinguishes these businesses from their competitors? What was the intent of business leaders who pursued social purpose? Is this a practical proposition? If such responsible businesses have existed in the past, why have they never become the norm? Does good business always, or ever, translate into good profits? Is business acting beyond its specific domain if it seeks to be beneficial to society? At a more fundamental level, we need to ask whether meaningful change on poverty or climate change can only come from governments.

This book takes as its starting point Donham's call for individual business leaders to have a "higher degree of responsibility" and explores what this enigmatic phrase might mean today by looking at specific examples from the past two hundred years, when business leaders operating under radically different conditions have gone beyond narrow profit seeking in ways that Donham envisaged. I term these endeavors "deep responsibility" to distinguish them from the superficial rhetoric of "corporate social responsibility"—a language available to any corporation that sprinkles a few good deeds on top of its not-so-good works.

My central hypothesis is that deeply responsible business leaders are motivated by a set of values that shape their practices. For some, it is the bedrock of virtuous character in leaders that prompts them to act in a fashion that promotes human flourishing, a term the management scholar John Ehrenfeld has defined as "the full realization of the human potential."[11] Honesty, fairness, loyalty, compassion, courage, and generosity are among the most important of these. These virtues are reinforced by practical wisdom, what Aristotle called "phronesis," which enables the virtues of character to be exercised. The philosopher Alasdair MacIntyre has dismissed the possibility that a manager in a for-profit business could ever be virtuous.[12] My book will challenge that assumption. Meanwhile, Ikujiro Nonaka and Hirotaka Takeuchi's *The Wise Company* argues that businesses have no place for virtue, because practical wisdom alone is the key. They find such practical wisdom most often in Japanese management, but my aim is to show it can be seen in many contexts.[13]

Perhaps the most influential critic of a purpose-driven business model was Milton Friedman, a Nobel laureate economist at the

University of Chicago and apostle of the free market, who insisted in a widely cited article published in the *New York Times Magazine* in 1970, as the title proclaimed, that "The Social Responsibility of Business Is to Increase Its Profits." The responsibility of corporate executives, Friedman argued, was to "make as much money as possible while conforming to the basic rules of the society."[14] Friedman's view helped transform business leaders' perception of their purpose and function not only in America but around the world. We will look at its impact and consider the arguments and evidence, in purpose-driven businesses, of those who fundamentally disagreed.

I describe another type of value driving deep responsibility as spirituality. As this might evoke misleading images of unworldly saints and raise doubts about the relevance of my historical cases to the present day, I would like to stress that my meaning is broad and holistic. While a minority of the business leaders studied in this book held strong religious beliefs, including Christian, Jain, and Muslim, others were influenced by secular philosophies or by their own life experiences. I define "spirituality" broadly as an implicit or explicit belief in the interconnectedness of all life and the planet that translates into a set of guiding principles and values.[15] Such values promote genuine moral commitment, reduce fear of unknown futures, benefit others besides the individual actor, and encourage a holistic understanding of problems and solutions.[16]

This book will underscore three elements common among deeply responsible business leaders. The first is the choice of an industry with some form of social value that is not actively harmful. The second is the nature of the interaction with stakeholders beyond investors, including employees, suppliers, customers, and government. Deeply responsible business leaders do not engage in exploitative and harmful relationships with these stakeholders and choose instead to interact with purpose and humility. Finally, deeply responsible business leaders support communities. Community is a profoundly important component of human society, yet it is a construct that has often been undermined by the ongoing rise of individualism and the forces of globalization.

The business leaders I have chosen to profile should be seen as the progenitors of the socially responsible businesses of today. The important lessons, and valuable warnings, that these stories reveal are the subject of this book.

Varieties of Business Purpose and Responsibility over Time

Donham was not the first person to ponder the purpose and social responsibility of business. There is a long historical tradition of debate dating back to the social reform movements inspired by the social hardship that accompanied the Industrial Revolution, which many of the business leaders profiled in this book contributed to in important ways. One finds recurring themes, with the only constant being a lack of consensus. Certainly the view, widespread in the United States and many other countries from the 1980s on, that the sole purpose of business was to maximize value for shareholders was never dominant historically. Part of my aim with this book is to put that now-dominant view into historical perspective and to show that what many take to be an article of faith is in fact an extreme and problematic proposition.

Businesses of one sort or another have been around for millennia, long before modern capitalism, and so have questions about corporate ethics and responsibility, even if they weren't expressed in that language.[17] The greed of merchants and financiers has been an abiding concern across all societies, offending morals so deeply that bad business behavior is a feature of comic literature across cultures and proscribed by religious taboos. Merchants and financiers were rebuked in medieval Europe for feeling no responsibility for anything beyond their own selfish interests.[18] "Although it is hard to imagine today," the accounting historian Jacob Soll has written, "guilt weighed heavily on medieval bankers and merchants."[19] As modern industry emerged in eighteenth-century Britain, there were breathtaking examples of skullduggery and moral failure, as well as extravagant financial swindles like the South Sea Bubble of 1720. Fraud was a regular occurrence. But so was the push for greater benevolence.[20]

It is widely thought that in *The Wealth of Nations*, published in 1776, the Scottish philosopher Adam Smith cast aside concerns about the destructive aspects of financial speculation, suggesting that making money should occur regardless of ethical consider-ations, ushering in a new age of capitalism.[21] A businessperson's pur-suit of self-interest would, in Smith's famous phrase, work through the "invisible hand" of the market "to promote an end which was no part of his intention." Smith continued, "By pursuing his own interest he frequently promotes that of the society more effectually than when he really intended to promote it."[22] But Smith wasn't really saying what many today want to believe he said. Often overlooked, especially recently, is that he excluded from this benefi-cial cycle of cause and effect a category of financial speculators he called "projectors" who sought "extraordinary profits." He sup-ported legal restrictions on interest rates for that reason and also made clear his disdain for gross inequality. "No society can surely be flourishing and happy," he observed, "of which the far greater part of the members are poor and miserable."[23] The economic his-torian Emma Rothschild has made it clear that the idea that Smith was simply saying, that unfettered market forces would lead to an optimal general equilibrium, is a skewed reinterpretation of his more complex and ethically informed views.[24]

Smith mentioned the invisible hand only once in *The Wealth of Nations*, but in the 1790 edition of his first book, *The Theory of Moral Sentiments*, first published thirty-one years earlier, he addressed the subject at greater length and was more specific about the bene-fits it delivered. It led, he wrote, to "nearly the same distribution of the necessities of life, which would have been made, had the earth been divided into equal portions among all its inhabitants."[25]

While Smith's first book stressed the distributional role of the in-visible hand in later editions, the original volume featured an actor called the "Impartial Spectator." This was an imaginary figure who might be equated with the conscience, within each person, that en-couraged an interest in the fortunes and happiness of others.[26] The Impartial Spectator provided an ethical framework within which capitalist markets could best function.[27] The character nurtured the virtues—temperance, justice, prudence, courage, benevolence, love—that Smith saw as essential to building "flourishing" societies. This emphasis on the importance of virtue placed him in a philosophical tradition extending back to Aristotle.[28]

The apocryphal father of capitalism's belief that business had a responsibility to operate within an ethical framework was echoed by subsequent generations, although there were many different opinions on the form this responsibility should take. As industry transformed the world, changing social and economic conditions placed the question of the responsibility of business leaders in a stark light. Wealth soared in the industrializing West during the nineteenth and early twentieth centuries, but with gross inequalities as the owners of capital grew rich while urban factory workers found themselves living and working in squalid conditions with little to no social protection. A mixture of ethical considerations and self-interest encouraged some large employers to provide welfare benefits for their workforces. Others used their new wealth to engage in philanthropy.

Among the most radical proponents of philanthropy was Andrew Carnegie, who became hugely wealthy building a steel business in the United States. Carnegie argued in an essay entitled "The Gospel of Wealth," published in 1889, that business leaders had a responsibility to use their wealth to promote social good. True to his word, he gave away almost all of his personal fortune of $145 million (around $10 billion in 2021 dollars) to establish the Carnegie Foundation in 1911, whose mission was "to promote the advancement and diffusion of knowledge and understanding."[29] Meanwhile, another type of stark wealth gap cropped up between the industrial nations of the West and most of the rest of the world, which lagged in developing modern industries and became—often under Western colonial tutelage—suppliers of commodities and food to the affluent West.

The first three chapters of Part I of this book, "A Question of Responsibility," consider how leaders of large businesses in Britain, the United States, and Germany responded to the central challenge of inequality that arose in this era. George Cadbury, Edward Filene, and Robert Bosch, the three central characters in these chapters, addressed different aspects of this broad challenge and proposed different solutions. They shared a commitment to radical ideas about the social responsibility of business and a willingness to execute on those ideas. They held a common commitment to ethical behavior and cared deeply about the welfare of their employees. Crucially, they also recognized the limits to what could be achieved by a single business enterprise and shared a belief that their responsibility extended beyond the borders of their firms. Shibusawa Eiichi, one of the central characters in Chapter 4 along with India's J. N. Tata, was their contemporary, and shared these qualities and beliefs, though he was born in a country (Japan) that had not taken part in the first wave of industrialization. As a result, he pursued a vision of business contributing to a more affluent and more equitable future for his society.

While in Smith's time thousands of small, family-owned firms competed mostly in their local markets, by the first half of the twentieth century some American and European businesses had become huge corporations that spanned the globe, dominating new industries such as automobiles and oil. This is the historical backdrop of Part II, "Turbulence." Although family ownership remained important, a growing separation of ownership and control precipitated calls for the professional managers of large corporations to address perceived societal ills. These trends in the corporate world took place in the context of major political and economic shocks that reverberated around the world: two world wars, the Great Depression, the Cold War, and decolonization.

The three chapters in Part II explore developments in business responsibility in this new era. The growth of big business occasioned wide-ranging debates about the societal responsibilities, if any, of what had become very large organizations.[30] Chapter 5 examines the interwar endeavors to incorporate social and ethical responsibility into the education of the next generation of professional managers of large corporations, spurring the rise of the first business schools. This chapter focuses on Wallace Donham, the dean of the Harvard

Business School whose speech opened this introduction, and the philosopher Alfred North Whitehead, who wanted the leaders of large corporations "to think greatly" about their role in society.

Chapter 6 considers the responsibility of business leaders in the interwar struggle for independence in India and the subsequent building of a new nation. It shows that the leader of the independence struggle, Mohandas Gandhi, held well-developed views concerning the responsibilities of business to all stakeholders, as well as a belief that it was its obligation to uphold the highest ethical standards. The chapter focuses on Kasturbhai Lalbhai, who built a profitable textile manufacturing business while supporting the independence struggle, operating it to high ethical standards and navigating the new complexities of independent India in a restrained fashion.

Chapter 7 brings us back to the United States after the end of World War II, when the view that business leaders had a social responsibility was becoming formalized. In interwar Britain, Quaker business families associated in particular with Benjamin Seebohm Rowntree had already become prominent proponents of the view that business should subordinate private gain to public good. Rowntree and his associates published powerful and influential books on the responsibilities of business.[31] Oliver Sheldon's *The Philosophy of Management,* published in 1923, was especially wide ranging. The third chapter, entitled "The Social Responsibility of Management," maintained that the output of industry needed to be assessed by a "double valuation" of "ethical" and "economic" standards.[32] In the wake of America's victory in World War II, as a result of the desire to make capitalism as attractive as possible to offset Soviet propaganda in the Cold War, such ideas moved into the mainstream. Jeremy Moon has described Howard Bowen's *The Social Responsibilities of the Businessman,* published in 1953, as the first study "to formally examine corporate responsibility in detail."[33]

The business leaders profiled in Chapter 7 operated at a time when the view that large corporations should be socially responsible was prevalent in the United States, although there were considerable disagreements as to what this actually meant. The chapter focuses on a number of cases of deep responsibility, including the automobile manufacturer George Romney, who pursued strategies to combat wasteful consumerism by promoting the compact car, and computer pioneers William C. Norris and An Wang, who used their businesses to provide employment and other opportunities to people from impoverished urban neighborhoods.

Part III of this book, "New Paradigms," addresses this recent era, when shareholder capitalism was the norm. Milton Friedman's skepticism about the social responsibility of business did not operate in a vacuum. He was a prominent figure in the Chicago school of free-market economists who made the case for laissez-faire capitalism, extolling the virtues of relying on unfettered markets with minimal government intervention. Two economists working in this tradition, Michael Jensen and William Meckling, developed agency theory, which saw shareholders as principals who hired executives as their agents, whose purpose was simply to maximize financial returns for their principals. Executives were to be incentivized by stock options, focusing their minds on share prices and stock buybacks. Although during these decades corporations increasingly proclaimed their commitments to sustainability, the assumption that the purpose of business is to maximize shareholder value spread widely. Accompanying these developments were broad shifts in the political economy, as, beginning in the 1980s, many governments liberalized and deregulated their economies, perceiving the market rather than public policy as the most efficient means of wealth creation.

The chapters in Part III feature business leaders who sought alternative paradigms to shareholder value and agency theory, instead stressing the broader social responsibilities of firms. Chapter 8 looks at a cohort of self-identified values-driven businesses that flourished during the 1970s and 1980s and reflected the new belief that markets were better placed than governments to solve societal ills, but disagreed profoundly with the view that the purpose of business was to maximize shareholder value. Instead, the founders of businesses like Patagonia, Ben & Jerry's, and The Body Shop believed that a for-profit business could be a vehicle to achieve a more just and sustainable world. The focus here is on Anita Roddick, whose beauty retail business The Body Shop became synonymous for a time with radical social and ecological responsibility of business, though it was later shown that her impact in raising awareness of social and environmental issues was more laudable than some of her business practices.

A recurring issue in many chapters is the reliance on founders or charismatic individual business leaders to ground a vision and practice of deep responsibility in their organizations. This often raised the challenge of sustainability once that individual retired or otherwise left a firm, or if the firm sought access to finance from outside investors or the capital market.

The final two chapters consider strategies to build systems and institutions in which individual deeply responsible business leaders and their firms could find validation and support. Chapter 9 considers the oldest endeavor to build such a system. The focus is on an Egyptian biodynamic food business created by Ibrahim Abouleish and a biodynamic tea business in Darjeeling, India, developed by Sanjay Bansal. They were among the contemporary manifestations of a set of businesses founded since the 1920s under the influence of Rudolf Steiner's Anthroposophy. This movement experienced considerable growth beginning in the 1980s and played a formative role in emergent sectors such as organic food and sustainable finance.

Chapter 10 turns to more recent efforts to institutionalize deep business responsibility by defining it, measuring it, benchmarking it, and developing communities with its value. Here I will look at environmental, social, and governance (ESG) investing, pioneered by Joan Bavaria and others; the B Lab Movement and especially its important Latin American outgrowth, Sistema B; the Economy of Communion; and the recent momentum behind diffusing and supporting the steward-ownership model.

My aim is to provide concrete examples of deeply responsible business leaders operating at different times and in different contexts. This is not a textbook suggesting how to reimagine such a complex system as capitalism. My concern is rather to show how individual efforts to pursue what Donham called an "increased sense of responsibility" have succeeded and failed, and why. There is no boilerplate model for such leaders. Deeply responsible business leaders are regular human beings with all the foibles of people in general. Some are inspirational, but some of the experiments in social purpose examined here were not successful, and some were not sustainable. In some cases, virtue signaling was not borne out by virtuous practices.

The rich historical evidence presented here will do a service if it punctures facile assumptions that doing good will necessarily be good business. Pursuing profits and purpose is never easy, and sometimes the two goals are in conflict. I hope, however, to show that deep responsibility is not an idealistic fantasy but rather an essential path for the future.

PART I

A QUESTION OF
RESPONSIBILITY

CHAPTER I

THE VALUE OF HUMAN DIGNITY

GEORGE CADBURY AND QUAKER CAPITALISM

Britain, as the first industrial nation, was also the first to see the massive social and economic changes caused by industrialization. Small-scale craft manufacturing had taken place in rural cottages and workshops, but the new manufacturing industries depended on factories operating in urban areas. Factory workers received little, if any, extra income from the first stage of industrialization. Between 1770 and 1830, there was no rise in average real wages, and working and living conditions were grim. Twelve-hour workdays were the norm. Laborers worked under far more rigid supervision than had previously been the case, as employers needed a disciplined workforce if factories were to function. Child labor was widespread. There was almost no state-level protection from exploitation. It was only in 1875 that Britain passed legislation controlling the employment of children to clean factory chimneys, and in 1891 that the minimum age of employment for a factory job was raised to eleven. The poor and destitute were placed in workhouses after 1834, where they toiled under brutal conditions managed by so-called guardians, who were often local business leaders. Because men, women, and children were assigned different living areas, families were split up.

These social conditions could prevail in part because Britain was a highly constrained democracy where voting was limited to male property owners. Despite successive reforms backed by popular movements to expand the vote, by the early 1860s only just over 1.4 million could vote out of a total British population of 30 million. By 1884, two out of three men had the right to vote. It was not until

1918 that all men over eighteen could vote, plus a limited number of women determined by age and property ownership. Women had to wait ten more years to gain equal voting rights as men.

In 1750, 23 percent of the total population of Britain lived in cities. By 1850, it was 50 percent. This was far higher than elsewhere in the world. At midcentury, London was one of only three cities in the world—alongside Beijing and Paris—with a population over one million. Britain's cities were squalid and unhygienic. Manchester, a small market town that would soon become the second-largest city in Britain, was a prime example. In the early eighteenth century, Manchester had fewer than ten thousand people. By 1800, that number had shot up to ninety thousand. The population soared to four hundred thousand by 1850 as the city became the center of a giant cotton textiles industry. Manchester's cheap cotton textile exports went around the globe, contributing (among other things) to the collapse of the once-giant textile industry in Bengal, India.[1]

The living conditions for most of Manchester's workforce were dire. Housing was poor, and the supply of clean water and waste removal was left to private companies. The worst conditions were in low-lying districts of the city near factories and railroads, where houses were flooded by polluted rivers.[2] Most houses had no flushing toilets until the end of the century. The novelist Charles Dickens described "Coketown," a fictional English industrial town similar to Manchester, in his famous novel *Hard Times*, published in 1854. It was a fearful and brutal place. Friedrich Engels, the coauthor of *The Communist Manifesto*, described Manchester in 1844 as "Hell on earth."[3]

Experiments in Social Responsibility

A handful of business leaders responded to this dire social situation with a belief that new industrial profits should not come entirely at the expense of their impoverished workers. Almost as soon as industrialization began, a number of employers began experimenting with using some of the funds they generated to make the lives and work of their employees better. Typically, these benefits far exceeded the minimum required by contemporary law and regulation. In some cases, they included the building of complete residential villages for employees and their families. In effect, these employers offered a visible helping hand, because they did not believe that the market was going to lift all up, as Adam Smith did. This first wave of experiments in social responsibility is widely seen as an antecedent to present-day corporate social responsibility.[4] Often termed "industrial paternalism," these policies were sometimes enforced by employers who desired a disciplined and productive workforce even more than a happy one.

Strong Protestant beliefs motivated many early experiments in ethical business. The Congregationalist Titus Salt, the Quaker John Grubb Richardson, and the Unitarian Samuel Greg built model villages near their factories in Saltaire, England; Bessbrook, Ireland; and Quarry Bank, England, and built houses, schools, shops, and recreational facilities for workers. Josiah Wedgwood, a Unitarian and one of the earliest of such figures, pioneered factory production in the pottery industry in Etruria, located outside the town of Stoke-on-Trent, England, in 1769. He introduced the innovation of specialized tasks for his workers and enforced authoritarian controls over their lives, including heavy fines for a range of things extending from lateness to bringing alcohol into the factory and writing on the walls. He also paid high wages; built free housing for workers that was a great improvement on the mud-and-wattle huts that were the norm in rural areas; and subsidized an early form of health insurance.[5] These investments in the well-being of his employees helped Wedgwood build a profitable and sustained business.

Robert Owen's textile mills in New Lanark, Scotland, twenty-five miles southeast of the city of Glasgow, offered extensive facilities, including schools, a company-owned general store, and an educational and cultural center. Perhaps the most famous of these early experiments, the village was an example of urban planning. Owen was so convinced New Lanark was a model for a future society that he opened it up to the public. In the decade after 1815, it was one of the most popular tourist destinations in Europe.[6]

Owen, described by his son as a "free-thinking Unitarian," was motivated by a secular conviction that the root of social ills lay in the existence of private property, coupled with a lack of educational opportunities. He believed that the poor and working class were victims of their circumstances and that, if their living and working conditions were improved, they could become more functional members of society. At the same time, he rejected the idea of enfranchising people within these groups, as he believed they were too ignorant and needed guidance. Following New Lanark's success as a profitable company and model community, Owen expressed a desire to expand his vision throughout Britain and to other countries to create a "New Moral World."[7]

Owen has been described by some contemporaries and later historians as a "utopian," but the term hardly does justice to a man who saw business as a means to bring about a far more equitable society.[8] Owen believed in creating self-sufficient communities with a fairer distribution of wealth and higher living standard. He was unusual among his peers for condemning corporal punishment in his mills, and he worked to advance legislation creating new child labor protections that mirrored those at New Lanark. His employees were well fed, were healthier than the norm, and, starting in 1813, were expected to work only a ten-and-a-half-hour workday, a marked improvement on the twelve hours or more that was the standard. Children in the village received eight years of schooling on average, and both girls and boys learned a wide variety of subjects, including history and geography, that were typically only taught to children from wealthy families. Out of admiration or loyalty, many of the workers at New Lanark named their children after Owen and his wife.[9]

Owen's experimental village attracted favorable attention. Social reformers and even royalty came to observe New Lanark.[10] Many contemporaries hailed Owen as an iconic figure, even a saint. He has been less admired by later historians, who have branded his experiments as an exercise in "paternalism" and dismissed his self-proclaimed ethical motivations as a cover for self-interest. New industrial employers like Owen needed a disciplined, stable, and sober workforce.[11] Because many factories were built outside major towns, sometimes to secure better sources of waterpower, it made sense to attract and keep a labor force.[12] Paternalism in factories served, as British business historian John F. Wilson concludes, as "a vital means by which employers were able to inculcate middle class virtues into their workers." Wilson is particularly critical of the close supervision of workers. "They [employers] were capitalists first and philanthropists second," he concludes, "and it seems likely that industrial paternalism facilitated the process of worker-indoctrination which had been going on since the mid-eighteenth century."[13]

Owen strongly favored order, discouraging disruptive behavior and drinking, both in public and at home. He overlooked (as many others did) the dangers of work in his mills and established powerful mechanisms of social control. He instituted surveillance practices such as the "silent monitor," which publicly displayed each worker's daily performance. Visitors to New Lanark were often invited to attend the children's dance and singing classes. Some who saw these displays believed that Owen manipulated or coerced the children into putting on a cheerful show for outsiders.[14]

Entrepreneurs faced a huge challenge to turn preindustrial workforces into industrial ones. The response of even the most enlightened figures appears heavy-handed today, yet their concern for workers' welfare was notable compared with most of their peers. When the overbearing Owen intruded too far on his workers' personal and family lives, they resisted and even went on strike.[15] Still, it should be remembered that the communities created by paternalistic and sometimes utopian industrialists were far better off than others at the time. The New Lanark factory community, a recent study observed, was "unparalleled in terms of working and living conditions."[16] But these experiments were hardly the norm. Most small and less profitable businesses could not afford to invest in their workers, let alone build model villages.[17]

Owen's own legacy included his experiments with cooperatives, a movement that grew as an important alternative corporate structure to for-profit business. He opened a cooperative store at New Lanark and subsequently developed grand schemes to create cooperative land-based communities that would eventually displace capitalism. During the 1820s he established short-lived communities in Orbiston, Scotland, and New Harmony, Indiana. Although his own initiatives came to nothing, Owen's ideas were among the inspiration for the creation of the Rochdale Equitable Pioneers Society in a Lancashire mill town in England in 1844. Twenty-eight textile workers formed the initial membership. They founded a store based on the idea of aggregating their purchasing power to obtain discounts from suppliers and returning profits to members. Over the following two decades many other consumer cooperatives were founded, especially in the north of England. In 1863, the Cooperative Wholesale Society (CWS) was formed to supply the retail cooperatives. By 1914 over three million people were members of cooperative societies, the CWS was one of Britain's largest businesses, and cooperatives accounted for almost one-fifth of the sales of groceries and provisions in that country.[18]

Meanwhile, as businesses grew in size and complexity over the course of the century, employee welfare schemes such as sick pay and pensions were sometimes adopted by the more profitable, although they never became the norm.[19] Altruism and self-interest continued to coexist. A classic example was the soap manufacturer William Lever, the founder of one of Britain's largest companies, Lever Brothers. He endowed numerous schools and hospitals and, when he died in 1925, left a share of his equity to create the Leverhulme Trust, which became one of Europe's largest educational foundations. In 1888, he began building a large model village beside the manufacturing plant at Port Sunlight, outside Liverpool.[20] A pension scheme opened in 1904, and five years later he started profit-sharing with employees. Lever, who was not particularly religious, also opened a church for interdenominational worship in 1904. The church was closely controlled by Lever himself and was employed quite consciously as an instrument to shape the values of employees and to keep down any socialist tendencies. The company welfare of-

ficer served as the minister in the church, which excluded nonem-
ployees.[21] Lever also had a testy relationship with the cooperative
movement. In 1910–1911 he unsuccessfully sued thirty-eight cooperative societies for passing off their own products in place of Lever
brands they refused to stock.[22]

As factory industry spread in Britain, a handful of new business
leaders provided support beyond wages for their employees, at a time
when the state provided little or no welfare support, and when hygiene conditions in the new industrial towns were very bad. Spiritual and ethical motivations coexisted alongside self-interest. Even
the most benign figures wanted to enforce their own views on the
people who worked for them. Still, they were prepared to share some
of their profits to give their employees better and more dignified
lives, hopefully in return for loyalty. Owen, for one, went further,
articulating a vision of a better society, first by his community at
New Lanark and later through his promotion of the concept of cooperative societies.

Quakernomics

It has long been a staple of British business history to observe that a
disproportionate number of early influential entrepreneurs belonged
to Protestant sects outside the established Church of England. As
with other minority groups that have become prominent in business, the reasons for this were multifaceted. The networking advantages of minorities, and strong emphasis on integrity and honesty,
were likely beneficial. Protestants outside the established church,
like Catholics and Jews, were also initially restricted from many
spheres of public life, including standing for public office, working in
the civil service, and obtaining university degrees.

Members of the Society of Friends, or Quakers, were especially
prominent in business in the eighteenth and nineteenth centuries.
They were visibly different from members of the Church of England.
Founded in England in the 1650s by George Fox, Quakers wore
plain and distinctive clothes, adhered to the principles of pacifism,

avoided alcohol, and refused to take oaths.[23] They did not marry non-Quakers. The sect was small—there were fewer than fourteen thousand Quakers in Britain in 1861—but Quakers had an outsize impact as entrepreneurs. During the eighteenth century, they included pioneers in the iron industry, with such businesses as the Darbys and Ransomes, and in finance, founding banks such as Pease, Backhouse, Gurney, Lloyds, and Barclays. In the nineteenth century, Quaker families were prominent in chemicals and pharmaceuticals, including Joseph Crosfield and Sons and Allen and Hanburys, and in foodstuffs, including firms such as Huntley and Palmers, Jacob's, Cadbury, Fry, and Rowntree.[24]

Why Quakers were so prominent in business has been much debated. Some point to the fact that pacifism kept them out of the armed services or that, unable to attend universities, they established their own schools and developed apprenticeship schemes within their communities.[25] Business remained one of the few avenues open to Quakers, and they had the advantages of strong family and trust networks to raise funds. Quakers were also known for their diligence and energy, as well as modest lifestyles. Quaker financial networks existed across the country, which was a major advantage at a time when institutional capital markets had not yet formed. Quakers were also concentrated in the north of England, where industrialization began.[26]

Quakers created innovative businesses and operated them in a highly ethical fashion. They became renowned for honesty and innovation, such as introducing fixed prices rather than the traditional system of bargaining.[27] Their "hyper-morality," as the business historian Leslie Hannah calls it, "created a climate conducive to rapid economic growth" by raising levels of trust.[28] The Quaker businesses of this era have come to be seen in recent years as models for more responsible business practices today.[29]

Quaker morality rested on strong beliefs and strong organization. The Society of Friends monitored the behavior of its adherents with exacting discipline. Quaker congregations—known as meetings—disowned members for bankruptcy if they had engaged in speculation or failed to pay their debts.[30] Fox insisted that his followers behave honestly in business. This mandate translated into a culture noted for high ethical standards. The church's so-called Yearly Meetings provided detailed advice, such as on the importance of clear and accurate accounts, and the members of the Society believed there was a collective responsibility to help one another and ensure that the group was not brought into disrepute. Both advice and sanctions were in copious supply.[31] That said, it took a major reputational crisis in the mid-eighteenth century for the Quaker movement to reform itself and really commit to the principle of honesty in business.[32]

The Quakers were badly persecuted and suffered discrimination into the nineteenth century. This influenced a business culture noted for "antagonism to inhumanity and institutional cruelty."[33] Unlike some other minority religious groups that have been successful in business, Quakers focused less on specific religious practices and sought instead to uphold a set of values, which they called "testimonies," based on the ideals of truth and equality. They believed they had a direct relationship with God, whom they sometimes called "the Light within." Quakers became prominent campaigners against slavery, although some members were involved in the slave trade.[34] Later Quakers were prominent campaigners for prison reform. Although most Quakers shared the general Christian belief in an afterlife, they were heavily focused on doing good on earth. A present-day Friends website for North America observes, "The emphasis of a Quaker's life is on present time—on experiencing and following the leadings of the Light in our lives today."[35] Quakers did not share the belief in predestination so central to the Presbyterian faith and instead emphasized human agency and the need to live a good life on earth.[36]

Given this emphasis on trust and honesty, it is not surprising that Quaker enterprises became some of the earliest examples of socially responsible businesses.[37] As they generated resources, many Quaker business owners invested in social provisions for their workers. At Coalbrookdale in England, the Darbys provided health insurance and constructed the first forty houses for workers in 1792. In 1846, the firm built a large school for seven hundred children of workers.[38]

The Pease family of Darlington, England, which owned a large coal-mining, iron, banking, and railroad business that employed seven thousand people, built extensive worker housing and many elementary schools.[39]

Such examples should be kept in context. Most Quakers did not create highly successful businesses, and those who did varied widely in their adherence to Quaker principles. While most Quakers avoided alcohol, there were noteworthy breweries such as Hanbury, Barclay, and Gurney managed by Quakers in the eighteenth and early nineteenth centuries.[40] Nor were all Quaker businesses paragons of ethical behavior and social purpose. The collapse of the Quaker-owned bank Overend and Gurney in 1866, with debts exceeding $1 billion in 2021 US dollars, was one of the major financial crises of the nineteenth century. The directors were acquitted of the technical crime of fraud, but there was an abundance of lax behavior and lack of proper auditing.[41] Business success also placed stresses on faith, and a number of successful entrepreneurs, such as most of the Crosfield family, who owned the chemical company Joseph Crosfield and Sons, resigned from the Society of Friends. Others, such as the Bryant family of the match manufacturer Bryant and May, stayed as Quakers but became "worldly," enjoying their wealth and manifesting less interest in the welfare of their employees. A final group, with the Cadbury family prominent among them, remained strict or what contemporaries called "plain" Quakers.[42]

Notwithstanding these caveats, Quaker businesses stand out as exemplars of deep responsibility. They reflect the influence of clearly articulated and truly held values on every aspect of decision-making.[43] The Said Business School economist Colin Mayer has written that the Quakers "led the way in some of the most enlightened and purposeful companies that Britain has had over the past 200 years."[44]

George Cadbury and Responsibility in Making Chocolate

George Cadbury shared the spiritual and ethical beliefs of many Quakers, which led them to pursue experiments in business responsibility. He stood out more for the scale of his ambition and his commitment to translate those beliefs into practice. The family firm was founded in 1824 in the city of Birmingham, England, by John Cadbury, George's father. Cadbury initially traded in tea and coffee and only later moved into chocolate beverages. John's health deteriorated after the death of his wife in 1855, and he suffered from crippling arthritis. By 1861, the business faced collapse, and he handed control over to his two sons, George (then twenty-one) and Richard (twenty-five). He lived quietly in retirement until his death in 1889. The close partnership of George and Richard lasted for fifty years, until Richard's death in 1899, and they transformed their father's faltering business into Britain's leading chocolate manufacturer.[45] George was the more daring and entrepreneurial figure, and he was always supported by Richard, who had a more restful and artistic temperament. Richard enjoyed foreign travel, wrote a lot of poetry and painted watercolors, and designed many of the illustrations used on the company packaging.[46]

George and Richard had a strict Quaker upbringing—their father would not allow a piano in their house, even as it became a standard feature of status in middle-class Victorian homes. While Richard and another older brother, John (who was to die at the early age of thirty-two in 1866), were sent to boarding schools, George attended a local Quaker day school known for its tough discipline. His mother died from tuberculous when he was fourteen, and the following year he left school to apprentice in the family firm. This had not been his first career choice, which had been to train as a doctor. However, the declining health of his father led him to join Richard in trying to save the firm.[47]

The small firm of Cadbury faced larger and longer-established competitors, including the Quaker firm of Fry's in Bristol.[48] The Cadbury brothers worked energetically to save their firm, which almost went bankrupt in 1863. A first breakthrough came in 1866 with the launch of Cadbury's Cocoa Essence, the first unadulterated cocoa powder to be sold in Britain. George Cadbury had learned that a Dutch firm had developed a machine capable of extracting most of the cocoa butter and eliminating the need for additives used previously to reduce the fat content. He went to the Netherlands and bought a machine to make his new Cocoa Essence. There was widespread concern at the time about the dangers of food additives, so the emphasis on pureness was well received, although it was not until 1891 that Cadbury actually stopped selling the last of its "adulterated" brands.[49]

Cadbury began using surplus supplies of cocoa butter to make eating chocolates, challenging the dominance of Continental European firms. Chocolate remained primarily a beverage in Britain before 1914, but Cadbury's strategies were important both in democratizing consumption and in creating the growing market for chocolate as we know it today. Market growth was encouraged by rising living standards and the temperance movement, and advertising campaigns stressed the nutritional qualities of drinking and eating chocolate.[50] George Cadbury's competitor Joseph Rowntree, another Quaker whose chocolate business was based in York, disliked advertising on ethical grounds, believing that focusing on product quality was the appropriate strategy. Cadbury had no ethical concerns about advertising, and this drove the firm's rapid growth.[51] The firm was a late entrant into milk chocolate, but effective advertising soon made Cadbury Dairy Milk, launched in 1905, the market leader. By 1908, Cadbury sales had reached £1.6 million ($200 million in 2021 dollars) and exceeded those of Fry. Rowntree, who remained focused on cocoa powder, was also overtaken by Cadbury.[52]

Chocolate may not seem to some to qualify as a responsible choice of industry. The sugar used in chocolate causes tooth decay and obesity, both of which rose sharply in nineteenth-century Britain.[53] For Quakers at the time, however, drinking chocolate was both morally and medically healthier than drinking alcohol. Cadbury also sought to make chocolate that was purer than the "adulterated" chocolate sold previously—cheaper ingredients such as potato starch, wheat, and powdered dry peas were frequently added to products. The milk used in Cadbury Dairy Milk was always highlighted for its health benefits. Much later scientific research would show that the cocoa plant contains a substance called flavanols that might promote blood circulation, as well as other positive health benefits.[54] Unfortunately, many of the nutritious properties of cocoa flavanols were removed in the process of making chocolate bars.[55]

Whatever the health impact of chocolate, George and Richard Cadbury inherited their father's interest in improving both the spiritual and material conditions of their workforce. In 1866 George, who had breakfast with his employees every day, initiated the practice of starting each working day with a brief, nondenominational religious service. Departing from industry norms, the firm closed the factory on public holidays. It also became the first employer in Birmingham to make Saturday a half day at work.

As the business grew, Cadbury needed larger premises than its central Birmingham location. In 1879, the firm moved the factory four miles out of the city center to a rural greenfield site that they called Bournville (named after a local stream, the Bourn). It soon needed even larger premises. While George Cadbury considered how to accommodate his growing business, he was also considering how he might support the well-being of his workforce. From the age of twenty-two until the end of his life, he was personally involved with the adult school movement of the Quakers, which aimed to teach reading, writing, and scripture to the poor. He personally taught hundreds of men to read and visited their homes, typically located in slums. Seeing these conditions firsthand encouraged him to commit to building a healthier and cleaner environment for his factory workers, and one with greater educational opportunities.[56]

When the new factory opened, it featured facilities such as a kitchen for heating food. This was needed in part because the new factory was far from where most workers lived. The company offered sick pay and covered all or most of the cost of hospital stays for employees and their dependents.[57] Cadbury was eager, like other large industrial companies, to secure a stable and loyal workforce, but the company invested more than others in the welfare of its workers, paying wages above local rates. Unlike most of the responsible businesses of the era, including Rowntree, it supported the right of workers to join trade unions.[58] The factory complex was notable for its sports facilities, which included soccer and cricket fields for men, playgrounds, a gymnasium, and an outdoor swimming pool. This reflected George Cadbury's views on the importance of sport for health. Cadbury was himself extremely active in sports, playing golf, riding horses, and taking up tennis at the age of fifty. Young men and women under eighteen who worked in the factory had compulsory physical education, including swimming lessons. The level of sports activities was high at the plant, and several employees joined British teams competing in the 1912, 1924, and subsequent Olympics.[59]

Cadbury shared a deep dislike for social inequality and poverty with other Quaker business leaders. Joseph Rowntree began an active campaign against the root causes of poverty in the 1860s, critiquing successive governments and the Church of England for supporting wealthy vested interests that he believed blocked progress relieving poverty.[60] In 1901, his son Seebohm published a book called *Poverty: A Study of Town Life* that showed that 60 percent of York's population lived at or below the poverty line, a concept he developed to describe people living below a calculated minimum subsistence level. The book was primarily a sociological study designed to show the extent of the problem rather than make policy recommendations, but it has been credited with exercising a considerable influence on the welfare reforms of the Liberal government elected in 1906, which included the introduction of an old-age pension for people seventy and over in 1909.[61] The subject was also one that George Cadbury had strong feelings about. In a letter to the bishop of Birmingham in 1907, he reflected on the "overwhelming" problem of "the existence side by side of great wealth and extreme poverty."[62]

These concerns lay behind George Cadbury's extensive philanthropic giving and also motivated his firm's welfare policies. When asked by the bishop in 1907 to articulate his "theory of giving," Cadbury responded, "Begin at home with your workpeople, see to their comfort, health, and so far as you can their general prosperity. See that your workshops are light and well-ventilated. As far as you have the means, give your people the advantage of living where there is plenty of space."[63]

The move of the factory to Bournville was motivated by these beliefs. In 1895, Cadbury personally bought 140 acres of land near the factory. Within twelve months, two hundred houses had been built. Each house had its own garden whose trees and flowers were planted before they were occupied. Bournville in part inspired a growing preference for "garden cities" in Britain. In 1899, an association was formed to promote them.[64] Houses at Bournville were initially offered for sale at the cost of construction, with mortgages offered by the company. After a wave of speculative purchases and sales, they were instead offered for rent. Unlike most of the other model villages of the era, the houses were never restricted to Cadbury employees.

Cadbury personally designed the layout of the Bournville village with the help of a young architect, William Alexander Harvey. Harvey was not a Quaker, and it is not known why Cadbury chose him. However, they shared some similar ideals. Harvey was a young member of the Arts and Crafts movement, which was inspired by social reformers and critics of the perceived brutalizing effects of the Industrial Revolution, such as the writer John Ruskin and the designer William Morris. The architects and artists associated with the movement sought to reform design to make it beautiful, and they encouraged a new appreciation for traditional crafts at risk of dying out, and closer to nature.[65]

Cadbury's own vision reflected Quaker beliefs in simplicity, which had long influenced their attitudes to visual culture, and a belief in the moral basis of design. He explicitly sought to enhance the dignity and respect of the people who lived in the houses in Bournville.[66] In 1906, Harvey published a book in which he outlined the instructions he had received to design the village. Cadbury had insisted that each house should have a garden, as he believed that gardening was good for one's health. As a vegetarian, he wanted people to be able to grow their own vegetables because, as Harvey put it, "increased consumption of fresh vegetable food, instead of animal food, was further desirable." He also saw gardens as promoting frugality: "Instead of losing money in the amusements usually sought in the towns, he saved it in his garden produce." Cadbury explicitly promoted a socially mixed community: more expensive homes were scattered around clusters of smaller, more basic housing. He believed, Harvey observed, that the "amalgamation of the factory-worker and the brain-worker in the same district is highly desirable."[67]

Cadbury was sure his vision of society was the right one, and he both invested in it and enforced it. There were strict rules regarding alcohol, which could not be served anywhere on the estate, a ban that lasted until 2015. However, Cadbury also voluntarily relinquished some of his formal control. In 1900 he donated the entire estate to the Bournville Village Trust, a charitable trust that he initially chaired, with no formal relationship to the firm. He personally continued to invest in expanding the estate and its facilities. In 1904 he tried, without success, to persuade the village's inhabitants to plant yellow and blue crocuses in their gardens—the primary colors of the Cadbury brand.[68]

When Richard Cadbury died in 1899 while on a trip to Jerusalem, Cadbury Brothers became a private limited company, with George as the chairman and his two sons (Edward and George Jr.) and Richard's sons (Barrow and William) in executive positions. George at this point was convinced that the company's virtuous principles could only be upheld if it remained in private hands. "If we sold any of the shares," he observed before his brother died, "they would probably come into the hands of men whose ideals are not those of my brother and myself. We might realize our fortune, and relieve ourselves of responsibility, but our experiment would be imperiled."[69]

Cadbury constantly rolled out new schemes to empower workers, seek their input, and invest in their welfare. An employee suggestion program started in 1902. A works committee started in 1905, which evolved into a works council with elected representatives.[70] Men's and women's pension schemes began in 1906 and 1911, respectively, to which the firm and the employee contributed. When a woman married she had to leave her job, which was the convention at that time, because George Cadbury believed that "a married woman could not look after her home properly if she worked in a factory."[71]

Cadbury's welfare policies, and Bournville, were legendary at the time. Bournville became a model for some contemporaries, especially Joseph Rowntree, who established the village of New Earswick outside York. In 1904, Rowntree also followed the Cadbury example by gifting much of his shareholding in the chocolate company to the Rowntree Village Trust that governed the village.[72]

The extent to which Quaker ideals were the driving forces behind these actions later stimulated a scholarly discussion concerning how corporate cultures are shaped. An analysis by Michael Rowlinson and John Hassard of a centennial company history of Cadbury published in 1931 describes, critically, how the firm had retrospectively ascribed its labor management policies to perennial Quaker values. Instead, Rowlinson and Hassard argue that the policies were actually developed in response to particular circumstances at the time they were introduced, and were also influenced by other factors, including George Cadbury's political views.[73] Policies evolved over time and were evidently shaped by contextual events. A number of the innovations followed a visit in 1901 by George Cadbury Jr. to the United States to specifically study industrial organization; they included a suggestion scheme, a company magazine, and a decentralized committee system.[74] There is no suggestion, however, that Cadbury's welfare policies were not genuine.

Cadbury Brothers relied on raw materials, especially cocoa, that were grown in equatorial areas of Africa. Firms that were generally well respected in their home countries often engaged in deeply unethical behaviors when they encountered colonized peoples. A vivid example is William Lever, whose search for secure supplies of palm oil used in soap manufacture led to the creation of large-scale plantations, beginning with the British colony of the Solomon Islands in the Pacific in the 1900s. The plantations had poor working conditions.[75] The situation was even grimmer for the tens of thousands of Congolese employed in the 750,000 hectares of natural palm groves for which Lever was awarded a concession in the Belgian

Congo in 1911. The British colonial government in Nigeria regarded palm groves as the property of Africans, but the palm groves in the Belgian Congo were given to Lever. Lever's company, Huileries du Congo Belge, became, in the words of one historian, "a sordid affair of large-scale profiteering, not heeding the harm done to Africans."[76]

One of the five concessions was called Leverville, but this was not an African version of Port Sunlight. Colonial officials forcibly recruited people to work as virtual slaves. Palm cutters who failed to meet their quotas were sent to prisons where the chicote, a type of whip, was in regular use. The rations offered to workers were considered insufficient by Belgian doctors, and hygiene standards were also criticized by public health officials. Violence, illness, and hunger stalked the concession.[77] Unilever (the successor to Lever Brothers) finally divested from the plantations in Lusanga (the renamed Leverville) in the 1990s, leaving behind a legacy of decaying infrastructure and poverty.[78]

Cadbury did not follow Lever's strategy of acquiring its own plantations, but this did not save the company from a major controversy about the working conditions of the people who grew and picked its cocoa. In 1902 the firm received the first reports that its major supplier of cocoa in the Portuguese-colonized islands of São Tomé and Principe, which were located off the coast of West Africa, employed slave labor. The colony was the world's largest exporter of cocoa, and Cadbury Brothers received 45 percent of its cocoa from it in that year. George's nephew William was sent to Lisbon in 1903 to investigate. He talked to relevant government ministers and planters, who assured him that the reports were the "work of men who were jealous of their own success." The British ambassador recommended that the firm give the Portuguese government "a year of grace" to resolve any problems.[79]

When it became clear that nothing had changed, an independent agent (a Quaker) was sent to São Tomé in 1905 and went on from there to Angola, another Portuguese colony. Cadbury, Fry, Rowntree, and the German chocolate company Stollwerck, all of whom sourced cocoa from the region, shared the cost. Although it proved difficult to obtain strong evidence, it was apparent that laborers were being forcibly recruited from Angola and shipped by armed guards to the islands, "from which they never return."[80] As Quakers had been prominent in antislavery campaigns—the slave trade had been abolished in the British Empire in 1807, and slavery itself in 1833— the story hit a very raw nerve. In October 1906 George Cadbury wrote to the British foreign secretary, Sir Edward Grey, about the situation. Grey, like Cadbury, was a member of the Liberal Party, which had swept to power against the Conservative Party the previous February. Cadbury noted that the group of British cocoa makers were "anxious to act together" and were "prepared to make some sacrifice in the interests of the natives." He added that he wanted to know that "any step we take will be in harmony with any premediated action of the British Government."[81] Cadbury did secure a twenty-minute meeting about the issue with Grey on October 20, but he was told "to refrain from calling public attention to the subject" until a full report had been received.[82] There was no support from the British government for any action. Grey wanted hard proof and was concerned to preserve the supply of laborers from Mozambique, another Portuguese colony, to South Africa, which Britain fully controlled after winning the Boer War six years earlier.[83]

The conditions in São Tomé were a growing international scandal. The prominent New York–based *Harper's Monthly* magazine commissioned the British war correspondent Henry Woodd Nevinson to report on the conditions, and his account was serialized monthly from August 1905 and published as *A Modern Slavery* in 1906. Nevinson documented in great detail the shocking conditions on plantations, including children's death rate of up to 25 percent every year.[84]

In September 1908, the affair became headline news in Britain when London's leading newspaper, the *Evening Standard,* which strongly disliked the Liberal political beliefs of George Cadbury, splashed the news that Cadbury was profiting from slavery. Cadbury sued for libel. When the case came to court in the following year, Cadbury Brothers was accused of stalling and covering up. George

Cadbury was able to show in court that his company had devoted considerable resources to trying to find out what labor conditions were really like in the Portuguese colony. It had also shifted its supplier source even before the desired clarity was achieved. The firm had reduced the share of its total consumption of supplies from São Tomé from 60 percent in 1903 to 32 percent by 1908, and it had begun locating a new source of supplies in the British West African colony of the Gold Coast (now Ghana). In March 1909, Cadbury, Rowntree, and Fry instituted a temporary boycott of all São Tomé cocoa.[85]

Cadbury's arguments under cross-examination were classic, and are much repeated to this day. He claimed that he wanted to avoid hurting plantation workers in São Tomé if the accusations were not true. He also argued that the issue was one for governments, not individual firms, and that a boycott by his own firm would not be effective, as he believed most US and German cocoa producers would not honor it.[86] Cadbury won the case but was only awarded derisory damages, reflecting the rather slow response of the firm to widespread allegations of very bad conditions in São Tomé, and the expectations that a Quaker firm would avoid anything associated with slavery. However, the jury did order Cadbury's legal costs, which were substantial, to be paid by the *Evening Standard*.[87]

The lack of interest by the British government, in particular, put Cadbury in an awkward position. In September 1914, the British foreign secretary observed to another government department that "it was highly desirable from the political point of view" to end the boycott of Portuguese cocoa. The primary reason was that neutral Portugal was being helpful to the British cause after the outbreak of World War I.[88] In 1917 the British government formally stated that it wanted the boycott to end, but Cadbury Brothers noted that as the death rate of workers was still very high, it would continue to avoid supplies from São Tomé.[89] The cocoa industry of the Gold Coast had been developed by local farmers and merchants, and there were none of the ethical challenges seen in Portugal's African colonies.[90]

If Quaker businesses operated along a spectrum of beliefs about the extent to which they should allocate resources to achieve a positive social impact, Cadbury was among the most committed to such a view. The design of Bournville reflected George Cadbury's vision of a future society in which people lived in pleasant and dignified conditions, with "brain workers" living side by side with people engaged in factory work and other trades. The investment in employee welfare and the commitment to high ethical values were noteworthy. Perhaps the most striking feature of George Cadbury was that he never saw any of the firm's pro-worker policies, or its investigation of labor conditions in São Tomé, as a cost. The move to Bournville, he observed in 1906, "was morally right and proved financially to be a success."[91] This is one of the earliest and clearest statements from a business leader that deep responsibility could be an asset for a business.

Meanwhile, the corporate culture and commitment to deep responsibility that George Cadbury had fostered long outlived his death in October 1922 as the company remained led by his sons and their sons. There was a slow dilution of the ownership. In 1912, two hundred thousand preference shares were offered to the public with priority to customers and staff, but no ordinary shares were offered. A merger with J. S. Fry in 1919 left the Cadbury family with just over 50 percent ownership. However, the loss of family control began in earnest in 1962 when the company finally went public, following pressures from some members of the Cadbury and Fry families to cash out. Cadbury family influence continued in the company until a merger with the Schweppes beverages company in 1969, and even afterward family members continued to serve on the board.[92] Sir Adrian Cadbury, an active Quaker and upholder of the firm's values, was chief executive of the company between 1965 and 1989. He was a noted proponent of ethical management and chaired the committee that developed an influential code on best practice in corporate governance in 1992.[93] However, the dilution of family ownership left the firm open to acquirers, and it succumbed to a hostile takeover by the US-based Kraft in 2012. The US-based Mondelez now owns the company, but the brand name remains familiar in Britain and internationally.

George Cadbury beyond the Boundaries of His Firm

A major characteristic of the deeply responsible business leaders featured in this book is their recognition of the limitations of what their single firm could achieve. This was certainly true of George Cadbury, whose sense of responsibility to contribute to a fairer society did not end at the boundaries of his firm. He pursued his vision through his church, in philanthropy more generally, and, with reluctance, in politics.

Cadbury was one of the great business philanthropists of his time. Many Quaker business leaders were active philanthropists, which some have seen as a way of reconciling their success in business with their dislike for material prosperity, but Cadbury's commitment to philanthropy came particularly early in his career and grew exponentially over time.[94] As the business overcame the difficulties he inherited from his father and then expanded, George Cadbury gave away his income nearly as fast as he made it. He explicitly sought to avoid passing great wealth on to his heirs, saying that he had "seen many families ruined by it, spiritually and morally."[95]

As a devout Quaker, it is not surprising that George Cadbury became involved in what was a time of change and renewal of faith. He was an important supporter of what has become known as the Quaker Renaissance. John Wilhelm Rowntree, Edward Grubb, and Rufus Jones led a movement to renew the vitality of the Quaker movement and align its values more clearly with the contemporary world. These reformers promoted new scientific theories such as the theory of evolution, argued for a critical understanding of the Bible, and encouraged Quakers to follow the example of Jesus in performing good works in society. Cadbury was wholly aligned with these views. At the Manchester Conference in 1895, when one thousand

Quakers met to discuss the future of the Society of Friends in Britain, he spoke of the "dead formality" of many Quaker meetings. He stressed how important it was for the Society of Friends to have an "earnest, life-giving, educated Gospel ministry."[96]

Cadbury lent both his energy and substantial financial resources to plans to revitalize the Society of Friends. He supported the creation of an academy to train Quaker pastors who might lead a movement of spiritual revival, donating his Woodbrooke estate, to be maintained at his family's expense, and convincing a leading scholar from the University of Cambridge to become the first director with a financial package sufficiently large to persuade him to move. He also donated equity in his newspaper, the *Daily News*, to create an endowment to support lectures and scholarships and provide free tuition fees. He continued to invest in the endeavor, providing funding for American Quakers to attend Woodbrooke.[97]

Cadbury was also an important benefactor of Christian missionary work. Support for foreign missionaries would not be on many people's list of socially beneficial spending today. Historians have documented the role of missionaries as agents of empire building, but for Cadbury, supporting spiritual life was just as important as supporting material being. He contributed substantial sums to the Society of Friends' Foreign Mission Association, but he was also a large benefactor to non-Quaker missions, and his choice of what to support was informative. He had a particular interest in China, partly a reflection of his disdain for the opium trade, and he became a supporter of the China Inland Mission, a nondenominational Protestant organization created by James Hudson Taylor in 1865, which became the largest missionary organization in China, deploying hundreds of missionaries. Taylor sought to dissociate the mission's work from Western governments, and he himself adopted Chinese dress and learned multiple Chinese dialects. This made him a radical figure among Christian missionaries in nineteenth-century China.[98] Cadbury was one of twelve people who financed the first one hundred missionaries sent to China, at a total cost of £10,000 ($1.1 million in 2021 US dollars).[99]

Most of Cadbury's philanthropy went to secular rather than religious causes. He made large gifts to the Bournville Village Trust,
as well as numerous gifts to much smaller programs. Cadbury had
a particular interest in improving the lives of poor children in the
city of Birmingham. After moving to Woodbrooke Farm in 1881,
he began holding parties under a large tent for poor children from
the city. When he moved to the larger Manor House in 1894, he
erected a large hall called the Barn, which could seat as many as seven
hundred people, and hosted daily events there during the summer
for children. There were also sporting facilities open to the public,
including an open-air bath.[100] In 1907 he purchased a large estate
known as Woodlands, which included a house and six acres of gardens, and transformed it into a hospital for crippled children that
he gave to the local charity, the Birmingham Cripples Union. When
this charity merged with a local hospital to form the Royal Cripples
Hospital in 1925, Woodlands became the location for inpatient services for the new hospital.[101] In the 1900s, Cadbury and his sons
also bought a large amount of land in the south of the city, which
had been threatened by urban development, and gave it to the City
of Birmingham. Further donations were made over the following
decade. They became the basis for a large recreational area that
became known as the Lickey Hills Park.[102]

Cadbury's aversion to unfair labor practices also led him to support social campaigns as a prominent member of what one historian
has called the "counter-elite" behind the large-scale social and welfare
reforms undertaken by the Liberal government between 1906 and
1914. The members of this counter-elite varied and included Liberals,
socialists, and women's and religious groups. The Cadbury and
Rowntree families, one study notes, were at "the storm center of the
movement for social reform."[103] George Cadbury supported (and
became president of) the National Anti-Sweating League, an organization formed in 1906 to oppose the exploitation of workers in
sweatshops, or factories in which workers were employed in poor
conditions for very low wages. He was also an active campaigner
for an old-age pension, convening a large conference at Browning

Hall in London in December 1898 that launched a national campaign for Britain to follow the precedents in Germany and New Zealand. He and his son Edward provided half the funds for the National Old Age Pensions League, which helped secure the legislation that created an old-age pension in Britain in 1909, widely regarded as the foundation of the country's social welfare system.[104]

Cadbury was a supporter of the Liberal Party. For a brief period at the end of the 1870s, he was elected to Birmingham City Council and Worcestershire County Council. But his interest in politics was limited, and in the 1890s he declined suggestions from leading Liberal politicians that he should stand for election to Parliament. This stance changed when the Anglo-Boer War broke out in South Africa in 1899, pitting the British government against the white Afrikaners who ran the states of Transvaal and the Orange Free State. It provoked a wave of patriotic sentiment in Britain, fueled by the popular press, which supported the rivals of the Liberals, the Conservative Party. The Liberal politician and future prime minister David Lloyd George reached out to Cadbury and asked him to fund the purchase of an old Liberal newspaper that had switched to supporting the war, the *Daily News*. Cadbury strongly disliked British imperialism and armed conflict. He was particularly opposed to the Anglo-Boer War, which he believed was provoked by mining companies seeking to secure access to gold and diamonds. He joined a syndicate to buy the newspaper and, when others pulled out, became the sole proprietor in 1901.[105]

Cadbury experienced large losses on the *Daily News*. Subscriptions fell by over half when the newspaper switched back to opposing the war. A new editor opposed to gambling insisted that there should be no news of horse racing, which further reduced the number of readers. Cadbury himself insisted that there should be no advertisements for alcohol, also reducing revenues.[106] Annual losses reached £60,000 (around $8 million in 2021 US dollars). Cadbury's radical views on social issues made him powerful enemies, including the conservative *Evening Standard*. There was discussion of the "Cocoa Press," which was publicly attacked by Conservatives in

Parliament.[107] In 1910, Cadbury invested more in publishing when he purchased an evening paper, the *Star*, from the Rowntree family in order to advance the Liberal cause. The following year, he put his press ownership under a trust, the Daily News Trust, with his son Edward as the chairman.[108]

The outbreak of World War I was something of a personal crisis for George Cadbury, but he made no attempt to impose his antiwar views on his firm. Employees were permitted to serve in the armed forces—two thousand did—and grants and allowances were made to their families if they experienced hardship as a result. Two of his sons joined the armed forces. He strongly opposed the Liberal government's decision to enter the war, withdrew his financial support, and increased his contributions to the Union of Democratic Control, which included disaffected Liberals and a group of socialists known as the Independent Labour Party. The Union, which was unable to make any leeway, criticized the secret nature of British diplomacy and instead advocated international disarmament and the formation of what became the League of Nations.[109]

Cadbury continued his philanthropy until the end of his life. After reading of the plight of impoverished children in Vienna following the end of the war, he paid for a group of them to spend a year in Bournville. He also continued an active program of support for children and the disabled, including regular parties at Manor House.[110]

Cadbury knew that there were limits as to what he and his single firm could accomplish, even if it could serve as a role model for other businesses. He understood, as a consequence, that it was essential for policy makers to address the big issues that concerned him. The result was his advocacy of social policies to address poverty and political campaigning against wars. He used his reputation and his money to promote policies that were of no immediate benefit to the firm and, in the case of his antiwar stance, were in fact very unpopular. This was clearly a case of selfless advocacy, rather than self-interested lobbying.

Meanwhile, Cadbury's philanthropy created or cocreated institutions outside the private sector that have lasted to the present day. The municipal-owned Lickey Hills Park continues to provide recreation for tens of thousands of Birmingham's residents each year. The Royal Cripples Hospital is now the Royal Orthopaedic Hospital, owned by Britain's National Health Service, and is one of the largest specialist orthopedic units in Europe. The Woodlands campus is still in use. The Bournville Village Trust is one of the largest nonprofit housing trusts in Britain, renting eight thousand properties in Bournville and other locations as well as providing community facilities and landscaping areas.

George Cadbury and Deep Responsibility

The development of modern factory production in Britain was accompanied by the emergence of a small cohort of business leaders who demonstrated a deep commitment to securing the well-being of their workers and improving society rather than just making profits for themselves. Motivated by values, many of them informed by their faith, they provided their employees with support beyond subsistence wages, and sometimes built whole communities. Robert Owen envisaged his experiment at New Lanark as a step toward a better and more equitable world. This is not to deny that self-interest and concern for social control (as in the case of William Lever) could coexist. Even so, relatively few business leaders were willing to invest much in their employees beyond wages.

The Quakers offered a noteworthy example of a group of business leaders pursuing deep responsibility. There was considerable variation among individual firms and individual leaders, but as a group they produced many successful businesses that acted with social responsibility. George Cadbury himself combined spirituality with a veritable checklist of virtues—honesty, fairness, loyalty, compassion, and beneficence among them. This did not mean he was perfect—he could be controlling—but it does mean that he was a virtuous leader who combined virtue with practical wisdom. He knew how to build a successful business, and how to learn from other companies and countries as he grew his business. He understood that he could not impose his pacifist views on his employees during World War I, even as he personally continued to oppose the war. His choice of industry; concern for other stakeholders, beginning with employees; and support for the communities of Bournville and Birmingham more generally were hallmarks of deep responsibility. Cadbury's insistence that policies that were "morally right" could also be "financially successful" marks him as a pioneer of ethical capitalism. He also understood that changing public policy was the key to making society as a whole more equitable.

Cadbury was, like today's mega-rich business philanthropists, in the business of "world-making."[111] But there was little self-interest in the world he sought to make. His focus on the material benefit of the less privileged members of society offers one of the more convincing examples that business can coexist with the local community and society more broadly in mutually beneficial ways.

Quaker entrepreneurs of this era proved successful at building firms and brands that lasted. They demonstrated that ethical behavior and responsibility to employees could be a competitive advantage and not a costly burden. Businesses and brands survived even when they passed out of Quaker hands. Barclays Bank and Lloyds Bank, founded by Quakers in the eighteenth century, still remain two of Britain's largest brands. However, as family ownership and influence declined and firms went public, so the distinctive beliefs and cultures in them faded, and businesses became vulnerable to hostile takeovers. Cadbury's own experience in this regard was preceded by that of fellow Quaker chocolate manufacturer Rowntree, which was acquired in 1988 in a hostile takeover bid by the Swiss multinational Nestlé, a firm whose marketing of baby foods to mothers in developing countries made it a byword for corporate irresponsibility. The Cadbury brand survives, but merely as part of the portfolio of the US-based Mondelez, whose proclaimed mission is to "lead the future of snacking by offering the right snack, for the right moment, made the right way."[112] If this sounds a far cry from the vision of George Cadbury, it is comforting that Cadbury contributed to a formidable and permanent legacy beyond the for-profit sector. Lickey Hills Park, the Royal Orthopaedic Hospital, and the Bournville Village Trust speak to his commitment to community. A survey in 2003 identified Bournville as "one of the nicest places to live in Britain."[113]

CHAPTER 2

REDISTRIBUTION OF POWER

EDWARD FILENE, RETAILING, AND THE
CREATION OF CREDIT UNIONS

The concerns about poverty that so preoccupied George Cadbury in Britain were echoed in the United States, where this chapter will show that there were parallels in the responses of some business leaders who, motivated by a familiar combination of values and self-interest, sought to address the problem. There were also more radical plans to extend the responsibility of business. Edward Filene lived at a moment of deep public skepticism about business and the concentration of power and wealth in American society. He perceived that business could be part of the solution rather than just a problem. "The modern business system, despised and derided by innumerable reformers," he observed in *The Way Out*, published in 1925, "will be both the inspiration and the instrument of the social progress of the future."[1] The caveat, he conceded, was that this could only be achieved if business was conducted in the right way, as "people are more important than profits."[2]

Filene was born in September 1860 in Salem, Massachusetts, and witnessed firsthand the extraordinary population and economic growth in the United States following the end of the Civil War. The population more than doubled from 31.4 million in 1860 to 76.2 million in 1900 as millions of immigrants poured in. The economy boomed, shaped by supportive local, state, and federal governments that facilitated the construction of railroads, expropriated Indigenous peoples' lands to make room for white settlers, and imposed high tariffs to protect domestic manufacturing.[3]

46

The spread of the telegraph and the expansion of the railroads from the midcentury onward unified the growing domestic market. Mass marketing and mass production became possible, facilitated by technological innovations that permitted continuous flows on production lines and the scaling of firms. By the turn of the century, Andrew Carnegie's Carnegie Steel Company (which in 1901 became part of the U.S. Steel Corporation) and John D. Rockefeller's Standard Oil Company had become industrial behemoths. These large corporations were known as "trusts," as they initially used the legal device of a trust to consolidate a slew of smaller companies under a centralized administration.[4]

The growth of these large corporations set alarm bells ringing in the distinctive political culture of the United States, which was traditionally decentralized and egalitarian, although most people's extension of equal rights did not extend to people of color or women. Farmers, laborers, and owners of smaller businesses looked askance as "plutocrats" like Carnegie and Rockefeller became rich and powerful. The big cities of the United States—Boston, Chicago, New York, and San Francisco—became visible expressions of deep inequalities. In 1890, the pioneering muckraking photojournalist Jacob Riis revealed the torrid conditions of New York's slums in his book *How the Other Half Lives*.[5] Economic historians have largely confirmed the widespread contemporary belief that inequality was increasing over time.[6]

The term "robber baron," first used to describe the plundering of feudal lands, was revived and rebranded to describe industrial titans like Carnegie and Rockefeller, on the assumption that their wealth must have been earned dishonestly. Mark Twain and Charles Dudley Warner coined a new phrase to describe the gross materialism and political corruption of the era in a satirical book, *The Gilded Age: A Tale of Today*, published in 1873.[7] The name was taken up by later historians to describe the last decades of the century, although the period saw a great deal of diversity in business practices and in the conduct of the new business elite, and—as the historian Richard John has suggested—it may well exaggerate the levels of corruption, vulgarity, and materialism of the period compared with previous and subsequent historical eras.[8]

The public image of big business in some quarters reached new lows as muckraker journalists wrote critically of big business's corrupt practices, poor working conditions, false advertising, and use of child labor. This trend began in 1902, when a number of prominent magazines, including *McClure's, Collier's,* and *Cosmopolitan,* began featuring crusading exposé articles of business and political corruption. These pieces often evolved into major books attacking specific corporations and industries. Classics of this genre included Ida Tarbell's *History of the Standard Oil Company* (1902); Lincoln Steffens's *The Shame of the Cities* (1904), which attacked corruption in municipal governments; and Samuel Hopkins Adams's *The Great American Fraud* (1906), which exposed troubling conditions in the patent medicine industry. Some muckrakers made their case through fiction. Major works of this genre included Upton Sinclair's *The Jungle* (1906), a fictionalized account of the Chicago meatpacking industry, and David Graham Phillips's *Lightfingered Gentry* (1907), on the insurance industry.[9]

There were attempts at various levels to counter the power of big business and the perceived inequality of wealth and power. The labor movement was an obvious source of opposition, but it was weaker in the United States than in Western European countries, where unions had larger memberships and faced fewer legal obstructions. In Britain, trade unions were legalized in 1871. In the United States, conspiracy laws were used to ban and disrupt labor organizing for several more decades, and the number of states that recognized unions were few. The American Federation of Labor, the main force in the labor movement by the end of the nineteenth century, focused on direct bargaining by craft workers with their employers and often worked at cross-purposes with other social reformers. It opposed legal protections for male workers, for example, because it believed that these laws undermined its own approach to worker protection.[10]

Strikes and unionization were a risky business and were often met with force and violence, including from the police.[11] The National

Association of Manufacturers, formed in 1895 and soon the largest business trade association, became a virulent campaigner against trade unions. It encouraged employers to invest in employee welfare schemes to keep workers satisfied, and it launched an "Industrial Betterment" program in 1914 designed to persuade employers to invest in worker education, factory safety, and other improvements.[12]

With the expansion of the franchise, political movements sought the redistribution of power and wealth. Populists won control of the state legislature of Kansas in 1890, and the Populist or People's Party was formed as a national party in 1892. The Populist Party gained support from farmers and others from rural areas who suddenly had a voice in the process. It demanded more regulation of big business, railroad companies, and Wall Street. Following a brief surge of enthusiasm, the party largely collapsed after supporting the failed presidential campaign of radical Democrat William Jennings Bryan in 1896.[13]

A more sustained political force known as the Progressive movement saw the emergence of city politicians, often in the upper Midwest, who fought to require utility monopolies to charge fair prices for transit, water, and electricity. Many Progressive leaders came from Protestant (often clerical) families and championed what they called views about the "Social Gospel." The movement drew support at the federal level when President William McKinley was assassinated in 1901 and replaced by his vice president, Theodore Roosevelt, a patrician populist who was elected on his own in 1904. Roosevelt was sympathetic to the early efforts of the muckraking journalists and supported efforts to break up large trusts, regulate the production of food and drugs, and protect public lands. He made use of the Sherman Antitrust Act, which made attempts to monopolize trade illegal but had lain largely dormant since it passed into law in 1890. In 1911, Standard Oil was broken up into thirty-four separate companies after a legal battle. However, the federal government lacked authority in most areas of the economy, and social reforms remained limited.[14] The United States entered World War I as an affluent nation and a profoundly unequal one.

Business Responsibility in the Gilded Age

Some aspects of the business response to the social challenges of the industrial age in the United States were quite different from those in Britain. The scale of corporate philanthropy, beginning with the creation of the Carnegie Foundation, had no parallel elsewhere. At the same time, as in Europe, there were a number of business leaders who were willing to invest in facilities for their workers. As far back as the early nineteenth century, a group of New England merchants (much later described by historians as the Boston Associates) created new mill towns such as Lowell and Waltham in Massachusetts and Manchester and Nashua in New Hampshire, where they provided decent housing for workers and educational facilities. They sought to make profits, but they had a strong social vision, aiming to design a workplace that could shape virtuous characters.[15]

As the century progressed, quite a few company towns were built. In some cases, such as the town built just outside Chicago during the 1880s by George Pullman, a railroad manufacturer, the primary desire to create a highly disciplined workforce was explicit. Life in the town he named after himself was so repressive that a strike broke out in 1894, which only ended when the US Army was called in to quell it.[16] A more benign endeavor was embarked on by the chocolate entrepreneur Milton Hershey, a member of the Mennonite sect, who established a company town called Hershey in his home state of Pennsylvania in 1903.[17] His aim, as he explained, was to create a place where "the things of modern progress all center in a town that has no poverty, no nuisances, and no evil."[18]

Some of the most active investors in employee welfare were founders of the department stores that emerged during the second half of the nineteenth century. As pioneering ventures such as Wanamaker in Philadelphia, Marshall Field's of Chicago, and Macy's in New York grew, they erected iconic buildings featuring the latest technological wonders such as elevators, telephones, and luxurious restrooms. Department stores offered consumers a dazzling array of products, typically at lower prices thanks to the advantages of mass production and bulk orders.[19] They also became major targets of critics of the new concentration of power. Smaller retailers and manufacturers took the lead in demanding greater fairness in retail and other American industries.[20] Small retailers could not compete with the lower prices offered by large department stores. Manufacturing companies found their recommended prices discounted against their will and beyond their control. The campaign for fixed prices and against the ability of dominant firms to set their own prices came to be called fair trade, and a lobbying group called the American Fair Trade League was formed in 1913.[21] There were unsuccessful attempts in some states to regulate department stores, which came under criticism for offering poor working conditions and low wages to female workers.[22]

Faced with such criticism, large retailers developed a vast array of new employee welfare programs. There were profit-sharing plans, short paid vacations, company-owned vacation camps, company magazines, and other policies and initiatives aimed at improving the experience of the salespeople and inventory clerks. The term "employee" was phased out and replaced by "store family." As satisfied employees were likely to deliver a more positive experience to customers, the business case for such an investment was felt to be particularly strong. The overall result, as one historian has written, was that department stores had "probably the most elaborate employee welfare programs in the country."[23] But they seldom recognized trade unions.

Macy's, in New York, developed a particularly elaborate welfare system. The store was started by Rowland Hussey Macy, a Quaker, in 1858. He leased out space, including to the brothers Isidor and Nathan Straus, who sold crockery. After Macy's premature death in 1877, the influence of the Straus brothers grew. They became partners in 1888 and acquired full ownership of the company a decade later. The Straus brothers originally knew most employees personally, but as three thousand people were employed by 1900, this was no longer possible. Welfare policies became institutionalized.

At the heart of the new arrangement was the Macy Mutual Aid Association, formed by employees in 1885, which paid health and life insurance benefits to its members. After 1904, all employees were required to belong to Macy Mutual Aid and the dues were deducted from weekly pay envelopes. The firm started so-called gratuity lunches in 1888, supplying milk, tea, or coffee free of charge to junior employees, many of them young women. Anyone occupying a higher position paid one cent for such beverages. Among other benefits, the firm provided an annual sleigh ride for the cashiers and a summer picnic for the entire store. Internal interviews with staff in 1913 uncovered great skepticism regarding the moral intent behind these policies, and resentment at heavy-handed surveillance by the "matron" who ran Macy's welfare department.[24]

While the welfare policies at Macy's and other department stores might be seen as a response to public hostility and a means to develop a loyal and stable workforce, it would be cynical to maintain that they were devoid of moral purpose. John Wanamaker, an active evangelical Presbyterian, was concerned about the public image of his business, but he also had a strong sense of stewardship. Under his leadership, the company set up pensions, employee restaurants and clinics, athletic facilities, and an array of musical activities, from singing choruses to an orchestra and a bagpipe band. The working day began at Wanamaker stores with employees singing "morning songs." Still, at Wanamaker too there was no acceptance of labor unions.[25]

Edward Filene and the Democratization of Choice

Edward Filene and his younger brother Lincoln transformed a small family-owned business into one of the largest mass retail companies in the United States, although they preferred that their company— Filene's—be known as a "specialty store in fashion" rather than a department store. Filene's had some of the best welfare schemes for employees in the retail industry, but those were in some respects the least remarkable dimension of the story. Filene treated his business as an experimental laboratory for bringing to life his vision of how business could achieve a major social impact. His experiment entailed a direct assault on the concentration of power and wealth that he saw in the United States.

Toward the end of his life, Filene recalled that he had developed over time a distinctive perspective when it came to profits and social purpose. The purpose of business, he wrote in a book published in 1931, was to "serve people, not merely to support the business man concerned in it. I was not an idealist. I wanted profits. I even had a strong preference for becoming rich. Nevertheless, this discovery of what business really is did strange things to me. It made me want to serve."[26] This quotation neatly summarizes Filene's career as a retailer. He built a profitable, innovative business using a business model that he believed could serve as a model for a more egalitarian society. He made it clear that he was not seeking a radical change in the political system. "I don't believe that socialism is best for our country," he told an audience in California, before adding a warning that "unless we can achieve economic democracy, our political democracy must be a sham."[27]

Filene's father, William, a German immigrant, opened a store in downtown Boston in 1881 after a series of small ventures in wholesaling and garment manufacturing.[28] Edward Filene had a tough childhood. A fall at three left him with a permanent limp, and he suffered from repeated attacks of eczema. Additionally, at the age of nine his mother sent him—and two of his brothers—to spend an unpleasant year at her former school in Germany, which was noted for its harsh discipline.[29] In 1880, at the age of twenty-one, he passed the entrance examinations to attend Harvard University, but his father had a stroke and he was compelled to give up his academic ambitions to play a larger role in the family business. He later called this one of the "great disappointments" of his life.[30] His younger brother Lincoln left high school at the age of fifteen to assist with the family business.[31]

William only technically retired in 1891, but the brothers took a leading role in developing the business. The retail goods store was reorganized as William Filene's Sons Company, with Edward and Lincoln sharing control as general partners and William designated as a special partner. After William's death in 1901, the business was incorporated, and the two brothers initially owned all the stock.[32] By 1899, sales had reached over $472,000 (over $14 million in 2021 US dollars).[33]

There were many innovations. The brothers took advantage of the large garment industry in Boston to build a high-turnover business in women's fashion, and they worked to counter existing biases against machine-made apparel. Alongside such apparel, the store sold glamorous handcrafted European luxury products that Filene procured in his overseas travels. Display was a key feature of the business. There were large windows at street level to highlight the latest fashions. Sometimes new outfits were displayed in the upper floors of the store and illuminated at night.[34] Inside the store, glass cases were used to display items for sale, whereas traditionally stores had kept their merchandise stored away in wooden boxes. There was also extensive use of mirrors throughout the store to heighten the perception of abundance and reinforce the appearance of plentiful choice.[35]

The company innovated in employment practices, too. When Filene learned how much time management had spent correcting mistakes during the busy Christmas season in 1902, he introduced the first employee training system in American retail history. Courses could be taken during working hours and were open to every employee.[36] This proved a particularly valuable means for women to become buyers and managers. Filene's also took the highly unusual step of hiring college graduates. These human resource development policies were accompanied by attention to the management structure. The business was divided into subunits that were required to report daily on inventory and sales. Filene was a great believer in planning, and the four broad divisions of the business had to produce six-month plans.[37] Filene always emphasized the importance of providing good service to customers. He encouraged his employees to treat customers as they would treat their own parents, with proper consideration of both what they needed and what they could afford.[38] "Poor service is immoral," he told an audience at the University of California, Berkeley, in February 1934.[39]

Filene had a particular dislike of waste, and he returned to the issue repeatedly. He believed that better management and mass production would contribute a great deal to eliminating the wasteful practices that kept prices on basic necessities high and wages low. In his 1934 book *The Consumer's Dollar,* Filene observed that he had "no room . . . to detail these staggering wastes." He added, though, that it was "enough to say that the consumer is robbed as efficiently by inefficiency as he could ever be by outright crookedness."[40]

This concern about waste led him as early as 1909 to pioneer another innovation, the Automated Bargain Basement. The concept of a bargain basement—a part of the store where goods were sold very cheaply because they were imperfect or old—was not new. Marshall Field had introduced the first bargain basement in 1879, but Filene managed his bargain basement differently. It operated as a separate unit from the main store, providing minimal service and few fitting rooms. Its buyers purchased items that could be sold at low prices, such as items from discontinued lines, overstock, and factory waste. Filene also developed an automated markdown system. If a good remained unsold in the bargain basement for twelve days, the price was cut by 25 percent, and six days later, the price fell by another 25 percent, and six more days later it fell by 25 percent again. If the good remained unsold after thirty days, it was given to a charity. This innovation was not immediately profitable, making its first profit only in 1919. But it generated immense publicity. Many years later, and after Filene was no longer involved in management, the bargain basement stayed profitable even as the main store was ravaged by the huge unemployment and falling incomes caused the Great Depression.[41]

Filene's Automated Bargain Basement aroused the same ire from smaller retailers and manufacturers as it did from other department store price-cutters. Filene was convinced that low prices were key to the challenge of redistributing power and wealth in American society. This view was prompted by contemporary concerns that inflation—which ranged around 1 to 2 percent between 1897 and 1914—was making the cost of living harder for the urban poor, many of whom were immigrants, while others had come to the cities from rural areas.[42] Like Henry Ford, whom he admired, Filene saw lower prices as the key to increasing consumer purchasing power and bringing about greater employment and societal well-being.[43] He believed that businesses should continually seek to raise rather than lower wages. During the 1900s his store paid a quite high wage of eight dollars a week, and he supported the campaign of the National Consumers League, a social justice advocacy group formed in 1899, to secure a state-level minimum wage. Between 1912 and 1922, Filene's workforce grew from one thousand to three thousand and wages doubled.[44] It was only in 1938 that the Fair Labor Standards Act created a federalized minimum wage system.

It is perhaps not surprising, given these views, that the Filene brothers were actively concerned with employee welfare. This was a family tradition. William Filene had organized regular, informal meetings at his home on Fridays so that employees could enjoy refreshments and offer their perspective on the store's operations.[45] Lincoln, writing in 1924, observed that he and his brother had systematized the "habits of business thought" that "were always my father's guide."[46] These included the idea that any company or industry should be driven by "high purposes," including giving employees "a just place in the business."[47] As so often, this family belief system appears to have been very important in shaping the virtuous character of the Filene brothers.

The welfare programs adopted by the Filene brothers started early and were particularly ambitious. In the early 1890s, the position of welfare director was created with specific responsibilities for employees. By 1898, employees could insure themselves against illness and received free health care services. The store experimented with bank-like services, enabling employees to deposit their savings and paying them interest. When a recession hit in 1908 and some employees suffered falling sales commissions, these funds were used to make loans to those employees, who were otherwise vulnerable to loan sharks.[48]

Edward Filene and the Vision of Industrial Democracy

Filene was a passionate supporter of "industrial democracy." He envisaged this as a business organization in which employees have an "adequate voice in the determination and control of the conditions of work, an adequate stake in the results of work, and as near as humanly possible a guarantee that the management of the business shall be efficient."[49] For Filene, social responsibility was the prerequisite to profitability, not a distraction from it. The company was used as an experimental laboratory for this idea.

Filene became a great champion of the Filene Cooperative Association (FCA), a cooperative organization for the company's workers, which had been launched under his father in 1891. The FCA operated all the employee welfare activities and provided a forum for discussing store policies and issues. Every employee who wanted to join was welcome. The Filene brothers belonged to it, but like everyone else, they only had one vote each. Members could modify any store rule if at least two-thirds of the FCA's elected council supported the change. If management vetoed the change, the veto could be overturned if all of the store's members united against it. In 1901, a formal arbitration committee was established by the FCA to resolve worker disputes.[50] Unlike most of its competitors, the company hired unionized workers in occupations where unions existed.[51]

Edward and Lincoln Filene owned all the equity of the store before 1907. In that year, the Filene brothers began a more radical experiment in industrial democracy, as they began to give shares to twenty managers and to the FCA.[52] Edward Filene assumed that others would share his views, but this proved a problematic assumption. As the company grew, managers were recruited from beyond the firm, and some were more concerned with generating profits. In 1911, while Filene was absorbed in trying to improve the City of

Boston's governance, Lincoln Filene hired Louis Kirstein as a vice president to help them build their business in men's fashion. Kirstein was a successful clothing retailer, with his own professional network, and was allowed to invest $250,000 in nonvoting stock in the company.[53]

In 1913 the Filene brothers, now middle aged, reorganized the firm again with the ambition of making sure its leadership would be secure in the long term. The new firm issued one hundred shares of common stock. Edward and Lincoln took fifty-two shares, with which they agreed to vote jointly, and the remaining shares were distributed among four vice presidents, including Kirstein, who headed different parts of the business. Under the terms of the agreement, in 1928 the Filene brothers would end their control of the firm by giving four common stock shares to the four vice presidents and the remainder to other employees or the FCA. Many of the details concerning what should happen to vice presidents who left the firm or died were left vague. The company acquired the shares of two former vice presidents, but things were more complicated, as we shall see, when another vice president died in 1925.[54]

There were other challenges to Edward Filene's goal of democratization. In 1916, as the firm moved into profitability again after initial losses on the Automated Bargain Basement had hurt the company financially, it was decided that dividends should be distributed between the management and the employees. Problems arose concerning which employees should get the money. An initial system decided by the FCA leadership led to many complaints. The following year, the assistants to the six partners organized as an operating committee and came up with a new plan, awarding most of the money to supervisors and specialists in order to provide them with an incentive to spur profitability. Filene opposed this, but it went forward. It was ironic that a system meant to increase employee involvement ended up reducing it, as lower-level employees did not have authority in deciding how the money would be allocated.[55]

The FCA never developed the kind of proactive role in the management of the company that Filene had envisioned. Members made use of the facilities but appeared reluctant to engage in their active management. The arbitration process was used, but it had considerable flaws, not least the fact that the executive secretary of the FCA was paid by the management, putting him in an awkward position if he fought the management on behalf of employees.[56] To Filene's consternation, few workers appeared interested in exercising their voices in the management of the store.[57]

Despite his good intentions, Filene himself did little to create a culture that would encourage most of his staff to feel comfortable assuming a more proactive role. He lacked the warmth of George Cadbury. He was personally abrasive and prone to annoy people around him. He never married, and on occasion he expressed regret about not having a family.[58] At his memorial service, one acquaintance observed that he "was a saint who sometimes seemed egotistical."[59] While abrasive personalities can deliver inspirational business leadership, they are unlikely to foster genuine employee participation.

Lincoln, who served as the store's general manager after 1908, found his brother excessively domineering, especially as Edward was frequently absent from the store doing other things outside the firm, discussed later. Where Edward was prickly, Lincoln was warm and good-humored and naturally talented at resolving conflict. Lincoln had long worked in his older brother's shadow, but over time, he grew more independent and assertive.[60] His initiatives often encouraged cooperation, but he seemed better at persuading others to join his endeavors.[61] Like his brother, he also wrote and published books and sought to be active in areas outside the family business on a national and international scale. In 1924 he published *A Merchant's Horizon*, which advocated for the wider use of the management policies in place at Filene's.[62] In 1926 he helped found the American Arbitration Association, a nonprofit that provided arbitration and mediation services to individuals and organizations that wanted to reach settlements out of court, and later assisted in bringing about an international arbitration commission. Lincoln married Therese Weil, a women's rights advocate and philanthropist, and had two daughters.[63] Edward and Lincoln were rivals as well as partners, and the emotional distance between them increased over time.

At work, Lincoln grew closer to Kirstein both professionally and personally. As early as 1922, Lincoln proposed to Kirstein the possibility of allowing his brother to retain his share of the company's profits but taking away his voting shares.[64] Kirstein, for his part, felt no loyalty to Edward. Kirstein was good at merchandizing, but he was more conventional in his thinking and the two men irritated each other. Edward seems to have favored the Automated Bargain Basement, which was his idea, while Kirstein's specialty—the men's store—was loss-making until the mid-1920s. Edward allegedly rankled Kirstein by continually bringing up its lack of profitability. There was also hostility between him and Edward Frost, the company's chief financial officer, on matters related to the company's finances.[65] When a vice president died in 1925, Kirstein and Frost purchased his equity, with Lincoln's blessing, giving them thirty-six shares (together) in the company, considerably more than Edward's twenty-six.[66]

In 1928, the management structure at Filene's changed quite dramatically. Edward was effectively removed from executive authority in a new agreement, supported by Lincoln, that ended the firm's cooperative plan. Edward retained the post of president until 1940 (when he would be eighty) and was given a $100,000 (around $1.5 million in 2021 dollars) annual salary. The company went public and the 100 shares of voting stock were replaced by 500,000 shares of new common stock. Edward was given 150,000 shares, but his brother and the other two partners secured 250,100 shares together. The five members of the operating committee together received 20,000, while just 4,900 shares were distributed among 150 employees to be selected by the company's management. The remaining 75,000 shares were offered to members of the public. This left employees with 5 percent of the stock, falling far short of the 1912 partnership agreement that would have left them with nearly half of the voting stock.[67]

In 1928, Kirstein promoted the merger of Filene's with three other regional department stores: Abraham & Straus of New York;

F. & R. Lazarus of Columbus, Ohio; and Shillito of Cincinnati. Bloomingdale's of New York joined the following year. The scheme involved the formation of a holding company with common ownership, but it allowed the retention of individual store identities. Lincoln supported the project because he favored its cooperative approach, but Edward vehemently opposed it and his relationship with his brother broke down for good.[68] Edward filed suit to oppose the project, but the lawsuit failed because the judge found his arguments to be without merit. In 1929, Federated Department Stores was formed with Walter Rothschild of Abraham & Straus as president and Lincoln as chairman of the board of directors.[69] Edward remained president of Filene's, but by this point the title was purely honorific. The merger, one historian later noted, severed him "from the management of his own store and relegated [him] forever to be a rich, powerless old man with an empty and meaningless but high sounding title."[70] The new holding company weathered the travails of the Great Depression. In addition to the profitability of Filene's Basement, the company innovated by beginning to offer credit to shoppers.[71]

Edward Filene had made a substantive contribution to the growth of one of the preeminent mass retailing firms in the United States. The welfare programs he established for employees continued after 1929.[72] The name Filene continued to be found on many American main streets until 2007 when the stores were rebranded as Macy's. Filene's Basement, which had become separately owned, closed in 2011. This was an impressive legacy. But Edward Filene's wider ambition of using the store as an experimental laboratory to show the benefits of offering employees more say in running the business did not ultimately succeed. The low prices of the store did democratize consumption to an extent, but they failed to redistribute wealth and power on a greater scale. Edward's attempt to democratize power within Filene's firm was undermined by poor execution, and perhaps by his own inability to motivate others to follow his vision. At times it was a story of good intentions more than results.

Advocating for Redistribution

Filene, like George Cadbury, did not see business as an isolated enterprise. He saw it as a vital part of the community and, even as he was building the retail business, he sought to use his wealth and reputation to improve civic institutions and to give more people access to capital. He chose to forgo many personal luxuries, although he did own a yacht and provided his mother with a stylish car and chauffeur, which he frequently borrowed.[73]

As early as the 1890s, Filene leveraged his reputation as a successful business leader in the interest of civic reform. The flashpoint was a conflict with the Boston Elevated Company, which had secured control over most of the city's streetcar lines. In 1899, the firm attempted to use its substantial political leverage to build a new streetcar line along the city's popular Washington Street, with the proviso that it could operate the line indefinitely and set the rates.[74] Filene objected, and he recruited the services of his firm's recently hired lawyer, Louis Brandeis. Brandeis was a talented Harvard Law School–trained lawyer who was to build a career as the "people's lawyer" crusading against big business.[75] Brandeis, whose parents were, like Filene, German and Jewish, would in 1916 become the first Jew to be appointed to the US Supreme Court.[76] Filene and Brandeis persuaded other prominent business leaders and others to fight for popular control over public transportation franchises. Together, they got the governor of Massachusetts to call a public referendum to prevent Boston Elevated from carrying out its plan. The plan was subsequently defeated in the referendum.[77] Filene and Brandeis engaged in other campaigns, usually (but not always) on the same side. Their outlooks were not entirely aligned. Brandeis disliked bigness, of either business or government, while Filene saw size as a way to secure efficiency. Their differences became explicit when Brandeis became the main force behind the American Fair Trade League in 1913.[78]

Brandeis did join Filene's ambitious project, launched in 1909, called Boston 1915 to make, as an article in the *Boston Herald* described it, "the Boston of 1915 the finest in the world."[79] An ambitious five-year plan was developed to address the overcrowded and unsanitary housing in the fast-growing city and to challenge corruption in the city government. Boston 1915 featured a spectacular program of social reforms, including old-age pensions and the building of a transportation infrastructure for the whole region.[80]

Filene also worked with the Catholic archbishop of Boston on a spinoff venture, the Boston Dwelling House Company, that sought to provide low-income housing in the Woodbourne area of the city. It developed a new, thriving community, although one that became primarily middle class due to the higher-than-expected costs of construction and, ultimately, the purchase prices.[81] A more ambitious plan to achieve comprehensive urban planning for the whole metropolitan region floundered in the face of local communities seeking to retain their individual identities. The election of the notoriously corrupt James M. Curley as mayor of Boston in 1914 served as the final nail in the coffin of the Boston 1915 project.[82]

Filene was also deeply involved in the cause of promoting credit unions. These nonprofit cooperative institutions provided credit to small farmers or craftsmen who were unable to secure credit from conventional sources and were thus vulnerable to exploitative moneylenders. The concept of the credit union emerged in nineteenth-century Germany and spread to other European countries, although not always successfully, as in the case of Ireland.[83] In 1909, Pierre Jay, the first commissioner of banks in Massachusetts, took up the idea, inviting the founder of Canada's first cooperative society to testify before the Massachusetts legislature. Filene soon supported the proposal. He may have encountered the concept when visiting Bengal in 1907, as the British colonial government was experimenting with credit unions.[84] Later that year, Massachusetts became the first state to pass a statute enabling credit unions to be incorporated.[85]

Even after the Massachusetts law was passed, there was little progress in launching a credit union. Filene was more focused at that time on the Boston 1915 project, but when this failed, he turned his attention to credit unions. In 1914, he and a group of other business leaders formed the Massachusetts Credit Union, a credit union in its own right, with the wider mission of encouraging the formation of other credit unions and lending them money. In April 1915, Filene helped draft a set of eight principles that credit unions should follow to achieve good practice. In the face of continued slow progress, Filene led a reconstruction of the organization, forming a new entity—the Massachusetts Credit Union Association—in 1917.[86]

Because Filene was devoted to the goal of redistributing wealth, his engagement with credit unions was understandable. Yet his interest also reflected his ambiguous relationship with Judaism. His nonreligious father, William, had taken the children to visit Christian churches to "see and hear and ask questions."[87] Edward Filene is known to have only attended Jewish services a few times during his entire life, and his observations on the subject were ambiguous. He noted enigmatically that he believed "intellectually in God," but saw religion as "the motive power of human progress, not the steering gear."[88] In 1913, the secular and assimilated Louis Brandeis became an active supporter of Zionism—advocating for Jews to return to Palestine—but Filene stayed silent on the issue. In general, he seems to have considered his Jewishness less a badge of honor than a distraction.[89] He felt, he wrote in 1932, "it was not good for my public work and my reputation for intellectual honesty that my being of Jewish origin should be so emphasized as to bring it into consideration when my other public work is being considered."[90] Filene was aware that he was, for many Americans, an outsider. He was also aware that anti-Semitism was intensifying.[91]

All of the founders of the Massachusetts Credit Union were Jewish, and only Jews were asked for contributions to the Credit Union Association in 1917.[92] A Boston rabbi observed in 1916 that support for credit unions helped "to make the people realize that not all Jews are alike, that not all are bad, that not all are money lenders or usurers."[93] Filene himself revealed in 1933 that his interest in credit unions was partly motivated by his desire "to fight an age old prejudice that all Jews were usurers."[94]

In 1920, Filene hired the Harvard-educated Massachusetts lawyer Roy Bergengren as managing director of the new association. Bergengren had been serving impoverished workers, but he had struggled to make ends meet. He found his passion for serving the poor could go hand in hand with a higher income by promoting credit unions.[95] Filene launched the Massachusetts Credit Union League, yet another attempt to create a super-organization to promote credit unions, in 1921. He asked Bergengren to head a new campaign whose ambition was to pass laws in every state to authorize the chartering of credit unions. The entire campaign was financed personally by Filene.[96]

The credit union movement made rapid progress over the course of the 1920s. By 1930, thirty-two states had credit union legislation and 1,100 individual credit unions had been organized. The credit union movement survived the stock market crash of 1929 and its aftermath with few collapses compared with the thousands of mainstream banks that went bankrupt during the early 1930s.[97] This success did not prevent regular conflicts between Filene and Bergengren. They argued over finances, over Bergengren's own salary, and over strategy. Bergengren wanted to push for a federal credit union law, but Filene thought it might create more problems than it would solve. Filene was much more concerned with working with established institutions such as the US Chamber of Commerce and the American Bankers Association. He believed a more promising strategy was to push for the organization of credit unions in states with credit union laws, and to continue efforts to pass credit union legislation in the remaining states.[98]

Bergengren finally got his federal legislation under the presidency of Franklin D. Roosevelt. The Federal Credit Union Act of 1934 enabled any group of seven people to form a credit union society and placed supervision of the society under the Farm Credit Administration.[99] Bergengren pressed on to form a national association, in part at least to free himself from the direct supervision of Filene, who continued to finance the Credit Union National Extension Bureau, the umbrella organization he had formed in 1921 to push for states to charter credit unions. In 1935, the Credit Union National Association was formed. Filene was elected its first president.[100] By that time, there were approximately 3,600 credit unions in the United States, with 750,000 members.[101]

Filene's endeavors to create institutions that could facilitate the redistribution of wealth and power had mixed fortunes. The grand vision for Boston 1915 was not achieved. His plans to democratize money were much more successful, and much more radical. He was successful in getting the credit union movement launched, even though Bergengren was responsible for much of its execution, and credit unions became an established part of the financial system of the United States. In 2010 the country had 7,500 retail credit unions, with ninety-two million members. Credit unions did not transform capitalism, but these community-based cooperative financial institutions provided many millions of people, typically less affluent, with loans for household expenses and the purchase of consumer durables, and have made it possible for people to secure higher interest rates on savings and pay lower interest rates on loans and, later, credit cards.

Advocating Cooperation and the Promotion of Truth

Filene's support for the credit union movement was intimately related with his wider and transformative social agenda, which he believed needed to be based on cooperative institutions and robust knowledge. He promoted both generously and enthusiastically.

Filene's philanthropic strategies to support these wider social goals grew out of one of his many efforts to kick-start the credit union movement. He and his brother Lincoln founded the Cooperative League as a nonprofit in 1919 to encourage cooperative credit unions. Edward was president, and he gifted several thousand shares of second-preferred stock of his company to the League. The organization's ambitions widened as Filene brought others, such as the paper manufacturer and ardent Christian Henry Denison, into the organization. The Cooperative League was renamed the Twentieth Century Fund in 1922 to reflect its wider goals. This was explicitly not a Carnegie-type foundation, for which he felt little sympathy. Filene believed that engaging in philanthropy after amassing great wealth, especially if that wealth was generated by unfair practices, was not a solution to the underlying problems of distribution.[102]

The Twentieth Century Fund moved to support a range of progressive causes. The first grants were given to support the League of Women Voters, established in 1920 after women had secured the right to vote, and to investigate efforts to stymie academic freedom. Grants were subsequently made to Bryn Mawr College to develop "a department of economics and research" and to study "industrial history and labor development."[103] Credit unions naturally received considerable support also. The Twentieth Century Fund provided the Credit Union National Extension Bureau, a foundation also established by Filene, with $1 million ($19 million in 2021 US dollars) between 1920 and 1934.[104]

The Twentieth Century Fund reflected Filene's near-obsessive reverence for "fact-finding," or what may be described as disinterested research for the purpose of seeking truth. As he observed in 1934, "When one is fact-finding, he had better take note of all the facts, no matter how they may interfere with his easy theories."[105] So greatly did he value fact-finding that he hired a number of "bright young men" as fact-checkers to help him prepare his public speeches, including the muckraking journalist Lincoln Steffens.[106]

The "truth" was coming under serious attack by this time. During the 1930s in Nazi Germany and the Soviet Union, the news media and cinema were instruments of propaganda that were used to support the regimes.[107] Filene's hero Henry Ford was a rampant anti-Semite who owned a newspaper, the *Dearborn Independent,* focused on anti-Jewish stories. In his book *The Way Out,* Filene complained that Ford had "been misled and hoodwinked in his warfare against the Jew."[108]

The advent of the Nazi regime further deepened Filene's awareness of the growth of anti-Semitism, especially after he visited Germany in June 1933. He observed that what was happening was "a crime against civilization."[109] He began contributing to organizations that sought to relieve the plight of German Jews. He also sought, in vain, to raise the profile of the issue, even attempting to persuade the celebrity science fiction writer H. G. Wells to visit Germany to expose what was going on.[110] In 1920, Filene had played a significant role in the founding of the International Chamber of Commerce, which sought to promote stronger trade relations between countries in order to build greater prosperity and preserve peace.[111] He vocally opposed the holding of the annual meeting of the International Chamber of Commerce in Berlin in June 1937. At the event, T. J. Watson, the chief executive of IBM and new president of the International Chamber of Commerce, received a medal from Adolf Hitler and gave him fulsome praise in return. Filene was one of the very few American business leaders to voice criticism of the Nazis. Many of the largest US corporations, including General Motors, Ford, Standard Oil of New Jersey, Coca-Cola, and many others, retained large manufacturing and other businesses Germany. With the single exception of Warner Brothers, even the major Hollywood studios—all of which were founded by Jewish immigrants from Europe—studiously avoided criticism of the Nazi regime out of concern for their profitable German market.[112]

At a meeting in Boston in March 1937 on the topic of "education for democracy," Filene shared his concern that Americans were losing the ability to discern the truth because of all the propaganda they encountered. In alliance with Kirtley Mather, a Harvard geologist and enthusiast for adult education, and Clyde R. Miller, a crusading journalist against propaganda who taught at Teachers College, Columbia University, he established the Institute for Propaganda Analysis in New York City and funded it for three years.[113] Filene died before the institute got started, but it subsequently issued publications exposing the activities of nativist, anti-Semitic, and fascist groups before being closed after the United States entered World War II.[114]

Filene's enthusiasm for cooperative businesses also increased toward the end of his life. The growth of credit unions reinforced his faith in cooperatives, and he began to consider ways of extending their role in the retail sector. He envisaged a chain of cooperative retail stores that would work with credit unions "to improve our social and political life by forcing the democratization of the control of money and the wider distribution of money."[115] In January 1936, Filene announced a plan to open the Consumer Distribution Corporation to serve as a procurement hub for a chain of cooperative department stores. He established a new foundation, the Edward A. Filene Good Will Fund, to finance the plan. He funded the corporation with $1 million (over $18 million in 2021 dollars).[116] The organization continued after Filene's death, with Roy Bergengren serving as vice president. During the first half of the 1940s, it published a series of management manuals for cooperative stores.[117]

In the summer of 1937, accompanied by his personal assistant Lillian Schoedler, Filene set off for his annual trip to Europe, against his doctor's advice. He went on a hunting expedition in the Austrian Alps. Afterward, Filene and Schoedler drove through France en route to Britain, but he became ill with a cold that quickly turned into pneumonia. He was taken to the American Hospital in Paris and died on September 26, 1937. His remains were cremated and sent back to Boston, where a small group of friends scattered them in the Charles River.[118]

According to George W. Coleman, who delivered a memorial eulogy in his honor, Filene was not satisfied with his achievements in his later years. Coleman claimed that Filene believed he had failed as a retail distributor because he had not been able to bring to fruition a key outcome he had hoped for: "the lessening of the great gap between the cost of producing merchandise and the cost the consumer had to pay for it." He also regretted that he had not been able to achieve industrial democracy as the leader of a large retail company.[119] Steffens, in his own autobiography, validated these two points and wrote that Filene called his life "the failure of a successful millionaire."[120] It was a harsh self-assessment, excessively so. Quite apart from whatever was achieved or not achieved in his department store, Filene's legacy was not a failure. Credit unions, which he did so much to foster, became a vibrant and important part of the American financial system. The Twentieth Century Fund, renamed the Century Foundation in 1999, became an important research institution funding projects aimed at influencing and improving public policy. After the September 11, 2001, terrorist attacks, the foundation sought ways to keep American civil liberties intact in the face of growing infringements on grounds of national security. Filene's warnings of the threat to democracy posed by the devaluation of truth remain as relevant today as they did in his time, and perhaps more so.

Edward Filene and Deep Responsibility

The United States entered the Great Depression in 1929 with the top 1 percent owning 24 percent of pretax income.[121] The newly wealthy were not the scions of old aristocratic land-owning families as in Europe. They were the bankers and industrialists who had made fortunes as the American economy grew.

Filene felt his responsibility as a business leader was to counter this concentration of wealth and power. He and his brother Lincoln built a successful mass specialty retail business and invested heavily in employee welfare. Department stores had a vested interest in such spending, but Filene's vision of the role business should play in leveling the playing field was far broader than most of his peers. He sought not only to improve the working conditions of employees but to share decision-making authority, profits, and ownership with them. He believed that business could be a vehicle for delivering the country from the inequality of wealth and power. By offering high wages and decision-making authority to workers, and low prices to customers, Filene believed he could widen access to—and democratize—wealth and power. He used his own firm as a laboratory for these ideas, although ultimately he was outmaneuvered from within.

This could be taken as evidence that the democratization of decision-making is a delusion in a large for-profit business, and that worker-owned cooperatives, which he favored as his career progressed, are a more promising vehicle. Yet arguably it was Filene's lack of the necessary personal qualities more than anything else that stood in the way of convincing others to sign up to his radical stance. Either way, Filene's experience does illustrate the challenge one individual faces in convincing less altruistic colleagues to truly invest in social purpose.

Filene understood that society needed changing, not just his own firm. This was not driven, as was the case with George Cadbury, by explicit religious beliefs, but he evidently held and pursued a holistic view of the world and its problems. From his first campaigns against a monopolist exploiting Boston's local transportation system onward, Filene sought ways to use his standing and wealth to challenge what he perceived as unfair distributions of power. In being a prominent champion of credit unions, he promoted an idea that he believed would democratize access to capital, particularly for those of limited means. This was a radical leveling measure, and a major legacy. Paralleling the case of Cadbury and the Bournville Village Trust and other institutions, some of Filene's most enduring impact lay in his work beyond the for-profit sector.

Filene's philanthropy was motivated by the insight that democracy could only function if citizens were well and truthfully informed. Later in life, he donated much of his fortune to counter the scourge of propaganda and misinformation. Sadly, he lived to see the whole concept of truth progressively undermined during the 1930s, and he even lived to see the International Chamber of Commerce, which he helped found, hold its annual meeting in Hitler's Berlin against his wishes. It is perhaps not surprising that at the end of his life, Filene believed he had failed. Yet his own warning about the threat to human civilization posed by the Nazi regime soon after it came to power was notable and brave. Filene was a business leader who believed that purpose and profits were interdependent. He offered a new approach for business leaders to make the world a better place, even if few chose to follow him.

CHAPTER 3

PROMOTING CHOICE AND
FACING DICTATORSHIP

ROBERT BOSCH IN IMPERIAL AND NAZI GERMANY

Until the middle of the nineteenth century, the region we know as Germany consisted of numerous smaller states, many of them relatively poor and agrarian. Then, quite suddenly, the expansion of the railroad network beginning in the 1850s brought rapid growth of the coal, iron, and engineering industries. Over the following decade, Otto von Bismarck, a politician in the state of Prussia, masterminded the unification of Germany, primarily by provoking three short wars with Denmark, the Habsburg Empire, and France. Kaiser Wilhelm I, the king of Prussia, headed the new German Empire created in 1871, and Bismarck served as chancellor until 1890.

Manufacturing flourished under the authoritarian rule of Bismarck and his successors, who imposed high tariffs to protect the domestic market. German business excelled in many of the new capital-intensive industries of the era, catching up to and often even overtaking Britain. Two-thirds of the two hundred largest German companies in 1913 were clustered in the chemical industry, electrical engineering and heavy machinery, and metals.[1] These firms went multinational with enthusiasm, building large businesses in the United States and around the world.[2]

Amid this change and in response to growing domestic turmoil, Germany forged a new path in its effort to dampen the rougher edges of capitalism by giving workers a stake in the nation's prosperity through social legislation. This turn toward workers' welfare was not solely state driven. As we will see, the business leaders explored in this chapter pushed far beyond the requirements of reformist legislation. They did so in difficult times—and sometimes made moral compromises, simultaneously resisting and abetting the more nefarious policies of the state.

As elsewhere, industrialization created a new urban labor force that initially experienced degrading working and living conditions, lacked any security in the event of illness or old age, and had no place in the political system. Workers' poor living conditions and lack of social protection began to be addressed by Bismarck in the 1880s, when Germany became the first country in the world to organize a state-sponsored and comprehensive social security system that covered blue-collar workers and white-collar workers whose annual earnings did not exceed 2,000 marks (around $13,000 in 2021 dollars). Compulsory health insurance, to which the employer contributed one-third and the worker two-thirds of the funds, was introduced in 1883. Compulsory accident insurance, entirely financed by employers, followed in 1884. In 1889, compulsory old-age insurance—to which the employee, employer, and government contributed—was passed. The insurance boards were composed of both managers and workers, allowing workers to influence policies directly. These measures formed the basis of what was known as the "social state."[3] Another twenty years would pass before Britain passed such welfare legislation: in 1908, the British government, after much campaigning by George Cadbury among others, introduced noncontributory pensions for people over seventy. In the United States, there was no national social security until the Social Security Act of 1935.

Bismarck, who was a devoted Lutheran, described these measures as "practical Christianity."[4] But his motivation appears to have been more pragmatic than spiritual. He was engaged in state-building and prioritized national unity. He also sought to suppress the potential enthusiasm of workers for socialism. Germany's Social Democrat Party was the most prominent socialist party globally, and it embraced Marxism and revolutionary goals. Considerable political repression accompanied Bismarck's welfare policies. Between 1878 and 1890, trade unions and the Social Democratic Party were illegal.[5]

Under Leo von Caprivi, Bismarck's successor as chancellor, the government introduced further social legislation, banning the employment of children under the age of thirteen, prohibiting work on Sundays, and establishing a guaranteed minimum wage. In 1891, Germany passed its first federal law giving workers participatory rights in some corporate decisions. The Bavarian and Prussian mining industry introduced mandatory participation rights in 1900 and 1905, respectively, after significant coal miner strikes.[6]

As Germany's economy expanded, its political ambitions grew, alarming neighboring countries. In 1894, France and Russia formed a military alliance. Germany's relations with Britain deteriorated after 1898, when Germany began to build a battle fleet to rival Britain's Royal Navy. An arms race developed centered on a new type of battleship, the dreadnought. Britain allied with France in 1904 and with Russia in 1907. Germany had a close alliance with the Habsburg monarchy of Austria-Hungary. By 1914, Europe was composed of competing and hostile military alliances. Armed hostilities were an accident waiting to happen—and they finally did with the outbreak of World War I on July 28, 1914.

The war and Germany's ultimate defeat sparked decades of turbulence. When hostilities broke out, the assets and trademarks of German businesses in foreign countries were expropriated.[7] In the chaotic last days of the war, the monarchy was overthrown in the November Revolution, and the Kaiser fled the country. The Weimar Republic, a new democracy, was born, offering new political and civil rights for citizens. But the war was followed by crippling hyperinflation, causing a massive economic and social shock. A recovery period and cultural flourishing followed before the Wall Street Crash. The resulting worldwide financial crisis caused massive unemployment, which, in turn, fueled support for extreme left-wing and right-wing political parties. In January 1933, Adolf Hitler and his ultranationalist National Socialist (hereafter Nazi) Party took power, albeit through backroom maneuvering rather than a democratic majority. There followed twelve years of one of the most notorious and murderous political regimes in modern history.

As will be seen throughout this book, deep responsibility takes different forms in different conditions. In Germany, as in Britain and the United States, business leaders faced the challenges of responding to the social consequences of rapid industrialization, but the conditions were different, as government provided much greater social security and forced businesses to contribute to financing it. After the outbreak of World War I, the challenge for German businesses was how to respond to economic and political turbulence. Apart from the brief interlude of the Weimar Republic, business leaders also faced authoritarian governments and, in the case of the Nazi period, a genocidal one, raising the issue of the responsibility of business leaders in the face of a coercive and amoral government.

This chapter begins with a survey of the social responsibility of German big business, which instituted social welfare programs for employees. Here we will look particularly at Krupp, which had one of the most extensive programs, albeit one primarily focused on serving the interests of the firm. The following sections turn to the career of the engineering entrepreneur Robert Bosch, an outlier who charted a different path from most of the other contemporary German business leaders. He called himself a socialist, and his understanding of his social responsibility was different from Krupp's. However, the Nazi era saw Bosch and his company tested under extreme circumstances, and the results were highly ambiguous.

Krupp and Experiments in Social Responsibility

German companies experimented with welfare provisions for their employees even before Bismarck introduced his first protective legislation in the 1880s; some companies offered insurance and provided company housing and stores. However, there was a great diversity of practices, reflecting the heterogeneous nature of business in unified Germany. "Upper Silesian magnates, Rhenish-Westphalian entrepreneurs, Hamburg merchants and shippers, Berlin bankers, Saxon textile industrialists, inventive entrepreneurs of the machine-building, electro-technical and chemical industries," the economic historian Gerald Feldman observes, "are not easily lumped together."[8] If there was a common driver to all of the new employee welfare programs, it was to bind workers to their companies and attract skilled workers by offering attractive benefits.[9]

The iron and steel firm of Krupp, based in Essen in the Ruhr region, became the poster child of corporate social spending. The Krupp family business was long established, but it was Alfred Krupp who made it into a significant industrial force during the middle decades of the nineteenth century. He developed breech-loading cannons that the firm supplied in large numbers to the Prussian army. At the time of his death in 1887, Krupp had 75,000 employees, 20,200 of whom were in the city of Essen. The firm provided extensive social services for its employees. The first voluntary sickness fund began in 1836, and this evolved into an extensive worker insurance program. A hospital, which began as a temporary facility for wounded Krupp workers in the Franco-Prussian War of 1870–1871, became a fully equipped facility. A company store, started in 1858, evolved into a system of separate shops for each factory and housing complex that sold food and clothing at low prices.[10]

In the words of historian Eugene McCreary, Alfred Krupp's motives were a "combination of humanitarianism and self-interest."[11] He wanted, and expected, complete loyalty to his firm. In a letter to the board in 1873 asking for the family of a worker killed in an accident to be well taken care of, he suggested that it would "strengthen the fidelity and attachment of all others to the establishment."[12] He also supported educational and cultural activities in the city of Essen. As Krupp aged and the firm grew, the self-interest dimension seems to have grown. His letters spoke of "chaining" workers to his factory. Krupp was obsessively secretive and terrified of knowledge leaks. He hounded important employees who left the firm in a determined effort to get them back.[13]

When Friedrich Krupp took over the firm on Alfred's death in 1887, he shifted the emphasis to providing recreational and educational opportunities. In 1890 a casino, surrounded by a large garden, was built for the office workers' social association. A library, the first free library in the city, opened in 1899, and it had fifty thousand volumes by 1914; by then, three-fourths of employees held library cards.[14]

Friedrich Krupp started to build worker colonies (as they were called) as early as the 1860s with parks, schools, and recreational grounds. The first houses, built for supervisors and workers, were made of wood and regarded as temporary. The provision of company housing was not unique, but soon Krupp was outpacing other firms in both the number of dwellings and their quality. From the 1870s, the buildings were built with brick and regarded as permanent. The number of Krupp dwellings expanded from 154 in 1870 to 2,680 in 1873. By 1900, one in eight people in Essen lived in a Krupp company apartment. Rents were kept lower than the norm in the city, and the apartments were a sought-after perk. Twenty thousand homes were built by 1914. Most colonies had a grocery shop, a beer hall, a school, and public green spaces.[15]

The most famous of Krupp's housing projects was the village of Margarethenhöhe, built in 1911. This undertaking reflected a new stage in welfare policies in Germany that was influenced by recent social reform movements, especially Deutsche Werkbund (German Association of Craftsmen), sponsored by Robert Bosch. These endeavors linked large manufacturing companies with prominent architects and industrial designers around the concept of "quality work."[16] Margarethe Krupp, four years after the death of her husband, Friedrich, in 1902, established a housing foundation with a 1-million-mark private donation. The Deutsche Werkbund–affiliated architect Georg Bettendorf designed Margarethenhöhe as a picturesque rural village featuring cottages on meandering tree-lined streets with a central square as well as a grocery store, hotel, post office, and church. The village was not restricted to Krupp employees: other citizens of Essen could rent houses. The population was mainly middle class, and it became, in effect, an architecturally distinct suburb of Essen. In an era that valued access to nature and fresh air as essential components of good health, Margarethenhöhe took advantage of its natural surroundings to support the most up-to-date thinking on maintaining a healthy workforce. The village was connected to natural spaces reserved for its residents' enjoyment.[17]

Krupp's worker housing schemes became part of its public image: the nicest homes were featured in its public relations campaigns, and the company offered directed tours of the factory and the connected factory housing. This promotional tactic known as *Besucherspolitik,* literally "the politics of visiting," became a tradition. The list of notable foreign visitors who came away with glowing reviews of the work included Secretary of State Alfred von Tirpitz and representatives of the prestigious *British Medical Journal.*[18]

Worker housing notwithstanding, there was plenty of coercion in the world of Krupp. Housing leases were often linked to employment contracts. The libraries were kept free of religious, philosophical, or political works, and workers living in the colonies were forbidden from receiving journals associated with the Social Democratic Party. Krupp's housing inspectors could enter homes at any time to check that inhabitants were following the rules.[19]

Powerful electrical companies like Siemens and AEG were another cohort of big firms that invested in welfare spending for employees. They were less blatantly coercive than Krupp, although they were hardly examples of surveillance-free living. Werner von Siemens, who founded the Siemens & Halske company in 1847, was motivated by a strong desire to provide security for his family, and he prioritized his family in the company's affairs. He avoided interfering in the private lives of workers, unlike Krupp, but gave careful thought, as company historian Wilfried Feldenkirchen notes, to "harmonizing the interests of his employees with the goals of the company."[20] Siemens noted in his memoirs that it had become apparent to him "at an early stage that a satisfactory development of the continuously growing company could be brought about only if the contented and spontaneous cooperation of all employees aimed at promoting their interests could be ensured." Therefore, he concluded, "all the members of the company should participate in the profits according to their achievements."[21]

This belief yielded a steady growth of welfare spending. In 1855, Siemens started giving employees at his Berlin factory a Christmas bonus based on their own and the firm's performance. In 1872 the firm established a pension fund, funded by Siemens, his brothers Carl and Wilhelm, and their then-partner Johann Georg Halske. This fund gave workers who had worked at Siemens for three decades or more a pension based on two-thirds of their wages. In 1872, a cooperative society was founded to provide its members with improved shopping facilities and a canteen. In 1873, Siemens introduced a nine-hour workday.[22] But these benefits came with strings. During the 1900s, when there were considerable labor disputes at the company, it was company policy that employees who took part in strikes would lose their vested rights to social benefits. If they were subsequently reinstated, their period of service at the company was deemed to start afresh. Siemens was aggressively anti-union and established a company union to keep the labor force under control.[23]

The war and the new legal order of the Weimar Republic changed the options available to Siemens' management. The Stinnes-Legien Agreement, named after the industrialist Hugo Stinnes and the trade union leader Carl Legien, signed on November 15, 1918, sought to defuse the conflict-riven industrial relations at the end of the war. Members of the business community were concerned not only by revolutionary socialism but also by some radical ideas being proposed by their own class. In 1917, Walther Rathenau, the son of the founder of Siemens' competitor AEG, published *Vom Aktienwesen: Eine geschäftliche Betrachtung* (From the stock market: A business perspective), which argued against the dominant power of shareholders. Instead, he made the case that corporations should be responsible for society as a whole.[24] Under the terms of the Stinnes-Legien Agreement, employers agreed to recognize trade unions, bargain with them over working conditions and wages, and introduce the eight-hour workday. In exchange, the trade unions acknowledged the continued existence of private property and agreed to join with employers in creating an *Arbeitsgemeinschaft,* or social partnership, designed to institutionalize future joint economic and social policies. The latter lasted until 1924, when employers pulled out of the eight-hour workday, but collective bargaining persisted until 1933, when it was abolished by the new Nazi government.[25]

In this new legal situation, Carl Friedrich von Siemens, Werner's younger son who headed the company between 1919 and 1941, accepted trade unions and collective bargaining. In 1928 the firm introduced a profit-sharing system, started funding annual recreational trips for employees, and invested in extensive health education.[26] The company also moved, much later than Krupp, into employer-provided housing. At the turn of the century, Siemens had transferred most of its production facilities to northwest Berlin in an area known as Siemensstadt. In 1921, construction of a residential estate at Rohrdamm in Siemensstadt began.[27] Hans Scharoun, architect and cocreator of the new workers' village, described it as "a space that a pedestrian crosses in about a quarter of an hour, a space big enough to accommodate the joyful experience of a child's adventure and small enough to create a feeling of home."[28] The project became one of Germany's best-recognized worker villages. Housing was designed by the Deutsche Werkbund–affiliated architect Walter Gropius, a founding member of the Bauhaus art school. While Krupp created rural cabins in a natural setting, Gropius designed more functional apartments with larger kitchens and bedrooms, built-in furniture, and timesaving appliances.[29] Still, the new commitment to social partnership, the historian Heidrun Homburg notes, "did not prevent the Siemens management from silently accepting the trade unions' dissolution after Hitler seized power."[30]

Krupp and Siemens were just two of the many large German firms that invested heavily in the social welfare of their employees. The benefits they offered were more extensive than those of most of their British and American counterparts at the time, even though German state insurance was also more robust. German corporate responsibility was motivated by self-interest and infused with patriarchal values, and it involved a heavy dose of coercion. There were plenty of parallels elsewhere. William Lever and George Pullman were also controlling and driven by self-interest in crafting welfare policies for employees, but Krupp, in particular, embraced a form of coercive paternalism on steroids. Bosch stands out as believing in a different form of responsibility, one that offered employees a wider measure of freedom and choice.

Robert Bosch and the Promise of Choice

Unlike George and Richard Cadbury and Edward and Lincoln Filene, who inherited their companies from their fathers, Bosch created his own company after working through engineering apprenticeships in Germany, the United States, and Britain. His firm introduced multiple innovations, including a spark plug that was an essential component of the internal combustion engine. His corporate welfare policies became some of the most progressive in Germany. Unlike many of his contemporaries, he sought to preserve the personal freedom of those employees who benefited from them. He also became a prominent philanthropist and an active promoter of international economic collaboration. Yet however earnest he may have been in his commitment to workers' welfare—and, later, to supporting resistance to the Nazis—he would not fully escape the moral compromises with the evils of his time.

Bosch's early life gave little sign that he would be successful in business. He was born in 1861 in Albeck in southern Germany to an affluent farmer and his wife. His family was decidedly middle class, not just in economic circumstances but also in its trappings and priorities. He later described his father as "a man educated beyond his class," saying, "He possessed a library of all the German classics and had also read and digested them."[31] Bosch's father was a dedicated Freemason. According to one of Bosch's biographers, Peter Theiner, this association "provided a refuge of cultivated civility, a liberal humane association, in which friendship, tolerance, solidarity, and cosmopolitan views were valued."[32] Bosch was an avid reader, like his father, but he did not do well at school. Instead of going on to high school and university, he became an apprentice precision mechanic at the age of fifteen. After three years, he left, disappointed in how little he learned, and went to work for his brother Karl, who was eighteen years older and owned a gas and water pipe company. He did a year of compulsory military service starting in 1881 and continued aimlessly changing jobs afterward. He briefly enrolled as a nonregistered student at Stuttgart Polytechnic, where a tutor gave him a letter of recommendation for the electrical company of Thomas Edison in New York.

While at Stuttgart Polytechnic, Bosch was impressed by one of the professors, Gustav Jäger, a doctor and zoologist. Jäger believed that woolen clothing was best for living a healthy life. Bosch adopted this view and, as his business developed, continued to wear woolen clothing and a wide-brimmed carpenter's hat.[33] Jäger also introduced Bosch to the principles of the contemporary *Lebensreform* (life reform) movement, which urged people to eat simple, healthy food and preached the virtues of nature. Bosch became a believer. Later, when he had money, he became, and remained, an active financial supporter of homeopathic medicine.[34]

Formal religion played a limited role in shaping his beliefs. Born and raised a Lutheran, he left the church in 1908. This appears to have reflected a dislike of organized religion more than anything else. His comments on religion were enigmatic. "I allow the Jew, Turk, Christian, and Buddhist to adhere to their God and idols," he once wrote. "As long as they are good people, I love them."[35]

The United States provided other formative experiences. Bosch arrived in New York in May 1884. He was briefly let go during a subsequent recession and experienced "bad times in New York," as he wrote home. He eventually found work again at Edison. He joined the Knights of Labor, originally a movement of Philadelphia craft workers that had grown into a mass trade union, and supported its demands, including eight-hour workdays, an end to child labor, temperance, access to education, and healthy living.[36] His time in the United States was formative, and he wrote home to his fiancée, Anna

Kayser, that he was "a socialist."[37] After a year, he crossed the Atlantic and worked at the British affiliate of Siemens in Woolwich, London, between May and December 1885, before returning to Germany at Christmas.

After working, again unsuccessfully, for another electrical company, Bosch launched his own workshop in Stuttgart in November 1887, one month after getting married. His father had died six years earlier, and funding came from his estate. The small business undertook electrical repairs and sold electrical medical devices. He invented a magneto—a small electric generator—for stationary engines in 1887, but by 1891 the business was only kept afloat thanks to loans from his family, especially his mother. Despite making low profits, Bosch invested heavily in machinery and stressed quality, punctuality, and discipline in his workshop.[38]

Bosch's prospects improved when the company began making magneto ignition devices to generate the electric spark that was necessary for the air-fuel mixture in an internal combustion engine to explode. Asked by a customer simply to copy an exciting machine, Bosch chose instead to steadily improve the technology. In 1897, his team adapted the magneto device and invented the first spark plug, a magneto-based ignition system. The invention revolutionized the operation of automobiles due to its reliability. Bosch's business took off. He opened a factory in Stuttgart in 1900 and soon opened outposts in Britain and France. The United States ultimately became the company's most significant market. In 1907, an American subsidiary was launched with a factory in New York. A second factory, in Massachusetts, followed in 1912.[39]

Bosch's employment policies were distinctive from the start. He referred to his employees as associates rather than wage earners because he wanted them to feel they were fully integrated into the business. He sought, he later wrote, "to cultivate eager associates by letting each individual work independently as far as possible while at the same time delegating the responsibility that goes with the task."[40] In 1896 he introduced nine-hour workdays and, ten years later, eight-hour workdays; Bosch was one of the first employers in

Germany to take these steps. He added free Saturday afternoons and graduated vacation time.[41] He invested heavily in the training of apprentices, so much so that he became known within the company as "Father Bosch." In 1913, he established a separate apprentice-training department.[42] Bosch paid high wages and claimed that doing so was good for business. "I don't pay good wages because I am rich," multiple sources record him as saying, though none give a date. "I am rich because I pay good wages."[43] Despite such assertions that generous wages and welfare provision were just good business, it is evident that broader social considerations were also at work.

Bosch's engagement with socialism in the United States continued on his return to Germany. He developed a close relationship with Karl Kautsky, the editor in chief of *Neue Zeit,* the central publication of the Social Democratic Party, but his view of socialism did not include support for widespread state intervention, which he disliked.[44] He was always discreet about his political views and maintained that he had no particular political affiliation. However, his circle of friends and actions made his progressive views quite explicit. He was good friends with the feminist and Social Democratic politician Clara Zetkin, who persuaded Bosch to provide work for political refugees who fled Russia in 1905 after the country's failed revolution.[45] Bosch opted not to join a new metal employers' association formed in the Württemberg region in 1907. This step contributed to his reputation among fellow business leaders as "Bosch the red."[46] Unlike most German business leaders and the federal government, Bosch welcomed the growth of trade unions.[47]

Bosch was not motivated by a strong urge to control people. Before 1914, as a matter of policy, he built no company housing and provided no company-owned recreational facilities or stores. He believed that housing would corrupt his relationship with his workers, and he was mindful of their need for "personal freedom" and maintaining "personal responsibility."[48] Instead he offered construction loans. The one exception was when an apartment building had to be destroyed to make way for the company's expanding campus. In that case, he rebuilt the structure a short distance away to provide houses for those who had been displaced. Bosch also did not create a dedicated athletic field for employees. Instead, he donated a large locker room to Stuttgart's most prominent soccer club on condition that his workers could use it when it was otherwise not occupied.[49] In 1913, on the twenty-fifth anniversary of Kaiser Wilhelm II's coronation, a book was prepared for publication that presented the noteworthy social activities of German industrialists. The publishers asked Bosch to send information and photographs. He answered that there was nothing to photograph at his company, as he did not engage in any "charity" for his workers.[50] Bosch did not want to solve his workers' economic and social problems: he wanted instead to create the conditions that would make it possible for them solve those problems for themselves.

This did not prevent Bosch from facing a large-scale strike at his factories shortly before World War I, after he let eight workers go in the face of an economic downturn and refused the union's demand to reinstate them. The dispute could not be resolved quickly and satisfactorily. There was much discussion in the press and in the state assembly given that the firm held such a stellar reputation for paying good wages and providing good welfare benefits. In the spring of 1913, Bosch locked his workers out of the factory. Eventually, some 1,800 of the 3,700 total workers before the lock out returned, creating a split in the workforce that Bosch deeply regretted. A settlement was ultimately reached, and Bosch promised returning workers that their salaries would not be reduced. He joined the employers' association he had previously spurned, and declined to negotiate further with the union on policies. However, he also rejected overtures to join a conservative group dominated by big business that was lobbying for stricter legislation against industrial strikes. He later described the "experience" of 1913 "as one of the worst" in his life.[51]

The remainder of Bosch's life saw him responding to constant economic and political turbulence. The company's sales boomed following the outbreak of World War I, growing from 27 million marks to over 77 million by 1917 as manufacturing switched from ignition systems for internal combustion engines to making detonators for grenades, which came to represent 70 percent of total production.[52] But the war was a disaster for his international business, which had provided 82 percent of the company's total sales in 1913. The company's factories and intellectual property in Britain and France were expropriated, and he lost the assets of the American business after the United States entered the war in 1917. Nothing was returned after the war.

Bosch undertook major restructuring of his company in these years, focused on finding a solution to the challenge of succession. His implicitly designated successor, Gustav Klein, was killed during a test flight with a new type of aircraft in 1917. His hopes that his son Robert, born in 1891, would succeed him were dashed when Robert was diagnosed with multiple sclerosis, from which he would die in 1921. In 1917, working with his friend and lawyer Paul Scheuing, Bosch turned his sole proprietorship into a stock corporation, Robert Bosch AG. Bosch retained 51 percent of the equity, and six senior executives held the remaining shares. This was only the first stage of the corporate reorganization.

Hans Walz, Bosch's private secretary, cooperated with Scheuing to work out the basis for a philanthropic approach to the management of Bosch's personal assets. This led to the establishment of an asset management company called Vermögensverwaltung GmbH (VVB) in March 1921. It was intended not only to control his personal assets but to eventually hold all the shares of Robert Bosch AG and to ensure in perpetuity that the company's strategy remained aligned with Bosch's beliefs. VVB's founding guidelines also made explicit the philanthropic intent behind the organization. "Apart from the alleviation of all kinds of hardship," it was noted, "support should be given to promote health, education, programs to help the gifted, international reconciliation, and similar objectives and his commitment to philanthropy."[53]

During the Weimar Republic, Bosch provided funds for the reformist Social Democratic newspaper *Sozialistische Monatshefte* and tried to get other industrialists to lend support also. Between 1917 and 1920, he also purchased a majority stake in the Deutsche

Verlagsanstalt, a regional publishing house that controlled leading newspapers in Württemberg. Acquiring a majority share in the firm was an explicit strategy to block entry into southwest Germany of the media mogul Alfred Hugenberg, a right-wing nationalist who by the late 1920s was financing the Nazi Party.[54] Bosch himself and Hans Walz, who became managing director of the company in 1926, joined the newly founded Association for Defense against Anti-Semitism in Stuttgart in that year.[55]

Bosch had to find new markets. The demand for war-related products in Germany wholly disappeared. In 1921 a new American company was launched, and Bosch traveled to Buenos Aires to start building a new business in Latin America and an Argentinean subsidiary in 1924.[56] The search for new markets encouraged the company to diversify its product portfolio into fountain pens, wrenches, typewriters, and other goods.[57] A downturn in the automobile industry in the mid-1920s caused a dramatic fall in sales of spark plugs. This was followed by further rationalization of the company governance structure, which included forming a quasi-board of three members to take over the primary executive responsibility for the company, and Walz becoming managing director. Under Walz, the company diversified more radically beyond the automobile industry through acquisitions and new investments and began manufacturing heating systems, refrigerators, radios, and televisions.[58]

The onset of the Great Depression and the consequent spread of tariffs and exchange controls radically changed the company's strategies abroad. In 1932 Bosch published a pamphlet, eventually translated into English in 1937, in which he reflected on preventing "future crises in the world economic system." The pamphlet reflected his continued optimism about the benefits of technical progress and his disdain for economic nationalism. "The world has become so small," he wrote, "that no sensible nation can think of cutting itself off from other nations." His recommendations included introducing reduced and flexible working hours, enabling people to do whatever they want in their leisure time to make themselves happier, and forming cartels designed to lower prices rather than raise them.[59]

By the time the English edition was published, his own country, led by Hitler since 1933, was well on its way to an extreme form of economic nationalism.

Bosch's Philanthropic Commitment

Bosch engaged in extensive philanthropic activities focused on education, alternative medicine, the city of Stuttgart, and pan-European collaboration. His first biographer, Theodor Heuss (a longtime friend selected by Bosch to write the biography, which was published in 1945, three years after Bosch's death), suggested he "was uncomfortable when he heard someone use idealistic views to blur the hard realities of workaday existence."[60] Instead, Bosch preferred to finance projects that would give concrete and visible assistance.

The promotion of education, both for his employees and more generally, was an abiding concern. This fit with his desire to help people help themselves, and with his broader ideas about the demands of citizenship. He noted that education enabled people "to make the right political decisions and to recognize false doctrines as such."[61] His more substantial philanthropy began in 1910, when he gave 1 million marks to his first significant foundation to support research and teaching at the Stuttgart Polytechnic (later the University of Stuttgart). Supporting this institution became a long-term commitment. In 1912 he purchased a literary newspaper called *Die Lese,* which had sought to make literary works more accessible but experienced financial difficulties. In 1916, he came to the financial rescue of the regional Social Democratic newspaper *Schwäbishe Tagwacht.*

Bosch's philanthropy intensified during World War I. His concern for the social consequences of the war, and his guilt at profiting from it, grew alongside sales. Soon after the war broke out, he gave 100,000 marks in cash to the mayor of Stuttgart to ameliorate the poverty and destitution that was spreading in the city, and he turned over a newly constructed factory to be a field hospital. He was eager to alleviate the poor housing conditions caused by rising rents, and in 1915 contributed two-thirds of the initial capital of 1.5 million marks to the Swabian Settlement Association, a nonprofit established to construct affordable housing. It had built almost three hundred new residential buildings by 1920 before the political and economic chaos following Germany's defeat halted the project.[62]

"When the war came and brought with it new military contracts," he later wrote, referring to his growing business in detonators for grenades, "it appalled me to think that I was making money while others were sacrificing their lives."[63] Toward the end of 1916, Bosch established the Robert Bosch War Foundation to canalize the river Neckar to improve shipping. The city of Stuttgart had long sought to undertake such a project but never had enough funding. By now a wealthy industrialist, Bosch donated 20 million marks for the project. Aware that the money might simply go into the coffers of the state of Württemberg if the war delayed construction, Bosch came up with an innovative legal structure for his gift, stipulating that the capital would only flow to the state when construction of the canal started. Meanwhile, the considerable annual interest of 650,000 marks was donated to the city and used for social welfare, education, public health, and beautification.[64]

Education remained a major priority. In 1916, Bosch founded the Association for the Advancement of the Gifted and donated 2 million marks to fund scholarships for talented individuals selected through a transparent process. The association began by sponsoring seventy-seven applicants, most of whom were between the ages of fourteen and twenty-six, who sought to go to a technical school or to acquire a commercial skill. The association later added a foundation for sponsoring music pupils. In 1918 Bosch also founded the Association for the Advancement of German General Adult Education, which had a broad agenda, including investing in pedagogical research in adult education, training relevant teachers, and expanding adult education to theater, music, cinema, and the arts. Bosch specified that the state should provide at least matching funds to complement his support. As part of his commitment to continuing education, Bosch launched a company library, which had amassed as many as eight thousand volumes by 1937. In marked contrast to Krupp's, Bosch's library included Karl Marx, Friedrich Engels, Vladimir Lenin, Leon Trotsky, and Rosa Luxemburg.[65]

Bosch was a fervent believer in alternative medicine, and he both funded institutions devoted to best practices and sought to spread the word. His father trusted greatly in homeopathy, and Bosch later recalled that during his childhood he was only ever given homeopathic treatments, which he judged to exercise a "powerful impact."[66] He remained a lifelong believer. During the war, he supplied 3 million marks to set up a homeopathic hospital near his home. The war halted the project, and in the chaotic postwar period he funded a homeopathic "interim hospital" in Stuttgart. In 1925 Bosch founded Hippokrates Verlag, a medical publishing company designed to promote a dialogue between conventional and alternative medicines. He also started buying books on the history of homeopathy and natural medicine, intended to be the basis of a new museum on the history of natural medicine, but that never materialized. In 1936, he donated a further 5.5 million marks to the project to mark his seventy-fifth birthday. Finally, in 1940, two years before his death, the full-scale homeopathic Robert Bosch Hospital was opened in Stuttgart. It was the largest homeopathic hospital in Germany and contained an X-ray department and a surgical unit, reflecting Bosch's wish for conventional and alternative medicine to coexist side by side.[67]

After World War I, amid rampant deprivation, Bosch made further investments to support his employees. In 1921 the Bosch Assistance Fund introduced life insurance for its salaried employees, which required the firm to pay a surcharge of 5 percent of an employee's annual salary to the insurance company. Unlike with most other companies at the time, the employee would not lose the company's contributions if he or she moved to another company. In the following year, Bosch launched a fund for children of employees who had died in the war. Later the benefits were extended to the children of sick and deceased employees. Both funds had to be recapitalized after the era of hyperinflation. A particularly innovative dimension was the nomination of honorary godparents from among employees to provide advice to fatherless children.[68]

Bosch was severely affected by the loss of close friends and associates during the war, and he actively supported efforts to prevent further conflicts. In 1923, Count Richard Coudenhove-Kalergi published a controversial book titled *Paneuropa* that called for the creation of a unified European state. Bosch provided financial support for Coudenhove-Kalergi and financed his Paneuropa movement. He brought together German business leaders and reached out to their French counterparts to discuss the creation of a single market, but the low trust between the parties meant that little was achieved.[69] Coudenhove-Kalergi described Bosch as "Pan-European for moral, rather than economic reasons . . . seeking not to sell his goods better in other countries, but to protect Europe from another war."[70] Bosch continued to support the movement even as growing Franco-German tensions rendered it increasingly irrelevant. In 1932, Bosch joined a group that included the novelist and Nobel laureate Thomas Mann, which nominated Coudenhove-Kalergi for the Nobel Peace Prize.[71]

The ascension of Hitler to power in 1933 put an end to the Pan-European movement. Coudenhove-Kalergi, half-Austrian and half-Japanese and married to a Jew, was personally loathed by Hitler. When the war began, he narrowly escaped from the Gestapo and eventually resettled in the United States. His biographer claims he was the inspiration for Victor Laszlo, the Czechoslovakian resistance leader in the iconic film *Casablanca*, released in 1942.[72]

Bosch and the Nazis

Bosch worked actively against the Nazis and deplored their policies. In the March 1932 election for the German president, he voted for Paul von Hindenburg, a conservative candidate who successfully beat Hitler.[73] Historians have long established that few of the leaders of large German companies supported Hitler's ascent to power; rather, they supported conservative parties, and most of the moral compromises and irresponsibility of business leaders came afterward. As Hitler undermined the institutions of democracy, abolished trade unions, stripped Jews of their rights, introduced conscription, and began large-scale rearmament, German capitalists were overwhelmingly silent.

Foreign business leaders with large operations in Germany were also silent. When Edward Filene warned that Nazi policies posed a "crime against civilization," he stood out as a lone voice. In Germany itself, each company had its own unique story, but the general response was silence and complicity. Historian Ralf Banken's main conclusion from surveying two decades of intensive research on business and the Nazis by German scholars is that business leaders were primarily motivated by their own economic self-interest.[74] The authors of an exhaustive history of Deutsche Bank observe, "Confronted by a world that no longer appeared to need them, bankers explained their compliant position to themselves by saying that they were doing nothing more than facing realities and then trying, however ineffectually, to mold them as best they could."[75] A subsequent study by the historian Harold James showed that a younger generation of Deutsche Bank managers became actively aligned with Nazi ideology.[76]

Even companies with a strong Jewish presence in ownership and management sought to survive rather than resist. This was the case of Beiersdorf, the maker of Nivea skin cream and other well-known personal care products. The company's Jewish managers resigned and were transferred to the firm's foreign affiliates after the Nazis came to power, and company marketing was aligned with the beauty ideals of the Nazi regime. Advertisements featured blonde, athletic models with no visible makeup and adopted the blackletter type favored by the Nazis.[77]

Hans Mommsen's definitive study of German resistance to Hitler concludes that "representatives of skilled trades, commerce and industry, and even the liberal professions, were completely absent from the resistance."[78] It is a sobering judgment of the ethical collapse of a business elite that prioritized profit over morality.

As the Nazi regime descended into full-scale genocide and lawless looting of occupied territories, many prominent German firms, including the chemicals giant IG Farben, followed in the footsteps of the German army and sought to acquire and absorb competitors in conquered countries.[79] At least four hundred companies employed hundreds of thousands of slave laborers from conquered territories and concentration camps.

Alfred Krupp, who effectively ran the steel company after his father's stroke in 1941, was a committed Nazi and an enthusiastic advocate of using slave labor from concentration camps until they died from exhaustion. The firm employed over one hundred thousand slave laborers recruited from 138 concentration camps in nearly one hundred factories.[80]

These profound ethical lapses were not unique to Krupp. The Degussa corporation processed and controlled the production and distribution of Zyklon B—the pesticide used to gas the inmates of the Auschwitz and Majdanek concentration camps.[81] The staff of the Bayer chemical company paid the SS, Hitler's private army responsible for the most egregious human rights abuses, for Auschwitz concentration camp inmates on whom they conducted experiments. The results of these experiments were often fatal or had life-changing consequences.[82] The giant insurance company Allianz insured SS-owned production facilities in camps. The engineering company Topf and Sons built crematoria for the camps.[83] As Banken acknowledges, there is ongoing scholarly debate about just how much freedom business leaders had to maneuver in the Nazi era. Whatever the academic merits of the question, there is no doubt that many leaders embraced the Nazi Party's policies and actions.[84]

Bosch's actions should be set within this context of overall moral depravity. He and Walz, who was a committed Lutheran, were not immediately aware of the depth of evil that was to come. At first, they welcomed Hitler's commitment to expanding the German automobile industry. Over the following years, however, they and their colleagues walked a fine line between complicity and resistance. In an endeavor to head off political interference, Walz joined the

Nazi Party and in 1935 became an honorary officer in the SS. Subsequently, he was invited to become a member of the Circle of Friends of the Reich leader of the SS, Heinrich Himmler. Bosch himself built a personal relationship with Hjalmar Schacht, the minister for economic affairs. Inside the company, partly because of these contacts and affiliations, the Nazi influence was kept at bay. Bosch and Walz hired young Jews and others facing persecution, including former members of the Communist Party; provided financial support to Jewish charities; and helped Jews get out of Germany. Walz's position, the historian Johannes Bähr has observed, became one of "hopeless contradictions," as he was "in association with the perpetrators of genocide when at the same time he was helping persecuted Jews."[85] There was little doubt where his true sympathies lay. In 1969 Walz became one of the few former members of the Nazi Party, alongside Oskar Schindler, honored by the State of Israel with the title Righteous Among the Nations.[86]

In 1937, Bosch appointed Carl Goerdeler to be an adviser to the company. Goerdeler was a conservative monarchist, a former mayor of Leipzig, and an activist in the German resistance to Hitler. When Bosch's efforts to convince the Nazi war minister Werner von Blomberg of the dangers of war failed, Goerdeler was sent around Europe and the United States on an unsuccessful mission to warn foreign leaders about what was happening in Nazi Germany.[87] Goerdeler and the top management at Bosch, including Walz and Willy Schlosstein, Bosch's private secretary, formed a passive resistance group within the company. After Bosch's death, Goerdeler became directly involved in the July 1944 plot to assassinate Hitler and was executed. Out of respect for the company and its founder, Walz and the others were protected by elements within the regime.[88]

There is little doubt that Bosch as a company benefited from the Nazi regime. The Nazis liked the high quality of Bosch's products, the high wages it paid, and its family ownership. The expansion of the automobile industry led to rapid growth in sales and profits. The company was also essential to rearmament plans. In 1936, Bosch erected a new factory to manufacture aircraft engines outside Berlin and founded a subsidiary to run it. In 1937, the regime constructed another new factory to produce equipment for military vehicles, which Bosch then operated. By 1940, armaments represented two-thirds of Bosch's total sales.[89] Bosch was initially optimistic that the Nazis would soon fall from power when war broke out in the fall of 1939. "I am happy that the war has arrived," he wrote. "Only in this way will we be able to rid ourselves of these criminals."[90] Instead, his company was dragged into the moral cesspit of the Nazi war economy. After 1940 and through Bosch's death until the end of the war, the company employed a growing number of slave laborers, including captured prisoners of war and concentration inmates. The numbers probably reached twenty thousand. At least some of them, especially Russians and inmates of concentration camps, were treated cruelly.[91]

Despite Bosch's personal disdain for the Nazi regime, his company ended up playing a significant role in the German war machine and in the human rights abuses that lay at its heart. The company kept the German army on wheels and the German air force flying, and Robert Bosch found himself hailed by the Nazis before his death in March 1942. On Bosch's eightieth birthday, Hitler called him a "Pioneer of Labor," and he ordered a state ceremony for Bosch's funeral.[92]

The leaders of the Bosch company protected vulnerable employees and, more startlingly, provided cover for the German resistance by posing as Nazis and developing contacts in the regime. But Bosch also offered services to the regime and profited from them. When Robert Bosch died, slave labor was being used in his factories. He may be judged as having made a pragmatic response to a horrible situation beyond his control, but his actions can hardly be considered a model for how a business leader should act in the context of an authoritarian and morally bankrupt government. His firm was too complicit with the Nazi regime for such an accolade. Bosch's pragmatism ultimately compromised his sense of deep responsibility.

The context was the ethical collapse of almost the entire German business system. As David de Jong's *Nazi Billionaires* demonstrates, Ferdinand Porsche, Friedrich Flick, August von Finck, Rudolf-August Oetker, and Günther Quandt were among the industrialists who laid the basis for vast family wealth in postwar Germany from the money they made from fulfilling Nazi orders, using slave labor, and stealing Jewish property.[93] Forty-two leading industrialists were put on trial at Nuremberg after the end of the war, and twenty-seven were found guilty of human rights abuses and other war crimes and sentenced to between eighteen months and twelve years in jail. Alfred Krupp received a twelve-year sentence plus forfeiture of property. He was pardoned by the American high commissioner for occupied Germany in 1951 in the context of the emergent Cold War and the American desire to strengthen Allied-occupied Germany against the Soviet Union. Thirteen members of IG Farben's management were also found guilty, including Hermann Schmitz, the chairman of the managing board, who received a four-year sentence. They were also pardoned in 1951, but IG Farben was dissolved and broken up into its constituent companies. No member of Bosch was put on trial.[94]

Over time, the new German Federal Republic became a model for stakeholder capitalism. A broad stakeholder view was reinforced by a legally mandated codetermination system that began in 1951 when a law required codetermination in businesses with more than one thousand employees in the coal, steel, and mining industries with workers' representatives making up one half of supervisory boards. This mandate drew on the long history of German legislation going back to Bismarck.[95]

Reaching back to the era of Bismarck, German big business had pursued notably progressive welfare policies, but in many cases (like Krupp) coercion and repression accompanied these investments and commitments. In this respect, Bosch stands out as significantly different from most of his contemporaries. Living through the unification of Germany as a nation-state, the overthrow of the Kaiser, the establishment of the Weimar Republic, and the murderous Nazi regime, he grew his business in more turbulent conditions than

George Cadbury and Edward Filene. Nevertheless, he shared their concerns for the less fortunate and their sense of social responsibility as the leader of a big business. Bosch cared for his employees and wanted them to work in good conditions. He invested in education in the city of Stuttgart and articulated the case for peace and cross-national collaboration. Unlike many of his peers, he emphasized supporting individuals and empowering them to make their own choices rather than mandating their actions. In this respect, he can be seen as a forerunner of the business leaders who characterized the post-1945 German social market economy.

But unlike Cadbury and Filene, Bosch built a successful business in an industry that benefited from war. He found himself making big profits in World War I and assuaged his guilt by giving money away. The situation was much more challenging in the Nazi era. Even as the elderly Bosch clandestinely supported the resistance to Hitler, his company profited from Germany's aggressive military buildup and helped make it possible. Most troublingly, his company employed slave labor. He and his colleagues saved individuals but were complicit in supporting the Nazi war machine that killed millions of people.

In his last years, Bosch gave more thought to his legacy and to ensuring that his business, and the values he thought it represented, would persist after his death. In 1937 he changed the legal structure of his company to a GmbH, a private limited liability company. In his will, drawn up the following year, Bosch expressed his wish for the company to remain independent and autonomous. The directors of the VVB asset management company he had created in 1921 were appointed as executors and given thirty years to reach a decision on the fate of his 86 percent ownership stake. Walz oversaw the postwar reconstruction of the company and led it until 1963.[96] Between 1962 and 1964 Bosch's family heirs helped to facilitate the institution of a new structure. They sold all but 8 percent of their shareholding to VVB (renamed Robert Bosch Stiftung in 1969). In return, VVB waived the voting rights from these shares, which were transferred to a new trust set up especially for this purpose, Robert Bosch Industrietreuhand KG.[97]

The resulting structure provides a model of long-term steward ownership. Robert Bosch GmbH had three shareholders. Robert Bosch Stiftung held 92 percent of dividend rights and no voting rights. The dividends were used in philanthropy. Robert Bosch Industrietreuhand held 93 percent of the voting rights and no dividend rights. It had ten steward-owners who served for limited periods, and whose positions could not be sold or inherited. Finally, Robert Bosch's heirs held 7 percent of voting rights and 8 percent of dividend rights. The structure removed any incentive to maximize profit over the company's long-term development, the welfare of employees, or environmental impact, and it protected the company from being taken over.[98] Bosch flourished as an innovative technology company noted for long-term vision with sales of over $80 billion and four hundred thousand employees in 2020. Robert Bosch Stiftung distributed over $90 million for philanthropic causes in that year.[99] Bosch, in light of its ownership structure, has been described by the Saïd Business School's Colin Mayer as one "of the most successful European corporations."[100] The deep responsibility of the founder persisted and was even strengthened after Bosch's death.

Robert Bosch's story shows us that capitalism limits the possibilities for choosing responsibility over the exigencies of the market or, in the 1930s and 1940s, the demands of the fascist state. When does palling around with Hitler undo whatever karmic bonus points are accrued from supporting the resistance?

CHAPTER 4

THE CHALLENGE OF LATECOMER STATES

J. N. TATA AND SHIBUSAWA EIICHI

George Cadbury, Edward Filene, and Robert Bosch shared a belief that business had a responsibility to address the social inequalities of wealth and access that accompanied the new industrial age. Shibusawa Eiichi, in Japan, established his business around the same time, but he faced different challenges.[1] Most of the world outside northwestern Europe and North America missed the first wave of industrialization and the explosion of wealth that followed from it. Many countries had been colonized or threatened with colonization by Western countries. This raised different challenges for business leaders. Was it their responsibility to help their countries catch up and modernize? How far should patriotism or a desire for political independence influence their business decisions? What role should these leaders play in shaping their societies as the country modernized?

This chapter looks at a cohort of business leaders who faced the common circumstance of living in societies that desired to catch up with the West. This did not generate a common response. We see some entrepreneurs focusing on wealth creation for themselves and their families while others prioritized the national good. Shibusawa was one of those who felt compelled to take on deep responsibility for creating wealth and contributing to the social and ethical development of his society, and we will look at his experience in greater detail.

The scale of the challenge faced by entrepreneurs who built businesses outside the developed West in the closing years of the nineteenth century and early years of the twentieth was enormous.

Although debates on numbers and chronology continue, it seems that income gaps between the more developed North Sea economies and those elsewhere, including China and India, opened up several centuries before the nineteenth century.[2] And while industrialization spread rapidly in Western Europe and across the Atlantic, it took hold much more slowly elsewhere. The second half of the nineteenth century saw people, trade, and capital move around the world on a scale and with a speed not seen previously. International transport costs fell with the arrival of railroads and steamships, while the speed of communication was transformed by the telegraph. Rather than bring economic growth, this wave of globalization facilitated international specialization. While northwestern Europe and North America manufactured goods and exported them, the rest of the world specialized in cultivating food and mining for minerals and gems that were exported to the industrialized world.[3] These countries were by and large much less technologically developed, much less urban, much less educated, and much poorer than Western Europe and the United States, magnifying the challenges faced by would-be entrepreneurs.

The gap in wealth between the industrialized West and the rest was huge by the time of World War I. According to the authoritative Maddison statistical database, which converts historical macroeconomic statistics into contemporary US dollars, the real GDP per capita of the United States stood at $10,108, while that of Britain was $8,212 and that of Germany was $5,815 in 1913.[4] The rest of the world was far behind. Much of Latin America lost half a century of economic growth because of political turbulence following the overthrow of Spanish colonial rule. With the notable exceptions of northern Mexico and Argentina, there was little industry in Latin America by 1913. Instead, the region became a massive exporter of wheat, beef, nitrates, rubber, silver, gold, and other commodities to the industrialized West. A number of countries, especially Argentina, grew wealthy from exporting beef and wheat, but the wealth was skewed as it became highly concentrated in the hands of landowners and a few powerful families.[5] Argentina's GDP per capita was $6,052 in 1913—marginally higher than Germany's. But Argentina was an outlier. The GDPs per capita of Mexico, Peru, and Brazil were only $2,004, $1,645, and $1,046, respectively.

Asia was another story. Japan experienced considerable development from the 1870s, but its real GDP per capita was still only $2,431 in 1913, less than a quarter of that of the United States. The larger economies of Asia fared far worse. In 1800, the giant handicraft industries of China and India accounted for over one-half of world manufacturing output. By 1880, the handicraft industries of both countries had been decimated as cheap manufactured textiles from the West undercut their export markets and penetrated their domestic markets.[6] India and China became exporters of opium, raw cotton, raw silk, sugar, and tea. In 1913, the estimated real GDP per capita of India and China was $1,073 and $985, respectively.

Poverty and lack of modern industry left countries vulnerable to Western imperialism. From the late eighteenth century to 1858, a large area of the Indian subcontinent fell under the control of Britain's East India Company, which was privately owned although chartered by the British government.[7] Insofar as the Company, as it was known, was a protomodern capitalist firm, India might be seen as the victim of a particularly lawless form of capitalism that could enforce its power with a private army. The free trade policies imposed on India in the nineteenth century meant that its handicraft industry was unprotected from cheaper British manufactured goods.[8] After imposing direct control of India in 1858, following a rebellion that included many of the locally recruited soldiers working for the Company, the British built Asia's largest rail network in India, but it was constructed for military purposes and to facilitate the export of primary commodities. The colonial regime raised few taxes and spent them on railroads and defense. Education received little spending.[9] By 1901, only an estimated 5 percent of India's 240 million people were literate, and almost all of these were men.[10]

In the same period, China lost much of its sovereignty as a result of two opium wars with Britain and other Western countries that acted in support of opium smugglers (the first ran from 1839 to

1842; the second from 1856 to 1860). China's defeat in these wars led to the imposition of Unequal Treaties, which forced China to open ports to Western trade, granted foreigners extraterritoriality, and legalize the opium trade. By the end of the 1880s, China had an estimated forty million opium addicts.[11]

Make Money or Improve Society?

Building a successful business is challenging in the best of circumstances, and even more so in a world dominated by foreign forces. Institutional structures in non-Western countries were often weak and unstable; when they were stable, it was often because the country had been turned into a colony. There was no ready supply of skilled labor or managerial talent because education levels were low. According to a study of the average number of years spent in school in 1910, the figure was 1.2 years in China and only 0.4 years in India. In Japan children spent on average 2.5 years in school, a number matched by Argentina, the most literate country in Latin America (Brazil only mustered 0.9 years). By contrast, the number of years spent in education was 7.5 in the United States, 7.0 in Germany, and 5.9 in Britain.[12]

Then as now, many business leaders felt that their responsibility began and ended with the creation of wealth for themselves and their families. This sentiment appears to have been particularly dominant in Latin America. As modern businesses were developed during the second half of the nineteenth century, they typically took the form of powerful family businesses with close connections to the ruling political elites. Context mattered a lot. Spanish colonial rule bequeathed socially (and ethnically) hierarchical societies. Landowning white elites dominated power structures. Franchises were extended very slowly, which some historians believe explains the limited investment in public education compared with the United States.[13]

This was the case in Argentina. A small group of family-owned businesses developed that owned Argentina's largest firms in their respective sectors: Tornquist, Bemberg, Devoto, Bunge y Born,

Portalis/Bracht, and Soulas. People with strong connections with Europe through family and business ties built each of these groups. They diversified from merchant houses and commodity trading into finance, mortgages, sugar refining, tourism, and fishing. Close contacts with the political elite, the absence of regulatory controls, and high tariff levels enabled these groups to flourish during the country's commodity boom. They grew horizontally across different industries, rather than building innovation capabilities in a single industry. As a result, there was no Argentine equivalent of a consumer brand builder like Cadbury or a scientific innovator like Bosch. This pattern reflected in part the country's small domestic market—the population was less than eight million in 1913—and its geographical distance from developed markets, but it was also a reflection of the importance of political contacts who could deliver exclusive concessions and privileged access to European capital. It was more profitable to build quasi-monopolies than to engage in time-consuming brand-building or risky innovations. Ernesto Tornquist, for example, had close connections with French and Belgian financiers. He was also a close friend of several presidents, including Julio A. Roca, who granted him a privileged tax-free concession to build a sugar refinery.[14]

There is no evidence that the goals of Argentinean business leaders like Tornquist extended far beyond making profits and ensuring the continuity of their family businesses. Their implicit assumption appears to have been that what was good for them was good for the country. If they engaged in philanthropy, it has left no trace, although individual business leaders often donated to the Catholic Church, which was the principal provider of education, health, and social welfare to the poor throughout the region.[15]

A greater diversity of beliefs on the social role of business can be found around this time in India. There were certainly examples of deep responsibility by some business leaders. A perceived need to respond to the loss of sovereignty to the East India Company and the British Crown provided the incentive and, in some respects, the opportunity. The subcontinent also had a long cultural tradition of charity, as its various religions all encouraged charitable giving. In Hinduism, the belief in karma dictated that good deeds were rewarded in future lives. And *zagat,* one of the five pillars of Islam, called on individuals with holdings over a certain threshold to give a customary contribution of 2.5 percent on the value of all of their possessions to the poor during the month of Ramadan.[16]

The case of the small Parsi community, which mostly lived around Mumbai (then Bombay), is particularly interesting. The Parsi community developed close ties with the colonial administration and played an outside role in the beginnings of modern industry. From the middle of the nineteenth century, Parsi merchants sought to create a modern textile industry to replace the devastated Bengal handicraft industry.[17] By 1914, entrepreneurs from this small community had built thirty-four of the ninety-five cotton textile mills in India.[18] Yet the Parsis were more than effective entrepreneurs. Like the Quakers, their values predisposed them to assume broad social responsibilities. Zoroastrianism, their religion, praised self-help and the promotion of public welfare. Zoroastrians saw the world as a battle between a benevolent god and a wicked spirit, in which human beings had free will to do good or evil. Their behavior is believed to be crucial to the cosmic struggle. The teachings emphasize the importance of doing good works to improve life in this world.[19]

The Parsi community produced noteworthy philanthropists and advocates of social reform. An early example is Jamsetji Jeejeebhoy, a Parsi merchant in Mumbai, who grew rich trading opium to China during the first half of the nineteenth century and later endowed the first civil hospital, the first obstetric institution, and the first arts college. There were reputational rewards for such generosity. He became the first Indian to be awarded a knighthood by Queen Victoria.[20] A later example is Ardeshir Godrej, the founder of what would become one of India's largest business groups. The Godrej group began by making locks and safety deposits in Mumbai in 1897, starting a business that would later diversify into consumer products and stand out for its long-standing commitment to making a positive social impact. Godrej believed that India needed to free itself from Britain by becoming economically self-sufficient, and he felt his business should play a role in this. He became an early advocate of a movement called *swadeshi* that sought to replace British goods with India-made goods as a first step to independence.[21]

Jamsetji Nusserwanji (J. N.) Tata, who became the most prominent pioneer of modern industry in India, embodied the Parsi belief that business should be driven by social purpose. Tata was born in 1839 to a family of Parsi priests. His father had broken the family tradition and gone into business, making a fortune in the opium trade. This meant that he could afford to send his son to the prestigious Elphinstone College. After college, Tata spent his twenties working in his father's trading business and traveling widely, including to China and Britain, where he studied the textile industry. In 1869 he bought a bankrupt grinding mill for oil-bearing seeds in Mumbai, converted it to a cotton mill, and sold it two years later at a big profit. He then set up a huge textile factory in Nagpur, later named Empress Mills, where he introduced ring spindles, hugely increasing productivity. By the time of his death in 1904, he had built a large modern cotton textile business. He also founded the Taj Mahal Hotel in Mumbai, the first luxury hotel for affluent visitors to the city, and planned to create India's first integrated steel factory, having identified coal and iron deposits. The venture proved challenging because British investors had no interest in supporting it. Tata's elder son Daribi continued the project after his death, eventually raising money from other Indian businesses and affluent princely families. In 1908 the Tata Iron and Steel Company, India's first steel producer, opened at Jamshedpur in Bengal.[22]

Tata's textiles business made him wealthy. He appeared to enjoy his wealth, building large houses, among other things. But he saw money as a means to a broader end, which was to make India more self-sufficient and to provide support for its people. Tata was not an opponent of British rule as such—if anything, he was a supporter of the British Empire.[23] But he did embrace *swadeshi*, naming one of his textile companies, established in 1886, Swadeshi Mills.[24]

A striking feature of Tata's projects was that they always contained elements of social purpose. For example, his ambition to build
a hydroelectricity-generating plant for Mumbai went far beyond
providing a power source for his own factories. He expressed the
hope that this might help make the city a "smokeless city," by
replacing coal with cleaner hydropower. An extensive program of
tree cultivation and a sanctuary in the water-catchment area near the
plant reflected Zoroastrian concerns for the purity of the earth.[25] The
project, like the steel venture, was challenging, and it was left to
Daribi to bring to fruition.[26]

"In a free enterprise," Tata observed, "the community is not just
another stake holder in the business but in fact the very purpose of
its existence."[27] He invested in health, educational, and housing facilities for his workers. At Empress Mills, he introduced for the first
time in India eight-hour days, well-ventilated workplaces, a nursery
for young mothers, and a water filtration plant to provide clean
drinking water. In 1886, he instituted a pension fund and, in 1895,
began to pay accident compensation.[28] As he planned the Jamshedpur
steel plant, he envisaged a garden city with hospitals, schools, parks,
a soccer stadium, and playing fields. The company operated a free
hospital, which could be used by any of the city's inhabitants.[29]
These policies provided value to the Tata textile and steel companies, as they stabilized and motivated a new industrial labor force.
They were imposed on employees rather than being an object of
discussion.[30] But this does not change the fact that these welfare
measures were generous and well ahead of their time.

Tata repurposed the tenets of Zoroastrianism into a form of stakeholder capitalism infused with spirituality. He embraced capitalism
but saw it as a means to create wealth for more than just himself
and his family. Zoroastrianism teaches that poverty and suffering are
an affliction of evil, and that removing them deprives evil of suste-
nance. Tata interpreted this mighty task as requiring a dynamic
approach to the goal of social uplift. He disliked what he called
"patchwork philanthropy," which fed and clothed the poor and
destitute: he preferred what he called "constructive philanthropy."

"What advances a nation or community is not so much to prop up its weakest and most helpless members," he noted, "as to lift up the best and most gifted so as to make them of the greatest service to the country."[31] His investments in education reflected this belief. He launched the J. N. Tata Endowment for the Higher Education of Indians in 1892, which gave scholarships in the form of loans with nominal interest rates to deserving students for higher education in Europe. The scheme was initially limited to Parsi students, but it subsequently became merit based. Early recipients included women such as Freny Cama and Krishnabai Kelavkar, who were able to study medicine abroad.[32]

In 1894, Tata set aside fourteen of his larger buildings and four landed properties to create an endowment for a postgraduate university of science and technology in the city of Bangalore. His offer was taken up only after his death, when the land and buildings were repurposed to create the Indian Institute of Science, set up along the lines of the Johns Hopkins University in Baltimore. The Indian Institute pioneered advanced scientific education in India. Again, one could detect some element of self-interest in his benevolence: such an institute could provide his business with a much-needed supply of scientific and technological expertise. Yet Tata also had a wider vision of what the institute could do, envisaging, for example, a humanities department designed to provide a well-balanced education beyond strictly technical subjects. The colonial government's opposition to this idea was one reason why the institute was only launched after his death.[33] Notably, Tata insisted that his own name not be used for the institution.[34]

Tornquist and Tata represent two ends of the spectrum when it comes to the responsibility of business leaders in latecomer economies. Both built highly successful businesses, but their legacies were different. Tornquist's son and grandson carried the business on, but it collapsed during the 1970s, and few would recognize his name in Argentina today. In contrast, the Tata business remains one of India's largest, and one of its most respected names when it comes to ethical and social responsibility.

Shibusawa Eiichi: From Feudal Farmer to Venture Capitalist

Shibusawa Eiichi, who is often called the "father of Japanese capitalism," was almost an exact contemporary of Tata.[35] Both were pioneers of modern business practices in their respective countries who shared a deep commitment to wider social purpose. The two men actually met in 1894, when Tata traveled to Japan to discuss with Shibusawa the creation of a joint venture between his company and Japanese interests. The shipping of Indian cotton to the Japanese port of Kobe was dominated by a cartel called the Shipping Conference, a leading member of which was Britain's giant P&O Steam Navigation Company. Tata wanted to ship the cotton at a lower rate. Shibusawa was able to arrange an agreement with Japan's largest shipping company, Nippon Yusen Kaisha (NYK), but the venture only lasted two years before Tata had to withdraw after making heavy losses.[36] Still, the episode reflected their aspirations to build the business capabilities of their respective nations.

Shibusawa's personal journey was one of remarkable transformation. He was born in 1840 in a country that had largely cut itself off from the rest of the world. In 1603, after a period of civil war and social disruption coinciding with the arrival of Portuguese traders, Tokugawa Ieyasu, a warlord, defeated his opponents and became shogun, or military dictator, an office that dated back to the twelfth century. His family ruled Japan for the next two and a half centuries. The shogun lived in the city of Edo (subsequently renamed Tokyo), while the imperial family lived in seclusion in the southern city of Kyoto. During the 1630s, Ieyasu's grandson Iemitsu expelled Europeans from the country and persecuted and largely eliminated the hundreds of thousands of local Christians who had been converted by European missionaries. He also closed the borders of Japan, although some trade with China continued and a small Dutch trading post was permitted on an artificial island built in Nagasaki Bay. The shogun imposed a rigid social hierarchy. Feudal lords ran their domains under his watchful eye. They had to spend every other year in residence in Edo and were expected to leave their families behind as hostages when they returned to their domains. Samurai, a warrior class, were at the top of this hierarchy. Farmers, artisans, and merchants, who were at the bottom, followed them.[37]

Despite the ostensibly rigid social hierarchy, Japan experienced considerable urbanization under the Tokugawa shogunate. By the eighteenth century, Edo was the largest city in the world. Literacy also increased. However, by the middle of the nineteenth century, Japan remained a preindustrial society subject to periodic devastating famines.[38]

In 1853, when Shibusawa was thirteen years old, Commodore Matthew Perry of the US Navy arrived in Edo Bay with two sailing ships and two steamships demanding that the country open itself to international trade. The United States was sweeping across the Pacific at that time and was particularly interested in securing coal supplies to facilitate the journey to China, which was the main country of interest. The samurai were master swordsmen but in no position to defend the country against Western guns and artillery. In 1858, the shogun was reluctantly forced to sign the Treaty of Amity and Commerce with the United States. Similar treaties followed with Britain, France, the Netherlands, and Russia. These Unequal Treaties replicated what had happened to China during the Opium Wars and later. Eight ports had to be opened for trade. Japan lost the right to set tariffs. Foreigners were given extraterritorial rights.[39]

Shibusawa came from a family of farmers, but they were affluent. His father had built a successful business buying indigo leaves from farmers, processing them into indigo balls, and selling them. As a result, Shibusawa received a good education. He was able to learn calligraphy, reading, swordsmanship, and writing, which at the time were largely the province of samurai families. He also received a thorough education in the ancient philosophy of Confucianism, which influenced him throughout his life. In 1861, he went to study in Edo and became involved in a radical movement challenging the shogun's acceptance of the treaties whose slogan was "expel the barbarians." He came close to staging an armed rebellion but changed his mind and instead entered the service of a brilliant feudal lord,

Hitotsubashi Yoshinobu, who became the last Tokugawa shogun in 1865.[40]

It was in this capacity that Shibusawa joined a Japanese delegation, which included the shogun's younger brother, to attend the Paris International Exposition in 1867. The group stopped at several ports on the forty-nine-day journey to France, including Shanghai, Hong Kong, Saigon, Singapore, and Aden. On the journey Shibusawa noted the new Western technologies he saw, including gaslights and electric cables. Japan was one of forty-two countries to take part in the exposition. Shibusawa met Emperor Napoleon III, who presided over the seven-month-long event, and kept detailed records of the modern machines he encountered.[41]

Shibusawa ended up spending over a year in Europe. The Japanese delegation visited neighboring countries, including Switzerland and Italy, traveling on the new technology of trains. Shibusawa recorded his thoughts about the growing importance of modern industries, especially steel, and how political leaders could advance a nation's commercial interests. The long visit was hugely influential. He saw the technological achievements of Europe but also perceived a huge contrast between the disdain that Tokugawa officials held toward merchants in Japan and the high status that businesspeople appeared to hold in Europe.[42]

Shibusawa was still in Paris in early 1868 when he heard news that the Tokugawa government had been overthrown. The successful revolt, which was staged primarily by samurai from the south of the country, was a turning point in modern Japanese history. The emperor Meiji, who was fifteen years old and had become emperor the previous year, was "restored" to power and moved from Kyoto to Edo, which was renamed Tokyo. Real power in the Meiji Restoration lay with the new government, composed primarily of the coup leaders. They resolved to resist the fate of India and the humiliation of Imperial China, not by attempting to fight the West but by catching up with it through a strategy based on the slogan of a "rich country, and strong army." The next few years saw radical political and social changes, including the establishment of compulsory education and military conscription, a new prefecture system of government to replace the feudal domains, and the progressive reduction in the status and income of the samurai. These were years of rebellions and assassinations as disgruntled samurai resisted the changes.[43]

The reforms transformed Japanese society in a way that did not occur in British India, where traditional social structures remained firmly in place. There was broad agreement in the government that creating modern industries was essential if Japan was to fend off the Western powers. There was, however, no consensus on the path forward. There was no Japanese way of doing business but rather competing models of different business systems. Meiji Japan became a giant experimental laboratory, investigating different institutional forms to achieve modernization, including in business. At least three different types of business developed.

The first was state-owned enterprise. The new Meiji rulers had little confidence that the private sector had the expertise to build modern enterprises, and they opposed allowing foreign business to invest in Japan. The government set up and financed at least twenty "model" manufacturing plants in engineering, cotton spinning, silk reeling, glass, sugar, and beer. It also built shipyards and opened coal and copper mines. These were staffed in part by several thousand so-called hired foreigners, who were recruited on contract to provide technical expertise. These businesses helped kick-start industrialization, but they were unprofitable. During the 1880s, the government privatized most of them.[44]

A second, and far more durable, type of business enterprise was family-owned groups. A number of important businesses, notably Mitsui and Sumitomo, evolved from merchant houses active in the Tokugawa period. Others were products of the new Meiji era. A prominent example was Mitsubishi, founded by Iwasaki Yataro, which started as a shipping company. Iwasaki provided assistance to the government on several occasions, including when it faced rebellions from disaffected samurai, and was rewarded with more ships and subsidies. He remained independent, however, and at various times was challenged by no fewer than three government-backed shipping firms. Iwasaki, like Shibusawa, was convinced that creating locally owned industries was key to Japan's retaining sovereignty, and his company fought off competition from leading British and American shipping companies. The fate of China and India was on the minds of all late nineteenth-century Japanese business leaders and government officials. Otherwise, Iwasaki's motivation and behavior were broadly similar to those of the Argentinean businessmen discussed earlier in this chapter. The creation of personal wealth and the wealth of his family was his priority. Iwasaki, one classic history of Japanese business observes, "identified his own Mitsubishi with the good of Japan and believed in the benefits of monopoly and one-man power."[45]

Iwasaki died in 1885, but by then he had laid the foundations of a family-owned business conglomerate known as a zaibatsu. The shipping company NYK became Asia's largest, while Mitsubishi diversified into a range of industries and remained under the control of the Iwasaki family.[46] Mitsubishi and the other zaibatsu shared certain characteristics. They were private and owned and led by single families. As they expanded, they also recruited graduates from Japan's new university system as professional managers.[47] Shibusawa disliked the family-owned zaibatsu, especially Iwasaki and Mitsubishi. The Mitsubishi zaibatsu represented to Shibusawa, in the words of the historian John Sagers, "all that was wrong with closed family-owned conglomerates which greatly benefitted from crony capitalist relationships with government officials."[48]

Shibusawa developed a third type of business enterprise after a brief, if influential, time as a government bureaucrat. This took the form of a joint-stock company with a broad stakeholder view of the responsibility of capitalism. On his return from Paris, Shibusawa was appointed head of taxation at the newly created Ministry of Finance. He was initially reluctant to work with the new government, but he flourished in his new role, helping to establish the yen, a new national currency, in 1871 and creating a standardized system of weights and measurement. Shibusawa's eyes, however, were not on government service but on business. In 1871, he published a book called *Tachiai ryakusoku* (Guidelines on forming companies) in which he synthesized what he had learned in France about how to organize joint-stock companies and how such enterprises could advance the public interest.[49]

The founding of Japan's first modern bank marked the start of the country's halting transition to the private sector—and Shibusawa led the way. In 1872 the government passed the National Bank Act, drafted by a team led by Shibusawa, based primarily on US precedent. Banks established under the Act were to be private, like their American counterparts. In 1873, Shibusawa left the Finance Ministry and became president of Dai'ichi Bank (First National Bank), which was formed under the auspices of the Act. Dai'ichi Bank was the first bank, and first joint-stock company, in Japan's history. Its structure reflected many of Shibusawa's ideas. He wanted the bank to use Western methods of auditing and double-entry bookkeeping and—especially—to take the joint-stock form. He declined Mitsui's offer to organize and finance the bank, and eventually persuaded seventy-one stockholders to invest in it. He also broke with tradition by insisting that the names of the investors and the sums they invested be public.[50] Shibusawa saw the bank as key to the nation-building agenda of the government. In 1879, he told a shareholder meeting that the bank needed to be "managed both for profit and with concern for the benefit and loss of the country as a whole."[51]

Shibusawa's decision to leave government and become a banker upended conventional wisdom in Japan about desirable career paths. In Tokugawa Japan, officialdom was the most respected role, while merchants were some of the least respected members of society. Shibusawa explicitly rejected this ranking.[52] When colleagues tried to persuade him not to leave the bureaucracy in 1873, he articulated his view of the importance of business. "Commerce and industry are the foundation of the State," he observed.[53] This was the first of many times that Shibusawa changed his mind. He proved remarkably open to responding to new contexts with new ideas.

Dai'ichi Bank was just the beginning. Shibusawa launched five hundred companies over his lifetime. The industries in which he

chose to invest lay at the core of the country's economic development and often involved the application of new Western technology.
He followed a number of rules in making his investments. When he
took on the role of director, he mostly restricted himself to one
company in each industry; in the rare instance when he invested in
multiple companies in the same industry, he made sure they were
in different geographical regions. When he served as president, he
might hold up to 30 percent of a company's stock, but in many
cases he only held a small percentage. Shibusawa was typically very
active at the launch of a company and then settled into a less inter-
ventionist role, attending shareholder meetings and sometimes stepping in if a president became ill. It was only through this light touch
that he could be involved in the affairs of so many companies. He
also built a cadre of trusted managers and investors whom he relied on to watch over the companies in which he was involved.[54]
In contrast to the zaibatsu, Shibusawa did not seek to create a diversified business group owned by his family. Indeed, he often sold shares
in companies he had invested in to raise capital for new businesses.
He had a tense relationship with his son Tokuji, whom he formally
disinherited in 1912.[55]

Many of Shibusawa's ventures started new industries in Japan.
Tokio Marine Insurance, launched in 1879, was Japan's first insurance company not specializing in life insurance. The Osaka Spinning
Company, started in 1882, was the first Japanese company to
succeed in mechanized cotton spinning. Shibusawa was motivated
to start the company because he "sensed a danger in the rapidly
increasing imports of cotton manufacturers."[56] While these companies evolved as business giants, Shibusawa also helped found many
small local companies in regions across the country. He retained
long-term relationships with these smaller companies, often over-
seeing eventual mergers with other firms.[57]

In addition to founding individual companies, Shibusawa created
and led associations intended to provide an infrastructure for modern
business. In 1877 he convened the Takuzenkai, which later became
the Tokyo Bankers' Association. He also helped found the Tokyo

Chamber of Commerce and in 1878 became its chairman. He insisted that the creation of such national institutions should not be left to the government. Business leaders, he remarked in one speech about the Chamber of Commerce, had "the resources, indeed the responsibility, to participate in the planning of national society."[58]

Shibusawa partially retired in 1909, on reaching the age of seventy. He stepped down from the boards of sixty-one enterprises, remaining active only in a few institutions, including Dai'ichi Bank, where he continued to serve as president, and the Bankers' Association, where he served as chairman.[59] He retired fully from business in 1916. It was hardly a conventional retirement, however, as he remained very active.

Like Cadbury, Filene, and Bosch, Shibusawa had a strong interest in the physical nature of communities. He headed a company that developed large portions of central Tokyo, and after his retirement he became involved in another, quite different, project. In response to the growing problem of overcrowding in Tokyo, he embraced Ebenezer Howard's concept of the self-sustainable "garden city" supervised by a socially oriented corporation. He assembled a group of influential business leaders and, in 1918, Garden City Incorporated was launched, with Shibusawa as president. Construction began of Denenchofu Garden City, located on farmland between Tokyo and Yokohama. Social purpose ranked above profit. The corporation dedicated 18 percent of the land to the public use, notably higher than the norm of 10 percent for central Tokyo at that time. Construction finished in 1928. The project was a remarkable achievement, although in some respects it became too successful for its own good. The attractive houses and layout proved popular: over time, houses became very expensive, and any social mission was lost.[60]

In 1925, at the age of eighty-five, Shibusawa helped found the Japan Wireless Telegraph Company, and in the following year he began advising Nippon Hōsō Kyōkai (NHK), the national radio broadcaster. In 1928, he also helped the government establish the Japan Air Transport Corporation as a national flag carrier. This turned out to be the last company that he organized before his death in 1931. He headed the organization committee but did not become president once the company started.[61]

Shibusawa never lost his enthusiasm for foreign travel. Throughout his later years, he remained informed about and engaged by what was happening outside Japan. He became a regular visitor to the United States after his first visit in 1909, returning in 1909 and 1915 for audiences at the White House with Theodore Roosevelt and Woodrow Wilson.[62]

Shibusawa lived through remarkable social and political transformations over the course of his long life and underwent a personal transformation himself. Born the son of a farmer in a closed economy with a rigid class system, he experienced as a young man the forceful entry of Western powers into Japan's closed world and played a part in the political revolution that followed. In a country that had long considered merchants the least virtuous members of society, he sought to reinvent the reputation of business, understanding it to be a key component of Japan's aspiration to catch up with the West. When Shibusawa died in 1931, Japan's real per capita GDP, according to the Maddison data, was $3,321, a significant increase over the $2,431 it had been in 1913—although still far behind the Western powers, even as they reeled from the onset of the Great Depression. Catching up was hard to do. But the real per capita GDPs of India and China had hardly grown over the same period, while that of Argentina had fallen.[63] Shibusawa was far from solely responsible for Japan's economic success—there were a phalanx of noteworthy entrepreneurs, including Iwasaki Yataro, Toyoda Sakichi, Fukuhara Arinobu, and Hattori Kintaro, but there is little dispute that he played an outsize role in Japan's effort to become, in the words of the Meiji government's slogan, a "rich country."

The Analects and the Abacus

Shibusawa believed that business should not just foster economic development but also shape an economic system in which firms had a wide social responsibility. In this respect, he was among the most ardent believers in the deep responsibility of business in this book. He articulated this vision in a selection of excerpts from his past speeches that he published in book form in 1916. The title of the collection, *Rongo to soroban,* or *The Analects and the Abacus,* captured his commitment to reconciling two apparently irreconcilable traditions. The *Analects* of Confucius is a collection of sayings and ideas attributed to the Chinese philosopher that describe the role of virtuous people (*junzi*) in bringing harmony to society and leading others by example. Confucius identified five core virtues: benevolence, righteousness, propriety, wisdom, and trustworthiness.[64] The abacus is a traditional counting frame. "The analects and abacus may seem unrelated," Shibusawa explained, "but they are actually very close. When I turned 70, a friend gave me a painting depicting the *analects,* an abacus, a sword, a silk hat and white gloves. These were symbols of my work in which virtue, practical affairs, and profit were always united."[65]

Traditionally, Confucian scholars had a contested relationship with commerce. Confucius had said that a person of noble character understood integrity, while a petty person knew about profit.[66] The shoguns had adopted neo-Confucianism, a revival of Confucianism that had its origins in tenth-century China, as the official ideology of the regime. Profit and commerce were regarded as vulgar, and contentment with poverty was seen as a moral good. In contrast, Shibusawa maintained that business activities did not contradict the teachings of Confucius but, rather, that profits and wealth could accompany morality. He went back to the *Analects* to make his point and insisted that Confucius never said that the pursuit of wealth was bad. Instead, he argued that making people prosperous through economic activity was the ultimate virtue.[67]

Shibusawa considered the pursuit of profits as morally legitimate, and essential to providing incentives for action, but only so long as an individual did not monopolize them and they were shared with society. He praised Andrew Carnegie's philanthropy as an example of the harmony between morality and economy. In contrast, he criticized J. D. Rockefeller—before he established his own foundation in 1913—for monopolizing his wealth. Shibusawa himself donated extensively.[68] Like Tata, however, Shibusawa was skeptical of simple charity. He thought it was necessary to carry out philanthropy "systematically" and "economically" so recipients did not become lazy.[69] He became an institution builder in philanthropy as much as in the business sector. In 1874 he became secretary-general of the Tokyo Yoikuin, a city-run institution for orphans, the elderly, and the sick. He became chairperson two years later and retained this position for the rest of his life. Overall, he was involved in establishing around six hundred social welfare and educational institutions. In 1908, he also founded a central association to improve the management of charitable relief work (which later became the Japan National Council of Social Welfare) and was its chairperson until his death in 1931.[70]

The ethical foundations of business were central to the economic system that Shibusawa envisaged. He invented the term *gapponshugi* to describe this system. The concept was multidimensional, which is why it has proved challenging to come up with an English-language equivalent. One dimension was ethics, and one expert on Shibusawa's thought describes gapponshugi as "capitalism infused with moral values."[71] A recent book on him and his work was titled *Ethical Capitalism*.[72] Shibusawa himself never used the Japanese term for capitalism (*shihonshugi*). He in some respects envisaged another economic system entirely, one founded on a belief that it was not necessary to sacrifice ethical principles in the pursuit of private wealth but, rather, that these principles were essential. "Without business making things happen, the country will not develop true prosperity. "True wealth is wealth built on a foundation of the country's virtue," he observed. He believed that any wealth not built on virtue would not last.[73]

Shibusawa's insistence on the important of ethical behavior needs to be understood in the specific context of Meiji Japan. As modernization began, Japanese business earned an international reputation for being highly corrupt. This may have been influenced by centuries-old traditions of "gift-giving," but more concretely it reflected a country where modern institutions were still being created and the norms of appropriate behavior in business still being forged. The government, like business leaders, was anxious to pursue modernization, and there were plentiful opportunities for companies with the right connections to secure contracts and favors. There was a recognized group of "political merchants" (*seisho*) who used contacts with government officials to secure favors. Against this background, Shibusawa was determined to foster honesty in the business system and transform its image on the global stage.[74]

Shibusawa's ethics emerged particularly from his interpretation of Confucian philosophy. A key principle was that managers needed to follow Confucian virtues. He believed that virtue could be cultivated through education, in which he became extensively involved, as discussed later. Virtue, he argued, was more effective than regulation or policy in securing positive outcomes.[75] Shibusawa also had a transitory influence from religion. On his 1909 trip to the United States, he spoke to the YMCA in San Francisco about his vision of the "ideal man" as "one who can combine the material with the spiritual." Religion, he noted, "gives mankind an object."[76] In 1912 he cofounded the Association Concordia, with the aim of promoting understanding between countries, and at various times he expressed the hope that a new religion could be created, merging Western and Eastern faiths with Confucianism. By the 1920s, however, he had largely abandoned this dream of a unified religion and stressed his reliance on Confucianism for the foundation of his ethical framework.[77]

The concept of gapponshugi went beyond ethical behavior. The words, when written in Chinese characters—known as kanji—have multiple meanings. (Japan has three alphabets: kanji, which is a Chinese-based picture system, and *hiragana* and *katakana,* which are indigenous to Japan and based on syllable sounds.) The word *gappon* means "raising capital," but the character for *pon* can also refer to human capital and social capital. Shibusawa wanted the companies he started to prosper, but he also wanted them to be part of a broader process contributing to the development of Japan and its society as a whole.[78]

The joint-stock company was essential to Shibusawa's inclusive and holistic vision of a virtuous business. In contrast to the closed systems of ownership and governance of zaibatsu, which focused on maximizing the fortunes of individual families, Shibusawa envisioned gapponshugi as a system of joint ownership among multiple shareholders. In each of his projects, he consulted widely and sought a wide circle of investors. He always insisted on establishing an elected board of directors, which, he argued, would be more likely than an autocratic president to make decisions that were compatible with both public and private interests.[79]

Investing in people was as important as raising capital under gapponshugi.[80] Shibusawa actively supported the development of commercial education in Japan, founding some schools and supporting other educational institutions in various ways, including financially and as an adviser.[81] He believed that few students from the prestigious University of Tokyo wanted to work in business, so he sought to encourage an alternative, and more practical, system of higher education. He played a prominent role in supporting the leading commercial school in the country, the Tokyo Higher Commercial School, founded in 1875, the predecessor of Hitotsubashi University. Shibusawa liked the fact that the students at the Tokyo Higher Commercial School had practical training in business, modeled after commercial colleges in the United States, and made field trips to places like the stock exchange. He fought a long battle to get the Tokyo Higher Commercial School, and other commercial schools, upgraded to the status of university. Finally, after much resistance, the government upgraded the school to the Tokyo University of Commerce in 1920.[82]

Shibusawa also actively encouraged women's education. In 1888 he helped create the Tokyo Women's Institute, which was intended for daughters of samurai and noble families. In 1901 he was associated with the founding of the Japan Women's University, the first private university for women, promoted by the former Christian minister and passionate advocate of women's education Naruse Jinzo, who would also become a cofounder of Association Concordia.[83] Shibusawa's enthusiasm for women's education should not be taken as evidence of a strong belief in female social progress. It partly reflected his desire that Japan be seen as equal to the West, but he continued to believe (like many proponents of women's education in the West at the time) that women should be "good wives and mothers" who would provide suitable training for their sons to become the next generation of managers.[84]

While Shibusawa was eager to invest in the training of managerial talent, even to the extent of providing training for their mothers, his attitude to organized labor was far removed from that of Cadbury, Filene, and Bosch. Before 1914, he opposed laws to protect workers in the textile industry, arguing that workers needed to work long hours to maximize earnings. He argued that the exercise of Confucian benevolence by employers and employees rendered both government intervention and labor unions unnecessary.[85] At the end of World War I, as labor disputes intensified, Shibusawa joined with the government to create the Cooperation Society, designed to encourage collaboration between employers and workers. As both the government and Shibusawa were opposed to the legalization of trade unions, the group had no representatives from organized labor, limiting its credibility in mediating labor disputes.[86]

A final dimension of gapponshugi was that it was a national project. Given the threat posed by Western imperialism at the time, this was not surprising. However, it was problematic, as the Meiji government linked catching up with the West with emulating Western imperialism in its own region. Japan adopted Commodore Perry's strategy and sent ships to Korea in 1878, forcing the country to accept Unequal Treaties of its own, this time in Japan's favor. After winning the First Sino-Japanese War (1894–1895), Japan secured the removal of nominal Chinese sovereignty over Korea. When Japan went on to defeat Russia in the Russo-Japanese War (1904–1905), Korea became a de facto colony of Japan. In 1910 Japan formally annexed Korea, beginning a brutal era of forced cultural assimilation that lasted until 1945.[87]

As the Japanese government pursued its imperialist policy, Shibusawa generally spoke out against excessive military spending, arguing that the money would be better spent on infrastructure development and supporting business. Yet when war broke out, he was supportive and raised funds. In some instances, he benefited from Japanese imperial expansion. This was particularly the case in Korea, where he played an important role in expanding Japan's presence. Dai'ichi Bank opened a branch at Pusan in 1878. It took over handling maritime customs duty operations in 1884. By 1905 Dai'ichi Bank had become Korea's acting central bank, and it remained the issuer of currency for a time. Shibusawa appears to have believed that it was in both countries' best interests if Japan modernized the Korean economy. "The development of Korea's financial institutions and transportation infrastructure," he noted, "must be done by Japanese."[88] He used the same argument when he organized a company to build a train line between Seoul and Busan and became its president. He argued that this would help make Korean rice cheaper in Japan, growing the Korean economy, which would in turn enable Japanese companies to sell more manufactured goods there.[89]

He took the same approach in Japan's other conflicts. During the First Sino-Japanese War, Shibusawa formed a society to sell war bonds; he personally and Dai'ichi Bank both made substantial purchases. When China lost, it had to forfeit Taiwan to Japan and pay a large indemnity. Shibusawa made no objections, but he did campaign against the government's planned use of the indemnity for military spending and to nationalize the railroads, arguing that it would be better spent on infrastructure. Similarly, he did not oppose Japan's successful war with Russia in 1904–1905, but he did complain about the cost.[90]

Japan entered World War I on the side of the Allies and benefited from its choice by receiving mandates for the former German colonial territories in the Pacific. As the growth of Japanese naval power caused tensions with the United States, Shibusawa pursued conciliation. He attended the Washington Naval Conference in 1921—meeting his third president, Warren Harding, in the White House—and supported efforts to limit further naval expansion.[91] But by then Japan's path was set. Shibusawa died on November 11, 1931, two months after the Japanese army attacked Manchuria, launching a fifteen-year war against China and signaling a new military domination of the Japanese government, which led to the Pacific War, millions of deaths, and Japan's total defeat. We will never know whether Shibusawa would have criticized what Japan had become.

Shibusawa's gapponshugi offered a radical view of how an economic system should be organized. While the organizational structures he favored were based on what he saw in France and the United States, the ethics were inspired by his interpretation of Confucianism. Capital, people, and society were equally important in gapponshugi. The virtues of a company's leaders—benevolence, righteousness, propriety, wisdom, and trustworthiness—were essential to the functioning of the company and its commitment to public purpose. His role in the foundation of Dai'ichi Bank and so many companies made him a hugely influential figure in Meiji Japan, but it is important to remember that gapponshugi was only one vision of how Japanese business should operate. Iwasaki Yataro and other zaibatsu leaders favored strong rather than more democratic leadership and the generation of family wealth. Although he stood apart from many of the conventions of his own society, Shibusawa was a man of his time and place. His acquiescence to Japanese imperialism and his views on the role of women in society seem antiquated today, while many of his other views have recently acquired a new relevance.

Shibusawa, Tata, and Deep Responsibility

Business leaders in countries that did not participate in the first wave of industrialization faced important challenges, and they operated in a context in which the rules of the game favored the industrialized West. As a broad generalization, most of the business leaders in these countries shared Tornquist and Iwasaki's assumption that what was good for their businesses was good for their countries. Many were more focused on the well-being of their families and their own positions in society than on the social and economic development of their country. But Tata and Shibusawa repurposed the tenets of Zoroastrianism and Confucianism, respectively, to argue that profits and social purpose were not only compatible but mutually beneficial. They shared a vision of a more affluent, and more equitable, future for their countries.

Both men can be seen as role models of deeply responsible business leaders. They chose to work in industries that would help modernize their economies and had an extended view of their responsibilities extending to stakeholders other than their own families, making a commitment to their communities, and emphasizing the importance of acting ethically. Shibusawa and Tata were not lone outliers but rather foundational figures in the Japanese and Indian business systems. They provide rich evidence that good business can translate into good profits. Shibusawa's vision and actions were the most radical of the two men. While the Tata business remained in family ownership, Shibusawa sought to create a widely owned business system in which he personally retained few shares. *Gappon* capitalism broadened the concept of capital from money to human and social capital and suggested how business could make Japan develop in a holistic fashion.

None of this means that there were not moral ambiguities in the careers of the two men. As elite members of hierarchical societies, they were even more paternalistic than their counterparts in the industrialized West. Shibusawa's acquiescence in, and even support of, Japan's imperial aggression provides an example and a warning that an ethical framework that puts a great stake on national uplift can be blinkered by patriotism.

The legacy of these two business leaders provides powerful insights on the sustainability of deep responsibility. Tata's business was left in the hands of the family after his death in 1908, and his successors were committed to the values he espoused. The business remained resilient, though it reeled with the onset of the Great Depression in the early 1930s.[92] Still, it survived the crisis and is to this day one of India's largest business groups. Tata businesses in steel, automobiles, and information technology services are among India's largest firms.[93] J. N. Tata's extensive philanthropy and commitment to social responsibility were both embraced by his sons Dorab and Ratan, as well as by J. R. D. Tata (the son of a cousin of J. N. Tata), who ran the business between 1938 and 1993. The institutions Tata created beyond the firm remain vibrant components of Indian life: there are now over 5,400 J. N. Tata scholars all over the world, and the Indian Institute of Science is regularly rated the best university in India.

Shibusawa's legacy is more complex, and it illustrates some of the complexities of assessing the overall impact of many of the figures in this book. The "father of Japanese capitalism," he was hugely influential in his time, and a figure of such international stature that he was a frequent visitor to the White House. He chose to exercise his influence personally or through intermediaries, given that his strategy was to withdraw the equity from firms he founded in order to invest in new firms. After his death, the military regime that ran the country was focused on waging war, first on China and subsequently on the United States, and it worked closely with the zaibatsu such as Mitsui and Mitsubishi. This was not a context in which the ideals of gapponshugi and ethical capitalism could flourish, let alone in the absence of Shibusawa himself, and over time their influence in the companies he founded diminished. During the Allied occupation after Japan's defeat in World War II, the family-owned zaibatsu were broken up into multiple components that over time coalesced in networks of nominally independent firms with extensive cross-shareholding and trade relations with each other. The Mitsui, Mitsubishi, and Sumitomo business groups, or *kigyo shudan,* were joined by others affiliated with the large city banks DKB, Fuyo, and Sanwa. This system was different from the one Shibusawa had promoted of independent firms with widely dispersed shareholdings. The vision of societal responsibility was more constrained than the one promoted by Shibusawa; these firms offered lifetime employment for their employees and dividends to the bank in each group. Many of the companies founded by Shibusawa remained important components of the Japanese business landscape. Dai'ichi Bank merged with other banks (in 1971 and 2000) to form today's Mizuho Financial Group, Japan's third-largest financial institution. Oji Paper, Sapporo Beer, and Tokyo Gas are among the companies founded by Shibusawa that remain large and important enterprises today. There seems, however, little explicit impact of Shibusawa's gapponshugi in their postwar histories, although his role is remembered at least on corporate websites. Mizuho's website features Shibusawa among its founders and notes his advocacy of "a pioneering and socially responsible approach to financial services."[94]

It was not until the global financial crisis of 2008, as Japan entered its third decade of economic stagnation after the collapse of the bubble economy in the 1980s, and after multiple shocking corporate scandals, that interest in Shibusawa's ideas revived in Japan. His name was mentioned more often in Japan's leading financial newspaper, *Nikkei:* there were eight mentions in 2009 and forty-two in 2019.[95] In 2019, the Japanese government announced that his image would appear on the 10,000-yen banknote—the highest denomination—starting in 2024.[96] In 2021, his life story was the subject of a yearlong drama series on the prominent Japanese television channel NHK (which began as a national radio broadcaster, as mentioned earlier). That same year, Japanese prime minister Fumio Kishida announced plans to launch an expert panel to discuss a "new form" of capitalism focused on redistributing wealth and shrinking inequality, and he invited one of Shibusawa's descendants to serve as a core member. As talk of environmental, social, and governance (ESG) investing and stakeholder capitalism reverberated through global capital markets, Japan rediscovered a business leader who had set out the basic principles of ethical capitalism over a century earlier.

PART II

TURBULENCE

CHAPTER 5

EDUCATING FUTURE LEADERS

WALLACE DONHAM, HARVARD BUSINESS SCHOOL, AND THE PUSH FOR ETHICAL CAPITALISM

This book began with the stark call in 1927 by Wallace Donham, the dean of the Harvard Business School, for business leaders to adopt "a higher degree of responsibility," including a "social consciousness" and a "competently equipped intelligence and wide vision."[1] The time has come to return to Donham and consider why he made that statement and what he meant by it.

Donham headed one of the top business schools in the United States in the interwar years. Business schools were a new phenomenon and primarily an American one, although there were parallels with the Tokyo Higher Commercial School supported by Shibusawa Eiichi and schools of commerce established in France and Germany. For most of the nineteenth century, the skills needed to be a manager were gained through apprenticeship or on-the-job training. When firms were small and family owned, skills and values were passed down from father to son. The scaling of businesses created a new need for managers.

The new educational institutions developed to teach future managers took different forms in different countries. France was an early mover with the creation of the École Supérieure de Commerce in Paris in 1819. The chamber of commerce in Paris followed this with the École des Hautes Etudes Commerciales in 1881, which offered a professional education with an emphasis on practical topics and tough entrance exams designed to create a business elite. In Germany commercial schools called Handelshochschulen emerged in the late nineteenth century following a model already established for engineering, which was taught in specialist schools because of a disdain for vocational education in Germany's universities. The commercial schools were the home of a new discipline called business economics, which heavily emphasized basic accounting.[2]

In the United States, private for-profit colleges developed beginning in the 1820s to teach basic business skills. An example is Eastman Schools, founded by George Washington Eastman, whose son George built the Eastman Kodak Company, which operated in three upstate New York cities and in Saint Louis, Missouri.[3] By the end of the century, business schools started to be created within established universities. In 1881, the Quaker industrialist Joseph Wharton donated $100,000 to the University of Pennsylvania to help establish the Wharton School, the first successful university school of business. Albert S. Bolles, a lawyer, was Wharton's first professor. It offered an undergraduate degree within the University of Pennsylvania that included courses related to business, such as finance and business law. A separate master of business administration (MBA) degree was launched in 1921.[4] The model of Wharton was followed by other universities in the United States. The predecessors to the University of California's Haas School of Business and the University of Chicago's Booth School of Business date from 1898. Dartmouth College founded the Tuck School of Administration and Finance. It initially offered a supplementary two-year course in business to undergraduates, without any degree beyond the initial bachelor's, but in 1902 it was decided to award a master of commercial science.[5] Harvard founded the Harvard Business School in 1908 and launched the world's first MBA program.[6] The focus of management as a separate discipline and the core of the curricula made the American schools distinct from European counterparts.[7]

The creation of educational institutions to train managers posed the logical question of what their education should consist of. For Donham and others it raised the possibility that, while the current generation of business leaders could only be exhorted to behave with a "higher degree of responsibility," a future generation of managers could be educated to have ethical and social responsibility built into their professional formation. The goal was ambitious: to rebuild the whole business system on stronger ethical foundations.

Although Harvard was part of a broader trend among business schools anxious to encourage ethical capitalism, it is especially relevant here because of the radical nature of Donham's broader agenda to promote business responsibility. As we will see, Donham's ideas were enriched through his relationship with the philosopher Alfred North Whitehead, who wanted business leaders "to think greatly" about their roles and responsibilities. Together they developed a holistic vision of the deep responsibility of business. Donham's efforts to promote an appropriate pedagogy to transmit these values were given new meaning and urgency by the stock market crash in 1929 and the Great Depression.

Is Management a Profession?

The creation of business schools by universities across the United States was driven by a variety of motives. As fortunes were made in business, the opening of business schools was a way to attract large donations, and the idea of a business school as a source of income for universities was born. The growth of these new schools also reflected a rising demand from students and their employers. Companies' growing desire for competent decision makers was matched by a new enthusiasm among college graduates for pursuing business careers. At Harvard University, it was estimated that at most 20 percent of Harvard College graduates went to work in business in 1897. By 1907, the year before the Harvard Business School was established, more than one-half of the graduating class went into business.[8]

Few people at the time regarded management as a profession akin to the law or medicine. The new business schools saw their mission as changing this, but they faced huge roadblocks. In particular, there was no agreement about the intellectual foundation required to make business a profession.[9] The Tuck School at Dartmouth College was founded with the explicit goal of raising business management to the same status as established and academically respectable professions.[10] Harvard had the same goal. The president of Harvard University, Charles William Eliot, observed that a career in business had become a "highly intellectual calling."[11] The first dean of the Harvard Business School, economic historian Edwin F. Gay, the son of a rich business executive, strove to put the study of business on a strong intellectual footing. He wrote that his aim was to generate "intellectual respect for business as a profession, with the social implications and heightened sense of responsibility which goes with that."[12]

Gay's emphasis on the need for a "heightened sense of responsibility" reflected the widespread criticism of big business in the United States at a time when muckraking journalists were eagerly exposing the excess of plutocrats and their exploitation of workers. This drove an urgent concern to define the ethical responsibilities of business. In 1914, the National Civic Association—an organization formed fourteen years earlier by representatives of big business, organized labor, and consumer advocates—established the Special Committee on Business Ethics, chaired by I. G. Schmidlap, a Cincinnati banker.[13] Regional chambers of commerce and industry associations developed their own business codes of ethics. A handbook published in 1924 collected approximately 250 such codes from business and professional organizations.[14] In that year, the US Chamber of Commerce appointed a Committee on Business Ethics, which developed fifteen principles of business conduct, including the need for equitable consideration, to make fair profits, to avoid excess, and to fulfill the "moral obligations of individuals."[15] The Chamber's hope was that regulation could be avoided by greater self-regulation.

Lessons in business ethics appeared in many forms in the new business schools and in universities. In 1904, the University of California's College of Commerce launched a business ethics lecture series after receiving a donation from a prominent Sacramento-based retailer who believed that improving knowledge was the way to improve ethics. In 1908, Yale began to offer lectures on business ethics that were intended for a primary audience of senior students but were subsequently turned into a book called *Every-Day Ethics* to reach a wider audience. In 1905, New York University began a "special course of lectures on business ethics," and in the 1912–1913 academic year it hired an Episcopal minister as a professor of business ethics.[16]

A broader strategy was pursued at the fledgling College of Commerce (later the Booth School) at the University of Chicago. Leon Marshall, the dean from 1909 to 1924, worked to bring together studies in business, philanthropy, politics, and social studies with the goal of training management students to prepare to enter one of three professional areas, as determined by the school: "public service," "philanthropic and charitable service," and "business service," each underpinned by the intention to serve society. Marshall wanted his graduates to have "some idea of social needs, with some zeal for serving those needs, with some appreciation of the rights, the privileges, and the obligations of the other members of society."[17]

After the outbreak of war in Europe in 1914, these sentiments became more widely diffused. Roswell C. McCrea, dean of Wharton and later of Columbia's business school, gave a speech in December 1915 in which he said, "Every student who goes through a school of business should be brought to an appreciation of social facts that will leave him public-spirited and socially minded."[18] Despite the nice words, there was no consensus on the content or meaning of social responsibility among the leaders of US business schools. Some went so far as to reject this new emphasis on social purpose. Emory R. Johnson, who became dean of the Wharton School in 1919, progressively moved Wharton's curriculum from one focused on social concerns to one centered on the development of technical specialization. Wharton excelled in insurance and accounting during the 1920s, not social responsibility.[19]

Meanwhile, the "professional" status of business education slowly garnered acceptance. Particularly influential were a number of theories aimed at increasing industrial efficiency. The most important in the 1910s was Frederick W. Taylor's theory of scientific management. Taylor maintained that worker productivity could be sharply increased by carefully studying each component of a job, employing bonus systems, and improving the design of the workplace and tools. Taylor saw the system as a way to improve relations between managers and workers by establishing a set of rules that everyone would regard as legitimate, but it was efficiency engineers with stopwatches and extreme surveillance of workers that became the public symbols of the Taylor system. The Harvard psychologist Hugo Münsterberg, the progenitor of applied psychology, developed a theory of industrial psychology for managing workers that became influential a decade later. He elaborated the concept of vocational fitness and suggested that the solution to the problem of labor unrest lay in the use of modern psychology to change workers' attitudes.[20]

Institutionalization helped as well. In 1916, sixteen business school deans from both public and private universities formed the American Association of Collegiate Schools of Business, a governing body that devised educational standards and organizational requirements for business schools and created an honors society for graduates.[21] Still, plenty remained skeptical that management really was a profession, and questioned the quality of the scholarship in the new business schools.[22] In 1918, the economist Thorstein Veblen, best known for his concept of conspicuous consumption, published a book that opposed the expansion of business education within universities. In *The Higher Learning in America*, he decried the "diversion of interest and support from science and scholarship to the competitive acquisition of wealth" and questioned the "endeavor to substitute the pursuit of gain and expenditure in place of the pursuit of knowledge."[23]

At the Harvard Business School, Gay was very much part of the professionalization strategy. He made scientific management central to the MBA curriculum and also followed others in bringing ethics into the classroom.[24] By the 1915–1916 academic year, the Harvard Business School had added a course titled Social Factors in Business Enterprise to the MBA program.[25] Gay's successor was similarly committed to ethics in management education, but he developed a far more ambitious agenda.

Wallace Donham and the Teaching of Purpose

Donham, who succeeded Gay as dean in 1919, came from a far more modest background than his predecessor. Born in Rockland, Massachusetts, in 1877 to a dentist father with high aspirations for his three children but limited means to provide for them, Donham saw his father lose his savings during the financial panic of 1893 while he was still in high school.[26] This was a period when Harvard's president, Charles Eliot, was encouraging students in public high schools to apply to the university. Eliot relaxed entrance requirements, which had included knowledge of classical Greek, and Donham passed the entrance exams and enrolled in 1895.[27] His older brother and sister, who had by then completed their educations, paid his tuition and travel expenses. He traveled the nearly fifty-mile round-trip commute from the family home in Rockland to Cambridge every day in order to save on student housing expenses.[28]

Donham graduated summa cum laude in just three years. He was interested in legal studies, but he could not afford the cost of tuition and instead contemplated becoming a teacher. Upon learning this, Abbott Lawrence Lowell, then a professor of government at Harvard College under whom Donham had studied, offered him a loan of $2,000 so that he could pursue a law degree. Lowell had been impressed by the young man's academic tenacity.[29]

Donham enrolled in Harvard Law School, where he was introduced to the "case" method, pioneered by Harvard Law School's first dean, Christopher Columbus Langdell. Rather than follow traditional lectures, students studied appellate court decisions, or "cases," and followed the Socratic question-and-answer format in the classroom. This pedagogical method made a lasting impression on Donham, who graduated with a law degree in 1901.[30]

Lowell continued to act as his patron and mentor. When he learned that Donham planned to delay his marriage until he had repaid the loan, he forgave the loan on condition that Donham marry his fiancée, Mabel Higgins, which he did in 1903.[31] Donham's first job out of law school was at the Old Colony Trust Company in

Boston. He rose through the ranks quickly; in 1906 he was promoted to vice president, a position he retained until 1919.[32] In 1908, the year that the Harvard Business School was established, Donham served as a guest lecturer as part of a "corporation finance" course.[33]

Lowell became president of Harvard University in 1909. When Gay resigned as dean of the Business School in 1919, Lowell invited Donham to discuss the post with him and found that Donham's ideas aligned with his own. Later reflecting on his conversation, Lowell noted Donham felt that the Harvard Business School "should have its own atmosphere, its own temperament, its own standards, its own loyalties." Donham agreed to take on the role, motivated by his loyalty to Lowell, the opportunity to specialize in the academic field of labor relations, and the desire to help establish the institution as a professional school.[34] It helped, too, that Donham had been an effective fund raiser for Harvard College, and the Business School was in urgent need of more funding.[35]

Donham's long tenure—he retired as dean in 1942—saw an expansion of annual enrollment from four hundred students to over one thousand. He secured a large donation from George F. Baker to build a new campus that opened in 1927, located in a former swamp across the Charles River in the Allston neighborhood of Boston, at some distance from the rest of Harvard's campus in Cambridge. Donham promoted the adoption of the case method, something for which his deanship became primarily known.[36] He believed that, in the classroom, the case method would create a kind of "laboratory" setting in which students could participate in near simulations of real-world decision-making.[37]

Donham had ambitions beyond new pedagogies and buildings. He saw ethics as a key addition to the curriculum, but his analysis of what was wrong with American business, and what should be done about it, was more fundamental than just preventing unethical behavior. He believed that the new scale of business, and deficiencies of leadership in other parts of society, placed executives in a unique position to address social problems and gave them an obligation to do so. For him, management education had no point if it did not teach the next generation of business leaders to take their responsibility to society seriously.

In 1920, Donham circulated a memorandum to the school's faculty that expressed his desire to train MBA students to "fit the student into business and society." He proposed that each student be taught in relation to "business opportunity" and to understand the "relation of businessmen to society."[38] These proposals reflected his concerns that rapid scientific and technological progress, and the rising materialism that accompanied it, were overtaking society's capacity for moral self-governance. This, he believed, called for a reevaluation of the fundamental role of business in society.

Donham began to modify the Harvard Business School's curriculum to include a wider range of perspectives, including that of labor. He was, in part, motivated to do this by his experience as a court-appointed receiver of the Bay State Street Railway Company during his tenure at the Old Colony Trust Company. As the receiver, he had worked in collaboration with the railway workers' union.[39] In the context of a major postwar recession that saw intensified labor unrest, Donham hired labor leader Robert Fechner of the International Association of American Machinists, which was affiliated with the American Federation of Labor, a national federation of labor unions. This was not a popular move, both inside and outside the Harvard Business School. Some incensed critics urged Donham to reconsider his decision to bring the voice of labor into the classroom, claiming that the endowment would suffer and that Fechner's teaching would sow "the seeds of social unrest," potentially encouraging the spread of communist ideas.[40] Donham dismissed these critics, observing in 1921 that he did not want to lay "down the law about business and the way it must be done" but rather that an innovation such as having Fechner teach would provide MBA students with the "basis for sane thought and independent thought."[41] Donham was interested in stimulating creative and critical thinking in his MBA students, which he believed was necessary if businesspeople were to offer leadership and play a positive role in the effort to solve complex social problems. The episode also demonstrated the constraints under which Donham operated. Fechner's three-year appointment was not renewed in 1924 out of concerns for the negative impact on donations.[42]

Donham wrestled with the question of how to develop pedagogies that would equip businesspeople to take on this social responsibility. In 1922, he wrote in a report to Lowell that the subject of business ethics was "much on the minds" of faculty members.[43] He saw what he perceived as rampant cynicism and a "quite definitely mercenary point of view" among business leaders when it came to their social contributions. In order to change this social dynamic, Donham believed he had to change minds. "We must change the condition that exists in the business community from one where the typical practitioner of business thinks of it as a way to make money," he wrote in 1926, "to one where he realizes its social significance, and therefore is proud of his job instead of rather apologetic."[44] In a subtle way, Donham was insisting that the goal of making money should be no more important than the desire to improve society. He believed that such a shift in mind-set would allow people in business to feel a greater sense of pride in their work. In his eyes, ethics was not a marginal add-on to the business school curriculum: it was a core component.

Donham believed that management education was key to achieving the mind-set change that was so urgently needed. He argued in his landmark article "The Social Significance of Business" that it was essential that business schools provide ethical training to students, as this form of instruction would not be possible later in their professional lives.[45] In 1927 he appointed Carl Frederick Taeusch, an Ohio-born academic who had obtained his PhD in philosophy at Harvard seven years earlier, as a member of the school's research staff. The following year Taeusch became an assistant professor of business ethics, responsible for teaching a second-year elective.[46] A pioneer in the field of business ethics, Taeusch had caught Donham's attention with the publication of *Professional and Business Ethics* in 1926, which had been favorably reviewed.[47] The subject he had been recruited to teach was unusual. Only seven of the thirty-eight member schools of the American Association of Collegiate Schools of Business in 1926 required students to take courses that included ethics.[48]

Donham believed that Taeusch's work would be distinct from prior efforts to teach business ethics, which he compared to "Sunday School talks."[49] The 1928 the Harvard Business School course catalog stated that the objective of Taeusch's new course was to teach "the self-regulatory functions of business," which included "the development of business knowledge and integrity, commercial arbitration, association and corporation policies, and the elimination of trade abuses and of unsound promotion schemes."[50] Taeusch also took on the role of managing editor of the *Harvard Business Review* and acting editor of the *International Review of Ethics,* a journal published by the University of Chicago Press.[51] After years of research he published *Policy and Ethics in Business* in 1931, a six-hundred-page book covering everything from antitrust and competitive behavior to bribery and advertising malpractice. There was very little discussion of the changed context following the Wall Street crash in October 1929, though Taeusch did discuss the role of banks providing finance for speculative activities before the crash. Ever the academic, he spent most of the preface bemoaning how hard it was to generate reliable empirical evidence on most of these subjects.[52]

For all of Donham's emphasis on business ethics, it remained an afterthought in the curriculum and was confined to Taeusch's elective course. One former MBA student, A. D. Henderson, who went on to become dean of Antioch College, a liberal arts college, wrote to Donham in 1933 wondering why "so little headway" had been made in teaching business ethics at the Harvard Business School. He pointedly observed that other courses in the curriculum undermined what Taeusch was trying to do. "The large majority of instructors in the school," Henderson observed, "gave absolutely no thought to this important objective in any of their teaching."[53] Evidently, the enthusiasm for teaching business ethics had little support from the rest of the faculty.

Donham's reply indicated that he was as cautious in execution as he was bold in vision. He called for more research and said he feared losing the "chance of ultimate effectiveness if we went ahead without an understanding of the problem simply because we knew the world was wrong."[54] The combination of Donham's caution and other faculty members' indifference or hostility mean that the efforts had little impact despite the angst following the Wall Street crash. Taeusch taught the business ethics course until 1935, when it was dropped from the catalog, apparently because of insufficient student interest.[55] The annual fee for earning an MBA degree at Harvard in 1935 was $600 (over $11,000 in 2021 US dollars), and few students appear to have felt that the ethics course gave them value for their money.[56] That year, Taeusch left the Harvard Business School and joined the Federal Department of Agriculture. After World War II, he became head of the philosophy program at the American University in Biarritz, France, and later a professor at Saint Louis University in Missouri.[57]

Donham was more successful in his effort to introduce the discipline of business history. His innovation was partly driven by a wish to enhance the academic credibility of the Business School by associating it with established disciplines.[58] He also believed that business history could serve as a vehicle to educate future business leaders about their wider mission to pursue social purpose. In 1928, in "The Social Significance of Business," Donham expressed his belief in the need for "economic or business historians working in the environment of business faculties." He pushed for resources to be devoted to studies "of the genesis and development of business problems and the social currents which create them or which they create."[59] Four years earlier, he had reached out to a group of Boston business leaders to form a society that would collect business records and promote research on the history of business.[60] He endorsed the creation of the Business Historical Society in 1925, and the School's Baker Library became the home of the society's collections. Using a gift from the retailer Gordon Selfridge, Donham purchased the fourteenth-to-sixteenth-century business archives of a branch of the Medici family. He also persuaded the Straus brothers, owners of the retail company

Macy's, to endow a professorship in business history named after their late father, Isidor Straus, who had died when the RMS *Titanic* sank in the Atlantic in 1912.[61]

In 1927, Norman Scott Brien (N. S. B.) Gras was appointed as the first Isidor Straus Professor of Business History. Gras had previously been at the University of Minnesota, where he taught in the Economics and Business Department, and he had studied at Harvard under Gay. A full course was launched in 1928 aimed, as Gras observed, at providing MBA students with "a cultural background for their work and a perspective to their training."[62] Unlike the ethics course, Gras's business history course had high enrollments, suggesting that MBA students saw it as relevant to their future careers.

Gras shared Donham's view that history was one means of persuading students of the need for business leaders to embrace the social responsibility of business. He and his colleague Henrietta Larson, who joined the school in 1928 and eventually became the first female full professor in 1961, developed teaching cases to support the course.[63] Larson believed that business history offered students the opportunity to develop "integrative intelligence," or the ability to see problems forming a complex system. In notes for a lecture in 1953, she wrote that students could gain from history "a heightened perception of ethical issues and of the close interdependence of business and the society in which it operates."[64] In his textbook *Business and Capitalism*, published in 1939, Gras argued that while 90 percent of the task of business was to produce "goods and services at low prices," the remaining 10 percent was "social engineering—looking after the human element in the firm."[65] He offered readers exemplars from Britain—including Robert Owen, George Cadbury, and William Lever—and praised the philanthropy of Andrew Carnegie and the Rockefellers. Gras ended on a more controversial note, however, reflecting that some might see social engineering as industrial feudalism, before speculating (surely influenced by the Great Depression) that the return of feudalism might be worth it to achieve "security in employment and good conditions of work."[66]

Donham had a clear vision that business formed a key component of society as a whole and needed to be integrated into the moral governance of society. Throughout the 1920s, he experimented with various ways of encouraging creative thinking in the curriculum in an effort to convince future business leaders that this was the case. His strategies ranged from including the views of labor in the classroom to introducing the formal teaching of ethics and business history. These efforts amounted to an impressive experiment in how to teach deep responsibility to business students, but Donham struggled to gain traction and was constrained by the skepticism of his own faculty, the unwillingness of MBAs to sign up for an ethics course, and concerns not to annoy donors.

Donham and Alfred North Whitehead

Donham's views on the responsibility of business and ethical capitalism were influenced by his relationship with the philosopher and polymath Alfred North Whitehead, who was invited to join the faculty at Harvard in 1924. The British-born Whitehead had a distinguished career as a mathematician, publishing the pathbreaking *Principia Mathematica* with Bertrand Russell, before becoming interested in the philosophy of science and education.[67] Whitehead was thrilled by the prospect of joining Harvard's philosophy department, where he hoped to address questions "half philosophical, half practical, such as Education."[68]

A year after he joined the Harvard faculty, Whitehead was asked to deliver the Lowell Lectures, an august eight-session lecture series. He chose to lecture on the subject "Science and the Modern World" and published his lectures as a book later that year. In the book, Whitehead reflected that society's drive to possess "material things" had led to the abandonment of values, which he felt were only superficially "bowed to" and subsequently relegated to the domain of churches.[69] These views clearly echoed some of Donham's concerns. At the center of the book was his discussion of the "fallacy of misplaced concreteness," or the "error of mistaking the abstract for the concrete."[70]

In 1926 Whitehead delivered another set of Lowell Lectures, this time on the subject of "Religion: Its Passing Forms and Eternal Truths," which was also published that year as a book, *Religion in the Making.*[71] Whitehead's views on religion were complex. "Religion is the last refuge of human savagery," he observed, "the uncritical association of religion with goodness is directly negatived by plain facts."[72] But he also noted its "transcendent importance" and that it "can be, and has been, the main instrument for progress."[73]

In his 1929 book *The Aims of Education,* Whitehead argued that the goal of educators was to help ideas come alive through the "joy of discovery" and by demonstrating how ideas had immediate practical value.[74] He believed that the true purpose of education was to "stimulate and guide each student's self-development."[75] Whitehead conceived of a student's education as a process of self-development that he believed to be cyclical. Rejecting notions of linear and mechanic learning processes, he described a cycle of learning that began with a "romance" with new stimuli that involved the arousal of interest and emotions, followed by "precision" as the stimuli were investigated, and concluding with a phase of "generalization" as the acquired learning was applied to new stimuli.[76]

Whitehead's arrival at Harvard attracted the attention of Donham. Although their backgrounds were very different, they shared a number of things, including an interest in innovative classroom pedagogy and an ambiguous attitude toward formal religion. Donham was distressed by what he felt to be a general lack of reverence and piety, which he believed was largely driven by advances in science and technology that appeared to have rendered religion obsolete. He argued that religious individuals desired to "contribute to the orderly evolution of human society toward better things" and that reinvigorating the role of religion in society would help resolve "strains" to "our social organism."[77] Donham was personally not especially religious in a formal sense. In correspondence to Harvard College alumnus Rev. Logan H. Roots in the mid-1930s, he expressed skepticism about the power of "mystic approaches" to problem-solving, believing instead that employing one's own intelligence, in service to one's country, was a better way to achieve successful outcomes.[78] Donham, like Whitehead, cared less about reviving formal religious belief as such, and more about the restoration of a broad spiritual outlook to their materialistic age. In "The Social Significance of Business" he expressed the hope "to enlist the forces of religion behind and with the constantly increasing group of men who without definite church affiliations have a thorough, fundamental belief in the general purpose of life."[79] Material things had become "controlling objectives," he observed later after stepping down as the Harvard Business School's dean. "Materialism is often substituted for spiritual values and ideals."[80]

As Donham reflected on the purpose of business education, and before he "committed" himself on "some aspects of an overall philosophy of [his] job," he later recalled that he sought to enlist the aid of someone "of first ability whose experience was as far away as possible from my own."[81] After reading *Science and the Modern World*, Donham chose Whitehead for the role. The two agreed to meet regularly on Saturday afternoons, and they maintained a "close friendship," according to Donham, until Whitehead's death in 1947.[82] In many of Donham's letters and speeches, he referred to Whitehead's professional and personal ideas and comments.[83]

As their personal relationship developed, Whitehead grew in enthusiasm about the mission of the Harvard Business School. He embraced the "professionalization" of management education, with its emphasis on the marriage of theory and practice—a pedagogical approach of which he was a strong proponent—and he supported the inclusion of training in the social sciences.[84] With a well-developed understanding of history, psychology, and society, students could, Whitehead believed, more effectively contextualize ideas about business. As he wrote in *The Aims of Education*, "Commerce and imagination thrive together."[85] Certainly, a purposeful and responsible business required the imagination to envisage something beyond business as usual, and to imagine how an individual business leader could play a role in making that better world.

Whitehead believed that the aim of educators was to pay attention both to the lessons they were trying to impart to their students and to the subjective way in which each student engaged with those lessons, including by experiencing the "romance" of new ideas. For Whitehead, the process of learning was in some respects more important than the content, in particular the willingness to listen, doubt, and imagine. A business school pedagogy that would employ these insights had a huge potential to transform, for the better, the next generation of business leaders.

Although Whitehead devoted significant attention to the philosophy of education, he also became a significant contributor to the intellectual foundation of process philosophy, with the publication in 1929 of *Process and Reality,* based on the Gifford Lectures he had given at the University of Edinburgh during the 1927–1928 academic year.[86] Whitehead saw life as a stream of discrete moments of experience, each of which involved objective content and subjective experience of that content. The world was interconnected, in his view, and individual choices had consequences for the world. Whitehead's concept of "life" was not limited to human experience.[87] His relational and integrated philosophy spoke to the ecological concerns of later generations. (A conference of his followers in 2015 proposed that he could be considered "the philosopher of ecological civilization.")[88]

How deeply Whitehead influenced Donham is impossible to measure, but his ideas on the importance of imagination in business, the benefit that might come from exposure to different academic disciplines, and the need for creativity in pedagogy were clearly echoed in Donham's words and actions. This relationship would be cemented by the traumatic upheaval of the Wall Street crash and the economic depression that followed.

The Wall Street Crash and the Great Depression

While the Wall Street Crash in 1929 surely surprised Donham as much as everybody else, he had spent the previous decade warning about the dangers of an impending social, economic, and political crisis unless business took its societal responsibilities more seriously. "Twenty years ago, in the period of great prosperity around 1923–1927," he later wrote, "I felt this nation was one of the least stable nations on the face of the globe."[89] His message then was out of tune with public opinion at a time of considerable exuberance generated by a booming stock market and a resurgent confidence in laissez-faire capitalism.[90]

Donham's predictions proved prescient. On October 24, the Dow Jones Industrial Average on the New York Stock Exchange lost 11 percent of its value. By July 1932 it was 89 percent lower than in October 1929. Within a few years ten thousand of the twenty-five thousand banks in operation in October 1929 had failed. In the absence of mandatory deposit insurance, millions of people lost their life savings. The unemployment rate rose from 3 percent to 23 percent between 1929 and 1932. By early 1933 US real GDP had fallen nearly one-third from 1929 and industrial production had fallen by almost one-half. President Herbert Hoover, who was inaugurated in March 1929, was a reformist of sorts, but committed to a view about the benefits of limited government intervention in the economy. He considered direct government aid to people in need as "handouts," and instead urged people to work harder and be more frugal as the crisis bore down. It was a stance that turned him into a deeply unpopular figure as the human and social cost of the Great Depression rose. The homeless shantytowns that appeared across America became symbolically known as "Hoovervilles."

Donham made the case for increased government intervention in response to the crisis. In April 1931, in an article published in the *Harvard Business Review,* he supported government spending to save jobs, even though he maintained that business was more efficient than government.[91] However, his impact on policy was minimal. In January 1931 he wrote to Charles Francis Adams, Hoover's secretary of the navy and a Harvard graduate, to make the case that the government must step in during periods of high unemployment to provide jobs. He noted that he had "been over the subject in detail with Professor Whitehead."[92] It took another year before the Hoover administration committed to using federal government spending for job creation. In the summer of 1932, Hoover bowed to pressure and signed the Emergency Relief Construction Act, which provided $2 billion ($40 billion in 2021 dollars) for public works projects and $300 million ($5.7 billion in 2021 dollars) for direct relief programs run by state governments.

Franklin D. Roosevelt's defeat of Hoover in the November 1932 presidential election, and the New Deal program he launched after assuming the presidency in March 1933, marked a massive shift in politics. State intervention in the economy grew, social security was introduced, and the rights of labor unions were greatly increased.[93] Big business was skeptical of or hostile to many of these policies. In September 1934 Donham wrote to Roosevelt advising him on how to "restore business confidence." The president invited Donham to visit him personally, but the meeting, by Roosevelt's account, was unproductive. "I put several problems up to him," Roosevelt later recalled, "and he had not one single concrete answer to any of them!"[94]

Donham had more impact on the research and teaching of his own institution. Across American business schools, the economic crisis encouraged a renewed emphasis on social responsibility and a new interest in the legitimate role of public policy in the economy.[95] Harvard Business School was no exception. Donham renewed his calls for business to take a leadership role in addressing the social and economic malaise.

Donham published *Business Adrift* in 1931 as the Great Depression was ravaging the US economy.[96] The introductory essay was by Whitehead, who affirmed Donham's belief that the leaders of business were the leaders of the modern world. Change their education and you might just be able to change the world for the better. A "great society," Whitehead observed in his introduction, "is a society in which its men of business think greatly of their functions."[97] For both men, greatness in business was not measured by building a giant company or becoming a billionaire, but by demonstrating responsibility for society.

In *Business Adrift,* Donham wrote of the importance of preventing the business system from passing through costly economic downturns in the future "if capitalistic civilization is to endure."[98] Whitehead emphasized in his introduction the need to be flexible in response to turbulence. He suggested that organized societies rested heavily on stability and routines, yet such routines were undermined by exogenous shocks, including scientific and technological innovation. "Rigid maxims, a rule-of-thumb routine, and cast-iron particular doctrines will be the ruin of many people," Whitehead observed. Instead, the "business mind of the future" requires "foresight," which he described as "a philosophic power of understanding the complex flux of the varieties of human societies." In order to achieve this skill, Whitehead suggested that management education needed to embrace philosophy, in which "the fact, the theory, the alternatives, and the ideal, are weighed together," providing "a sense of the worth of life."[99]

Donham embraced Whitehead's concept of foresight as an essential component of business professionalism, writing that it could be possible to "construct a theory of foresight" that could address problems, "whether they are economic in nature or arise out of the complex sociological or political aspects of a changing world." He felt that, with foresight, the "complicated flux of things which is modern industrial civilization may be brought to some greater extent within the boundaries of rational thought."[100]

Training a Capacity for Leadership

Donham sought, with varying degrees of success, to align the curriculum of Harvard Business School with the economic crisis. In 1931, he proposed a third year of study for designated students to pursue a doctor of commercial science degree by engaging in research and specialized training in order to develop "the capacity for leadership in problems of the relation of business to civilization," as Donham told faculty members, many of whom were less than enthusiastic.[101] He argued that such a course of study would help support the social objective of the school, and the faculty ultimately voted to approve the plan. A preliminary report suggested that instruction in the third year could include such topics as biology, sociology, and government, as Donham believed strongly in the need for business school students to study the relationship of business management "to the various social sciences, to the structure of human society, to the behavior of human beings."[102] President Lowell strongly objected, believing these areas of research to be too far outside the domain of a school of business. Donham's proposed three-year curriculum was never launched.

Donham also pursued further significant changes to the MBA curriculum that had distinctly practical dimensions. In 1926 he had recruited Elton Mayo, a pioneer of the new field of human relations. Mayo had struggled to find a regular academic position after moving to the United States from Australia, but his work on the causes of industrial conflict did attract the attention and financial support of the Laura Spelman Rockefeller Memorial Foundation—named after J. D. Rockefeller's wife—and more particularly its head, Beardsley Ruml, who sought to encourage social science research about the social problems associated with industrial society. The business community was supportive of Mayo's research on the agitation-prone mind of certain workers, which he thought was caused by scientific management's breaking down of work into discrete tasks with measurable completion times, and Ruml got Mayo an appointment in Wharton's Department of Industrial Research. When Donham read Mayo's research about modern industrial problems, he reached out to him and secured funding from Ruml for a professorship. The appointment was initially rejected by Lowell, who said the university would not take over his salary after a guarantee of four years' support from Ruml ended. Donham secured further funding from Edward Filene and Owen Young, the head of General Electric, and was able to make the appointment. The outside funding gave Mayo a salary and research budget higher than those of any of the other faculty at the Harvard Business School, and Donham was able to relieve Mayo of teaching responsibilities.[103]

At the Harvard Business School, Mayo joined a nine-year study of workers at a Western Electric factory in the Hawthorne suburb of

Chicago. The Hawthorne Experiments, as the study became known, generated massive amounts of productivity data, and thousands of interviews were conducted with the employees. Mayo's best-selling book from this research, *The Human Problems of an Industrial Civilization,* was published in 1933.[104]

Donham and Whitehead liked Mayo's research because it presented management problems within the context of complex social systems rather than just production and technical systems, which they believed was an essential component of professional management training. Mayo extended the manager's role within such social systems to addressing issues such as norms and the status of employees.[105] A close relationship formed. Mayo even recruited Whitehead's son, Thomas North Whitehead, to work with him.[106] Donham strove to incorporate Mayo's research into the MBA program. The mandatory second-year course in business policy changed under Donham's watch in an effort to make it more relevant to the Depression years. By 1937, instead of devoting "its attention to logical problems of business policy," Donham wrote to Harvard's president, James B. Conant, who had replaced Lowell in 1933, "in practically every topic considered, the human aspects of problems are given primary emphasis."[107] Mayo's fundamental concern was to develop methods that would avoid social unrest and facilitate the smooth working of capitalist enterprise. This was not as radical as Donham's own vision of business serving society.

A more unorthodox approach came from a side project masterminded by a professor of business statistics, Donald H. Davenport. Together with Frank Ayres, the secretary of the Business Historical Society, Davenport began collecting photographs to illustrate modern "industrial life." This reflected the changed ethos of the New Deal era, which was more labor friendly, and made the role of workers in factories visually explicit. The project was particularly interested in documentary images of workers using machinery.[108] Davenport observed that the purpose of the collection, which contained thousands of images, was "the foundation for a better understanding of industrial relations." He added that this would enable viewers "to look upon the working man with some degree of respect and sympathetic consideration," rather than "to look upon labor as a commodity and to ignore the human relations involved."[109]

The work of other faculty also reflected a new concern for the social impact of business. In 1934, Professor Philip Cabot proposed as an "experiment" to Conant that he be given permission to launch a program for business leaders aged between thirty and forty.[110] Cabot, who like Donham thought businesses ought to serve larger social purposes, believed in the value of steering a new generation of business leaders away from a drive to maximize personal profits and toward cooperative endeavors in order to "stabilize our industrial system."[111] Although he had little hope of changing the minds of current business leaders, who had "been trained and conditioned for extreme individualism for at least fifty years," he thought younger generations were "still plastic." He proposed that the program meet on the Harvard Business School campus one weekend per month to discuss "how to provide greater economic security."[112] By January 1936 the group had met six times and included, on average, sixty to sixty-five people.[113] Some of the participants, who convened at the Harvard Faculty Club, included representatives from Filene's, Metropolitan Life Insurance, National Biscuit, New England Telephone and Telegraph, J. P. Morgan & Co., and Standard Oil Company of New Jersey.[114] In the January 1935 meeting, Donham gave a presentation titled "Social Responsibilities and Problems of Industry."[115]

By the end of the decade the conversation series was stronger than ever, with meetings six times a year and attendance consistently above the intended maximum of sixty people. Business leaders came from near and far, traveling from as far as Philadelphia to Chicago.[116] The outbreak of World War II in 1939 shifted the topics under discussion. By December 1939 they included "American Business Policy in War Time" and "Democracy and the Profession of Business."[117] The meetings grew in size to approximately 250 people; their membership was limited to men representing small, New England–based businesses. The aim of the New England Conference on Defense, as it was renamed in February 1941, became, as Cabot wrote to President Roosevelt, to provide these small-business leaders "with practical information which would enable them to cooperate with the Army, Navy, and other departments of the Federal government engaged in national defense."[118] The meetings appear to have come to an abrupt end with Cabot's death in December 1941.[119]

Donham had sought a greater presence for government and public policy in the school's curriculum some years earlier. In 1934, he proposed that the school add new courses on "public aspects of private business and the administration of public business."[120] This reflected his belief that the government would, and should, assume a greater role in the economy long before President Roosevelt's election and the launch of the New Deal. In 1932 Donham published another book, *Business Looks at the Unforeseen,* which made the case for "central thinking" involving both government and business. He saw a role for government in addressing "social questions" including old age, illness and disability, and employment stabilization. Donham foresaw that such policies would be bounded by a corporatist-type structure involving close collaboration between business and industry, an idea that was frequently expressed during the New Deal era. He suggested the creation of an "economic general staff," which would include "men chosen by representatives of the government, of business, and of labor."[121]

Donham's book was full of explicit criticism of an excessively narrow, profit-centered capitalist system. "The test of the administrative efficiency we need," he observed, "cannot be the last dollar of profits or the last pound of production."[122] Laissez-faire policies, he noted toward the end of the book, would in the long run lead to "revolution with all its costs." There needed to be a compromise, in his view, "between our existing over-emphasis on individual initiative and opportunity, and our under-emphasis on basic security for the great mass of our people."[123]

It was against this background that Donham sought to add courses on public administration, "problems in government and business," government accounting, and public finance to the curriculum.[124] These courses were intended to help educate future business leaders about the legitimate role that regulation played in promoting accountability and fair business practices in the economy.[125] The idea was not well received by Harvard University as a whole, perhaps because the New Deal was highly politicized and detested by most members of the business community and supporters of the Republican Party especially. President Conant wrote to Donham to note that while the plan had been approved, courses should not "raise controversial questions about the relation of Government to Business nor attempt to draw an undue number of students into this field."[126]

The outbreak of World War II, followed by the entry of the United States into the war in December 1941, shifted attention away from business and social responsibility. In 1942, the sixty-five-year-old Donham retired from the deanship, although he continued as George F. Baker Professor of Business Administration for another six years and started a human relations course for undergraduates at Harvard. Under his successor, Donald K. David, the Harvard Business School—in contrast to peer institutions such as Booth, Tuck, and Wharton—devoted itself entirely to the task of helping to win the war. While other business schools modified their MBA programs, David canceled Harvard's program and the School switched to training officers and factory managers. In February 1945 the faculty took the further dramatic step of voting unanimously to rescind all authorizations of existing courses. This represented a dramatic affirmation of a desire to commit wholeheartedly to creating the conditions for long-term economic prosperity, which it was hoped would prevent another war.[127] The complete sweep ended much of what Donham and Whitehead had sought to achieve. Donham himself continued to work as an educator, at Harvard and later at Colgate University. He published a book titled *Education for Responsible Living* in 1944 that attacked narrow specialization within the social sciences and the liberal arts.[128] He also continued to pursue his interest in Asia. He had raised the funds necessary to establish the Harvard-Yenching Institute for Chinese Studies at Harvard in 1928.

As chairman of the board beginning in 1934, he had forged new links with China and with Allahabad University in India. Shortly before his death in 1954, he had sought to learn more about how visiting scholars from China, India, Japan, and Korea were faring at Harvard.[129]

Donham and Whitehead wanted business leaders to think greatly about their roles in society and hoped business education could change the mind-sets of the next generation of managers. They saw a connected world in which business leaders played an important role within society, exercising responsibility for other stakeholders, including labor, and behaving ethically. They also argued, especially in the New Deal era, that business should have a collaborative, rather than adversarial, relationship with government. Donham and White-head identified why it was important for business to demonstrate social responsibility. It was not simply that it was the right thing to do, though both men believed it was; they argued that social structures could break down if inequality and unfairness were too great. If it did not exercise greater responsibility, they argued, capitalism would lose legitimacy. The positions of some business leaders today are strikingly similar.

Donham's vision was bold, and it deserves more attention from business school deans today who are urgently looking for ways to make their research and teaching relevant for the next generation of students, many of whom are seeking a close engagement with issues of ethics, purpose, and sustainability.[130] Yet his impact in many regards was limited. Despite his views on the need to bring business and government in alignment, he had no influence on policy makers and few business leaders appear to have paid much attention. He struggled even to execute his ideas at his own institution, as neither his faculty nor his students seemed to be very interested in his arguments about social responsibility. Perhaps Veblen was right that the pursuit of gain and the pursuit of knowledge were not compatible.

World War II largely ended Donham's experiments. He moved too cautiously while underestimating how hard it would be to change minds. He and Whitehead also overestimated their influence on the outlooks of a set of privileged people paying a considerable tuition fee to learn how to succeed in business. No one goes to business school to learn to be a virtuous or spiritual person. Many people's core value systems are well formed by the time of their mid- to late twenties, although there are always exceptions, as in the case of religious conversions or born-again experiences. Donham's new courses in business history and other topics were probably most valuable for their potential to enhance the practical wisdom of students as they faced real-world challenges and applied their analytical skills.[131]

Harvard Business School's commitment to stakeholder capitalism did not end with Donham's retirement, but it took a different form, less motivated by ethics and more focused on helping in America's Cold War struggle against the Soviet Union. In 1949, in a landmark article in *Harvard Business Review* titled "Business Responsibilities in an Uncertain World," Donald K. David insisted that American business had a responsibility to show it was a superior system to Soviet-style communism. This meant, in his view, avoiding a narrow focus on profits and treating employees fairly, combating racial discrimination, and assisting the development of poorer countries. The odds, he claimed, were high in the battle between "democracy and totalitarianism." It was a "war of methods and ideas."[132]

Donham became celebrated as the dean who introduced case method pedagogy to Harvard Business School, rather than as the dean who sought to change how American capitalism worked. In a book published by Harvard Business School in 1999, one chapter traces the "antecedents" of a required MBA course entitled Leadership, Ethics, and Corporate Responsibility, which was launched in 1987. Instead of going back to Donham's deanship, their story begins with a 1959 report on management education that had recommended that business education should be concerned "not only with competence but also with responsibility, not only with skills but also with the attitudes of businessmen."[133] Donham's legacy as a pioneering advocate of and thinker about the social responsibility of business was forgotten even within his own institution. Whitehead came to be lauded as a formative influence on process philosophy and environmental ethics, and his innovative contributions to management education were all but forgotten.

As we shall see in Chapter 10, during the 1980s the Harvard Business School abandoned its previous commitment to a form of business social responsibility, and it became an enthusiastic evangelizer of maximizing shareholder value over the following decades. A rediscovery of the role of business in society came very slowly, and partly as a result of pressure from millennial MBA students seeking greater societal relevance in their programs in the wake of the turbulent 2010s and the COVID-19 pandemic. In January 2022 a new dean, Srikant Datar, described how one of his central aspirations was to shift Harvard Business School's thinking "beyond notions of merely personal success toward becoming, collectively and individually, driving forces in redefining the role of business in society around the world—addressing inequality, exclusion, climate change, and other intractable problems."[134] Donham and Whitehead would have been pleased.

CHAPTER 6

BUILDING A NATION,
ADDRESSING DISPARITIES

KASTURBHAI LALBHAI IN COLONIAL

AND INDEPENDENT INDIA

During the interwar years, while Alfred North Whitehead was urging American business leaders to "think greatly" about their responsibilities to society, eight thousand miles away in India, business leaders found themselves facing even more immediate and extreme challenges. Ardeshir Godrej, J. N. Tata, and others had established the basis for economic independence and actively sought to address social ills, but Indian society remained overwhelmingly rural, poor, and unequal. In 1913 India's life expectancy at birth was only twenty-two, while it was forty in Japan and fifty-two in the United States, and the colonial state remained in place.[1] A mass independence movement had formed that was directly raising the question of the responsibility of business leaders, if any, for liberation from colonial rule. Kasturbhai Lalbhai, the textile manufacturer who is the main focus of this chapter, was one of a handful of business leaders committed to the independence struggle. He was later to play a significant role in building the nation after Independence in 1947.

When the India National Congress (hereafter Congress) was founded in 1885, its initial aim was not independence but creating a greater role for educated Indians in the British government structures. When the colonial government divided the province of Bengal into two separate regions in 1905, a step taken to reduce nationalist activity, Congress began supporting the boycott of British goods and

promoting the *swadeshi* movement.[2] The party was further radicalized when Mohandas Gandhi, who had gone to London at eighteen
and qualified as a lawyer, returned to India following two decades
of campaigning for the rights of ethnic Indians in South Africa, where
he had honed his strategy of *satyagraha,* or nonviolent resistance.[3]
Millions of Indians had shown their loyalty by volunteering to fight
alongside Britain in World War I, and there was outrage in April 1919
when a British general, Reginald Dyer, ordered the killing of nearly
four thousand unarmed civilians who had gathered for a fair in the
city of Amritsar.

In 1924, when Gandhi became president of the Congress Party
for the term limit of one year, he and his followers pursued a campaign of noncooperation with the British. He called for the boycott
of British goods; the wearing of homespun cloth, or *khadi;* and noncooperation with colonial institutions and courts. Gandhi declared
India independent on January 26, 1930, though this act had little
impact on the colonial government. Later, in March, he led hundreds
of thousands of people in a 240-mile march to the sea to protest
the salt tax. Highlighting a tax on a basic commodity consumed
by everyone was a masterstroke in delegitimizing British rule. The
events were filmed and shown in newsreels around the world, hugely
raising Gandhi's profile.[4]

Gandhi's successful campaign of nonviolent resistance against the
British captured attention at the time, but he campaigned rigorously
for social justice, especially the rights of women and the tens of millions of Dalit, or untouchables, in the lowest rank of the Hindu caste
structure, who were considered unclean and only allowed to perform
tasks that were thought to be dirty, such as sanitation, cleaning
drains, and scavenging. Gandhi also proposed a model for the role
of business in society.

Although he was supportive of private ownership and appreciated
the benefits that might come from the wealth created by capitalism,
Gandhi argued that business leaders should run their companies as
trustees and use the wealth they generated to improve society. This
was explicitly not a call for philanthropy: Gandhi once observed

that if the trustee model were widely adopted, philanthropy would be unnecessary.[5] Rather, he was advocating a business model based on ethical principles, believing that how it operated could change society for the better. He shared his contemporary Edward Filene's view that companies should aim to make and distribute products at the lowest possible cost so that poorer members of society could afford them.[6]

The origins of Gandhi's ideas about business were remarkably diverse. Although he was born a Hindu from a family of merchants, he grew up in the province of Gujarat, a religiously mixed region with significant Jain and Muslim populations. Gandhi settled in Ahmedabad, the largest city in the province, almost immediately after returning from South Africa.[7] Jainism, one of India's oldest and smallest religions, was an especially important influence on him. Charity is one of the six daily duties of followers. The four types of gifts—food, protection, medicine, and learning—encouraged wealthy Jain families to fund rest houses, hospitals, schools, and libraries. The faith puts a strong emphasis on asceticism (as does Hinduism), inviting a disdain for materialism among its most devoted adherents. Jains also have a deep commitment to nonviolence, adhering to a vegan diet so that no animal life is hurt.[8] Ahmedabad's Jain temples were managed by the Anandji Kalyanji Trust for their formal owner, Ādinātha, a saint said to have lived millions of years ago who was thought to be the first to have been reborn. The trust pioneered a sense of fiduciary responsibility; rules were developed for matters such as determining succession, preventing the misuse of office, and ensuring that funds could only be used to serve Ādinātha.[9]

Gandhi knew the law governing trusts from his training as a lawyer in London; he was also influenced by expatriate Quakers, some of whom worked with him in the years between the wars. Gandhi studied Quaker thought and came to adopt many of their bedrock principles: valuing simplicity, equality, and pacifism and strongly believing in the social responsibility of business. He had a particularly close relationship with Horace Alexander, a British Quaker teacher, writer, and ornithologist, who acted as an intermediary between

Gandhi and the viceroy of India, Lord Irwin, enabling Gandhi to participate in the Second Roundtable Conference on the Future of India in 1931. That year Gandhi visited the Woodbrooke Quaker College founded by George Cadbury, a journey he described as "a pilgrimage."[10]

Gandhi, Business, and the Struggle for Indian Independence

Neither Gandhi's campaign for independence nor his concept of trusteeship was widely supported by the Indian business community. Although Gandhi himself was not a socialist, Congress included prominent figures, such as Jawaharlal Nehru, who were highly critical of capitalism. This association did not endear the business elite. The Tatas, who were by now firmly established as India's biggest business group, were largely aloof. Although their businesses were owned by philanthropic trusts, they made no claim to practice Gandhian trusteeship and instead claimed an affinity with the Carnegie and Ford Foundations in the United States.[11] Beyond philanthropy, the group focused on building India's industrial capabilities. J. R. D. Tata, who took over leadership of the company in 1937, was a huge fan of aviation and started India's first airline—the predecessor to Air India.[12]

Gandhi did work closely with a number of business leaders, especially Kasturbhai Lalbhai, Ghanshyam Das (G. D.) Birla, and Jamnalal Bajaj. In the words of economic historian Tirthankar Roy, these men became "the public face of Indian business, and straddled nationalism and capitalism." But they were not, he cautions, "representatives of the business world at large."[13]

Birla and Bajaj were both members of the Marwari money-lending and trading caste, which flourished during the nineteenth century as small-scale, informal bankers to many different communities. They spread to cities all over India and became dominant forces in the jute trade in Kolkata before 1914.[14] During World War I, a handful of Marwari who prospered in jute trading made their first steps into modern manufacturing. The single most important figure was Birla, who made windfall profits by hedging transactions in raw jute and speculating in silver and stocks. During the war he entered jute processing, previously a monopoly of British-owned firms. Birla had been impressed by the organizational skills of the British and appalled by their racism.[15] When the colonial administration finally introduced tariff protection for the sugar industry, Birla also expanded rapidly in that industry, previously dominated by British firms.

Birla first encountered Gandhi in 1916, when Gandhi visited Kolkata as a guest of the Marwari community and was taken on a cart through the streets of the city. When the cart reached the business district, Birla and his friend Bajaj, both in their mid-twenties, unyoked the horses and began pulling the cart themselves.[16] Gandhi's austerity and authenticity appealed to Birla, who came from a closely knit and frugal family that followed a strict vegetarian diet.[17]

Birla became closely involved with Gandhi, although he was cautious about direct confrontations with the British.[18] He generally played a moderating influence on Congress, enabling the party to raise substantial sums from the business community and playing an intermediary role between Gandhi and the British.[19] Birla was the single most important financial donor to Congress.[20]

The relationship between Gandhi and Birla attracted critics. B. R. Ambedkar, an economist and leader of the Dalit community, who went on to head the committee that drafted Independent India's constitution, saw trustee capitalism as a self-serving device that would let wealthy people like Birla stay rich, so long as they gave money to good causes. If Birla financed Congress, Ambedkar observed, "it is because he realized and Mr. Gandhi taught him, that money invested in politics gives large dividends."[21]

Birla used both his time and money to support Gandhi's social campaigns. He became the founding president of the nonprofit organization All-India Anti Untouchability League (later renamed Harijan Sevak Sangh, or Servants of Untouchables Society), founded by Gandhi in 1932 to campaign against caste discrimination.[22] He also supported Gandhi's campaigns to encourage handicraft industries and the unity of Hindus and Muslims. Like J. N. Tata in an earlier generation, Birla also sought to improve access to education. The Birla Education Trust, which he established at his birthplace of Pilani, Rajasthan, in 1929, began by opening schools in the area aimed at promoting literacy, especially for girls. Over time, Birla's educational work grew. In 1946, he and his family conceived and financed the Birla Institute of Technology (now a university) at Pilani, modeled on the Massachusetts Institute of Technology. Birla was a very religious Hindu. He and his family gave away large sums for temple building, and from early in the century he was a supporter of the Hindu revival movement in north India and of the Hindu nationalist wing of Congress.[23] Yet his philanthropy extended to other faiths. He gave both to the Aligarh Muslim University and to the Benaras Hindu University.[24]

Jamnalal Bajaj, a friend with whom he shared strong religious and aesthetic values, grew even closer to Gandhi.[25] Bajaj was a successful cotton trader who, after meeting Gandhi, transformed his business and political activities. Although known for his highly ethical business practices before meeting Gandhi, he became a fervent supporter and followed Gandhi's advice, avoided industries that Gandhi believed had negative societal consequences, such as alcohol. He and his wife, Janaki, became prominent campaigners for the rights of women and Dalits. In 1915 Bajaj founded Shiksha Mandal, which launched schools and later colleges. He did not simply write the checks, but keep in frequent touch with the schools, went on picnics with the children, and ate with them.[26]

Bajaj also openly campaigned for independence, with the result that he, his wife, and other members of the family were jailed multiple times. If Birla provoked cynicism among some critics, Bajaj showed all the signs of being the genuine article. By the time of his early death in 1942, his business was totally financially drained by his philanthropy and support for Gandhi, although it was subsequently revived by his sons after independence.[27] Bajaj had no doubt that any business operating in colonial India had a responsibility to assist the independence struggle. He also believed that business should play a significant role in fighting social injustice.

Still, there were limits to their social justice agenda. Birla and Bajaj generally disliked trade unions, as did the Tatas, and made no effort to democratize the ownership of their companies. They enhanced their reputations and social capital by funding cultural, political, and educational institutions. This might invite the same criticism leveled at American philanthropists from Carnegie onward: they made self-interested investments in order to shape the future, so their philanthropy could be seen as an investment in "world-making"—a charade enabling rich elites to extend their control from economic matters to shaping social and political arenas.[28] Yet this would be unfair. Birla and Tata may have grown rich in a poor country, but they were driven by a genuine vision of what it would take to make India stronger, fairer, and more autonomous. Support for education and social justice was badly needed, and their contributions far exceeded those of most of their peers.

Kasturbhai Lalbhai Builds an Ethical Cotton Business

Lalbhai was a less prominent figure in India's struggle for independence than Birla or Bajaj, but he led an extraordinary life and his business had an impact that can still be felt today. He was born in 1894 to Mohini and Lalbhai Dalpatbhai, a prominent Jain merchant family, in Ahmedabad, a city known for its merchant community, both Hindu and Jain.

His family tree could be traced all the way back to the sixteenth century, when an ancestor had served the Mughal emperor Akbar as court jeweler. Another ancestor had earned the title Nagarsheth, or city chief, for saving Ahmedabad by paying off Maratha raiders in the 1720s.[29] Kasturbhai's father belonged to a branch of the family that had splintered from the Nagarsheth but remained prosperous.

Although Ahmedabad came under British control in 1817, it was far less influenced by expatriates than Mumbai, and the merchant community, or *banias,* was a dominant force in cultural and social life.[30] The merchant community in Ahmedabad did not follow Tata and other Mumbai merchants into textile manufacturing, leaving the occasional attempt to open a factory to British expatriates or Brahmins.[31] It was only in 1877 that a Jain merchant opened a mill. Another Jain merchant followed in 1880, but Hindu merchants waited another decade.[32] Lalbhai Dalpatbhai and two of his brothers eventually opened a modestly sized cotton mill called Saraspur in 1897, when Kasturbhai was three. They invited a member of the more prestigious side of the family to become the first chairman.[33]

Dalpatbhai was a devout Jain. He was prominent in Jain organizations, became president of the Anandji Kalyanji, and supported a variety of causes, constructing a free lodge for travelers in the memory of his father and establishing a school for girls in the name of his mother. At home he was frugal and the family was noteworthy for eating simple food. His wife, equally devout, went on pilgrimages to Jain shrines and donated generously to the community.[34]

Dalpatbhai became chairman of Saraspur in 1900, following the unexpected death of the first chairman. The venture focused on spinning until the emergence of the *swadeshi* movement, when it began weaving. A second mill, Raipur, started production in 1909. When squabbles between the brothers led to a split, Dalpatbhai was left with the second, unproven mill. Soon after, in June 1912, he had a heart attack and died.[35] In accordance with the custom at the time, Kasturbhai adopted his father's name, Lalbhai, as the family name.

The unexpected death of his father left the seventeen-year-old in a challenging position. He had just entered the prestigious Gujarati College, but his mother asked him to help run Raipur Mill, while his oldest brother, Chimanbhai, became the chairman. The business struggled until the outbreak of World War I, when wartime import duties protected the domestic market from foreign imports and profits rose. Lalbhai (as I will now call him) proved himself to be an effective manager, outshining his brother. Concluding that the quality of raw cotton really mattered to the success of the business, he made an unprecedented decision to go out personally to the villages and towns where cotton was purchased to engage in hands-on quality control.[36]

Lalbhai had inherited strong religious beliefs from his parents and was widely read in Jain literature. He fully observed Jain practices. Like all Jains, he was strictly vegetarian. He ate dinner before dark, a rule that meant that any guest who arrived late for a dinner invitation might go without food.[37] He developed a regular daily routine, getting up at five o'clock in the morning, performing yoga, and then praying for forty-five minutes before working all day. Even when his business became highly successful, he maintained this routine. His grandson later noted that he had seven sets of clothes "that he marked with numbers from one to seven, and wore them in sequence so that each set would get used equally and thus undergo the same number of washes."[38] This reflected Lalbhai's legendary reluctance to spend money, especially on himself.[39]

He prioritized ethics in all decisions, business or otherwise. "There is no substitute for integrity in business," he once observed.[40] When he entered into an oral agreement to sell cotton waste for a certain sum and then learned it was worth much more, he refused to go back on his word and went through with the contract, incurring a substantial financial loss. Throughout his life, his biographer reflected about this incident, Lalbhai "continued to enjoy the reputation for keeping his word once he had given it, no matter what the consequences."[41] His total commitment to ethical behavior became the stuff of legend. Spurning appeals to family loyalty, he chose to take his niece's husband to court in 1938 for embezzling funds from the Anandji Kalyanji Trust and even served as a witness for the prosecution.[42]

Lalbhai became a director of Raipur Mill in 1916. In the wake of the wartime boom, he and his brother began planning to create a new and much larger mill that was named Asoka Mill. Lalbhai ordered manufacturing equipment from Britain on the basis of a much-improved rupee exchange rate. The whole endeavor almost collapsed because of currency fluctuations and market instability, but Asoka Mill eventually started production in 1923. The rest of the decade was difficult, but the decision to invest in weaving proved a good one.[43] The Saraspur mill owned by his uncles, which was still spinning cotton but not weaving it, went into liquidation in 1924. Lalbhai developed a liquidation scheme and launched a new company in 1928 with himself as the chairman. He modernized the venture, replacing antiquated spinning machines and weaving equipment.[44] Still, his textile businesses remained one of the smaller Ahmedabad ventures. In 1929 Ambalal Sarabhai ran the largest single company in the industry, Calico Mills, which made finer, upscale products.[45] Sarabhai was also a Jain but less devout: he was excommunicated for a time after shooting a rabid dog on the factory grounds.[46]

The Wall Street Crash and the outbreak of the Great Depression gave a shock to the Indian economy. The sharp fall in commodity prices imposed a terrible toll on India's vast rural sector. However, the colonial government increased tariffs, including for British manufactured imports, and this provided a basis for a considerable amount of import-substitution manufacturing. Lalbhai saw an opportunity. In 1931 he launched two new mills, Nutan Mills and Arvind Mills. The latter was a distinctive departure, as it focused on fine and luxury textiles. Lalbhai took advantage of the economic crisis by ordering new machinery from Britain at a substantial discount.[47] Over the course of the decade, he became the owner of the single largest cotton textile business in Ahmedabad. By 1939, his companies controlled 24 percent of the total weaving capacity and 12 percent of the total spinning capacity in Ahmedabad. Arvind in particular was consistently profitable, as it sold to a more affluent market less affected by the Depression.[48] Arvind was pioneering in another way. Lalbhai recruited an economist named Balwantrai Mazumdar to help him run the new business. Mazumdar, who had been trained at the London School of Economics and was subsequently on the economics faculty of Banaras Hindu University, proved talented, but he also possessed a strong vision and had close links with Jayaprakash Narayan, a prominent socialist member of

Congress. At Arvind he introduced progressive welfare policies, including a bonus on profits earned in 1940 followed by a voluntary pension fund for lower-paid workers in the following year.[49]

Taking advantage of a crisis to leapfrog past his main competitor was a swashbuckling strategy, but there was little else that was swashbuckling about Lalbhai's approach to business. He remained committed to the "managing agency" organizational form that was widely used in India. This model, which had been developed in the nineteenth century, enabled promoters of new industrial ventures to float them as nominally independent joint-stock companies yet in practice retain control over them because the promoter's family firm would be appointed as the managing agency of the joint-stock company on a long-term basis. The managing agency form enabled business families to access outside capital, which was relatively scarce, while retaining control. Yet as a system it also had multiple imperfections. Managing agents frequently cross-subsidized between the nominally independent firms they managed, and there were multiple conflicts of interest. Lalbhai strictly adhered to this organizational form. Each of his textile mills was incorporated as a separate company and listed separately on the stock exchange. The family business was the managing agency, and he personally made important decisions for all of the firms.[50]

Lalbhai did not follow the diversification paths taken by Birla, Bajaj, and Tata, preferring to expand the textile business, although he did invest in starch. Starch is a basic raw material used in the textile industry to strengthen warp yarns, finish fabrics, and create prints. Anil Starch, launched on a very modest scale in 1938, was India's first starch manufacturing company.[51] In all his companies, Lalbhai paid moderate dividends, ploughed profits back into the business, and sought—like Filene—to avoid waste of any kind.[52] In this, his behavior was characteristic of Jain business leaders. Jains are suspicious of debt and leverage, preferring organic growth buttressed by strong family and community networks. A long-term outlook, and attendant focus on building sustainable businesses that could be handed over to the next generation, is their hallmark. Excessive risk-taking and bankruptcy are not an option.[53]

Jain businesspeople also have a strong belief that it matters how profits are made. Jains believe in the interconnection of all parts of society, including animals and nature. Given this worldview, it makes no sense to compartmentalize business as separate from society. As a result, Jains avoid professions that involve violence of any kind. They never trade animal products or weapons. Jains also avoid fermented foods such as beer and other alcoholic beverages, as they want to avoid killing microorganisms. (Not surprisingly given this fact, Lalbhai turned down a proposal in the interwar years to open a potentially profitable brewery.)[54] Like Buddhists, Jains believe in a cosmic law, dharma, that can only be perceived by humans if they attain enlightenment. The last person to have achieved such enlightenment, Jambu Swami, lived 2,500 years ago. Still, Jains believe that every living being has a glimpse of dharma, and so every perspective deserves respect. It is a recipe for humility, and for listening to others.[55] The vows taken by Jains guided Lalbhai in his behavior in business, including the vows of *satya* (to be truthful and honest), *asteya* (not to steal), and *aparigraha* (to avoid wasteful consumption and unnecessary accumulation of possessions).[56] They amounted to a checklist for virtuous behavior.

Lalbhai built a sound business but not a big one. This was not for want of talent. He had taken over his father's small business at an early age, sustained it during a period of family squabbles, and taken advantage of the Great Depression to become the largest textile manufacturer in his city. But he believed that the responsibility of business was not to grow at any cost, and certainly not to focus exclusively on maximizing dividends to shareholders. During World War II Lalbhai's companies scrupulously avoided the profiteering that became widespread in Indian business, as was confirmed by a subsequent government inquiry into wartime profiteering.[57] Jain ethics involve not just avoiding dishonest behavior but avoiding waste and only doing business in industries that do no harm.

Advocating for Independence and Building Institutions

Lalbhai shared Wallace Donham and Alfred North Whitehead's be-lief (though he would not have recognized it as such) that business was embedded in society rather than apart from it and that it needed to have a social dimension. A central question as he built his busi-ness was how to respond to the colonial state. He chose to become a strong supporter of the independence movement.

After Gandhi settled in Ahmedabad in 1915, Lalbhai and other mill owners began attending his public meetings, but the honeymoon period ended abruptly. During the wartime boom, the wages of mill workers had increased dramatically. As demand weakened in 1918, mill owners decided to sharply reduce wages, from 90 percent of prewar salaries to 20 percent. Gandhi opposed the move and orga-nized a strike. When the mill owners stood firm, Gandhi went on a fast, a tactic he had first used in South Africa and that he would later use against the British. The dispute was eventually resolved when the mill owners agreed to appoint an arbitrator, who increased the wages in steps: 20 percent on day one, 35 percent on day two, and 27 percent thereafter. Lalbhai's role during the standoff sufficiently impressed his fellow mill owners for them to recruit him as a member of the man-aging committee of the Ahmedabad Millowners Association.[58]

That year, Lalbhai joined a famine relief committee following se-rious food shortages in Gujarat after the monsoon rains failed. This was accompanied by a major outbreak of the worldwide influenza pandemic. He contributed a large amount of money from the relief efforts, collected more funds from the rich, and became directly in-volved in distributing supplies. He was to take a prominent role in relief operations in the region for the rest of his life.[59] This work brought him into contact with the Congress Party. In 1923 he was elected for three years to the Central Legislative Assembly, the lower house of the Imperial Legislative Council, created by the Govern-ment of India Act of 1919. The body had an extremely restricted franchise. The Ahmedabad Millowners Association was allowed to elect one member of the 144-person legislature, and Lalbhai narrowly won the seat, beating the son of one of the founders of the association, who was known for his British sympathies. Although Lalbhai stayed only three years—he shared George Cadbury's dislike of overt political activity—he made new connections with politicians, including Mohammad Ali Jinnah, the leader of the Muslim League, and Sir Purshottamdas Thakurdas, a cotton trader who was to become an important nationalist business leader.[60]

Lalbhai also became involved with the Tilak Swaraj Fund, established by Gandhi in 1921, which aimed to collect the huge sum of 1 crore of rupees (about $30 million in 2021 US dollars) to support India's freedom struggle and fund resistance to British rule. A number of mill owners gave more money, but Gandhi chose to nominate Lalbhai as one of the three trustees, perhaps indicating how much trust he placed in him. Within six months, forty-eight mills had promised to make financial contributions to the fund, although less than Gandhi expected and wanted. Lalbhai was hands-on in the fund-raising process, at one stage harshly chastising a mill owner who had changed his mind about making a contribution. The money went toward a primary school for cotton workers' children established by Anasuya Sarabhai, the sister of Ambalal and a pioneer of the women's movement in India. The sums collected in Ahmedabad were smaller than those collected in Mumbai, but many more people contributed. In Mumbai, two business leaders—one of whom was Ardeshir Godrej, the prominent Parsi industrialist—contributed almost all the money.[61]

In 1927 Lalbhai became a member of the first executive committee of the Federation of Indian Chambers of Commerce and Industry, the fruit of Birla's persistent endeavor to create a unified voice for Indian business to counter the influence of the Associated Chambers of Commerce, which was dominated by British interests.[62] Lalbhai became president in 1934. By then, he had accompanied a number of official delegations to international conferences, and in 1937 he became a director of the Reserve Bank of India. The bank was British controlled and the Indian directors were meant to be more symbolic than substantive, but when the governorship fell vacant, he successfully campaigned for the deputy governor, who was an Indian, to take on the role.[63] These appointments inside the British system did not preclude him from continuing to support the independence movement. Following Gandhi's historic Quit India campaign in 1942, he clandestinely helped organize a three-and-a-half-month strike of the Ahmedabad textile workers.[64]

Less clandestinely, Lalbhai was one of the eight leading industrialists, with Birla and J. R. D. Tata, who developed the Bombay Plan in 1944, outlining the role of the government in shaping the economic policy of a future independent India. The group envisaged a doubling of per capita income over fifteen years through a combination of increased industrialization and government-sponsored investment in infrastructure. The Bombay Plan proposed that the state take on a central, coordinating role, although it did not call for the nationalization of industry. Gandhi himself never endorsed the plan, nor did his rival Jawaharlal Nehru, India's first prime minister, but it is widely thought to have influenced Nehru's approach to the government regulation of industry.[65]

During the interwar years, Lalbhai became a core member of a small elite group in Ahmedabad that dominated the municipal government and took a leading role in redesigning the city. The group included Ambalal Sarabhai and the lawyer and politician Vallabhbhai Patel, a major figure in the Congress Party, who was notably more sympathetic to business than the secular and socialist-inclined Nehru.[66] Lalbhai's proactive engagement in municipal affairs was accompanied by extensive philanthropy. Although charitable giving had been a feature of his family for generations, he took advantage of a change in the law in 1922 offering individuals tax exemptions on 50 percent of their donations to charitable institutions. He formed the Lalbhai Trust, a charitable trust in the name of his father.[67]

Education was an enduring focus of both his municipal activities and his philanthropy. Ahmedabad had few institutions of higher learning beyond a handful of private schools established under the British. In 1920 Gandhi established the Gujarat Vidyapith, designed to encourage Indians to abandon institutions linked to the colonial regime, and in 1927 Lalbhai and a few close associates formed the Gujarat Law Society in an effort to start a college of law.[68] In 1936 Lalbhai became chairman of the newly formed Ahmedabad Education Society, which planned to develop a network of institutions to provide instruction in multiple disciplines. That year the society charted its first college, the H. L. Commerce College, and in 1937 the L. D. Arts College followed. The ultimate goal was to create a university, and the society acquired a large plot of land on which colleges, hostels, and sports grounds could be built.[69] A cluster of other institutions followed, including the M. G. Science Institute in 1946 and, after independence, the L. M. College of Pharmacy, A. G. Teachers College, and other institutions. Lalbhai provided one-half of the total donations between 1936 and 1962 to support these institutions and was active in recruiting talent.[70]

Like his father, he actively supported Jain institutions. In 1925 he became chairman of the Anandji Kalyanji Trust, a position he would hold for the next fifty years. He modernized the management of the trust, introducing budgetary controls, appointing accountants to audit receipts and expenditures, and ensuring that there were regular elections. In 1932 he launched a program to renovate Jain temples, many of which were in a state of disrepair. The work was in every respect hands-on: he paid close attention to the authenticity of the restorations, sometimes ordering work he considered subpar to be redone. He also shifted social norms at the temples managed by the trust. Jain temples had traditionally not allowed Hindu Dalits to enter their precincts. Lalbhai succeeded in changing this rule after threatening to resign as chairman.[71]

Lalbhai had no doubt that the responsibility of a business leader extended beyond making a profit. He chose to join the minority of business leaders actively supporting Gandhi and the independence movement. Unlike Bajaj, he did not break laws or go to jail; he worked within colonial institutions to advance the national interest. He stood out for having a clear vision for the future of the country, and the role industrialists such as himself should play in contributing to its development, once it was independent. The Ahmedabad Education Society provided a long-term strategy to broaden and deepen the educational base of the city.

The Business of Building a New India

India and Pakistan became independent on August 15, 1947. Partition, the separation of secular but majority-Hindu India and predominantly Muslim Pakistan, had been bitterly opposed by Gandhi, but he was sidelined by the leadership of Congress, who came to believe it was inevitable. This was also the position of some of the business leaders closest to Gandhi, especially G. D. Birla, who was an early believer in partition. This reflected in part Birla's close association with Hindu nationalism. However, he and other big business leaders also wanted a strong central government able to take the lead in promoting development, and they feared that if Hindus and Muslims stayed together, they would instead get a weak central government and strong provinces.[72]

Lalbhai shared Birla's position on the need for a strong central government, though he abhorred the violence that occurred as events unfolded toward Partition. He took a leadership position in responding to communal riots between Hindus and Muslims in Ahmedabad in 1941 and 1946. He headed the Ahmedabad Citizens Peace Committee, which worked to calm the disturbances, and on one occasion led a procession through the city urging an end to the rioting.[73] The cost of Partition in human lives when it happened turned out to be extraordinarily high, with fifteen million people displaced and up to two million dead. The cost for big business was much lower. Over 90 percent of the industrial assets of undivided India were located in Independent India, while ahead of Partition there was a massive capital flight out of the Punjab, which looked to be allocated to Pakistan.[74] Partition did result in some immediate problems, however, for Lalbhai's business. Not only was the market for textiles disrupted, but Partition separated his business from many of the finest cotton-growing areas on the subcontinent from where he had sourced raw cotton.[75]

Lalbhai's role in the independence struggle left him with high-level connections in Independent India. Gandhi was tragically assassinated within six months by a Hindu extremist. Nehru became India's first prime minister and Lalbhai's friend Vallabhbhai Patel his deputy prime minister, although within two years the latter too was dead. Nehru's proclaimed socialism made the business community uneasy, even those who had supported the Bombay Plan, with its recommendation that the state play a central role in guiding the economy. Although Nehru was initially cautious and there was no giant leap toward state ownership, over time a policy that combined protectionism, industrial licensing, and price controls was adopted and came to be collectively known as the License Raj. This lasted until the start of liberalization in 1991.[76] Private enterprise could, and did, continue, but within a heavily regulated context in which the state set the rules of the game.[77]

Lalbhai's support for Congress gave him a voice in these developments. Nehru would stop by the family house, where several generations lived together, for social visits, in part because his sister was married to the son of one of Lalbhai's sisters.[78] There were plenty of opportunities for rent-seeking, but Lalbhai appears to have avoided the temptation to ask for favors. One of his grandsons, who lived in the family house and occasionally encountered Nehru, much later observed:

My grandfather was part of the freedom movement. He had all these friends who finally became politicians and ran the country. They were more like friends and they could come without security, without the kind of paraphernalia that usually politicians would have. . . . My grandfather taught us that you have to stay non-aligned. So, all of your businesses should not be based on any kind of political patronage. . . . He had all these friends because he would only discuss things that would be relevant for the country or policy matters, but he would never ever raise the issue of his personal business.[79]

Lalbhai's business was not always helped by the new regime. As the government of a newly independent India moved toward a planned economy, the textile industry was subjected to a number of constraints. A ceiling was placed on the production of cloth in order to facilitate handicraft production. Wages were increased arbitrarily by government policies, and the government mandated a provident (pension) fund scheme for employees. By 1960, sales at Lalbhai's mills were lower than they had been in 1951, and profits as a percentage of sales were mostly lower, too. Profitability remained subdued over the following decade as inflation accelerated. The textile industry was subjected to statutory price control in 1964. The devaluation of the rupee two years later raised the cost of the imported raw cotton that was now needed after repeated crop failures.[80]

There were also new opportunities, however, as a result of the government's drive to industrialize India. In 1955, development rebates were offered to manufacturers who invested in new plants and machinery, and Lalbhai responded with a steady program of investment and modernization. The Lalbhai mills became some of the most modern in India and were now all producing fine textiles. This enabled Lalbhai to build an export business, facilitated by government incentives. In 1972 a formal Research and Development Department was launched in Arvind Mills, helped by a tax deduction on capital expenditure.[81]

On September 5, 1947, fifteen days after Independence, Lalbhai launched India's first dyestuffs manufacturer, Atul. The US company American Cyanamid agreed to provide technical know-how and to design the new plant in return for an annual royalty. Lalbhai also invited the Americans to take a 10 percent equity stake, both to cement the relationship and to provide extra capital. He secured, in the words of his biographer, "through government help," 900 acres of rural land at Valsad, almost two hundred miles south of Ahmedabad. Further land was later acquired to take the site to 1,200 acres.[82]

Lalbhai pursued a plan to create rural employment as he strove to make India self-sufficient in chemical production. He appointed

Balwantrai Mazumdar as the general manager of Atul, and a plan was pursued that included building a new residential community with a full range of educational, medical, social, and recreational facilities. One hundred thousand trees of two hundred different varieties were planted to protect against pollution and provide shade for the community. Land was leased to American Cyanamid to begin its own manufacturing in a joint venture in which Atul held 35 percent of the share capital.[83] The complex became, as the corporate website later proclaimed, "one of the greenest chemical complexes in the world."[84]

Nehru opened the Atul plant in 1952. It was the first Indian-controlled dye venture in a country otherwise dominated by foreign companies. The start-up was less than spectacular. It only produced small quantities of very cheap dyes, and progress was slow until it received government assistance.[85] In 1955 the Indian government offered a sizable loan, at 4.5 percent annual interest, which the group used to set up production plants for an important fast dye called naphthol. During the mid-1950s, Lalbhai lobbied for and secured changes to India's tariff structure, including a reduction of import duties on intermediate products used as raw materials by Atul and other dye manufacturers, and a rise on duties of finished dyes. During the 1960s, the firm invested more in intermediate products, albeit with repeated delays due to foreign exchange shortages and delays in licensing. Attempts to produce higher-quality products in joint ventures with foreign firms were blocked by the government.[86] Still, by the 1970s, Atul had become a substantial chemicals manufacturer—the largest in India—and also an exporter.[87]

Lalbhai's eldest son, Siddharth, a chemical engineer, moved to work at Atul in 1952, joined the board in 1957, and eventually replaced his father as chairman in 1977. He and Mazumdar oversaw a growing number of social projects, including the establishment of the Gujarati-language K–12 Kalyani School in 1953. In the same year Mazumdar set up Urmi Stree Sanstha, which aimed to empower women from nearby villages. It began modestly encouraging activities such as knitting, music competitions, and flood relief, and then in the following decade it facilitated the production and sale of hard spices as a means of raising the incomes of women in the rural areas surrounding the Atul complex.[88] Set in an area with large numbers of Dalit and disadvantaged tribal groups, Atul grew as a major force for social improvement. While the Government of India mandated that 15 percent of a company's workforce should consist of what it termed "scheduled castes and tribes," Atul had achieved 35 percent by the 1970s. They were housed at nominal rents on the campus, and their children had access to the educational facilities.[89]

Lalbhai continued to limit diversification into industries wholly unrelated to his main textile businesses. He also avoided industries in which government influence was paramount. An unintended consequence of the License Raj was a rapid spread of corruption in the bureaucracy.[90] Lalbhai sought to keep his distance from the government, avoiding industries that required extensive permissions from the bureaucracy.[91] The avoidance of industries in which the government was involved became a feature of Indian businesses that sought to avoid ethical challenges.[92] If opportunities were missed, there were also benefits from being known not to engage in corruption.

Lalbhai continued to oversee his business into his seventies and worked hard to integrate his family in the management of the group. It still consisted in the 1970s of nine independent listed companies—the seven textile companies, plus the starch and dye companies. Lalbhai gave each of his four brothers and three sisters one of these companies to manage. The role of his sisters was unusual; the norm at that time was for women to leave the family business after marriage. Lalbhai wanted to keep everyone together, "but at the same time," his grandson observed, "he gave them autonomy to operate their own units."[93] He did see the importance of developing managerial expertise, however. One indication of this recognition was his decision to send his two sons to the United States for their education. Siddharth trained as a chemical engineer at MIT and the Polytechnic Institute of New York University, while Shrenik went to MIT and the Harvard Business School.[94]

Lalbhai's vision of the purpose and social responsibility of business remained strong in Independent India. "Industry and trade have to discharge many responsibilities to the community," he told the Indian Merchants Chamber in 1963. "They should provide support—moral, personal and financial—to institutions and causes which make their towns and villages better for living and which are intimately connected with our spiritual heritage." In the same meeting he asserted, at a time of growing skepticism about the private sector in the socialist-inclined government, the need to make profits. "Profits are a measure of effective, efficient operation," he observed, "and should be worn as a badge of accomplishment and of honor."[95]

Lalbhai's vision continued to include building institutions. He headed a committee, for example, that built a new port at Klanda, to replace Karachi, which was now in Pakistan. This became one of the major ports on India's west coast.[96] But the city of Ahmedabad and state of Gujarat remained the focus of his efforts. He founded and became the first president of the Gujarati Chamber of Commerce in 1949.[97] He promoted research to upgrade the textile industry, using an industry-oriented, cooperative approach like that of Edward Filene and his brother. He was a major force behind the creation in 1947 of the nonprofit Ahmedabad Textile Industry Research Association, which was funded by the member mills of the Ahmedabad Millowners Association and received government support. Also behind the endeavor was Ambalal Sarabhai's son Vikram, who had completed a PhD in cosmic ray physics at Cambridge University.[98] As one later study notes, Lalbhai "spotted in Vikram a young person who could and would use his high social status and new educational credentials to make significant social changes."[99]

Lalbhai and Vikram Sarabhai collaborated again to create the Physical Research Laboratory in 1947, which was financed by the Ahmedabad Education Society and a charitable trust of the Sarabhai family. Lalbhai headed the governing council of the laboratory, and Sarabhai, as the second director, would develop the basis for India's space program.[100]

By the 1950s, the Indian government had become concerned that the country lacked any formal management education institute. It approached the Ford Foundation in the United States, which, in the context of the Cold War, was concerned to expand American-style executive education abroad, especially to countries considered strategic such as India. Ford sent two faculty teams to India, one from the Harvard Business School and one from the University of California, Los Angeles, in 1957 and 1959, respectively. They concluded that any new institution would have to be kept out of the underperforming university system.[101]

The government decided to establish two institutions, one in eastern and one in western India. While the Kolkata proposal went ahead, the idea of establishing a business school in Mumbai went awry when the University of Bombay refused to accept an institution outside its control. It was at this stage that Sarabhai began campaigning for Ahmedabad to be the location for the new Indian Institute of Management. He recruited Lalbhai, who committed to raising funds for buildings, and the chief minister of the state of Gujarat, who promised to find the land.[102] Prakash Tandon, a family friend and the chair of the Indian affiliate of the consumer products company Unilever, became the chairman of the board of the new institute.[103]

The Harvard Business School, which had first become interested in India through the approach of the Ford Foundation, became quite interested in the idea of replicating itself in India, especially if someone else would be willing to fund the experiment. By 1957, a committee on the school's international activities in India observed that, "despite the formal hostility of government to private enterprise," there was a "strong business community," which the committee believed needed more developed management talent. In 1962 another committee told George P. Baker, the School's dean, that there was more than "academic interest" involved. Citing the competition between Communist China and India, the committee noted that the "Free World cannot afford to have India fail under a democratic system" and that it was "most important that the institutions of the

Free World, of which we are one, examine carefully their opportunities to help Indian economic growth."[104]

The cost of establishing the Institute was shared between the Government of India, which committed to $240,000 annually; the state government, which provided sixty-four acres of land worth $400,000; and the business community, which committed $600,000 for buildings. The Ford Foundation provided a two-year $471,000 grant to develop the Institute's training and research, of which $466,000 was paid to Harvard for hosting Indians on its campus and sending faculty to India.[105]

Lalbhai devoted much energy to the Institute, although he declined the formal title of chairman.[106] During meetings of the board of governors, he led calls for the government to give the Institute the power of degree conferment.[107] He served through the 1960s on the personnel committee, which recruited faculty and took a hands-on approach to the construction of the Institute, planned by the American architect Louis Khan. Khan called Lalbhai "one of the greatest natural architects I have encountered."[108] At meetings of the building committee, Lalbhai would intervene on multiple issues, from the height of parapets to the floor coverings.[109] He was also a large funder. On a list of donors as of March 1965, the Sarabhai-owned Calico Mills appeared first, followed by Arvind Mills and seven of Lalbhai's other companies.[110] A year later, Arvind was the second-largest donor after Bombay Dyeing and Manufacturing, a company owned by the prominent Parsi Wadia family. Once again, several of the group's companies were substantial donors.[111]

The early years were challenging. The Harvard Business School staff members sent to the Institute found their views were not considered as important as they had expected. They were not impressed by Sarabhai's leadership and were particularly unimpressed by his "intimate personal relationship," in the words of one report, with the person he appointed as research director, the Harvard-educated sociologist Kamla Chowdhry.[112] Harvard ultimately blocked his plan to appoint Chowdhry his successor as director.[113]

There is no evidence that Lalbhai intervened in the personnel issues that so annoyed Harvard. This probably reflects how close-knit the Jain community was in Ahmedabad. When John Fox, the Harvard Business School's director of overseas relations, visited in 1963, he was full of praise for the "enthusiasm and support of the local business community." However, he went on to comment on the "kind of insulation and degree of self-satisfaction" he had encountered. He added that most of the people he met "seemed to be very devout and strict Jains, and these people make the assumption that their way of life is it" and lacked understanding "that some people hold other beliefs and have not done too badly."[114] Whatever the early problems and cultural tensions with Harvard, the Indian Institute of Management in Ahmedabad went on to become the premier management school in India.

As he approached retirement, Lalbhai remained extremely active in his business, and also in institution building. In 1972, at the age of seventy-eight, he became head of the Sankat Nivaran Society (Gujarat Disaster Mitigation Society) established by the Gujarat Chamber of Commerce and the Ahmedabad Millowners Association to coordinate famine relief operations. This became a long-lasting society that conducted relief operations in times of famine and other natural disasters.[115] After his formal retirement in 1977, Lalbhai remained chairman of Arvind Mills until his death, attending the office frequently while leaving day-to-day business to his sons. He continued to spend a day and half every month at the Atul complex in Valsad. He died suddenly in January 1980, at the age of eighty-five.

Lalbhai played a significant role in building the new, postcolonial India. Although connected at the highest level with government, he focused his lobbying on matters—such as tariffs or securing land at Valsad—that served higher goals than his bottom line. He played a significant role in creating India's new chemicals industry while devoting much of his energy and time to creating new educational institutions in Ahmedabad. There is little doubt that Lalbhai had a vision of the world he hoped to help bring into being, but he was not at the center of it. He wanted his city, and country, to be full of museums and educational institutions, proportioned and elegant buildings, and green spaces. He ran a respected and ethical business that employed large numbers of people, whose social conditions were steadily improved, especially under the influence of Balwantrai Mazumdar. Lalbhai's austere beliefs served him well as a check on the vanity and egocentrism that so often accompany material success.

In the face of oppressive poverty and a struggle for independence, some of India's business leaders concluded that they were responsible for building a new nation. Infused with religious convictions and inspired by Gandhi, Bajaj, Birla, and Lalbhai believed that they could and should play a part in securing India's autonomy. They created modern institutions, designed to give the independent state the infrastructure it would need to flourish. Contemporary critics such as Dalit leader B. R. Ambedkar were cynical as to their motives. With the exception of Bajaj, they built wealth for their families and named buildings after themselves. Yet these self-flattering tendencies do not take away the fact that they devoted themselves to a brave transformation of their country and sought to align their businesses with this vision.

Lalbhai was so austere he makes George Cadbury look like a flamboyant wastrel. His outlook was hardly cosmopolitan or global; although active in the nationwide struggle for independence, he focused his business and his philanthropy largely on one province, and even the single city of Ahmedabad. The Harvard Business School faculty saw him and other Jain business leaders as narrow religious individuals rather than their idea of responsible business leaders. Yet the visiting team certainly had blind spots of their own. Their institution had yet to admit female students, and in the mid-1960s there were fewer than ten African Americans at the Harvard Business School in a student body of over 1,600.[116]

Lalbhai's humility should not prevent him from being seen as a compelling role model of a deeply responsible business leader. He built a profitable business from a fragile inheritance, operated it ethically, made the right decisions in moments of turbulent upheaval, and navigated the new complexities of independent India in a morally restrained fashion. He avoided excessive debt and was an exemplar of patient capital, growing his businesses organically when doing so made sense. He wanted to help his poor, occupied country industrialize and achieve independence. He did so by helping his hometown of Ahmedabad to grow as a hub for the textile industry. He also started the country's chemicals industry, creating a green oasis at Valsad that sought to address the chronic problem of rural poverty among Dalit and tribal groups. In line with Jain beliefs, he saw business as a part of society.

It has recently been argued that corporate reputation is a major asset, and a key to longevity, in countries with weak institutional environments. Trust levels are lower in such countries, and alternative sources of information about companies scarce, so a reputation for honesty and ethical behavior will attract customers, employees, suppliers, and others.[117] Lalbhai's firm undoubtedly benefited from the good reputation that decades of hard work and philanthropy generated, but it would be a stretch to argue that securing a competitive advantage was his driving motivation.

Lalbhai's legacy certainly endured. The businesses he created remain in existence today, still controlled by his family. His grandson Sanjay reinvented Arvind as a manufacturer of denim. It is now a world-famous, billion-dollar company. Atul is a multinational chemical company that currently makes 1,350 products and has businesses in Britain, China, and the United States, among other countries. The decades-long commitments to social sustainability and rural development were brought together in the Atul Foundation in 2010, which is committed to helping those living below the poverty line, motivated by the five values of empathy, benevolence, collaboration, quality, and honesty.[118] The Ahmedabad Education Society, which still exists, created a rich educational infrastructure in a city with few opportunities before Lalbhai started. Although he was traditional in many ways, he played a crucial role in creating a modern business school in India that is now a premier educational institution in the country. As a "natural architect," he also left behind the building of the Indian Institute of Management and many other buildings in Ahmedabad, as well as the Atul campus at Valsad. His legacy can be seen in the skyline of Ahmedabad and in the actions and lives of the generations of students that have passed through the institutions he created.

The postindependence period saw the growth of some powerful businesses in India, such as Reliance, led by Dhirubhai Ambani, which are regarded by some as the epitome of rent-seeking.[119] Yet Lalbhai's values remained embedded in the corporate cultures of the businesses he founded throughout his life and after his death, as did those of Bajaj, Birla, and Tata in their family businesses. These values survived the long era of quasi-socialism and state planning that prevailed in India before 1991, and they survived the subsequent era of neoliberalism. At a time of political turbulence and institutional negligence, deep responsibility delivered benefits. The rewards of ethical and socially responsible business practices have arguably been much higher in emerging markets than in their developed counterparts.

CHAPTER 7

MODEST CONSUMERISM, URBAN BLIGHT, TECH SOLUTIONS, AND THE QUEST TO IMPROVE SOCIETY

A noteworthy feature of the search for deep responsibility has been its lack of continuity. There have been times and places where the idea and practice have flourished, only for interest to wane subsequently. The United States before, after, and long after World War II provides a striking example. In the interwar years Wallace Donham and Alfred North Whitehead could only implore business to think greatly, and by the 1980s the doctrine of shareholder value had become so ascendant that the affirmation that "greed is good" became the stuff of cinematic legend.[1] But in the first decades after World War II, the leaders of many large American corporations lined up to declare their belief that business had a role to play beyond making profits for shareholders.

The United States emerged from World War II as a uniquely powerful and wealthy country. The economies of Europe and Japan had been devastated by war and would take years to recover. American corporations dominated, for a time, many of the world's industries, and despite political competition with the Soviet Union and the new People's Republic of China, the United States had no economic peer or rival. Faced with limited competition from abroad, large American corporations could afford to be responsible.

Initial fears that the war would leave American industry in tatters and that tens of thousands of returning soldiers would be unemployed did not materialize. Instead, thanks in great part to the Servicemen's Readjustment Act of 1944 (popularly known as the GI Bill), the US government provided veterans, or more specifically primarily white veterans, with low-interest loans to start a business, low-interest mortgages to buy a home, and tuition to go back to school.[2] A rapid increase in home ownership led to booming markets for consumer products like washing machines, dishwashers, and television sets. By the end of the 1950s, three out of every four households had at least one car.[3]

The war had changed the mind-sets of business leaders and the reputation of business in general. Businesses had collaborated in important ways with the war effort, as firms were obliged to shift their production to support the national interest. In many industries the government became their main customer—and a lucrative one. Just as Bosch had redirected its operations in World War II, Ford made airplanes instead of automobiles, and General Motors made tanks and machine guns.

In 1942, the president of the automobile company Studebaker and senior managers from other large companies, including Kodak and Sears, formed the Committee for Economic Development, a nonprofit, nonpartisan, business-led public policy organization that became highly influential in policy formation. The committee initially promoted international organizations and American participation in them, but it soon branched out to other areas.[4] Among other initiatives, Winthrop W. Aldrich, the chairman of Chase National Bank, worked with welfare agency leaders in 1943 to establish the National War Fund to coordinate fund-raising efforts for relief and welfare programs. Three annual nationwide campaigns sponsored by the fund raised $321 million between 1943 and 1945.[5]

American business was proud of having delivered the products that enabled the United States to emerge triumphantly from the war. With their reputations much enhanced, concerns about the concentration of power that had so alarmed Edward Filene and others faded as large corporations began to be perceived as forces for good. One example of this new, less critical perspective can be found in the writings of John Kenneth Galbraith, a long-serving professor of economics at Harvard University and an influential public intellectual. In 1952 Galbraith published *American Capitalism: The Concept of Countervailing Power*, in which he explained that old concepts of competition no longer applied. Instead, he saw an economy run by big business, government, and labor unions that ideally offered a system of checks and balances. He argued that the power of corporations would be constrained by the countervailing power of the other two parties. Galbraith emphasized the role of corporations in driving economic growth. The "modern industry of a few large firms," he observed, is "an excellent instrument for inducing technical change."[6]

The Cold War added further incentives for big business to engage in socially responsible activities. While American industry was widely admired for having helped win the war, Soviet propaganda branded capitalism as ego-driven and fundamentally unfair. Some saw business as the "conscience carrier" of America. Others thought it should help America win the global popularity contest with the Soviet Union. As this chapter will show, the triumphant consumerism of the postwar era had a darker side, too, which many tried to atone for without disrupting the status quo, establishing company funds to support philanthropic activities and, not incidentally, lessen tax burdens. Meanwhile, a much smaller number of business leaders pursued deep responsibility by seeking to achieve a more sustainable, equitable, and ethical future.

The prevalence of the belief in postwar America that large corporations had a social responsibility was highlighted in this book's Introduction. We will explore further how this belief emerged and what forms it took to provide necessary context for the models of deep responsibility highlighted here. George Romney, who headed the automobile manufacturer American Motors Corporation during the 1950s, provides the first individual example. In his vision, he rejected what he perceived as excessive waste in the vibrant postwar consumer economy. When he became governor of Michigan, the crisis of housing, race, and class had triggered riots in blighted city centers. William C. Norris and An Wang, pioneers in the emergent computer industry, used their businesses to facilitate engagement with economically depressed urban neighborhoods and to help minorities who had been held back as white people prospered with government help.

The New American Business Creed

In 1949, Harvard University embarked on a lengthy investigation into the American "business creed." The results, published in 1956, confirmed that the business elite had cast aside its more individualistic past. To back up this claim, the report's authors pointed to the public statements of business leaders they had collected from the late 1940s onward. The authors revealed that the new creed focused on "the role of professional managers in the large business firm" to "consciously direct economic forces for the common good."[7]

Although real, these changes were more pronounced in rhetoric than in practice. Large US corporations had a history of paternalistic welfare policies accompanied by charitable donations. These tendencies ramped up and were more publicly celebrated in the postwar decades. This may have reflected a new confidence, but it also reflected, as the sociologist Rami Kaplan has written, a "desire to forestall the statist trend by appropriating responsibilities that would otherwise be government's."[8] Whatever the motive, corporate social responsibility became the fashion in American big business. General Electric, encouraged by new laws that made corporate giving to charities tax deductible, invested in social programs in local communities and in education. Meanwhile, higher tax rates, and especially an excess profits tax introduced during the Korean War between 1950 and 1953, prompted a surge in the creation of philanthropic foundations to reduce their tax obligations. Gifts of stock to family foundations also enabled continued family control over many businesses.[9] General Electric, Procter & Gamble, and U.S. Steel were among the large corporations that established foundations. There was also a great deal of business investment in education. Alfred P. Sloan, the long-serving chief executive of General Motors, and other business leaders such as Irving Olds of U.S. Steel and Frank Abrams of Standard Oil of New Jersey worked on the Council for Financial Aid to Education to encourage firms to give to universities.[10]

A number of companies distinguished themselves through their commitment to social responsibility. Among them was the Minneapolis-based retailer Dayton, which committed to giving away 5 percent of its pretax profits to philanthropy from 1946 onward.[11] The blue jeans manufacturer Levi Strauss, led by Walter A. Haas, pursued high standards of social responsibility, shortening the work-week during the Great Depression so that it would not need to lay off employees. In the 1940s the company ended racial segregation at its manufacturing plants in California. By 1960, when Levi's opened a new plant in Virginia, it was integrated from the start—four years before the Civil Rights Act of 1964 mandated the end of segregation. In the company's 1971 initial public offering, Haas noted that profits might be affected by "its commitment to socially responsible programs."[12]

A particularly notable example of social commitment can be found in the case of the Cummins Engine Company based in Columbus, Indiana. J. Irwin Miller, the chairman of this family-controlled company known for making quality diesel truck engines, committed to giving away 5 percent of pretax profits in 1954. Miller was a member of the Christian Church (Disciples of Christ) and devoted to its charitable mandates. Like the Jains, the Disciples of Christ believe that architectural space and design are important for a community to flourish. In 1954 Miller founded the Cummins Engine Foundation, which sponsored the design of new school buildings.[13] Other buildings designed by prominent architects followed. "He and the company were instrumental," his obituary in the *New York Times* observed, "in changing a decaying Columbus into a show-case for buildings."[14]

Miller cared about more than good buildings. During the early 1960s, he took the lead in prompting personnel heads to hire African Americans for more senior positions. Some years later he wrote to the mayor of Columbus, apparently with minimal effect, threatening to stop investing in the city unless action was taken to prevent white neighborhoods from blocking Black Cummins employees from purchasing homes.[15] In the early 1970s the Cummins Engine Foundation appointed five Black field officers in Chicago, Washington, Atlanta, Detroit, and Los Angeles and empowered them to make grants to local communities.[16]

Corporate paternalism may have reached its apogee during the postwar decades. Under T. J. Watson Sr., who led the firm between 1914 and 1953, the punch card manufacturer IBM developed a strong corporate culture, mandating everything from salespeople wearing blue suits to employees singing company songs. Watson's son, Tom Jr., took over the company in 1953 and led IBM into the computer age. He abolished company songs and some other excesses but otherwise codified the culture into three "Basic Beliefs": respect for the individual, superlative customer service, and the pursuit of excellence in all tasks.[17] Employees were always retrained and rarely dismissed. An open-door policy enabled anyone with a grievance to contact any executive. IBM also progressively diversified its labor policies. Persons with disabilities were hired after 1943, initially because of labor shortages. Women were hired as systems engineers and salespeople and by the 1970s were in management.[18] In 1972 the Fund for Community Service was established, under which employees could request money for community projects. Only the employee's manager and one other executive were needed to approve a project.[19]

A more radical agenda for business was proposed in Howard R. Bowen's book *The Social Responsibilities of the Businessman*, published in 1953, which has regularly been credited with introducing the concept of corporate social responsibility.[20] He was an educator with a somewhat turbulent career. He earned a PhD from the University of Iowa in 1935 and stayed to teach economics until 1942, then worked in the private sector and government until 1947, when he was recruited as dean of the College of Business Administration at the University of Illinois. His attempts to introduce Keynesian economics and topics related to business's responsibility to society led to a revolt by faculty, and he resigned as dean after three years, staying on the faculty for another two years before moving elsewhere, first to Williams College in Massachusetts, then to Grinnell College in Iowa, where he served as president; his last job was as professor of economics and education at Claremont Graduate University.[21]

Bowen's book, much cited subsequently as corporate social responsibility grew as an academic field, appears as rather an aberration in his own career. His own research was broadly focused in institutional and welfare economics, and in 1948 he published a textbook on welfare economics called *Towards Social Economy*.[22] His work was scholarly, yet *The Social Responsibilities of the Businessman* was meant for a general audience. His authorship may have been in part opportunistic in that the book formed part of a series entitled Christian Ethics and Economic Life that was funded by the Rockefeller Foundation and was sponsored by the interfaith National Council of Churches.[23] Bowen devoted an entire chapter to the Protestant view of the responsibility of business leaders. He maintained that Protestant doctrine had "fairly definite principles" about the "Christian duty" of business leaders to serve society rather than regarding the maximizing of profit as the sole end of enterprise. Bowen's checklist of the formal responsibilities of a business leader included—and it is worth remembering that segregation was still the law at this point in the South and informal segregation the norm almost everywhere else—the avoidance of discrimination "on grounds of race, religion, political views, national origin, social status, physical appearance or sex."[24]

If such ideas were radical for their time, Bowen floated a number of other ideas that would start to be taken seriously—though even now they are rarely executed—only a half century later. These included proposing five yearly "social audits" on companies by external experts, the development of business codes of good practice, the greater integration of business responsibility in management education, and the idea that business should be held responsible to society for externalities such as pollution.[25] These suggestions qualify Bowen more as a pioneer of deep responsibility than of conventional corporate social responsibility.

Bowen's book was no turning point in practice. It faded from view rather than starting a movement. As we have seen, the social responsibility of big business was already in the air in postwar America, so the broad topic, if not individual radical proposals, was not novel. Bowen himself provided a laundry list of things to be responsible for, but the overall framing was uninspiring. A manager's responsibility, he summarized, was to pursue strategies that were described vaguely as "desirable in terms of objectives and values of our society."[26] Bowen's next book, *The Business Enterprise as a Subject for Research* (1955), was sponsored by the Social Science Research Council and was designed to show how social science research can illuminate our understanding of the firm. It contained nothing about social responsibility, and less than a page on the "informal social pressures" exerted on the behavior of firms. He confined himself to a list of questions that "have not been investigated thoroughly," including, "What is the moral code of businessmen, and how is it developed and transmitted?"[27] Bowen spent the remainder of his career writing on the economics of education. The fact that he lost interest in the subject may have dented any impact of his ideas. Bowen himself judged his book to have had little impact. Invited to discuss the book at a workshop held in 1975, he noted that he "had observed few gains in the quality of business stewardship" since it was published. He went on to reflect that "an economy that serves the people" was only achievable "if corporate enterprise is brought under social control on terms such that the public and not the corporation controls the controller."[28] It was hardly a ringing endorsement of corporations' ability to uphold their social responsibility themselves. Bowen had clearly concluded that some form of government regulation was necessary, though he left the desirable boundaries between corporate responsibility and state enforcement unclear.

Bowen's radical ideas moved well beyond dressing a pig in a tuxedo, but his vision did not become reality in his lifetime. If American big business assumed slightly more responsibility for society in this era—and there appears to have been little to no discussion of the responsibilities of small and medium-sized firms—there was no redefinition of its social purpose. We now turn to the cases of some business leaders who came closer to making deep responsibility real.

George Romney and the Movement for Modest Consumerism

The postwar United States was the ultimate consumer society. As the cultural historian Gary Cross has observed, absent other common denominators such as inherited cultural traditions, a national church, or even a national educational system, Americans historically "defined themselves and their society through goods."[29] Lizabeth Cohen, who describes postwar America as the "consumers' republic," has suggested that the act of satisfying material desires through consumption became associated with serving the national interest and promoting the well-being of the economy. According to Cohen, many believed that taking on this "citizen-consumer" role would help promote greater equality, freedom, and democracy.[30]

Believing that being American meant more than shopping, George Romney, who was chief executive of the American Motors Corporation (AMC) during the 1950s, was one of the few business leaders who sought to address what he saw as the excesses of consumerism. He believed that the responsibility of business was to make products with enduring value, based on principles of integrity and honesty, in a fashion in which profits were not made at the expense of the public interest. This was a more modest view of social responsibility than that of Edward Filene, but in the context of postwar America, his efforts to promote smaller cars and less-wasteful consumption stand out.

Romney may have been unusual among American business leaders, but he fit squarely into a long tradition of skepticism of excessive consumerism. Rampant consumerism did not fit comfortably with the strong Christian morality prevalent in the United States. This tension manifested itself in various endeavors to restrict the consumption of things considered morally undesirable, most notably culminating in the fourteen years when the sale and consumption of alcohol were illegal, and the extensive controls introduced to curb gambling.

There were also strong critics of unrestrained consumption. A prominent example was Thorstein Veblen. Before he turned his attention to criticizing business education in American universities, Veblen had published *The Theory of the Leisure Class,* first released in 1899, with its searing critique of the "conspicuous consumption" of the rich who bought goods and services for status. He saw such buying as a threat to the American work ethos and called for a return to simpler living.[31] During the interwar years, consumer movements began contesting misleading information put out by manufacturers, which they sometimes linked to wasteful consumption patterns. Stuart Chase's book *The Tragedy of Waste* (1925) and *Your Money's Worth* (1927), cowritten by Frederick J. Schlink, attacked corporate advertising and advocated consumer protection. In 1929 Chase and Schlink founded the nonprofit Consumer Research, which exposed misleading advertising.[32] These efforts to expose misleading information had little practical impact. There were too many internal contradictions and countervailing forces. During the New Deal, spending came to be seen as a way to revive economic growth, legitimizing consumption as a national duty.[33] It was hard to succeed in making the case against consumerism in an America "largely constituted on the market."[34]

Nonetheless, during the 1950s there were further expressions of alarm about consumerist excess. Among the most prominent critics was Galbraith. Although his 1952 book *American Capitalism* offered a reassuring image of big business, his next book, *The Affluent Society,* published in 1958, launched an assault on misleading corporate advertising and excessive consumerism. Noting that basic needs had been met for virtually all nonimpoverished people, Galbraith wrote, "the fact that wants can be synthesized by advertising, catalyzed by salesmanship, and shaped by the discreet manipulations of the persuaders shows that they are not very urgent."[35] Galbraith worried that the effects of affluence would lead to increased disregard for those who were impoverished, as well as the development of socially accepted doctrines that would justify poverty.[36] *The Affluent Society* became a best seller, with 1.3 million copies sold within twenty-five years.[37] Whether Galbraith even found any irony in this commercial success is unclear, but the book, for all its impact, yielded no decline in overall consumer spending.

Among other voices critical of American consumerism was the journalist and social critic Vance Packard, who published a series of books that attacked business for turning Americans into manipulated "status-seekers."[38] *The Hidden Persuaders*, published in 1957, took aim at manipulative mass marketers, taking up the arguments first articulated by Chase and Schlink thirty years earlier.[39] Two years later, in *The Status Seekers*, he critiqued what he called "mass produced suburbs," the single-class, white communities fostering division in the country.[40] In *The Waste Makers*, published in 1960, Packard complained that "wastefulness has become a part of the American way of life."[41] The book criticized consumers for their pursuit of materialism on credit. Like Galbraith, Packard saw the business community as the central driver of wasteful consumerism because "they have a vested interest in its accelerated perpetuation."[42] He focused especially on "planned obsolescence," the deliberate and widespread practice of designing products to quickly become obsolete or go out of style. The book provoked an aggressive response from some companies and the trade press. The chemical company DuPont ran an advertisement titled "Waste-Maker Nonsense."[43]

This was the historical moment in which George Romney sought to promote smaller, less wasteful automobiles. His path to chief executive was neither linear nor easy. Born in 1907 in a Mormon colony in Mexico called Colonia Dublán, he had seen the colony subsumed by the chaos of the Mexican Revolution when he was five, after which his family resettled on a small parcel of farmland with poor soil in Oakley, Idaho.[44] As he was growing up, the family moved between Idaho, California, and Utah, depending on where his father could find work. Two of his brothers died as children, and when he was eighteen, his mother died of a cerebral hemorrhage.[45]

Between 1926 and 1928, Romney served as a Mormon missionary in Scotland. Upon returning to the United States, the near-penniless Romney secured a job on the staff of Senator David I. Walsh, Democrat of Massachusetts, in Washington, DC, and he eventually became his private secretary. The connections Romney made in Washington led him, in 1930, to be offered an apprenticeship at the Aluminum Company of America, a large aluminum manufacturing company.[46] In 1931, he became a full-time lobbyist for the company.[47]

Romney was neither the first nor the last Mormon to enter the business world. Indeed, many Mormons—members of the Church of Jesus Christ of Latter-Day Saints—flourished in the private sector. Although they were few in number—one million in 1947 and only three million worldwide by 1971—their success in business became legendary. Notable figures include J. Willard Marriott, the founder of the hotel chain; James LeVoy Sorenson, the medical device inventor and pharmaceutical entrepreneur; the chemicals entrepreneur Jon Huntsman Sr.; and the airline entrepreneur David Neeleman.

As with the Quakers, the causes of their success have long been debated. The Book of Mormon, published in 1830 by Joseph Smith, the founder of Mormonism, explicitly encourages ideals of self-reliance, a strong work ethic, and taking initiative within one's community.[48] Mormon rules prohibit drinking alcohol, keeping most members sober in an age of ubiquitous heavy drinking in the nineteenth century. The church actively incentivizes members to be successful, and they are expected to tithe one-tenth of their income.[49] Their missionary activity often requires young Mormons to learn a foreign language, and it may foster entrepreneurial skills, especially as they have to sell beliefs—including the teaching that Jesus Christ visited America after his resurrection—that many greet with incredulity or even hostility.[50]

There is another aspect of Mormonism that was particularly important in shaping Romney's views of the responsibility of business. The church is highly organized, and members are tasked with extensive duties from age three onward.[51] A strong hierarchy presides over the educational system, the worldwide missionary program, and the church's extensive welfare system.[52] As the historian of Mormonism Matthew Bowman has noted, a foundational idea within the Mormon church is that institutions are a means of transforming the individual. The church promotes organization and bureaucracy as a means of accomplishing social goals.[53] Romney's confidence in the power of business, and of other institutions such as churches and political organizations, to improve society seems to have rested quite heavily on this Mormon mind-set.

Romney's early career lobbying for the Aluminum Company of America was unremarkable. After being passed over for promotion, he left to become a manager of the Detroit office of the Automobile Manufacturers Association (AMA), an industry association, in 1939. It was in this position that he was exposed to the new spirit of cooperation in the automobile industry in the buildup to the war. He was appointed managing director of the Automotive Council on War Production, and it tasked him with organizing the automobile industry's transition to the mass production of war materials in the wake of the attack on Pearl Harbor. In March 1942 he was promoted to the role of general manager.[54] Under Romney's leadership, one of the council's first actions was to create an inventory of all of the idle machine tools in each of the automakers' factories. Then each company used the list of 198,000 items to facilitate machine-tool swapping among themselves, to ensure that every factory had what it needed to produce supplies and equipment for the war effort.[55]

Romney liked what he saw in wartime collaboration, and he became an evangelist for the benefits of what he called "competitive cooperative capitalism." He imagined an ideal world in which there was a balance of power between labor and management, with the two operating in cooperation with government. This balance came to be an essential ingredient of Romney's broader worldview in which people worked together to resolve larger social problems, just as the auto industry had during World War II.[56] After the war, Romney proposed that the AMA continue to facilitate cooperative industry activities and to speak out on public issues. But it ultimately chose not to do this.[57]

By 1948, Romney was ready to move on. He ended up with competing offers from two small, rival automobile companies, Packard and Nash-Kelvinator. Although Packard offered Romney a guaranteed promotion to chief executive, he opted for the less attractive offer from Nash-Kelvinator to be the assistant to the chief executive George W. Mason. Romney took Mason's offer because, as he later suggested in a letter to his father, he wanted a greater chance to educate himself about the industry before taking on a leadership role.[58] He did indeed get a hands-on education, including learning how to take apart and put together a car.[59]

Romney was a bundle of energy in his new position. He suggested various types of collaboration with Packard around the design and manufacture of automobile parts; Mason eventually implemented some of Romney's ideas.[60] By 1953 he was named executive vice president, making him the second most powerful person at Nash-Kelvinator.[61] When Mason died suddenly in October 1954, the board of directors made Romney the president, general manager, and chairman of the board.[62]

Earlier in 1954, Nash-Kelvinator had merged with Hudson, another automotive company, to form AMC. It was then the largest corporate merger in US business history.[63] The timing was not auspicious. AMC was far smaller than the top three firms—Ford, General Motors, and Chrysler—and a major price war was underway as Ford struggled to regain market leadership, which had been lost during the disastrous last years of Henry Ford's tenure as chief executive.[64] In 1954, the year Romney took over, AMC's revenue was $400 million, and the company reported a fiscal-year loss of $11 million.[65]

In 1950, Mason had put Romney in charge of marketing the company's new Rambler line of compact cars. Romney was among a minority of executives at the firm who were enthusiastic about the new cars.[66] He picked up the project. In many ways, the compact car represented values that he embraced and embodied: efficiency, self-restraint, and practicality over size and flashiness. It was also the opposite of prevailing trends in the industry. This was a time when cars became increasingly large and increasingly flashy, with large tailfins and hood ornaments painted in vibrant colors such as pink, blue, and green. A famous saying in Detroit was that small cars meant small profits. New models were launched every year. By the mid-1950s, owners were scrapping their cars three years sooner than in the previous decade so they could get a new Thunderbird or Pontiac to impress their friends and families.[67] The Rambler stood out. It was much shorter in its wheelbase (100 inches for a two-door and 108 for a four-door) than was customary at the time, when standard Ford models were 118 inches and more expensive models 124 inches. And it could run for more than thirty miles per gallon of gas—an industry-leading feature.[68] Romney was convinced that the Rambler represented the future of AMC, in combination with "a better spirit of cooperation and teamwork."[69]

Despite his committed efforts to promote the Rambler, the car was a weak performer in the marketplace. Romney decided to move up production of the 1957 model of the Rambler by a year—a strategy that proved unsuccessful as production problems and poor quality led to low sales. Operating losses in that year came to $19.7 million. Romney and other executives took voluntary pay cuts of up to 35 percent in response, while the company sold two executive airplanes, consolidated its dealerships, and even cleaned its offices less frequently.[70]

Romney found it difficult to sell the compact car even within AMC. In fact, he later noted the greatest challenge he faced was internal: "The biggest problem we had was to change the mental attitude of our own vice president in charge of sales and of our sales organization and our dealers."[71] He replaced his vice president of sales before releasing a new Rambler model in the fall of 1957. He also allegedly told the company's dealers, "If you have some men who lack enthusiasm, fire them with enthusiasm or fire them."[72]

Romney developed a strategy that he felt could beat out the bigger, flashier cars. At AMA, he had led the collection and analysis of nationwide car use statistics. He'd learned that most car trips were no more than a dozen or so miles—just far enough to run errands at local shops, drop a kid off at school, or visit a friend.[73] Romney became fixated on the idea that compact cars were more appropriate for such brief, local trips and that it was only a matter of time before American consumers realized that they might actually prefer smaller cars. Romney worked hard to persuade AMC's car dealers that the Rambler represented the future of the automobile industry. To popularize the idea that a compact car was a sensible consumer choice, he would hold up a loaf of bread in one hand and a single vitamin in the other to show how much value a smaller item could offer. He also took to calling competitors' vehicles "gas-guzzling dinosaurs," giving them names like "stegosaurus" and "dimetrodon." Industry executives started calling him a "dinosaur hunter" and gave him a plaque bearing the words, "To George Romney, critic, lecturer, anthropologist, white hunter of the American dinosaur."[74]

Romney was enthusiastic about the Rambler in part because he objected to the excesses he saw in the automobile marketplace, which he described as "the size and power craze."[75] "We faced at American Motors the kind of problem that Galbraith talked about," he would later recall.[76] In 1941, while working at AMA, he had observed that "refreshing change is one thing, but incessant change has a touch of idiocy."[77] He regularly associated the Rambler with the public interest, explaining how families that had saved money on gasoline could use their savings to pay for education.[78]

In 1961, Romney reflected that when he was appointed president "of a company on the edge of the grave," he came up with two strategies: to sell the Rambler concept and to build "a better spirit of cooperation and teamwork between the management, the employees, the union, the dealers, the stockholders, the suppliers and the customers."[79] In line with the second of these goals, he developed a pathbreaking—for the automobile industry—profit-sharing scheme. That year he reached an agreement with the United Auto Workers on a plan that would give employees 10 percent of before-tax net profits, after the company had set aside 10 percent of the stockholders' equity. Employees would also receive an additional 5 percent in the form of company stock (voting rights would be exercised by trustees selected by the company's board of directors).[80] Romney believed that profit sharing would incentivize productivity and profits.[81] The 1961 agreement was described by reporters as "revolutionary" and praised for bringing "profit sharing into greater prominence as a possible mode of worker compensation than it has been for many years."[82]

If Romney was in the minority of postwar American business leaders in his promotion of profit sharing, he was all the more so in his objections to consumerism and materialism. In a speech delivered in Los Angeles in 1959, he cited Alfred North Whitehead to bolster his critique of materialism:

> I get the distinct feeling that American people are getting fed up with trivialities, shoddiness and mediocrity. Most people want, need and respond to positive values. They want to find new and dynamic meanings to their lives. These words of Alfred North Whitehead, the English scientist, mathematician and philosopher, might well serve as America's challenge. He said: "We must produce a great age, or see the collapse of the upward striving of our race." I do not believe that our ability to produce material things should be established as the No. 1 symbol of our age. . . . Instead we must base our greatness on moral and spiritual values of enduring worth.[83]

Romney was in the business of selling cars, so he was far from opposed to material things. But as a Mormon, he believed that possession of material things should not be the main purpose of life. It was wasteful consumerism and planned obsolescence to which he particularly objected. The Rambler remained central to his vision of countering such excessive consumerism. Sales were helped by a recession in 1958, which made the Rambler's economical features, particularly its strong fuel economy, more salient to American consumers.[84] Romney's competitiveness led him to break with industry advertising norms. Beginning in 1956, AMC printed "X-Ray" booklets that compared the Rambler's features and prices with those of competitors. The booklets used disparaging words like "antiquated" and "ostentatious" to describe the cars of other companies. One

American automobile executive complained of this approach, "You plug your own product; you don't knock the other fellow's. Romney named names."[85]

Romney's efforts to promote the Rambler were rewarded, for a time. The company's overall production nearly doubled each year between 1957 and 1959. In that period, the company's overall market share increased from 1.76 percent to 6 percent. In 1960 AMC's revenue broke the $1 billion threshold, and profits in 1959 and 1960 were about double what they had been in 1958.[86] Romney made a speech to Rambler dealers in 1960 in which he lauded them for their contribution to a "revolution of basic proportions in the American economy" and called them "Ramblerutionists."[87] In 1961, he invited his dealers to join the company in building up their joint brand image. "We believe," he told them that year, "we are beginning to build a corporate image in America as a corporation that wants to be a symbol of industrial honesty and integrity."[88]

There were by then competitors to the Rambler. The German car company Volkswagen entered the American market in 1955 with its compact Beetle model, which was cheaper than Rambler models. The advertising agency Doyle Dane Bernback launched a "Think Small" advertising campaign to promote the Beetle, and later campaigns were critical of planned obsolescence and superficial design changes.[89] During the early 1960s, imports of Beetles grew rapidly as the car found a market in the emergent counterculture movement, whose followers found it a convenient statement against materialism.[90] Romney responded to the new compact car by "reskinning" the 1961 Rambler American—a subbrand introduced three years earlier—and making them slightly shorter and narrower. That year was a turbulent one for the auto industry, and AMC's profits fell by half—relative to 1960 levels—to $23.6 million. However, the company's profits recovered in 1962 to $34.2 million, as AMC sold over 478,000 Ramblers to its dealers, an increase of 24 percent.[91]

In line with his faith in competitive cooperative capitalism, Romney believed that concentrations of power and lack of real competition were a serious problem in many industries. He practiced what he preached. Although he was advised against it, in February 1958 he voluntarily appeared before the Subcommittee on Antitrust and Monopoly of the Senate Judiciary Committee to propose that Congress enact antitrust laws to curb monopoly power, including in the automobile industry. For good measure he also proposed that union power be reduced, criticizing the strategy of "pattern bargaining" used by the United Auto Workers as unfair to smaller automobile companies such as AMC.[92] He made the controversial argument that the Big Three automobile companies ought to be broken up. "Once a firm takes 35 percent or more of an established market, say in cars," Romney opined, "it would have to spin off part of its operations."[93] Media reactions were mixed. Some were convinced that Romney wanted the larger automobile firms broken up for his own gain. Romney brushed off detractors, stating, as one reporter later observed, "that he had long held his views but refrained from voicing them until his company was in the black."[94]

Business was not the only institution that Romney believed was important for achieving change. He was active in the Mormon church and consistently followed the rule not to work on Sundays. He also had a long-standing interest in politics and was vocal about his belief that citizens should be encouraged to overcome impediments to individual political action.[95] In September 1959, Romney spearheaded and led the nonpartisan organization Citizens for Michigan to assess the state government's economic problems and seek solutions. It attracted few supporters. He also participated as a vice president in Michigan's Constitutional Convention to rewrite the state constitution, which had been in effect since 1850. The new constitution was approved by voters in 1963.[96] In 1962, Romney's interest in politics brought him to a crossroads. On February 10, he announced his decision to become a candidate for the Republican gubernatorial nomination. In his announcement, he cited partisanship and the influence of special-interest groups as factors that had stifled previous administrations from representing the interests of all of their constituents.[97] He resigned as president and chairman of AMC and became vice-chairman.[98]

Romney went on to win the 1962 gubernatorial election—making him the first Republican governor for fourteen years—and was re-elected in 1964 and 1966.[99]

Within a decade, little remained of Romney's legacy at AMC. His immediate successor adopted a new strategy, introducing larger, more expensive cars for small-car buyers to trade up to and deemphasizing the Rambler brand. Company profits plummeted from nearly $38 million in 1963 to a loss of nearly $13 million by 1966.[100] Arguing that the profit-sharing agreement had raised AMC's labor costs eight to ten cents per hour above General Motors', the new management watered down the profit-sharing agreement in 1964, and employees were paid in cash rather than stock.[101] After 1969, the Rambler line was dropped from the North American market, although it was continued for a while in other markets, including Argentina and Mexico. The contrast with Volkswagen was stark. In 1968 Disney released its comedy movie *The Love Bug,* starring a self-driving, self-aware Beetle.[102] That same year the United States became Volkswagen's most important foreign market, with 563,522 cars—40 percent of total production—sold in the United States. In 1979 the French auto manufacturer Renault invested in AMC, eventually acquiring nearly half of the stock. In 1987, Renault sold the company to Chrysler. By the end of the decade, the company name had entirely disappeared.[103]

Romney's legacy at AMC was minimal, but this should not detract from what he sought to achieve. He believed that the responsibility of a firm was to achieve positive social changes, and that this choice could be a path to profit. His criticism of big cars and planned obsolescence aligned him more with Galbraith and Packard than with the mainstream of American big business, but he was right that some Americans would object to the "bigger, better, newer" mantra of mass consumerism and respond to a company that offered less flashy economy from a trustworthy brand. In fact, anticonsumerist consumers would in a few decades become a significant market. In the end, Romney failed to create a "Ramblerution," and the emergent hippie movement went for Beetles rather than Ramblers. Pursing profit with the purpose of constraining rather than encouraging wasteful consumption proved a lonely path, but Volkswagen had shown that it was possible to market a status symbol of anticonsumption—and to make a lot of money in the process.

Housing, Race, and Class: William Norris and An Wang

If consumerism and the resulting waste represented one major challenge for postwar America, the related problems of housing, race, and class represented an even greater one. While the country as a whole was affluent, many big cities experienced sharp demographic changes, triggering a growing economic and social crisis. There were multiple problems. Some so-called urban renewal programs in major cities such as New York, Boston, and New Haven falsely designated Black districts as "blighted" slums and demolished downtown blocks full of small businesses in order to build highways, department stores, and parking garages. These development schemes often decimated the social and cultural fabric of existing neighborhoods by displacing low-income, Black, and immigrant communities and diminishing or destroying the unique historical character of downtowns.[104] For-profit developers were among those most responsible for discriminatory housing practices. While many preferred not to see the problem, two eminent figures in the emergent computer industry, William Norris and An Wang, believed that for-profit business should be part of the solution.

The exodus of higher-income white families from cities to suburbs was facilitated by the availability of low-cost mortgages. The problem was that not everyone had access to these mortgages: 98 percent of the loans the Federal Housing Administration insured from 1934 to 1962 went to white Americans.[105] Automobile ownership grew, a trend that facilitated commuting over much longer distances. At the same time, the federal government embarked on a vast road-building program, launched with the Interstate and Defense

Highways Act of 1956. This triggered a huge building boom in the suburbs. The largest builder of family homes was the firm of the brothers William and Alfred Levitt, which mass-produced entire suburbs. Their first "Levittown," as they were called, was built between 1947 and 1951 on land previously used to grow potatoes near Hempstead on Long Island, thirty miles from New York City, and it came to host eighty thousand people. A second Levittown was constructed in Bucks County, Pennsylvania, between 1952 and 1958.[106] As affluent white families left cities, local tax bases were eroded. Because many public goods were financed at the county level, this had disastrous social consequences, resulting in sharply declining standards for schools and other services. To make matters worse, city governments were often incentivized to raze or prevent the building of low-income housing in order to build commercial or moderate-to-high-income housing that would generate greater revenue.[107]

Cities increasingly became the preserve of the poor and the non-white. The phenomenon of "white flight," which had started during the interwar years, intensified in this era.[108] Four million Black people immigrated to northern cities from the rural South between 1940 and 1970. Research has shown that every Black arrival in a non-southern city was correlated with two white departures.[109] Black people faced restrictions on where they could settle in the North. The tightly regulated Levittowns would not permit Black families to purchase property, and houses could only be rented, according to the rules of each community, to "members of the Caucasian race."[110] The racial segregation of housing led to the de facto segregation of public schools long after *Brown v. Board of Education* in 1954 outlawed it; segregation proved to be an enduring blight.[111]

As governor of Michigan, George Romney himself made a noteworthy contribution to addressing some of these issues. A new state constitution went into effect in 1964. It included the establishment of the first civil rights commission in the United States. This was one of several active civil rights policies he pursued: he also spent more on education and established the state's first minimum-wage law.[112] Romney forged a close relationship with Martin Luther

King Jr. and appeared at the front of civil rights marches.[113] These actions put him at odds with the leadership of the Mormon church, which had a terrible history when it came to African Americans, going back to its support of slavery. The Mormon church excluded Black men from the priesthood until 1978.

As secretary of housing and urban development following the election of Richard Nixon as president in 1968, Romney sought to pressure predominantly white communities to build affordable housing and to end discriminatory zoning practices. He instituted a housing scheme called "Open Communities" that rejected applications from states and cities that pursued racial discrimination in housing. This was kept secret from Nixon. After a brief and highly misleading flirtation with "Black capitalism," Nixon eventually concluded that fair housing was a vote loser, and Romney resigned from his post in November 1972 after Nixon won reelection.[114]

Business was also engaged in seeking solutions to the challenges of housing and race in inner cities. After the war, large manufacturing corporations, real estate developers, private investors, and banks became more active in the affairs of urban communities. In the late 1940s General Motors established "plant-city committees," which linked company officials with community leaders. But requests for financial support were usually rejected by the head office in Detroit unless the case could be made in Detroit of a direct corporate interest. In 1950, Ford followed with a community relations department in the thirty-five cities in which it operated. In fact, few of the corporate community programs of the 1950s and 1960s yielded concrete achievements.[115] Businesses stood out as the despoiler of communities and race relations rather than the opposite. The Levitts' firm was one of many builders of suburban homes that discriminated against minorities. Developers were closely intertwined with urban planners in engaging in "slum clearance." This was the case of the urban planner Robert Moses, who transformed New York City after World War II, and whose legacy of highways cutting across the city and consequent wrecking of neighborhoods tarnished his reputation for many. Meanwhile, mortgage lenders and insurance companies also engaged in discriminatory practices that reinforced segregation.[116]

Firms in the new computer industry sought a more positive role. Initially dominated by IBM after World War II, the industry was pried open beginning in the late 1950s by pressure from antitrust authorities that forced IBM to allow its customers to accept "plug compatible" accessories made by other companies for use with IBM computers. This opened the door to a surge of creativity by hardware and software firms.[117] This creativity helped fuel a new interest in the social purpose of business.

Among the earliest and most innovative new entrants was Control Data Corporation (CDC), led by William C. Norris, who had launched it with a team of navy codebreakers in Minneapolis in 1957. By 1958 CDC had secured a contract from the US Navy to develop the CDC 1604 computer, which was designed to be the most powerful computer in the world. Other contracts followed. The emergent market for supercomputers in this era was driven by contracts from government agencies, and Norris and his colleagues, with their military background, were effective at building contacts.[118] Norris led a string of innovations, including the groundbreaking CDC 6600 in 1964, which ran ten times faster than any other commercial computer. By 1965, CDC had become a *Fortune* 500 company. Two years later the company had twenty-three factories in eight states and four other countries.[119]

Norris had firsthand knowledge of hardship. He grew up on a farm in Nebraska and was educated in a one-room schoolhouse. In spring 1932, a month before he graduated from the University of Nebraska with a degree in electrical engineering, his father died and he had to take over the management of the family farm. The Great Depression had a disastrous impact on farmer incomes, and things were made worse by the "dust bowl" storms that afflicted Nebraska and the entire Southern Plains region.[120] This tumultuous experience appears to have shaped his view that business should contribute to society, not through philanthropy but as a profit-making opportunity. The nature of his business meant that the firm was affected by the Kennedy administration's decision in 1961 to mandate nondiscrimination and affirmative action in hiring by federal contractors. CDC and other contractors had to provide evidence of compliance. When riots broke out in Minneapolis Northside, a neighborhood with a large African American population, in August 1966, the company offered twenty scholarships to disadvantaged youths to engage in training for computer industry workers. When it became clear that one of the reasons for the low number of African American job applicants was that they could not travel to the factory in the suburbs on public transit, Norris devised a plan to establish a factory in Minneapolis Northside and began operations in 1967, the year of the "long hot summer" that saw 159 riots across the country, including a three-day destructive riot in Minneapolis Northside in July.[121]

The assassination of Martin Luther King Jr. in April 1968 and the subsequent rioting appear to have energized Norris. When news broke of the assassination, Norris was attending a ten-day course on future problems for managers at Columbia University.[122] Just over a week later, he wrote in an internal company memorandum about the need for an "acceleration of actions by business to help in a major way to solve some of the more urgent social problems—particularly poverty and rioting in the streets." The memo went on to argue that if business did not take steps, the government would do so, and that taking a proactive stance "might turn out in the long run to be good business."[123] Over the following years, Norris set up CDC plants in impoverished neighborhoods in Saint Paul, Minneapolis, and Washington, DC. The problem was that CDC's initiative did not encourage others to invest. Ten years after the Minneapolis factory opened, no other large employer had invested in the area. Norris responded by creating the for-profit City Venture Corporation in 1978, designed to provide management and consulting services to facilitate job creation by helping to start new businesses and expanding existing ones. By 1986 over one thousand companies employing more than thirteen thousand workers had been created, but the program experienced problems with local activists resentful of being dictated to, and it suffered from declining federal funds with the onset of the Reagan administration. In 1986, CDC divested the business to its management.[124]

Building factories in economically depressed parts of cities was not Norris's sole contribution to social reform. The company spent $1 billion over two decades to develop a computer-based education system, building on research at the University of Illinois at Urbana-Champaign. In 1976, CDC secured full rights over the use of PLATO (Programmed Logic for Automatic Teaching Operations). The company began to sell PLATO to public school systems and offered a range of options, from buying a computer mainframe and full PLATO software to buying a single PLATO course accessed at one of the company's Control Data Institutes.[125]

PLATO evolved over time, and by the mid-1970s had been described as "perhaps the most advanced online services platform in the world," with a set of tools that enabled collaboration, communication, and recreation. The staff working on it wanted to develop business applications for which there was considered to be a large market. Norris instead insisted that development focus on the education market.[126] He believed that PLATO could transform the American educational system, which he criticized for rising costs and fragmentation, and—rightly—saw as a major impediment to many children's success in economically depressed areas. He thought computerized education would enable more individualized instruction, increasing the speed of learning and freeing teachers from routine tasks, thus enabling them to pay more individual attention to students. He believed that companies could take the lead in meeting the needs of society by offering, as he noted in a speech in 1976, "higher-quality, more readily available education—at lower costs."[127] This fueled his core vision that business could and should help solve social problems. "The major problems of our society are massive, and massive resources are required for their solution," he noted in a speech in 1979. "The best approach is to view them with the strategy that they can be profitable business opportunities with an appropriate sharing of cost between business and government."[128]

Norris employed PLATO in a program called Fair Break to reach inner-city youths, primarily the disadvantaged, high school dropouts, and single mothers. Fair Break had begun operating in Saint Paul, Minnesota, in 1978. It consisted of four months of PLATO-based classroom work with sessions including trained counselors. Topics covered included basic math and reading, but also life management and job-seeking skills. Some programs were specifically designed to prepare disabled people for employment. Contracts were signed with state and local government agencies, and it was financed primarily by federal job training funds. By 1986 there were forty-five Fair Break centers in operation. PLATO was also extended to prisons in the early 1970s, beginning with the installation at CDC expense of PLATO terminals at the Minnesota State Prison in Stillwater. There was a marked improvement in inmate reading ability and math scores, which led to further experiments and, in 1981, a determined push to develop a market in prisons. By 1986 it had been introduced into eighty prisons.[129]

High costs and complex maintenance, however, meant that PLATO never lived up to Norris's dreams. It ended up being used primarily as an employee training tool in large companies. CDC, like other mainframe computer makers, including IBM, was thrown into crisis as the personal computer exploded onto the market. The first very basic personal computer, called the Altair, was marketed by a small calculator company in Albuquerque, New Mexico, in 1974. The real breakthrough in the new technology happened three years later when the small Californian start-up Apple launched Apple II, the electronic calculator company Commodore launched PET, and Tandy—then the largest mass retailer of electronics goods in the United States—launched its TRS model, sold cheaply at its Radio Shack stores for home education and video games. IBM launched its own personal computer in 1981. The market for personal computers soared.[130]

Norris was forced out as CEO in 1986, with his social programs seen as part of the problem facing CDC. He was fully aware that his social programs had long met skepticism in Wall Street. "If people don't scoff," he said in an interview concerning CDC's support for a small-scale farming venture in 1980, "I'd know immediately I was on the wrong track."[131] After he left, the firm was largely dismantled in the following years. PLATO was sold off in several pieces.[132] The system served as a remarkable pioneer of today's cyberculture: it offered multiplayer games, chat rooms, instant messaging, message boards, and screen savers all before the advent of the internet. However, Norris's stubborn insistence that PLATO be confined to transforming education meant that most of its potential was not realized, including the potential to deliver revenue streams that might have subsidized the work in the education sector.[133] For all of the hope and promise of tech-fueled innovation, inner-city education was not transformed.

Norris was not the only computer industry pioneer who sought to have a positive social impact by investing in communities. An Wang, an immigrant from Shanghai with a PhD in applied physics from Harvard in 1947, founded Wang Laboratories in 1951 in Cambridge, Massachusetts, and incorporated the company four years later. Wang Laboratories started modestly, making and selling memory cores. It grew as it invested progressively in calculators, word processing, and computers. In 1967, after launching the highly successful Wang 300 calculator, the company went public, with a market capitalization of $70 million. Wang transitioned into a minicomputer company when it launched Model 2200 in 1972. It called the 2200 a computing calculator, but it was actually a full-purpose computer. Wang's next step was into the new domain of word processing. In 1971, Wang launched the Wang 1200 word processor. He struggled to attract customers, but the much more accessible Wang Word Processing System, launched in 1976, was hugely successful. Wang, one study concludes, had an "astute sense of knowing when to get out of one market and into a new one about to open up."[134] At its peak in the mid-1980s, Wang Laboratories had annual revenues of $3 billion and employed over thirty-three thousand people.[135]

Wang's firm was, like most of the large electronics companies of the era, generous to employees, and it sometimes exceeded industry norms. Employees were given pension plans and stock through profit sharing, and by 1982 they held about 17 percent of the total equity. Wang also established childcare centers in his manufacturing plants and operated a country club for employees.[136]

Like Norris, Wang invested heavily in education. He established the Wang Institute of Graduate Studies in 1979 in Tyngsborough, Massachusetts, and funded it with $6 million. The institute launched a master's degree program in software engineering and provided scholarships to support Chinese students with graduate fellowships. Wang had benefited from a World War II initiative that had allowed him to take part in a training program in the United States. As the company's fortunes soared in the early 1980s, Wang intensified his philanthropic donations to educational, medical, and artistic institutions. For several years, he gave more to charity than he earned. There were large grants to Harvard, including support for the John K. Fairbank Center for East Asian Studies and for Massachusetts General Hospital, where the Wang building became—and remains—a prominent landmark. In 1983, he rescued the crumbling Metropolitan Theatre in Boston with a donation of $4 million and renamed it the Wang Theatre. The theater was managed by the nonprofit Wang Center for the Performing Arts (now the Boch Center).[137]

By the end of his career, Wang came to articulate explicit views about the social purpose of business. "I'm there to impart the philosophy I value," he told *Business Week* in 1982, and that was "to serve a useful purpose to society at large, and to make sure the people we serve—stockholders, employees, and customers—get a fair return."[138] He developed these themes in his autobiography *Lessons*, published four years later, which made reference, without much detail, to the influence of Confucianism on his thinking.[139] "Corporate behavior," he wrote, "should be judged by the same standards as personal behavior."[140] He noted that his "purpose in founding Wang Laboratories was to devise equipment and services that would increase worker productivity and make jobs easier." He went on to say, however, that "if in the pursuit of this goal, my company exploited its own employees or its surrounding community, or pursued business in an unethical manner, this would negate whatever positive contributions the company made through its products."[141]

Investment in communities in Massachusetts was one of the more distinctive features of Wang's business. As the firm became successful in the 1970s, it outgrew its original site in the small town of Tewksbury. Wang moved his manufacturing to the nearby city of Lowell, which had flourished as the center of the textile industry in the early nineteenth century but had been hollowed out since the end of World War II. By the mid-1970s, Lowell had the highest unemployment rate (at 13.8 percent) of any city in the United States. The city's officials had failed to attract a high-profile company to invest, even though Massachusetts was experiencing a tech boom. Seeing an opportunity, Wang acquired a building and property in Lowell at a very low cost and established the company's headquarters there. The buildings cost around $60 million to construct.[142] Manufacturing stayed in Tewksbury. Wang later explained that it was easier for the company's higher-paid employees to commute the seven extra miles to Lowell than it was for the blue-collar workers who lived near the plant.[143]

Wang's business grew so fast that he was soon constructing a tower block supported by the city government, which waived zoning rules and took other steps to accommodate the building. A second tower followed with an impressive penthouse suite on top.[144] Wang Laboratories became the largest employer in the city, and by the mid-1980s, Lowell had the lowest unemployment rate in the United States.[145] As the company continued to invest in the city, it attracted glowing local press. "What Dr. An Wang has done for this city can hardly be over-estimated," Lowell's newspaper, the *Sunday Sun*, observed in 1981. "He has given our residents more than high hopes for the future . . . if there is little real unemployment in the city at this time, it is due, in large part, to Wang."[146]

Wang chose not to follow other US electronics companies in outsourcing to Asia, although he did establish factories in Scotland and Puerto Rico in the 1980s. Instead, Wang invested heavily in a computer-assembly plant in Boston's Chinatown with the ambition of providing better-paying jobs to the local Chinese American community. The plant was opened in 1984 and employed three hundred workers.[147] The chief reason why he established a plant in downtown Boston, he told an audience at Babson College in 1985, after being awarded a Distinguished Entrepreneur prize, was "a desire to invest in the city where I did my early work. The decision is also an expression of faith in the potential of an urban area and its residents."[148]

The mid-1980s were a high point for the business and for Wang personally. In 1984 Wang and his family owned about 55 percent of the company stock, and *Forbes* magazine, estimating his worth at $1.6 billion, ranked him as the fifth-richest American.[149] Three years later the business was in trouble. The sales of the company's word processors, built around expensive minicomputers, were devastated by the spread of personal computers. As earnings stumbled, the Wang Institute of Graduate Studies was closed in 1987. Although Wang had previously proved adept at navigating shifting markets, a stubborn belief that he was always right prevented him from addressing underlying challenges. He declined to listen when his staff suggested the firm move into personal computers. By the time Wang finally took this step in the mid-1980s, it was too late and too costly. The company's personal computers were priced too high and were not compatible with IBM's dominant products.[150]

Wang's problems were not unique. His business was part of a cluster of companies located around Route 128 in Massachusetts that had flourished as a global center of electronics innovation during the 1970s, at the same time as Northern California's Silicon Valley. During the early 1980s the Silicon Valley microchip makers lost their semiconductor market to Japan, while Route 128 minicomputer companies began to be decimated by the rise of workstations and personal computers. However, later in the decade, Silicon Valley renewed itself, as firms such as Intel and Hewlett-Packard flourished and new start-ups entered the semiconductor and computer business. Wang and other Route 128 companies, such as Digital Equipment Corporation and Data General, sank further into decline and eventually failed. One study notes that while Silicon Valley's culture, with its dense social networks and an open labor market, encouraged new entrepreneurial ventures, Route 128's culture emphasized secrecy and independence, and a small number of vertically integrated corporations that kept to themselves. Wang's business was typical in this regard, and its secrecy and independence worked against corporate renewal.[151]

Wang's commitment to keeping his business in the family contributed to the business's challenges. In 1976 he delisted his stock from the New York Stock Exchange and moved it to the American Stock Exchange, which permitted him to create a separate limited-voting class of stock that kept the family in control. His commitment to his son Frederick as successor was probably a net negative. He made Frederick president in 1987, only to have to dismiss him two years later, shortly before he died of cancer at age seventy.[152] Wang Laboratories went into bankruptcy protection in 1992 and was subsequently dismantled. The impact on Lowell was disastrous. The unemployment rate reached 12.5 percent in 1991.[153]

Norris and Wang made real efforts to use their businesses to address the blight of race and class discrimination. Yet the deep responsibility programs of CDC and Wang Laboratories disappeared along with the companies. It is not hard to find fault with both men. Norris misjudged the ease of the PLATO system, and Wang put the interests of his family before the interests of his firm. Yet human frailty should not diminish our appreciation of the deep social impact the two men were able to achieve. Norris addressed head-on the fact that people in economically depressed areas of cities, often African Americans, needed jobs so they could build better futures. He took a risk by setting up factories in blighted neighborhoods and actively recruited from those neighborhoods. He recognized that systemic racism required proactive countermeasures and put a firm ethical foundation at the center of his business. Wang transformed the city of Lowell after decades of stagnation and decline. The factory in Boston's Chinatown took jobs to a minority urban community that needed them and faced the blight of racism. The easier path would have been to outsource jobs to cheaper countries such as

Southeast Asia, Hong Kong, and Mexico, as most of the American semiconductor firms beginning with Fairchild Semiconductor in 1963 did, but Wang chose to put social purpose ahead of profits.

The policies of Romney, Norris, and Wang emerged in the specific context of postwar America when big business as a whole followed a broadly stakeholder-minded approach. Firms like IBM offered their employees stable employment and encouraged wider social engagement. This was the agenda strongly supported by Donald K. David and his successors at the Harvard Business School, as well as many other business school deans. The broad mission of these endeavors was to make economic systems work more equitably—and to be seen to be doing so, to deflect critiques of capitalism coming from the communist world. The conversation about social responsibility did not extend beyond large corporations, and staving off government mandates to behave responsibly was certainly one motivation. There was no fundamental rethinking of the social purpose of business, although a number of proposed ideas were nevertheless quite radical, including some of the recommendations in Howard Bowen's *The Social Responsibilities of the Businessman*.

This chapter has explored the cases of business leaders who pursued a deeper responsibility. Romney, uncomfortable about materialism, translated some of his Mormon beliefs into efforts to reduce wasteful consumerism. He was one of the few American business leaders who rejected planned obsolescence and consumer excess. Few others spoke up, even as the dire ecological impact of consumerism became undeniable.

Most of the "community programs" created by large corporations made limited contributions to the racial crisis engulfing American cities. Yet this chapter has identified two business leaders who thought more radically and took concrete action. Norris developed a vision for taking manufacturing jobs back to depressed parts of cities to help solve the chronic problems of oppression they faced. He acted on this vision in Minneapolis and elsewhere. At least for a time, he offered opportunities and changed many people's lives for the better. He had an even more radical vision of how his PLATO educational computer service could transform the chances of inner-city youths. The execution was flawed, yet he forged a new path by suggesting how computer technologies could transform inner-city education. Wang's commitment to keep jobs in towns such as Lowell and in Boston's Chinatown demonstrated how a purpose-driven business can positively affect society. Wang's investments in education, health, and culture had a lasting, positive impact on society. It is hard not to compare Norris and Wang favorably to most current computer industry titans in Silicon Valley, few of whom seem interested in changing the world for the better, and some of whom are hugely harmful.

The facts that the Rambler car was discontinued, Norris lost his job, and Wang's firm went bankrupt soon after his death were indicative that times were changing. Skepticism about the social responsibility of business grew from the 1970s, culminating in agency theory and the shareholder value model of capitalism. As maximizing shareholder value became the official creed of large US public companies—albeit still accompanied by a veneer of corporate social responsibility programs—a new generation of entrepreneurial start-ups took up the mantle of deep responsibility, as will be seen in Chapter 8.

PART III

NEW PARADIGMS

THE RISE OF VALUES-DRIVEN BUSINESSES

ANITA RODDICK AND THE
CHALLENGE OF GROWTH

From the 1960s on, a new generation began to reset social and cultural norms. They did so in a changed, more globally connected, world. For the most part, this new generation had limited regard for "the establishment," a vague term of derision that included big business and often capitalism as a whole, despite often living in considerable affluence because of it. Some among them founded firms aligned with their anti-establishment values. The resetting of social norms and the emergence of a new crop of socially minded business leaders determined to use their companies to change the world for the better are exemplified by the remarkable—and cautionary—story of the British beauty entrepreneur Anita Roddick.

Challenges to accepted norms came from many directions. The new youth culture was most visibly epitomized by hippies, members of a countercultural movement that originated on college campuses in the United States but was really a transatlantic phenomenon.[1] Many hippies favored unconventional dress, cooperative living arrangements, vegetarian diets based on unprocessed foods, and hallucinogenic drugs. They challenged dietary norms by experimenting with alternative foods, including products such as granola bars and yogurt that in time became mainstream.[2] The "Summer of Love" in 1967 saw large gatherings of young people and musical concerts in big cities across North America and Europe, including London, Paris,

Amsterdam, Copenhagen, and even Prague and Warsaw in Communist Eastern Europe.[3]

Music festivals and rock music provided the sounds of the alternative society that this youth culture imagined. Rock music was at the center of the so-called Swinging Sixties, which transformed London from the dull capital of a country that had lost its empire to a countercultural global hub. The music of the Beatles, especially after the release of Sgt. Pepper's Lonely Hearts Club Band in 1967, caused a wave of experimentation and innovation. The lyrics of the 1960s encouraged rebellion and self-expression. The Beatles made their first appearance in the United States in February 1964—when the four band members were between twenty and twenty-three—and a wave of "Beatlemania" followed. When they appeared on the popular Ed Sullivan Show on February 9, 1964, two days after their arrival, an estimated seventy-three million people watched.[4]

The transatlantic impact of the Beatles reflected the new mobility of people and ideas. Regular commercial air service between London and New York began in 1958, making their visit possible. In 1970, the first Boeing 747 carrying hundreds of passengers flew between New York and London, the first step in the democratization of international travel. Blue-collar workers started traveling internationally on vacation for the first time, something that had previously been the preserve of elites.

Hippies and rock groups were not the only ones pushing the boundaries and challenging norms. Mass social protest movements convulsed the United States and Europe, as students took to the streets to demand changes to established ways. In the United States, the civil rights movement saw the earliest mass protests aimed at transforming both the social and political status quo. The 1963 March on Washington for Jobs and Freedom, led by Rev. Martin Luther King Jr., drew an estimated 250,000 peaceful demonstrators, who walked from the Washington Monument to the Lincoln Memorial to demand economic equality and civil rights for African Americans. Parallel streams of social activism animated student radicals and the New Left, a term that originated in Britain and crossed the Atlantic. This new movement, deeply critical of capitalist materialism, spontaneously arose elsewhere, as the Nouvelle Gauche in France and the Neue Linke in Germany.[5]

Protests against the war in Vietnam played an important role in the transatlantic student protest movements and were catalysts for action on both sides of the Atlantic, although the youths in each country had their own concerns. The riots that swept France in May 1968 centered on wide-ranging calls for the democratization of social and cultural institutions, from education to the news media.[6]

The 1960s also saw the emergence of social movements concerned with the natural environment, a topic that came to inspire many of the new values-driven businesses. This was not the first generation to worry about the environmental cost of capitalism. During the nineteenth century social elites in the United States and Europe championed a conservationist movement leading to the creation of national parks and the introduction of new regulations, especially on air pollution.[7] The momentum behind this nascent environmentalism dissipated with the arrival of World War I, as war and economic and social upheaval diverted attention elsewhere. Scientists' warnings about soil erosion, waste, and even climate change were ignored.[8]

In *The Social Responsibilities of the Businessman,* Howard Bowen went so far as to say that the "obviously wasteful use of natural resources is morally indefensible." But he quickly added that there were limits to what could "reasonably be expected of businessmen," and the "interests of future generations probably must be handled largely through government policy."[9] This reflected the long-prevalent assumption in law and accounting that environmental damage caused by a company was an "externality" that was up to others to deal with. It was an assumption that the new generation of values-driven entrepreneurs did not share, although most businesses continued to focus on profits and productivity and to pay scant attention to the environmental impact of their actions.

The revival of concern about the natural environment, sometimes described as the second wave of environmentalism, has often been dated to the publication of Rachel Carson's book *Silent Spring,* a warning against pesticides, in 1962.[10] The book rapidly reached an international audience. The release of the British edition, in 1963, coincided with a toxic waste spill in the county of Kent. Local activists linked the spill to Carson's book, triggering a nationwide debate on the use of pesticides.[11]

In December 1968 the crew of Apollo 8, the first spaceship to orbit the moon, photographed the earth against the darkness of space. The "Earthrise" photograph became a symbol of the earth's fragility and was widely adopted by the environmental movement. As environmental awareness grew, new nongovernmental organizations (NGOs) were formed, including the Friends of the Earth in San Francisco in 1969 and Greenpeace in Victoria, Canada, in 1971. When the first Earth Day was held in the United States on April 22, 1970, twenty million Americans demonstrated for a healthier environment.[12]

Initially there was little interaction between environmentalists, the New Left, and radical activists, but a convergence came in the 1970s around opposing nuclear power, in which many governments sought to invest in the wake of the oil price rises of that decade.[13] In 1972, the first-ever United Nations Conference on the Environment was held in Stockholm. Many nations committed to new environmental laws. The Environmental Protection Agency was founded in the United States in 1970, though public policies fell short of what was needed.

By the time the United Nations Earth Summit was held in Rio de Janeiro in 1992, the scientific evidence on the reality of climate change was mounting. Five years later the Kyoto Protocol became the first internationally binding treaty aimed at reducing global emissions. It largely failed, but by the new century, many acknowledged the reality of human-induced climate change, even if few were prepared to take serious steps to stop it.

Feminism also enjoyed a resurgence in the 1960s. Like environmentalism, campaigning for the rights of women had a long history. A so-called first wave of feminism in the late nineteenth and early twentieth centuries had focused on gaining the right to vote. In 1893,

New Zealand became the first country to grant suffrage to women. The United States followed in 1920, a full twenty-seven years later, with the passage of the Nineteenth Amendment to the Constitution. In many other countries, female suffrage came much later (1944 in France, 1946 in Japan, 1949 in India, 1953 in Mexico, 1971 in Switzerland, and 2015 in Saudi Arabia). Gaining suffrage did not end the cultural and social norms standing in the way of full equality, especially those governing work and business. With the spread of industrialization in the West, women—or rather, more affluent urban women—were steered into the household as wives and mothers, while wage earning was dominated by men. Many women did toil in factories and sweatshops, but they almost never appeared as managers of large-scale businesses. Businesses catering to other women, primarily fashion and beauty, were the exceptions, as well as professions such as teaching, nursing, domestic service, and clerical work.[14]

In the 1960s, a "second wave" of feminists fought back against repressive social values and normative gender roles so evident in the restricted options for women in business. They explored the depression and social isolation caused by repetitive household duties and spoke movingly about the pain of being intellectually underestimated. Betty Friedan's *The Feminine Mystique,* which sold one million copies in 1963, argued that women were deeply unhappy in their limited roles as wives and mothers.[15] Critics pointed out that the malaise Friedan described primarily afflicted white middle-class women, while less privileged women had no choice but to work outside the home. Still, the book energized the feminist movement in the United States and was influential elsewhere. Friedan went on to cofound the National Organization for Women in 1966.[16] After working undercover as a server at the Playboy Club, the freelance journalist Gloria Steinem publicly exposed the extent of male chauvinism and became a leading voice in the feminist movement. Her campaigns for legalized abortion and federally funded daycare made her nationally famous and contributed to a bitter rivalry with Friedan.[17]

Feminism was both a transatlantic and a global movement with different characteristics depending on national culture and circumstances.[18] In Britain, where the feminist movement expanded rapidly in the 1960s and 1970s, there was an overlap with peace movements protesting the Vietnam War and campaigning for nuclear disarmament. While the politics of race and class were intermingled with American feminism, in Britain feminism was most closely linked to class. Feminists campaigned for equal pay and in support of exploited female workers.[19]

Some of these convulsive challenges to social norms went nowhere. The New Left did not replace capitalism with a new socialist order, and students were unable to end the Vietnam War. But others, such as the civil rights movement, second-wave feminism, and the environmental movement, started processes that gained momentum and are still with us today. Perhaps the major common feature of these social movements—beyond their evident desire for change—was their disregard for capitalism. Business was at the core of a rotten system for New Left radicals, a polluter and a poisoner for environmentalists, and one of the guardians of male hierarchical privilege for feminists. While many business leaders chose to ignore this countercultural critique or actively scorned it, some sought to present themselves in more virtuous light, though public displays of social conscience were sometimes more veneer than substance. A third group of entrepreneurs put activism and social change at the heart of their business plans.

A New Generation of Values-Driven Businesses

The new generation of countercultural business leaders that emerged in the late 1960s and 1970s, many of them based in the United States although with counterparts elsewhere, were often critical of capitalism as a system and of the existing relationship between business and society. They saw founding an alternative form of business as the best way to achieve positive social impact and believed that such businesses were key to seriously improving society. These businesses came to be (self-)described as "values-driven."[20] Business leaders with values were not, as this book has made clear, a new phenomenon, but this post-1960s cohort distinguished itself from many predecessors by its vocal rejection of conventional norms and by its social goals. Ecological concerns were high on the agendas of many of the founders, most of whom also had views aligned with the civil rights and feminist movements.

These values-driven businesses tended to cluster in industries with the clear potential to drive positive ecological or societal change. Renewable energy was one such industry. From the nineteenth century onward, small numbers of entrepreneurs experimented with technologies in wind and solar energy with the ambition of bringing electricity to rural areas or countries with limited access to coal. This tradition gained new adherents as ecological concerns mounted. During the 1970s, values-driven entrepreneurs such as the American industrial chemist Elliot Berman—motivated by a desire to provide electricity to the rural poor in developing countries—were among the most important innovators driving down the cost of solar cells.[21] In the same period, environmental activists in the United States, Denmark, and elsewhere catalyzed incremental innovations in blade design for turbines, laying the foundation for the modern wind energy industry.[22]

It was not until the early 1980s that policy makers began to support renewables, beginning with California's pioneering feed-in tariffs. Danish companies such as Vestas turned out to be the largest beneficiaries of this Californian wind boom, not least because they developed more reliable technologies than their American counterparts. They were well placed when governmental support for the industry in Denmark grew in the second half of the 1980s, just as it fell in California.[23]

The food industry also attracted people who felt that a values-driven business could be a vehicle for societal improvements. The health of the soil and of human beings, and concern about the consumption of processed foods, were long-running concerns among those worried about the nefarious impacts of industrialization. Small organic food and farming businesses were formed beginning in the second half of the nineteenth century, especially in Europe and the United States, in reaction to the growing use of chemical fertilizers.[24] Chapter 9 will explore how businesses inspired by the Austrian philosopher Rudolf Steiner, who laid out the principles of biodynamic farming in the early 1920s, became significant forces behind the growth of the organic food market.

From the late 1960s, a new generation of countercultural entrepreneurs gravitated toward natural foods retailing. They sought to change minds about the health of people and the planet, not simply to sell products. The macrobiotic movement, which originated in Japan, was an important influence behind the creation of the first natural foods stores in the United States. Erewhon was opened in Boston in 1966 by Japanese immigrants Michio Kushi and his wife, Aveline. Michio Kushi saw healthier eating as forming part of a lifestyle change that would bring health and peace to the world. He hired the twenty-one-year-old Paul Hawken, who would go on to become a prominent green entrepreneur in his own right, to run the store. He pioneered the idea of contracting with farmers to grow organic crops, which was a crucial step in giving farmers the confidence to grow organic food.[25]

The herbal tea company Celestial Seasonings was founded in Boulder, Colorado—known for its intense countercultural community—by Mo Siegel in 1970 when he was twenty-one. Reading the *Urantia Book,* a spiritual and religious tome of unknown authorship that appears to have been written in Chicago in the first half of the twentieth century, Siegel later observed, "made me examine my values and commit myself to doing something worthwhile with my life. . . . I immediately turned to the health food industry." Collecting wild herbs that grew around Boulder, he began experimenting with herbal tea blends and launched a successful brand. While health foods had previously had a reputation for being earnest rather than delicious, Siegel focused relentlessly on making his teas taste good. The culture at Celestial Seasonings mirrored the counterculture of its time. Siegel rode to work on a bicycle, and employees walked around in bare feet. The brand was deeply ecological: organic, noncaffeinated, and free of all additives, each box of tea had detailed ingredient lists, health advice, and selected spiritual sayings.[26] If the venture was unconventional, it was also successful in the marketplace. Siegel, who declared his admiration for IBM, pursued growth. By 1978, Celestial Seasonings employed two hundred people and sales reached $9 million ($35 million in 2021 dollars).[27]

In that same year John Mackey, a college dropout who for a time lived in a commune studying Eastern religions and has manifested a lifelong interest in the occult, opened a natural foods store called Safer Way in Austin, Texas. He later described how he had previously held the view "that both business and capitalism were fundamentally based on greed, selfishness, and exploitation" in pursuit of "the goal of maximizing profits." He initially espoused cooperative movements as the way forward but found decision-making too politicized with little room for "entrepreneurial creativity." He opted to go into business, reading free enterprise economists like Friedrich Hayek, Ludwig von Mises, and even Milton Friedman. He concluded that "free enterprise, when combined with property rights, innovation, the rule of law, and constitutionally limited democratic government, results in societies that maximize societal prosperity and establish conditions that promote human happiness and well-being."[28] It is unlikely that many values-driven entrepreneurs of this era read free-market thinkers, at least with any enthusiasm, and this was typical of Mackey's eclectic outlook. However, his enthusiasm for capitalism was not combined at all with an espousal of Friedman's view that the sole purpose of firms was to maximize shareholder value. In contrast, over the years he developed a philosophy that he called "Conscious Capitalism" that envisaged "businesses galvanized by higher purposes that serve and align the interests of all their major stakeholders; businesses with conscious leaders who exist in service to the company's purpose, the people it touches, and the planet; and businesses with resilient, caring cultures."[29]

Mackey's single store became the basis of Whole Foods Market, which grew rapidly in the once highly fragmented organic food market consisting of mom-and-pop shops selling both organic food and the message of its importance for the world. By 1991 the company operated twelve stores around the United States and had annual sales of over $92 million ($173 million in 2021 dollars). The following year the firm went public, providing the funds to acquire other companies. It grew rapidly after that. Mackey, who is universally described as highly competitive, departed from the practices of early pioneers of the alternative food industry such as Erewhon, which only stocked organic foods and sought to actively promote organic values to its customers. Mackey stocked nonorganic products and celebrated consumerism by emphasizing the shopping experience as much as the food being sold. He did not allow unions but instead developed a culture of empowerment in which teams and stores made key decisions on hiring and product. This culture attracted highly motivated employees, or "team members," as they were described by the company, which helped drive the growth of the firm and of the entire organic food market. By 2000 Whole Foods' sales of $2 billion ($3 billion in 2021 dollars) represented one-third of the total organic food market in the United States.[30]

Over time, a pattern emerged that will be seen in many of the stories told in this chapter. Success and growth took a toll on mission. Erewhon experienced repeated labor issues during the 1970s, and as it grew in size—sales reached over $3 million in 1973 ($17 million in 2021 dollars)—early practices, such as meditation breaks, were phased out. In 1981, Erewhon went bankrupt.[31] Siegel gave motivational speeches to his employees at Celestial Seasonings, but they were paid less than the Boulder average, partly because he was opposed to trade unions. The pursuit of growth took the form that, as one historian notes, "seemed disloyal to the alternative food network." Celestial Seasonings started selling to conventional supermarkets rather than dealing exclusively with health food stores and cooperatives.[32] In 1984, Siegel sold the company to the consumer products giant Kraft for nearly $40 million ($98 million in 2021 dollars). The brand survived and remained organic, but it was stripped of the more mission-driven features that had characterized its early days. Even then, Kraft was so disappointed by the brand that it sold it back to its management in 1988. Siegel came back from retirement as chief executive three years later. He sold the company again in 2000 to Hain Pure Foods, a conventional company engaged in rolling up the still-fragmented natural foods business. Hain Pure was renamed Hain Celestial. Celestial Seasonings remains a premier organic tea brand, producing an estimated 1.6 billion cups of tea a year, but it is now part of the portfolio of a conventional large company with no ambition beyond having a successful and profitable business selling herbal tea.[33] In 2015, Hain Celestial settled for $9.4 million a California class action lawsuit alleging that it was falsely labeling cosmetic products as "organic" in order to mislead consumers.[34]

Despite its success, Whole Foods Market continued on its path of growth. It built bigger stores and made further acquisitions. By 1913, it was the eighth-largest food and drug company in the United States. The focus by now was more on selling organic products rather than ideas about healthy food and a healthy planet, although it did become noted for pioneering programs to support sustainable fisheries, animal welfare, and fair trade; eliminating plastic bags long before towns began to mandate the step; and creating programs to assist its staff in losing weight and quitting smoking.[35] Critics noted the important role of Whole Foods, with its huge demand for organic products, in creating an "organic-industrial complex" of large farms very different from the alternative and radical origins of organic farming.[36] As Whole Foods developed global supply chains—in and of itself a significant contributor to climate change—the pressure to keep costs low often resulted in low wages, and sometimes human rights abuses, for the workers picking fruit and vegetables in developing countries, and even the United States.[37]

In some instances, entrepreneurs developed values-driven businesses based less on their choice of product than on how they ran their businesses. The ice cream company founded by Ben Cohen and Jerry Greenfield in the state of Vermont in 1978 was an iconic example of this. Initially their social responsibility was limited to giving away a free cone of ice cream to anyone who came into their shop once a year, but after turning down an offer to sell the company in 1982, they resolved that their "purpose" was "to see whether a business could survive while being a force for progressive social change."[38]

Cohen and Greenfield proceeded to pursue their vision of making business "a force for progressive social change." In 1985, the Ben & Jerry's Foundation was established with a gift from Cohen and Greenfield and a commitment to give 7.5 percent of the company's annual pretax profits to fund community-oriented projects. The founders made it clear that their vision went beyond philanthropy. They sought to integrate "socially beneficially actions into as many day-to-day activities as possible."[39] They banned the use of recombinant bovine growth hormone in their products and screened the values of their vendors. They sought out minority-owned and female-owned businesses to support. In their 1997 book they described a holistic vision of the place of business in society. "In the world in which we live, the spiritual has been taken out of our day-to-day life," they observed. "So we go to work during the week and focus solely on earning our paychecks and maximizing profit. Then on the weekends we go to church or temple and devote what's left of our energy to the spiritual part of our lives. But the reality is that we will never actualize those spiritual concerns until we integrate them into business."[40] These words would have resonated with George Cadbury and many of the earlier business leaders seen in this book.

In the case of Ben & Jerry's, growth did not dilute mission. Cohen and Greenfield ramped up their commitment to their social mission. In 1988, Ben & Jerry's became the first American company to publish a social assessment. The annual report in that year included a "stakeholders report" that assessed the company's activities with employees, customers, suppliers, investors, and communities, defined as "the entire world." The stakeholder report in the following year was written by employees and audited by William Norris.[41] During the 1990s the company supported campaigns for the protection of children and addressing childhood hunger, and made direct investments in low-income housing. In 1992, Ben & Jerry's was an early signer of a new ten-point code of environmental conduct for businesses. (The origins of the Ceres Principles are discussed in Chapter 10.)

The problem of growth manifested itself in this case in increasing managerial dysfunction, as well as Cohen's erratic performance as chief executive. In 1993 the board decided to hire a professional chief executive, but that required abandoning the long-established corporate practice that no one would get paid more than seven times a new plant worker. Employees were offered stock options to give them a stake in the company's success, but these also began to be used to incentivize potential senior managers to work at the company.[42] After the first professional chief executive failed to work out, in 1997 the board appointed Perry Odak, then working at a gun manufacturer. He focused on cutting costs and preparing the company for sale.[43]

The organic chocolate company Green & Black's, founded in Britain by husband-and wife-team Craig Sams and Josephine Fairley in 1991, is another example of a company that sought to promote deep responsibility with a not particularly healthy product. Fairley was a successful glossy magazine editor in her early twenties when she converted to the cause of organic food. Sams was an expatriate American who had opened a macrobiotic London restaurant called Seed in 1967—which became a beacon for countercultural artists including John Lennon and Yoko Ono. Sams became a serial entrepreneur, founding new organic brands. These included Ceres Grain, Britain's first natural food shop; Ceres Bakery, which sold products made of organic wholegrain flours; Harmony, which sold Britain's first organic brown rice, buckwheat, and three types of miso; and Whole Earth, which made peanut butter.[44]

As we saw in the case of Cadbury, chocolate has potential health benefits but also downsides, as it can promote tooth decay and obesity. The downsides were even greater for the many people employed in exploitative cocoa plantations, whose incomes fluctuated widely with shifting world prices over which they had no control.[45] Fairley and Sams were particularly concerned about the environmental impact of forest clearances and the use of pesticides.[46] The chocolate bar they created aimed "to convey the ecological message about forest clearance, and the problems of pesticide use."[47] However, they wanted the product to sell. Although their chocolate was entirely organic, which at the time was highly unusual, they added raw cane sugar and a high cocoa butter content, which made it less than ideally healthy. This elevation of cane sugar and cocoa butter marked a break from traditional practices one was likely to find at natural foods shops, which the founders addressed by putting a health warning on the wrappers.

The cocoa was at first exclusively sourced from growers in the rainforest highlands of Togo, one of the few groups still growing cocoa organically. After a political crisis made procuring supplies from Togo challenging, Fairley and Sams reached an agreement with a farmers' association in the south of Belize in 1994. This became the basis for the new and successful Maya Gold brand. The cooperative was offered a five-year rolling contract at a fixed price, assistance in gaining organic certification, a cash advance, training, and incentives to encourage biodiversity, such as planting shade trees.[48]

Green & Black's was the first Fairtrade product sold in Britain. The Fairtrade movement started in the Netherlands in 1988 when the Max Havelaar Foundation launched Fairtrade coffee with Mexican coffee beans. The aim was to bypass the commodities markets by guaranteeing minimum prices and a long-term contract and including a premium so that profits could be used in long-term development projects.[49]

As it grew, Green & Black's became, as one later researcher put it, "a case study in compromise." The business did well. With this success, the farming community in Belize received an income boost. Within ten years the number of children receiving secondary education rose from 10 percent to 80 percent. Yet the ratio between purpose and profits appeared to shift over time. In advertising and packaging, the mention of organic and Fairtrade was replaced by an emphasis on the indulgent, sensual pleasures of high-quality chocolate.[50] This contributed to expanding sales and hence, among other things, to income flows to Belize, but it also diminished the ethical education role of the brand.

Values-Driven Businesses in Fashion and Beauty

There were some industries where it was less obvious how any business could drive positive social change—and some where the difficulties made such an outcome improbable. Fashion, for example, lay at the heart of the consumer culture so disliked by hippies and other critics of materialism. Consumers bought clothing for personal adornment or as status symbols, and many of the dyes, bleaches, and chemicals used in the industry had a devastating impact on the environment. Handmade clothes were the preferred option of the hippie movement, preferably made of natural fibers. Creating a values-driven for-profit business in the clothing industry was not so straightforward.

It was probably no coincidence that the entrepreneur who created one of the most ecologically and socially responsible fashion brands came from an industry far removed from fashion. The California firm of Patagonia started in 1973 as an offshoot of the Chouinard Equipment business founded by Yvon Chouinard.[51] Chouinard had developed a strong concern for the sanctity of the natural environment in his rock-climbing business, and his company sold climbing equipment. In 1970 he stopped selling steel pitons, his firm's staple product, as he realized they were scarring mountains as climbers hammered them into the rock face. He replaced them with aluminum chocks, which had the same function but did not damage the rock surface. Chouinard carried his environmental concerns into a new clothing business called Patagonia, which flourished even as Chouinard Equipment encountered legal difficulties and went bankrupt. Patagonia developed an attractive brand in outdoor clothing at a time when relaxing social norms brought sportswear into mainstream use. Sales reached $100 million ($196 million in 2021 dollars) by the end of the 1980s. Chouinard brought to clothing the same concern for the environment that had propelled his rock-climbing business. The company committed to a steady increase in environmental practices, including developing recycled polyester and printing catalogs on recycled paper, as the company matured. Patagonia became one of the first in California to provide on-site childcare, which was followed by the introduction of job sharing and flex time. In 1986, Patagonia began donating 10 percent of its profits to NGOs seeking to save or restore the natural habitat. It gave primarily to smaller ventures rather than what Chouinard derogatively described as "NGOs with big staffs, high overheads, and corporate connections."[52]

In 1991, a near bankruptcy caused by a recession made Chouinard reconsider his whole growth strategy at Patagonia. "I realized we were just growing for the sake of growing," he later commented, "which is bullshit." At the same time the company radicalized its environmental strategies, replacing the 10 percent donation with a self-imposed "earth tax" of 1 percent of sales, which was a much bigger number. The company included in its mission statement "Cause no unnecessary harm." Between 1991 and 1994 Patagonia mapped the environmental impact of its supply chain, focusing on the damage caused by cotton, wool, polyester, and nylon. In 1996, the company switched to making jackets out of recycled polyester and switched entirely to organically grown cotton. This was hugely difficult because at the time only a few family farmers in California and Texas grew organic cotton. The company had to work directly with farmers to increase supplies while seeking changes throughout their supply chain. Spinners, for example, disliked organic cotton because it was full of leaves and stems. They were asked to clean their equipment before and after running the organic cotton. An executive estimated that these sourcing changes tripled the firm's supply cost, and prices were increased as a result. It turned out that consumers were willing to pay the higher prices.[53]

Chouinard became increasingly explicit in his desire to engage in deeply responsible business practice. "The capitalist ideal is you grow a company and focus on making it as profitable as possible," he said in one interview. "Then, when you cash out, you become a philanthropist. We believe a company has a responsibility to do that all along—for the sake of the employees, for the sake of the planet."[54] Patagonia became a rare case of a values-driven business whose values, and their implementation, became stronger as it grew. And despite charging higher prices than competitors, it did grow. Revenues reached $800 million by 2020. Chouinard also continued to experiment. In 2012 he launched Patagonia Provisions, which sold food products using ingredients that claimed to be actively healing the earth by improving the health of the soil, enabling it to store more greenhouse gases. Chouinard hailed such "regenerative agriculture" as far preferable to what he termed Big Organic, "dominated by large companies searching for ways to grow more food and increase profit margins through technology."[55] In 2017, Patagonia joined with a group of farmers and others to form the nonprofit Regenerative Organic Alliance to develop a new certification program. This required farms to be certified as USDA Organic—produced without synthetic pesticides and fertilizers—and be audited for building soil health, sequestering carbon, and ensuring social fairness and animal welfare.[56]

Despite the firm's impressive commitments to ecological and social sustainability, Patagonia's growth might be seen as a paradox in light of Chouinard's skepticism about growth and inherent ecological cost. While some of its customers applauded the brand's environmental credentials, at least as many were just well-heeled admirers of a fashionable brand. For some, Patagonia was part of consumer society, rather than an eco-friendly alternative.[57] Patagonia's overall impact remained small in an industry that, as fast fashion took hold, became progressively more environmentally damaging and wasteful. The amount of textiles, much of it discarded clothing, put in landfills in the United States rose from 1.9 million tons in 1970 to 11.3 million in 2018.[58] If Patagonia did encourage consumerism, a more positive view would be that it offered a role model of what could be achieved in such a wasteful and destructive industry. The timeless aesthetic, functional features, and lasting quality of its clothes also meant that consumers would not need to buy new ones for a long time, while its premium prices discouraged a throwaway mind-set.

Beauty was another industry that appeared to present structural obstacles to advancing a social purpose. In many preindustrial societies, both genders had used perfumes and pomades, but as the industry developed over the course of the nineteenth century, it began to focus more exclusively on women.[59] The industry was a poor fit with ecological concerns, as it essentially prized the unnatural. The whole point was to enhance or alter the natural appearance of women. The industry shared none of the concerns of the organic food movement when it came to the use of chemistry to engineer products. Indeed, because some of the natural products traditionally used as homemade hair dyes and face creams were often harmful to people's hair and skin, the industry focused on using chemicals to make safer products.[60]

There was a particular paradox to the fact that the false promises and exaggerated claims that characterized the beauty industry often originated with the many talented female entrepreneurs who grew successful businesses. This phenomenon was exemplified by Polish-born Helena Rubinstein, one of the most formative figures in the American beauty industry between the 1920s and the 1960s. She fixated on age as a monstrous challenge for a woman. In 1915, she called the "problem" of wrinkles "the most important in the whole field of beauty work" and "the hobgoblin of womanhood."[61] In her marketing, she made women afraid of aging while suggesting that it was their own fault if they did not address the issue, combining guilt and fear. In her book *My Life for Beauty,* published in 1966, a year before her death, she noted that her favorite copy line was "There are no ugly women, only lazy ones."[62] Rubinstein promised scientific solutions to the challenge of aging. Early in her career she came up with the notion of "beauty as science." From the 1920s, she was regularly photographed wearing white coats in laboratories, though she had no formal scientific training. It was simply a good story.[63]

There was more evidence of responsibility beyond the mainstream industry. The global beauty industry developed in a profoundly racist fashion privileging the features of Western people of European ethnicity.[64] In the United States, the mainstream beauty industry made no provision for the distinctive hair textures or skin tones of African Americans because its leaders did not imagine they could be beautiful. This created an opportunity for Black entrepreneurs Annie Turnbo Malone and her former employee Madam C. J. Walker, who built large businesses before 1914 around the treatment of African American hair. Both women became self-made millionaires.[65]

The selling of tonics and instruments to straighten hair was seen by some at the time as deeply irresponsible in that it appeared to be an endeavor to make Black people look more like white people.[66] Booker T. Washington, one of the founders of the National Negro Business League, maintained that success in business would improve the political position of the Black community, a view W. E. B. Du Bois criticized for underestimating the deeply embedded nature of white racism.[67] Leaving that broader argument aside, both Malone and Walker were more values-driven than most of their white counterparts at this time. Malone was particularly concerned with combating scalp disease, which afflicted African American women because of insufficient access to bathrooms and clean water. Both women rejected the idea that social pressures or men should dictate what women did with their hair, face, and bodies. They built their business at a time when lynching was a regular occurrence in the South. In sharp contrast to the brutality of the society in which they operated, they defined a beauty culture for Black people, and thus made Black beauty more visible. Both Malone and Walker also saw the industry as a way for Black women to better themselves financially. In 1918 Malone opened Poro College, the first school dedicated to Black cosmetology, at the heart of Saint Louis's historic Black district of the Ville. The college's "aims and purposes" were "to contribute to the economic betterment of Race Women."[68] The name Poro, which Malone used for her business as a whole, was taken from a secret (and exclusively male) African society "dedicated to disciplining and enhancing the body spiritually and physically."[69]

The creation of jobs and empowerment of women was widely cited over the decades as the social justification for the industry as a whole. But it is hard to find examples beyond Malone and Walker of women who entered the industry with this goal in mind rather than the pursuit of profits. It was a favorite topic for David H. Mc-Connell, the creator of the Avon direct-selling company (known as California Perfume Company before 1939), but he seems to have stumbled onto hiring women as salespeople and discovered both that they were good at selling to other women and that employing independent women working on commission was a low-cost way to expand the business.[70] Some claimed that cosmetics and hair products gave women self-confidence and power. In a booklet entitled *The Secrets of Beauty*, Rubenstein wrote, "If you are pretty, you may twist the world 'round your fingers—but if you are not, you are one of the twisted!"[71] Her contemporary and hated rival Elizabeth Arden agreed. In her book *The Quest of the Beautiful*, published in 1920, Arden wrote, "Beauty is power."[72]

Although the jobs and opportunities were real, the industry's emphasis on youth and narrow conceptions of beauty drained the confidence of most women rather than enhancing it. Its products were marketed through a form of dubious storytelling that often amounted to little more than lies. They sold, in the oft-quoted words of the younger brother of Charles Revson, the founder of the Revlon cosmetics company, "hope."[73] The storytelling was closely guarded. Estée Lauder, the most successful postwar American cosmetics entrepreneur, took steps to ruin the writer Lee Israel upon hearing that she was writing a critical and unauthorized biography. Lauder published her own memoirs to dent the sales, sending Israel into a downward spiral of debt and, eventually, crime.[74]

The beauty industry attracted skepticism from feminists, although not as much as might have been expected given its restrictive notions of beauty and monetization of anxieties. It was not until the second half of the 1960s that it came under critical scrutiny. In 1968, in a demonstration against the Miss America beauty pageant, one hundred feminists filled a trash can with symbols of women's oppression, including *Playboy, Esquire,* dishwashing liquid, hair curlers, mascara, and false eye lashes, and crowned a live sheep America's beauty queen.[75] Yet it was another two decades before Naomi Wolf's *The Beauty Myth: How Images of Beauty Are Used against Women,* published in 1990, launched a full-scale assault on the industry. Wolf argued that as the social power of women had increased, the pressure they felt to adhere to unrealistic physical standards of beauty had grown stronger due to commercial influences on the mass media.[76] Wolf lumped the cosmetics, diet, cosmetic surgery, and pornography industries together, claiming that they were all financed "from the capital made out of unconscious anxieties."[77]

Well before Wolf's best-selling book, a handful of values-driven entrepreneurs had sought to develop a more socially productive industry. An early example was the British fashion designer Mary Quant, who revolutionized young women's fashion during the 1960s with the promotion of the miniskirt as part of her drive to create affordable and accessible fashion. Quant's high hemlines became literal manifestations of women's emerging freedom and a symbol of sexual liberation following the advent of the birth control pill. Miniskirts were quickly adopted by Gloria Steinem and other second-wave feminists.[78] Quant entered the beauty industry in 1966, working with the British company Gala Cosmetics. Instead of packaging her makeup in soft pastels, she used the hard colors of black and silver. Romantic names were replaced by names she considered appropriate for the new liberated woman, such as a cleanser called Come Clean. In 1970, her brand Make-up to Make Love On challenged a convention that women removed their makeup and put on a night skin cream before going to bed.[79]

Within a few years, small natural cosmetics businesses appeared in the United States. A forerunner was Tom's of Maine, launched by Tom and Kate Chappell in Maine in 1970, which started by making phosphate-free laundry detergent. The Chappells disliked the use of toxic chemicals in products and believed that, as Tom Chappell later wrote in *The Soul of a Business,* "environmental protection and profit could be merged." The couple next turned their attention to toothpaste. They wondered, he later wrote, "why all toothpastes were full of complex abrasives, dyes, artificial flavors, preservatives, binders, fluoride and worst of all saccharin, long suspected as a cause of cancer." In 1975 they launched a natural toothpaste, followed by chemical-free deodorant, mouthwash, and shaving cream. The firm emphasized the recycling of packaging and gave 10 percent of its pretax profits to charity. The brand met with success, and after diversifying from health food stores to supermarkets and drugstore chains in 1981, sales increased from $1.5 million to $5 million ($12 million in 2021 dollars) in five years.[80]

Growth again took a toll. By 1986 Tom Chappell felt overwhelmed by "numbers, numbers, numbers." He was in constant conflict with the professional management, who were focused on more growth, and wanted to leave the business. Instead Chappell, a lifelong Episcopalian, went to earn a master's degree in theology at Harvard Divinity School. He was reinvigorated. In 1989, the board agreed to a mission statement and statement of beliefs designed to keep the company tethered to its core values. The statement of beliefs included "We believe that our company can be financially successful while behaving in a socially responsible and environmentally sensitive manner."[81]

In 1978 the hairdresser Horst Rechelbacher, inspired by his encounter with Ayurveda in India, launched the Aveda brand with a clove shampoo initially sold through his chain of hair salons in Minnesota. The brand popularized the concept of aromatherapy, which linked health and well-being with the sense of smell, and more broadly can be seen as the principal creator of the natural cosmetics industry in the United States. More products followed—lip gloss, hair conditioners, mascara, fragrances, herbal teas, coffee beans, nontoxic household cleaners, nutritional supplements—which were always organic and never toxic. Rechelbacher increasingly placed his business in the wider context of sustainability. Aveda became a vocal supporter of ecological and social causes and was the very first company to sign up to the Ceres Principles.[82] "Sustainability is not an eco-Band-Aid for affluent Westerners, nor pie in the sky idealism,"

Rechelbacher observed in *Minding Your Business*, published in 2008. "It is the necessary life-blood of a new era of enlightened capitalism on which our collective future many depend."[83]

While American and European brands dominated the marketplace, the push to environmentally sustainable cosmetics resonated around the world. Natura, one of Latin America's leading examples of a deeply responsible company, was started by Antonio Luiz Seabra as a small cosmetics store in the city of São Paulo, Brazil, in 1969. It evolved into a direct-selling model that competed with Avon, a company with a large market share in Brazil. Seabra was a self-taught philosopher who believed that cosmetics played an important role in the relationships between people, communities, and the natural environment. Over time, Natura forged partnerships with schools and NGOs, and developed expertise in the sustainable use of ingredients from Brazil's teeming and biodiverse natural environment. Natura avoided manipulative advertising, which Seabra denounced as a "cultural crime." In 1992, a decade before Unilever's Dove brand introduced its Real Beauty campaign featuring (photoshopped) senior women, Natura introduced the concept of the "Truly Beautiful Woman," insisting that beauty was not a matter of age but of self-esteem.[84]

The values-driven entrepreneurs who emerged between the late 1960s and the 1980s were mostly on the margins of the business world, but not entirely. Patagonia's sales became substantial, as did those of Natura, which came to employ hundreds of thousands of sales associates. Even small start-ups by entrepreneurs like Elliot Berman, Mo Siegel, Craig Sams, and Mary Quant exercised an outsize influence in the early stages of solar energy and organic food, provided new ways of running businesses in the chocolate industry, and challenged long-established norms in the beauty industry. These entrepreneurs actively wanted to improve the world, whether by bringing electricity to the rural poor in developing countries or taking toxic chemicals out of products people consumed. Yet there were early signs that combining such deep responsibility and profit in this type of firm could be problematic if the businesses were successful.

While Chouinard reset the business model at Patagonia, and Natura progressively increased its commitment to the environment, the indigenous community, and society, in other ventures like Celestial Seasonings and Whole Foods Market, business success was accompanied by a weakening of original values. The tensions between values and growth become starkly apparent in the case of Anita Roddick's The Body Shop.

The Body Shop and Business as a Force for Social Change

The Body Shop, started by Roddick in Britain in 1976, expanded rapidly compared with most of the businesses I have discussed so far. By 1991 it had revenues of £116 million ($360 million in 2021 US dollars) and pretax profits of £20 million ($62 million). Over fifteen years, it had grown from a single store to 586 shops operating worldwide, from Germany and Spain to Australia, Saudi Arabia, Taiwan, and the United States, of which 90 percent were franchised. The Body Shop was awarded industry accolades, such as UK Company of the Year in 1985. Three years later Roddick was given a fancy if archaic title—Order of the British Empire—bestowed by the Queen.[85]

Roddick herself became a poster child for values-driven business. In a magazine interview in 1990, she observed that it was possible to "rewrite the book on business. I think you can trade ethically; be committed to social responsibility, global responsibility; empower your employees without being afraid of them."[86] The company's annual reports were full of bold and visionary statements. The Body Shop, the annual report for 1993 declared, "doesn't believe in profits without principles." Those principles were identified as concern for human and civil rights, care for the environment, and opposition to the exploitation of animals.[87] It was a story that a generation of consumers, influenced by the social movements of the 1960s and 1970s, found attractive.

Born Anita Lucia Perella in the small town of Littlehampton on the south coast of England in 1942, Roddick was the daughter of

Italian Jewish immigrants. People like her were rare in the quiet town that her family called the "home of the newly wed and nearly dead."[88] She grew up helping to run the family business, a café, and went on to have a hectic early adulthood, training as a teacher, working briefly as an educator, getting a scholarship to study in a kibbutz in Israel for three months, and taking a position as a library researcher for the *International Herald Tribune* in Paris. She then spent a year in Geneva in the department of women's rights at the International Labor Organization. Illustrating the new mobility of the era, Roddick used her savings to travel extensively in Southeast Asia and southern Africa. Returning to Britain, she met Gordon Roddick, who also liked to travel. They married in 1970 and she took his name. The birth of two daughters obliged them to settle down, at which point they opened a restaurant and then a hotel in Littlehampton.[89]

Her foray into the beauty industry began in 1976, when her husband announced his intention to ride a horse from Buenos Aires to New York City. They sold the hotel and restaurant, and, after deciding not to accompany him, Roddick resolved to open a shop selling cosmetics. She began The Body Shop—in her own words—as a way to "survive" and care for her young daughters while her husband galloped away on his trip.[90]

Roddick later described in *Body and Soul* (1994), one of several autobiographies, how she encountered a challenge faced by many female entrepreneurs. She recalled visiting her local bank to ask for a small loan to get her business started. She dressed in casual clothes and took one of her babies. She was denied the loan. She returned to the bank dressed in professional attire and wearing makeup, accompanied by her husband. This time she secured a loan to rent a shop in Brighton, a larger city seventeen miles along the coast from Littlehampton.[91]

In *Body and Soul*, Roddick described how she had a vision for the company even before the store opened. She disliked how the conventional beauty industry sold products in large containers, so she wanted to offer multiple size alternatives. She did not like "fancy packaging" in general and wanted to offer a cheaper alternative. She also said she wanted to use natural ingredients, having seen them used effectively by women in developing countries, and she identified ingredients that she had seen most commonly used, such as cocoa butter.[92] Because she had almost no money, everything needed to be done on the cheap. She found a local herbalist who could supply small quantities of the natural ingredients she wanted to use. She located a supply of cheap containers in the form of the plastic bottles used by hospitals to collect urine samples and developed the idea of offering to refill empty containers. She got friends to fill bottles and handwrite all the labels. The whole approach was iconoclastic. She said that the company name, The Body Shop, was inspired by seeing auto repair shops in California while on a trip with her husband.[93]

It was an inspiring story, but like those told by many of her predecessors in the beauty industry, it was not true. In 1994, the journalist Jon Entine offered another version of the origin story in an article for *Business Ethics* entitled "Shattered Image: Is The Body Shop Too Good to Be True?"[94] The article critically examined many aspects of the business and disclosed the likely origins of Roddick's business plan.

Entine agreed that Roddick had been inspired by what she saw in California, but not by its auto repair shops. In 1971, Roddick visited a small but cool hippie shop in Berkeley, California. It was owned by two sisters and called The Berkeley Body Shop, and it had been founded the year before Roddick's visit. The shop was very close to Roddick's ultimate design in multiple respects, including the small bottles that could be refilled and the handwritten labels. The Berkeley Body Shop also made widespread use of the color green. The first catalog for Roddick's The Body Shop repeated the copy of the Berkeley shop almost word for word, including spelling mistakes.[95] In 1987, the Berkeley sisters were offered $3.5 million by The Body Shop to change the name of their shop to Body Time. As part of the arrangement, they agreed not to talk further on the matter.[96] The editor of *Business Ethics*, which was threatened with legal action by The Body Shop, confirmed the "uncanny similarities" between the literatures of the two shops and circulated copies to the entire editorial board to enable them to see with their "own eyes."[97]

This turned out to be typical of Roddick's conduct and motivations. She was in a hurry and believed—like so many of her predecessors in the beauty industry—in the power of storytelling in brand-building. Unfortunately, the stories she told were often true only in her own mind.

Roddick's first store opened in Brighton in March 1976 and did well. Almost immediately, she decided to open a second shop in a neighboring town. After the bank again refused to finance her, she sold half the business to a friend's boyfriend, Ian McGlinn, a used-car salesperson, who offered her £4,000 ($40,000 in 2021 US dollars). "Giving away half the business is considered by many as the biggest mistake I have ever made," she later reflected, but she wanted to grow the business and she needed capital.[98] McGlinn, who became a recluse living a luxurious and dissolute lifestyle around the world, remained a silent partner in the business. He died in 2010 in his apartment in the tax haven of Monaco. Having sold his shares four years earlier, he was one of Britain's richest men at the time of his death.[99]

A desire to grow was the most conspicuous feature of The Body Shop in the following years. When Gordon Roddick returned from South America after his horse died, he joined the business. "We never even gave a thought to slowing down," he later noted. "We wanted to see how far we could push the boundaries of possibility."[100] The layout of the store itself was at the center of the business model. Each store was brightly lit with open spaces and a black-and-white-tiled floor. The shelves had cards offering information about each product, and a large Product Information Manual, which gave detailed descriptions of the ingredients, was available in the corner. There were also informational packets on the counter about matters such as animal testing. Staff were knowledgeable but never overbearing.[101]

In 1978 The Body Shop began a franchise system in order to accelerate growth, and the first international store was opened, in

Brussels. By 1984 one-fifth of sales were outside Britain, and the company had eighty-three international stores and forty-five in Britain. Roddick sought to keep control of her vision for the company through the franchise system. "We didn't want businesspeople," she later recalled. "We wanted teachers. We wanted activists. We wanted partners, because that's what we cared about."[102] She later described how she imagined creating a "moral network of thousands and thousands, hundreds of shops all around the world all fighting for human rights bringing issues into the shops not just selling The Body Shop shampoos and lotions like everybody else can do." She was particularly interested in the potential of giving the young people who worked in her stores a "safe place to practice activism."[103]

The desire to grow drove a decision to list the company in 1984 on the Unlisted Securities Market, which had been established by the London Stock Exchange for companies regarded as too small to qualify for a full listing. The initial public offering (IPO) made the company worth £8 million ($36 million in 2021 US dollars). The stock doubled in value after one day of trading. This made the Roddicks and McGlinn rich and gave the firm ample funds to expand. By 1991, the company's market value was £350 million ($1 billion).

In retrospect, Roddick regretted the decision to go public. It meant, she later commented, that control was given to "financial intermediaries who were contemptuous of what we were trying to do."[104] In a subsequent interview she described the City of London— shorthand for the financial sector—as "financial fascists who could only see the bottom line."[105] But there was little actual loss of control after the IPO, as the Roddicks retained 30 percent of the equity and McGlinn held another 30 percent.[106]

In *Body and Soul*, Roddick recalled a conversation with her husband on the night of the flotation. "Should not a business that relied on the community for its success," she remembered saying, "be prepared to give something back to the community?" The couple realized "that The Body Shop had both the potential and the means at its disposal to do good."[107] In contrast, she was largely dismissive of the investors in her company. "Most are only interested in the short-term and quick profit," she told a Harvard Business School case writer in 1991. "They don't come to our annual meetings and they don't respond to our communications. As far as I am concerned, I have no responsibility to these people at all."[108]

Roddick's determination to "do good" was multidimensional. Like Mary Quant, she took aim at many of the long-established fundamentals of the beauty industry. This represented some of Roddick's most socially positive innovations. "I hate the beauty business," she wrote in *Body and Soul.* "It is a monster industry selling unattainable dreams. It lies. It cheats. It exploits women."[109] At issue was marketing that played on women's fear of aging, fear of not being beautiful, fear of the types of things both Arden and Rubinstein promoted with their "beauty is power" ethos. "It is immoral to trade on fear," Roddick observed. "It is immoral constantly to make women feel dissatisfied with their bodies. It is immoral to deceive a customer by making miracle claims for a product."[110] In contrast, Roddick largely avoided advertising, never used conventionally attractive young models in posters in shops, embraced wrinkles and gray hairs, and offered products to "protect skin," not to alter it.[111]

In 1997, The Body Shop launched the most celebrated of its marketing campaigns using a plump doll with a Barbie-like face called Ruby.[112] Roddick noted in the company's annual report that Ruby looked "like a girl who enjoys life to the fullest—and that's what self-esteem is all about. Fret about who you could be and you're merely wasting who you are."[113] It was a startling image for the beauty industry, although it was aligned with growing campaigns against the objectification of women in the media.[114] Mattel, the maker of the Barbie doll, took issue with Ruby and how much her facial features resembled those of the impossibly slim Barbie. The company secured a cease-and-desist order in 1998 and forced The Body Shop to remove images of Ruby from the shop windows of American stores. According to Roddick, "Ruby was making Barbie look bad, presumably by mocking the plastic twig-like bestseller."[115]

Roddick disagreed with feminists who rejected all forms of adornment, saying that the real problem was not the beauty industry per se, but the fact that men ran it.[116] She sought to celebrate sexiness and to stop shaming women who were concerned with how they looked. "If you are a woman you've gotta talk womanly things. . . . So bring back sexiness in the office I would say. Bring back flirting."[117]

Like many other values-driven entrepreneurs, Roddick paid attention to employee welfare. Inspiring her young employees—in the 1980s three-quarters of the employees were women—was key to the business, as they were the face of the brand in each shop. Roddick visited stores regularly and encouraged upward communication through a suggestion scheme. A large daycare facility was opened at the Littlehampton head office, with the cost linked to salary level. The company established its own training center in London, which was open to franchisees as well as employees, and which focused on the products rather than selling them. It also addressed wider social issues, including care of the elderly and AIDS.[118] Roddick expected her employees not just to be inspired but to put that inspiration to work. In aid of this mandate, she paid every The Body Shop employee a half day to do community service once a week.[119]

This system became strained as The Body Shop scaled, especially after it built a large business in the United States where, by the early 1990s, it faced growing competition from companies that emulated parts of its business model. Bath and Body Works, created by the fashion retailer Limited Brands, was especially successful in this regard.[120] It was complaints from employees and franchisees in the United States that triggered the journalist Jon Entine to investigate the firm. While working for ABC News in 1993, Entine was approached by two Chicago franchisees in the same week who wanted him to do a report on the "mean-spirited" company. He was next contacted by a graphic designer in New Jersey who claimed to have "been forced to print things that weren't true."[121] Entine's article and subsequent investigations revealed disturbing patterns that went beyond lying about the origins of The Body Shop idea. He established, for example, that the often-idealistic young staff in the American stores received low wages and fewer benefits than the norm. There were other problems. In 1993, a manager in the American business complained of widespread sexual harassment of female employees. After being dismissed, she sued The Body Shop in federal court. The Body Shop paid a large settlement in return for a gag order.[122]

Entine was skeptical, too, about The Body Shop's Trade Not Aid strategy, which Roddick launched in 1987. The idea, like the Fairtrade movement, was that it was better to help people in developing countries by buying their products at enhanced prices than to donate to charities. People needed jobs and livelihoods, the logic went, not handouts. The first experiment was conducted with a group of farm communities established by a British expatriate to train homeless boys in Tirumangalam, in the southern Indian state of Tamil Nadu. Roddick made Boys Town the primary supplier of Footsie Rollers, pieces of acacia wood sold as foot massagers. Wages were four times the local norm. Further contracts followed, in new locations. Beeswax was sourced from traditional beekeepers in Zambia, babassu oil from a cooperative in the Brazilian rainforest, and cocoa butter from community groups in Ghana.[123]

Roddick made much of this program, but Entine estimated that in 1993, The Body Shop was sourcing no more than 0.165 percent of its purchases from fair trade in developing countries.[124] The Brazilian babassu oil turned out to be made from refined oil. The Boys Town orphanage turned out to be run by a pedophile. Roddick later wrote of the "cruel deception" she had experienced.[125] Entine also took aim at The Body Shop's claim that it made "extraordinary" donations to charity, using the company's own annual reports to show that the firm contributed between 0.36 percent and 1.24 percent of pretax profits annually between 1986 and 1993.[126] Entine's initial publisher, *Vanity Fair*, which had a British edition, received threatening letters from two law firms alleging libel. The magazine paid him in full but did not publish his article. The Body Shop applied similar pressures against *Business Ethics*, though the magazine chose to go ahead with publication.[127]

Entine's revelations caused a clash between Roddick and Joan Bavaria, the Boston-based pioneer of socially responsible investment, whom we will meet properly in Chapter 10. Bavaria's firm, Franklin

Research and Development Corporation, had awarded The Body Shop its highest social rating in 1991. Three years later, Entine's report caused consternation.[128] Franklin Research conducted its own investigation, which concluded that "certain recent criticism of The Body Shop is justified." The report accused The Body Shop of cultivating an image inconsistent with "the company's sometimes less than impressive performance," and of defensiveness when criticized. Franklin Research sold its fifty thousand shares in The Body Shop and recommended to clients that they do the same. As The Body Shop's share price fell by 20 percent over the summer of 1994, there was an unpleasant public argument between two of the most prominent advocates of socially responsible business. Roddick was quoted in the *New York Times* as saying that "Franklin has a vested interest in taking a shot at us."[129]

There was in fact a more concrete, if modest, achievement, closer to Roddick's home. In 1988, the company opened a soap factory in a run-down suburb of Glasgow called Easterhouse, where the unemployment rate was 37 percent. A young man from Easterhouse heard Roddick speaking in London and asked if there was anything she could do to help his community.[130] "It's not economic in terms of transport," Roddick observed, "but it's easier to inculcate our ideas here."[131] Roddick paid her Glasgow employees the same wages as she paid those in Littlehampton—a third higher than local rates—and put 25 percent of post-tax profits from products made there back into the community.[132] Soapworks employed more than 120 people in 1994.[133] As usual, Roddick hyped up the impact of a relatively small investment. However, it remained a feature of the area and became Britain's largest soap factory.[134] In addition to the Glasgow factory, Gordon Roddick founded a weekly newspaper to be sold by the homeless and unemployed in London. Launched in 1991, the *Big Issue* eventually became a self-financing current affairs magazine providing income for street vendors.[135]

The biggest test of The Body Shop's authenticity as a values-driven company lay in its environmental achievements. Roddick was in her twenties when the second wave of environmentalism accelerated during the 1960s. For her—as for many of her generation—the environment mattered in ways it had not for most business leaders previously. "Not a single decision is ever taken in The Body Shop," she wrote in 1991, "without first considering environmental and social issues."[136] This commitment was not just talk. The avoidance of waste and recycling were front and center from the beginning, and other measures were adopted over time. In 1993, for example, only two years after the first wind farm had started in Britain, the company took a 15 percent stake in a wind farm near Rhayader in Mid Wales to support the development of renewable energy and offset carbon dioxide emissions from the company's operations. Roddick opened the facility in person.[137] The Body Shop's involvement, however, ended after a few years. It basked in the publicity and moved on.

The Body Shop was also an early mover in environmental reporting. During the 1980s Joan Bavaria and others in the socially responsible investment community had started to explore ways for companies to report their social and environmental performance alongside their financial performance. In 1992, The Body Shop developed its first Eco-management and Audit Scheme environmental statement. Bavaria knew the British management consultant John Elkington, who proposed that environmental and social reports be integrated with financial ones. In 1997 he published *Cannibals with Forks,* which introduced the concept of a "triple bottom line" involving profitability, environmental quality, and social justice.[138] The Body Shop launched its first attempt at producing such an integrated report in 1995. Two years later, the effort yielded *The Values Report,* a pioneering effort that was more than two hundred pages long.[139] It was awarded the highest ranking by the United Nations Environment Program and by Elkington's consultancy SustainAbility in international benchmarking surveys of corporate sustainability reports.[140] As with similar endeavors over the following years, gaps in data, fuzzy metrics, and a lack of comparative information from other companies made *The Values Report* more of a statement of principles than a precise audit. Two decades later academics were still trying to make the case that integrated reporting provides the key to "re-imagining capitalism" in a more sustainable fashion.[141]

As usual, real achievements were balanced by hyperbole. In 1989, the German government successfully sued The Body Shop for using the phrase "Not tested on animals" on its labels. As a result, the company adopted a new phrase, "Against animal testing." In practice, the firm used many of the same ingredients that had been tested on animals as the rest of the industry. In 1992, an estimated 46.5 percent of the firm's ingredients had been tested on animals.[142]

Meanwhile, Entine argued in "The Shattered Image" that The Body Shop's "most basic myth is that it sells 'natural' products." He noted that many of the lotions and makeup used petrochemical ingredients, synthetic dyes, and artificial colors.[143] The criticism was widely shared by people who studied the ingredients of cosmetics. Mark Constantine, an herbalist who worked for Roddick in the 1980s before founding the natural cosmetics company Lush, noted, "Roddick never could care less about ingredients."[144] Rodolphe Balz, a pioneer of biodynamic farming in France who founded the organic cosmetics company Sanoflore in 1986, later remembered meeting Roddick. She "had great ideas, and a lot of ethics," he recalled, "but her ethics were focused more on people than the composition of her products." In fact, the ingredients of her products, he added, "were absolutely disgusting."[145]

Roddick's record as a values-driven entrepreneur was distinctly mixed. She and her husband built a successful international brand that rejected the restrictive norms of the beauty industry. The avoidance of wasteful packaging and the rejection of gender stereotypes were concrete examples of values-driven decisions in an industry that exemplified wasteful consumption and manipulative advertising. Roddick raised the profile of natural cosmetics and promoted the idea of sourcing from poor communities in the developing world. She found innovative ways to support working women by providing daycare facilities for employees, and she pioneered the concept of benchmarked environmental reporting. It was a story many found inspiring, attuned as it was to the progressive social voices and values of the era. Yet it was also a story full of hyperbole, overclaiming, and outright lies designed to create a halo effect. Large profits were generated and far less was offered in return than was suggested by the company's slick self-presentation. It would be possible to conclude from the empirical evidence that the Roddicks were more charlatans than deeply responsible. Or, more charitably, that Anita Roddick started telling stories about her own firm because she needed a good story in order to have a voice in the social and environmental matters that really concerned her.

Business as Advocacy

Roddick stands apart from many of the previous business leaders in this book in her vision of business as a form of advocacy. From the start, she insisted that the primary responsibility of a business was to have a positive impact outside its own narrow boundaries. "You're never ever remembered for what you do in business," she once observed. "What you do in civil society is what you are remembered for."[146] This view rested on her belief that business shaped the world, and that it had not done a great job. "Today's corporations have global responsibilities," she wrote in 1991, "because their decisions affect world problems concerning economics, poverty, security, and fear."[147] She was dismissive toward the organizations that represented big business—commenting in one interview that the International Chamber of Commerce was "in bed with the devil"—and insisting that campaigning had to be done not at a high level but rather as a grassroots movement, "which was lively and sexy." Roddick's belief that the world was suffering from a form of "spiritual poverty"— an inability to care about injustice—drove her to make a positive difference, by using her storefronts to proselytize caring.[148]

Roddick's relentless campaigning was integral to building the Body Shop brand. The reciprocal relationship between the brand and the campaigns was evident from her first campaign, launched shortly after the IPO, to "save the whales." Roddick allied with the NGO Greenpeace, an unusual move at the time, and filled her shops with posters about the issue. Talking up the whales when more and more companies sold brands claiming to be natural was also a useful piece of marketing—The Body Shop's jojoba oil products were promoted as an alternative to cosmetics products made from sperm whale oil. The promotion worked well, but after two years disagreements with Greenpeace led Roddick to switch allegiance to Friends of the Earth. The following years saw campaigns on recycling, acid rain, and the depletion of the ozone layer.[149] These campaigns may have absolved consumers' guilt at consuming, but they were still buying—in Balz's words—products with "disgusting" ingredients, and few whales were saved as a result.

In 1987, Roddick decided that The Body Shop should define and execute its own campaigns, and over the following decade there were many of them. In 1989, a Stop the Burning campaign collected almost one million signatures in a petition asking the Brazilian government to stop burning its tropical rainforests. In 1994, The Body Shop collected three million signatures to help protect endangered species from illegal trade.[150] In 1995, The Body Shop started a Make Your Mark human rights campaign—opened by the Dalai Lama— asking customers to leave a thumbprint as a signature to testify to their support of human rights globally. Roddick wrote, "A campaign like this is part of the DNA of our business. Not only does it fire up our day-to-day lives, but it embodies our conviction that business should be about social responsibility as well as profit."[151]

It is hard to judge whether all these signatures really changed anything, but in one instance at least, advocacy does seem to have changed behavior on the ground. Between 1993 and 1998, The Body Shop supported the Ogoni people of Nigeria, whose natural environment was devastated by oil exploration by Shell and who were subject to human rights abuses by their own government. The Body Shop launched a very active campaign, paying for Ogoni representatives to fly to Geneva to address the UN Sub-Commission on Human Rights, lobbying Shell, and protesting outside Shell offices and the World Petroleum Congress. None of this stopped the Nigerian military government from executing Ken Saro-Wiwa, the leader of Ogoni protesters, in November 1995. The previous June, while imprisoned, he had dedicated a poem to Roddick:

Had I a voice
I would sing your song
Had I a tongue
I would speak your praise
Had I the time
I would live for you[152]

Roddick claimed a "partial success" when, three years later, Shell responded to the subsequent global outcry with a new Profits and Principles advertising campaign.[153]

In 1990, The Body Shop Foundation was established and funded by an annual donation of profits from the company. Between 1990 and 1996, the foundation (according to Roddick) donated £3.5 million ($8 million in 2021 US dollars) to more than 180 charities. Annual corporate donations were modest.[154] In 1998, The Body Shop made an operating profit of £38 million ($100 million) and donated £800,000 ($2.5 million), or just over 2 percent of its profits, to the foundation. Still, small sums could have large consequences. Soon after the foundation was established, Roddick visited Romania and came across a number of abandoned orphanages. She organized a small group of volunteers to refurbish three orphanages, and this project grew over time, spreading to neighboring countries with similar challenges, including Bosnia and Albania. Children on the Edge was set up in 1994 as part of the foundation before becoming an independent charity in 2004.[155]

In November 1999, Roddick joined the mass protests that took place in Seattle in an effort to disrupt a meeting of the World Trade Organization (WTO) to negotiate a new range of world trade agreements. Two years later, in an edited volume Roddick observed that she was "probably one of the few international retailers to be baton-charged and tear-gassed by American policemen" during the event.[156] The book had chapters by prominent critics of globalization such as Naomi Klein and Ralph Nader, and it represented a shift in her thought. Although she argued that alliances between companies and NGOs had brought positive dividends, her new focus was the "democratic deficit" represented by institutions such as the WTO, the World Bank, and the International Monetary Fund.[157]

Roddick's campaigning was an important part of her brand's image as an iconoclastic force for good in the world. The social movements of the 1960s and 1970s had created a new customer segment of people with disposable incomes who cared about the plight of the Ogoni people and Romanian orphans. They were more likely to buy a brand that they perceived to be helping to make the world a better place than one that just made its owners richer. Despite her shortcomings, the fact remains that Roddick was able to raise the profile of multiple causes by lending her name and The Body Shop brand in support. Over the following decades, other companies would follow this path in recognition of the reputational advantages. It was not long until this spilled over to multinational companies, generally with little real commitment to environmental sustainability or human rights. Ethical consumerism soon became just another form of consumerism. We would see tobacco companies become active campaigners against child labor, domestic violence, and much else. Roddick offers a more genuine example.

From Values-Driven to Traitor Brands

The Body Shop's last decade as an independent company proved to be an anticlimax. It continued to grow, but the glory days were over. Between 1992 and 2002, revenues rose from £147 million ($440 million in 2021 US dollars) to $380 million ($910 million), but pretax profits halved over that period, and retained profits fell from £13.4 million ($40 million) to—£1.4 million (–$3.4 million). A collapse in market capitalization reduced Roddick's personal share in the company from £90 million ($270 million) to £20 million ($48 million) over the course of the 1990s.[158]

There was no single cause. Negative press took a toll on The Body Shop's public image and its bottom line. The business in the United

States—larger than Britain's in terms of share of total revenues in 1996—experienced growing competitive pressure from new companies in the "natural" category. No longer eager to be involved in the day-to-day management of the business, Anita and Gordon Roddick brought in professional managers. In an interview given before her sudden death in 2007, Anita claimed that she and Gordon were "bored shitless" with the "details of the business."[159] In 1998 a new CEO, Patrick Gournay, a former executive of France's Danone dairy group, was appointed. His assessment—as recorded by Roddick— was that "the company was too cumbersome and heavy."[160] Under Gournay, the company sold its manufacturing plant at Littlehampton. There was also a severe deterioration in relations with franchisees as the brand faced increased competition, and the company started buying back underperforming franchises. Lawsuits in the United States subsequently alleged that company-owned stores were given preference in supplies.[161] Roddick later said that under Gournay the company lost "its soul."[162]

In 2002, after multiple failed attempts to sell the company, including to the Mexican nutritional products company Grupo Omnilife, the Roddicks stepped down as cochairs but remained nonexecutive directors. Gournay also left. The Body Shop came under the leadership of two men, Adrian Bellamy, a director who had overseen the North American business, and Peter Saunders, the former chief executive of that business. Both men came from conventional retailing backgrounds. Bellamy was already the chairperson of Gucci, and the following year he became chairman of the consumer products company Reckitt Benckiser. A company that had highlighted its support for women's issues in previous annual reports was left with only two women on its board of directors, one of whom was Roddick herself. Still, over the following four years, the new team raised The Body Shop's share price by 300 percent from its low in 2002.[163]

In 2006 the Roddicks and McGlinn were able to sell The Body Shop to L'Oréal, one of the largest beauty companies in the world, for £652 million ($1.4 billion in 2021 US dollars). The Roddicks made £130 million ($277 million) from the sale and McGlinn £150 million

($320 million). L'Oréal, which had invented the first safe chemical hair dye before World War I, owned many luxury and mass French and American brands, including Lancôme, Maybelline, and Kiehl's, none of which claimed to be green. Roddick claimed that L'Oréal's ownership would not change The Body Shop's ethical values. "It's not deemed in nature that because they're big and huge that they're going to diminish our DNA. It can't be done," she said, calling the deal "the best safe place" for the business.[164] She also claimed that she hoped the sale would act as a sort of "Trojan Horse" move allowing an ethical company to slip in among the ranks of the very companies she hoped to change.[165]

Roddick received a huge amount of criticism for the sale, not least because L'Oréal engaged in widespread animal testing. It was also partly owned by the Swiss consumer goods company Nestlé, which had long been criticized for promoting infant formula in the developing world.[166] The sale formed part of the accelerating trend for values-driven, eco-friendly companies being acquired by large corporations, which began to see a profitable market niche in owning such brands. Aveda was acquired by Estée Lauder in 1997 for $300 million ($484 million in 2021 dollars). Unilever acquired Ben & Jerry's in 2000 for $326 million ($490 million). Cadbury acquired Green & Black's in 2005 for $36 million ($48 million) and was itself acquired in a hostile takeover by Kraft in 2009. The toothpaste company Colgate-Palmolive acquired the majority of Tom's of Maine in 2006 for $100 million ($128 million), with the Chappells initially keeping 16 percent of the stock along with securing a promise not to change the culture. There were many other such cases, culminating in Amazon's purchase of Whole Foods Market in 2017 for $13.9 billion. In 2013, the Organic Consumer Association in the United States began compiling lists of "traitor brands"—values-driven brands that fell under the ownership of parent companies that, for example, campaigned against mandatory labeling of foods containing genetically modified organisms (GMOs).[167]

In most cases, the Trojan Horse theory proved false. The values-driven brands became one component of a large conventional firm's portfolio and often lost their social activism as a result. The impact of Amazon on Whole Foods Market became a subject of regular commentary. Most observers agreed that the focus on employee agency and social mission gave way to greater centralization of decision-making, an adoption of Amazon tactics of promotions and discounts, and experimentation with more automated retailing formats.[168]

Occasionally, there were other outcomes. The Ben & Jerry's sale agreement had, unusually, left the wholly owned affiliate with an independent board with legal authority to protect the social mission. In a remarkable episode, this board was able to push back against Unilever's attempt to corporatize the firm. In 2008, the board prepared a lawsuit against Unilever for breaching the sale agreement, and two years later the parties reached an agreement to affirm the affiliate's continued autonomy.[169] In 2012, Ben & Jerry's became the first wholly owned subsidiary to become a certified B Corp, a movement I will examine in Chapter 10. In 2021, the company's decision to end the sale of ice cream to Palestinian territories occupied by Israel resulted in a huge furor for Unilever as Jewish lobby organizations protested the decision, and multiple US state pension funds, including New Jersey and New York, sold positions in Unilever under laws combating attempts to encourage boycotting or divesting from Israel.[170]

The Body Shop languished under L'Oréal's ownership, as the values of the two organizations were so different. "When L'Oréal took over," the chief executive of The Body Shop Foundation noted, "the pendulum swung massively towards a drive for commercial benefit, which meant that a lot of the organizations we'd worked with in our 27-year history wouldn't get a look-in in future." In 2013, The Body Shop stopped funding the foundation entirely.[171] Four years later L'Oréal sold The Body Shop to Natura for $1.1 billion. Natura had publicly listed 20 percent of its capital in 2004, but the founders had retained control over the business. The Body Shop brand's new owners promised to revive the spirit of Anita Roddick.[172] In 2019, The Body Shop followed Natura's path and became a licensed B Corp.

The story of The Body Shop followed a general pattern for the values-driven firms of this era. They made powerful statements, but they remained minnows in a big ocean. In 1987, a nonprofit organization called the Social Venture Network was formed in San Francisco to provide a place for values-driven firms to meet and share ideas. Early members included Ben Cohen and Anita Roddick. But such associations could not address some basic challenges. Values-driven ventures experienced organizational issues as they grew, as tight managerial controls and hierarchies were generally antithetical to their corporate cultures. They needed capital to grow, but once ownership was shared with people who were primarily driven by commercial considerations, the temptation to sell to a large public company was great. By the 1990s there were many willing corporate buyers of green, ethical, and responsible brands. Yvon Chouinard stood out for his realization that growth could be more of a problem than an opportunity, and his determination to keep the ownership of Patagonia in the hands of himself and those of his wife. "I used to think that if we could show that being a responsible business is good business then others would follow," he noted in 2019. "And some do, but they're tiny little companies. But the public companies, they're all green-washing."[173]

The assault on conventional social and cultural norms that began during the 1960s helped spawn a new cohort of businesses that pursued deep responsibility. The founders of these firms believed that a for-profit business could be a vehicle for achieving a more just and sustainable world. They were no fans of capitalism as such, but they perceived that through purchasing decisions, marketing messages, and the actions of employees, business could be a vehicle for positive social impact. They also believed that the resources they generated could be deployed to support the work of NGOs and other actors supporting civil society. The protection and healing of the natural environment was now a far greater concern. Horizons were no longer bounded by geography. People and ideas were traveling globally, and what happened in the rainforest no longer stayed in the rainforest.

The companies created by these entrepreneurs spoke to a new generation of younger consumers far more concerned about the environment and societal inequities. The values-driven entrepreneurs were a product of this climate, and they found markets because of it. Over time, weaknesses in their model inevitably emerged. It was not easy to retain a values-based culture as a company grew in size. Challenging existing social and cultural norms was not really compatible with making profits. In many cases, growing the business seemed to become more important than growing the social impact. Large conventional companies were willing buyers of successful values-driven brands as they sought to reach the new demographic of socially conscious consumers. Those that retained and even strengthened their mission, like Natura and Patagonia, were the ones where the founders retained control.

Roddick pursued bold ideas about corporate responsibility, rejecting harmful gender stereotypes, excessive packaging, and reliance on chemical ingredients that characterized most of her industry. Both her business and the causes she embraced were truly global. Above all, she demonstrated that the voice of a charismatic business leader and a popular brand could be used to advance just social causes, especially if thousands of employees could be motivated to engage also. She demonstrated how a business enterprise could become a force for positive social change in a way that was democratic and spiritually fulfilling.

Yet Roddick's story was also a striking example of the tendency of some of the values-driven entrepreneurs to fall in love with their own narratives while behaving a great deal more like a conventional business than their rhetoric implied. The Roddicks were people in a hurry, and their urgency was to grow the business. From the start, the rush to grow pushed them to make questionable decisions with long-term consequences, such as the sale of half the company to pay for a second shop. This meant that a significant amount of the wealth generated by The Body Shop ended up with their tax-avoiding, silent partner. Realizing the power of a good story to build a brand and promote a cause, Roddick repeatedly exaggerated her achievements.

The company that promoted itself as natural did not invest in costly organic ingredients, but instead sold conventional products with a few herbs and exotic oils thrown in. In the long run, this lack of authenticity drained the life from the company, which under the influence of professional managers became a conventional business even before the Roddicks sold it to L'Oréal. Anita Roddick emerges as a poster child of the values-driven businesses of this era, but also a prime example of the temptation to let hype to triumph over execution.

CHAPTER 9

SOCIAL THREE-FOLDING

BIODYNAMIC FARMING AND
HOW TO BUILD A FLOURISHING COMMUNITY

Parallel to the growth of values-driven businesses, another set of businesses grew with a commitment to pursuing deep responsibility. Our focus in this chapter is the Sekem organic farming business created by Ibrahim Abouleish in Egypt and the Ambootia organic tea business developed by Sanjay Bansal in Darjeeling, India. What these firms had in common, and what makes them distinct from others seen previously, was their adherence to a set of beliefs about the importance of fully integrating business into a flourishing and balanced community, and their adherence to a global certification system introduced by the followers of the eccentric Austrian philosopher and institution builder Rudolf Steiner.

Steiner formulated his philosophy in the early twentieth century, but his ideas gained a new relevance as accelerating environmental degradation and rising wealth inequality beginning in the 1970s were accompanied by the hollowing out of communities. As barriers to trade and capital movements fell with deregulation, corporations moved resources across borders in pursuit of profitable opportunities. Although new technologies enabled the dispersal of economic activities, global firms tended to cluster higher-value-added activities—and the jobs that accompanied them—in a few locations. These "global cities" included Silicon Valley, New York, London, Singapore, and Mumbai.[1]

In contrast, cities and regions that relied on lower-skill manufacturing jobs saw those jobs outsourced to places with even lower labor costs, leaving behind former industrial communities, like the Midwest of the United States and the north of England, with few jobs, less hope, and a proclivity for supporting populist politicians who promised salvation.[2] Meanwhile, vast swaths of Africa, Latin America, and rural India almost completely missed the wealth creation of the new globalization wave. Many of the young and unemployed came to feel that their only hope was to leave their communities and migrate to urban metropolises such as Lima, Lagos, or Mumbai, where a life of poverty and degradation usually awaited them. The decimation of communities, the "third pillar" of society (alongside nation-states and markets) in the analysis by Chicago economist and former governor of the Reserve Bank of India Raghuram Rajan, was all too evident across much of the world.[3]

Against this reality of disintegration and injustice, followers of Steiner saw in his ideas an alternative, holistic vision of the future, which started with renewing individual lives, and then local communities, and up through ever-larger communities until one reaches the planet. Because his ideas have been so influential in the creation and dissemination of the sustainability movement, this chapter begins with Steiner, his philosophy, and how he came to see the creation of a new business system based on what he called "social three-folding" as a means of creating harmony within communities, between humans and nature, and between the material and the spiritual worlds. Next we will consider his impact more specifically on organic farming practices before turning to consider the growth of businesses influenced by Steiner's ideas and the surprising resurgence of his ideas half a century after his death.

Steiner's Philosophy and Social Three-Folding

Steiner had what most people would consider to be some crazy ideas, and some repugnant ones, but his concern for communities and disdain for materialism spoke to people hungry for a more fulfilling sense of integration in a world of galloping materialism and de-humanizing conditions. Perhaps more importantly than the man himself, his followers converted some of his ideas into actual insti-tutions—schools, medical communities, and for-profit businesses—that pioneered organic farming and integrated communities sustained by a new type of financial institution. Steiner became an unlikely inspiration for a new cohort of entrepreneurs who believed that ethical business practices could be the key to sustaining a more har-monious world.

Born in 1861 in present-day Croatia, then part of the Austro-Hungarian Empire, Steiner was formally educated in math and physics in Vienna and obtained a doctorate in philosophy from Rostock University in Germany. As a man of his time, he was heavily influ-enced by German idealism, especially the work of Johann Wolfgang von Goethe. His life took a less orthodox turn when he moved to Berlin in 1897 and became involved with a new religious movement called Theosophy, founded by the eccentric Helena Petrovna Bla-vatsky, a Russian immigrant to the United States who revived the old notion that Plato knew of a "wisdom religion" that offered the secrets of knowledge and enlightenment.[4] Blavatsky was heavily in-fluenced by South Asian religions, especially Buddhism, and diffused concepts such as karma and reincarnation to the West.[5]

Steiner led the German section of the Theosophical Society be-tween 1902 and 1912, but he diverged from the movement's leaders in his insistence on the importance of scientific investigation. Although the Theosophists were highly influenced by Eastern religions, Steiner insisted on the unique importance of the incarnation and crucifixion of Jesus Christ. In 1913 he founded his own school of thought, in which he called Anthroposophy a "science of the spirit" that sought to occupy a middle ground between science and religion.

In highly simplified terms (and Steiner was anything but simple), he believed that humans had lost awareness of their ancient under-standing that they had bodies, souls, and spirits. Like Blavatsky, Steiner believed that humanity was engaged in an epic struggle against materialism, which had caused this loss of awareness, and that a demon called Ahriman, an evil spirit in Zoroastrianism, had diverted humanity from its true path by preaching the virtues of the material and technological world.[6] Steiner believed that human beings lived both on earth and in the spiritual world and he was convinced that they needed to operate competently in both realms. There was an optimism in his work arising from his belief that there was a spiritual dimension to human beings that could be a source of hope for future possibilities and new beginnings.[7] Steiner believed that humans were continuously reincarnated, changing genders and cultures as they evolved over time. Capacities acquired in one incarnation became new talents in the next, while misdeeds also came back. Reincarnation and karma meant, in Steiner's view, that everything in life had a meaning.

Steiner's philosophy was regarded at the time by almost anyone who encountered it as outlandish. It was not, however, wholly exceptional. At some level it fit into a long tradition of Western esotericism that shared a belief that some form of ancient wisdom and knowledge that had been largely lost had been kept alive by small groups of initiates who sought to save humanity. This intellectual heritage did not make Steiner's views any less weird or problematic. While accounts of encounters with celestial beings and goblins appear harmless, there was a much darker side also. Steiner believed that over the course of repeated reincarnations, souls passed through successively "higher" racial stages until race as such ceased to exist. He explained to an audience in Oslo in 1910, that the "black race" was shaped by forces associated with childhood, the "yellow and brownish races" of Asia by the characteristics of youth, and Europeans by the "ripest characteristics" of adulthood. The belief in racial hierarchies, though held in various forms by some of his contemporaries, can only be considered malign.[8] In other writings he was explicit that the list of negative qualities a student of his spiritual science needed to guard against included "the tendency to discriminate on the basis of such outer characteristics as social status, gender, race, and so on."[9]

Steiner was a passionate supporter of Germany's cause during World War I, and after the country's defeat he used occult language to explain that the war had been a battle between "Germandom" and Slavic and Romanic "spiritual elements." The German "spirit" was seen as key to humanity's future. His views formed part of a wider cultural reaction to the country's defeat, which emphasized the unique importance of the German people, a view that would end badly with the advent of the Nazi regime.[10]

Steiner's near contemporary Alfred North Whitehead avoided propagating racial myths and stories about goblins and has, consequently, been much more influential in academic philosophy. But the parallels in some of their ideas are quite striking. Despite being trained in math, both emphasized the importance of the spiritual as well as the material. Both took a holistic view of the world and saw connections rather than differences. Both saw life as a continuous learning experience and argued that human perceptions always simplified complexity. Openness to learning and a belief in the endless potential for creativity were key to both thinkers. Finally, and most importantly for this book, they shared the belief that these ideas should be put into practice. Whitehead was attracted to the Harvard Business School because it brought theory and practice together. Steiner, particularly in the last two decades of his life—he died in 1925—invested heavily in developing practical applications of his worldview.

Steiner's worldview was centered on achieving harmony between humans and nature, and between matter and spirit. In the wake of World War I, influenced no doubt by the turbulence of the postwar period, Steiner formalized his views in the concept of social three-folding. He distinguished between three spheres of society—the economic, the political and legal, and the cultural. He argued that economic activity needed to be organized and carried out in the spirit of cooperation with the objective of meeting the needs of all human beings. The political and legal sphere was concerned with the protection of human rights and equality. The cultural sphere was concerned with the cultivation of human capacities. It included teaching, the arts, and religion, and it facilitated creativity and made freedom of the individual a fundamental principle. Steiner believed that society was best served when these spheres were autonomous, even though every adult took part in all three spheres. He was equally opposed to the economic (that is, business) dominating the other two spheres, as he was to a socialist state dominating economic life. Instead he saw the three spheres as interdependent. He believed that the economic sphere, for example, generated surpluses as a gift to the cultural sphere.[11]

Steiner thought business should retain full control over the allocation of capital and considered state intervention to be disastrous. This view was no doubt influenced by the fact that he was developing his ideas against the background of war and postwar turbulence, with fragile governments in Germany and elsewhere, and a radical experiment in socialist government underway in Russia after the Bolshevik Revolution. However, he did not believe that market forces should allocate capital. Instead, he argued that bankers and other figures in the cultural sphere, who had developed the ability to recognize who could use capital most effectively for the benefit of the entire community, should place capital at the disposal of these promising individuals. Although he believed that successful business-people should keep the financial rewards of their endeavors, he felt that money, like goods, should "wear out" and be returned after a certain period of time (he suggested twenty-five years), either for new investments or to be gifted to the cultural sphere.[12]

Even before he came up with the formal concept of three-folding, Steiner was actively developing practical applications of his philosophy. Although he was not formally trained as an architect, in 1913 he began constructing the Goetheanum, a double-domed wooden building in Dornach, Switzerland, as a school for "spiritual science." The Goetheanum, and the replacement building after the first wooden building was destroyed, allegedly by arson, in 1922, was a radical endeavor to introduce his spiritual philosophy into architecture. He wrote four mystery plays, which told his story of spiritual development, and developed eurythmy, a new expressive movement and dance form, in partnership with his second wife, Marie.[13] He also researched the healing power of ingredients derived from plants, working with Ita Wegman, a Swiss-trained medical doctor who had grown up in the Dutch East Indies (now Indonesia). The school at the Goetheanum included departments run by pharmacists and chemists, who sought to develop products of Anthroposophical medicine.[14]

Steiner's emergence as an entrepreneur came in the aftermath of World War I. In October 1919 he gave a speech to Anthroposophists at Dornach calling for an international movement of renewal based on his views of three-folding. Also speaking that day was Emil Molt, a German entrepreneur who owned the Waldorf-Astoria Cigarette Company and who was in the process of cofounding with Steiner a school in Stuttgart to serve the children of factory employees. Steiner's ideas on education ran against the norms of his time. He felt that a school should be open to all children and be coeducational, that it should be a unified twelve-year school, and that teachers should be given primary control of the classroom and curriculum with minimum interference from the state.[15] His first school became the forerunner of the Waldorf educational system, which put a heavy emphasis on music, arts, movement, and stories in the early stages of the program and was designed to inspire imagination and holistic understanding.

Molt suggested that businesses could be established to provide the financial means for supporting the diffusion of Anthroposophy. In accordance with his views of social three-folding, Steiner proposed that a "bank-like institution" be created to support such businesses, which would promote Anthroposophical values by providing other companies with financial and managerial support in the hopes of building a new business culture. Although the bank was intended to be profitable, the profits were not an end in themselves so much as to repay loans and support educational and cultural institutions.[16]

It proved challenging to execute such a project in financially and economically unstable postwar Germany. The proposed bank,

Der Kommende Tag (The Coming Day), was launched in 1920 with Steiner as chairman. A number of small companies and laboratories were also launched in Germany and Switzerland to make natural medicines. The ventures struggled to grow, which was hardly surprising given the precarious financial state of the country and the threat of social upheaval. The earlier ventures were rolled up in 1924 into a joint-stock company that came to be known as Weleda. Steiner had been alarmed by Adolf Hitler's attempted coup in Munich in the previous year, and this seems to have prompted his decision to base the firm in Switzerland. Steiner did not join the board, as he wanted to focus on his spiritual work. The Anthroposophical Society and individual Anthroposophists were the shareholders. He saw the company as an "economic-spiritual enterprise."[17]

By then, Steiner had also developed ideas about a new agricultural system based on Anthroposophist principles. Working with a group of German farmers, he gave a series of lectures on agriculture in 1924, incorporating ideas then in circulation in Germany, such as seeing farms as organisms and avoiding chemical fertilizers. Unsurprisingly, he added his own twist. The health of the soil, plants, and animals depended, he argued, on their connection with cosmic creative forces.[18]

Steiner's lectures on farming provided the basic principles of what became known as biodynamic agriculture, one of the primary systems of organic agriculture. Steiner promoted the use of nine so-called preparations designed for soil health to stimulate plant growth alongside crop rotation, manuring, and the integration of crops with livestock. A mixture of minerals, plants, and animal manure, the preparations were fermented before their application and left in the soil for either six months or a year, two of them in cow horns and five in different animal parts, such as the bladder. Three were then sprayed on crops and six blended into compost. In addition, the method emphasized that plants came under astrological influences and that planting and harvesting needed to coincide with movements of the moon and planets.[19]

In 1923, Steiner became ill. During his last months, he was cared for by Wegman as they jointly wrote his last book, which provided a theoretical basis for the new medicine they were developing. Weleda's product line included remedies against a wide variety of illnesses as well as dietary supplements and digestive teas. Hair tonic and shaving soap were also made from ingredients grown according to biodynamic principles.[20] The business was the forerunner of the modern natural beauty industry that Anita Roddick and others would take into the mainstream half a century later.

Anthroposophy survived the death of its founder, although not without considerable traumas. The Anthroposophical Society, originally founded in 1912, was refounded as the General Anthroposophical Society in 1923, based in the Goetheanum in Dornach. In time national affiliates were founded. Steiner established a First Class of fully committed members—one estimate is that it came to form 10 to 30 percent of the membership—which was secretive and appeared cultlike to outsiders.[21] The Nazi era caused splits in the movement, as some elements were sympathetic to Nazi ideas. Still, in 1935, the German society was formally banned for its alleged association with Jews and Freemasons.[22] Wegman herself was expelled from the society after a power struggle, along with the entire British and Dutch branches, in part for her vocal opposition to the Nazis. Steiner's wife, Marie, was on the opposite side.[23] The movement was eventually reunited in the early 1960s, but differences remained between the German- and English-speaking traditions.[24]

While the relatively small group of committed followers argued among themselves, experiments in the practical applications of Anthroposophy persisted. Weleda issued its first dividend in 1929 but did not issue another one until after World War II. It remained in business and continues so today, selling skin creams and other personal care products in some forty countries. The company also remained closely held within the Anthroposophical movement, and 40 percent of its shares are still held by the General Anthroposophical Society.[25]

Meanwhile, work continued on the practical application of Steiner's agricultural ideas. The Anthroposophy movement created institutions and established rules. Demeter, founded in 1927, advised farmers and engaged in the marketing of biodynamic products. The Demeter trademark was developed in 1928 to certify products, and for half a century, it remained the only certification scheme for organic products. To this day, it is one of the most rigorous and uncompromised organic certification schemes and the only one enforcing the same standards worldwide. The entry ticket to securing Demeter certification was and remains high. The starting point was that land had to be free of chemicals for three years before certification would be granted. The standard has no requirement for a farmer to have knowledge of, or accept, Anthroposophy.[26] In 1938 Ehrenfried Pfeiffer, a German chemist who had worked with Steiner before moving to the United States, published *Bio-dynamic Farming and Gardening*, coining the term "biodynamic" and creating a publicly available textbook for the first time.[27]

The Waldorf school movement also grew, though slowly. New Waldorf schools opened in Britain and the United States in the 1930s, although the schools were closed down in Nazi Germany.[28] Anthroposophical ideas also inspired the foundation in Scotland in 1939 of the Camphill movement for children with development disabilities.[29]

Steiner has inspired some passionate followers, but he has puzzled most. The same reactions have persisted after his death. Few were convinced that human history was advanced by battles with demonic forces, and his belief that reincarnation followed a racial hierarchy is a distasteful reminder of a long tradition of Western racism. But his disdain for materialism, his belief in the value of holistic solutions and vibrant communities, and his insistence on the integration of creativity and the arts into education struck a chord. However strange Steiner's philosophy may appear to us now, his followers were adept at translating some of his ideas into actual institutions. His vision of a beneficial role for business in healing society and building

balanced and healthy communities has inspired many ethical entrepreneurs and left an enduring legacy.

Anthroposophy and Business

In the immediate postwar decades, Anthroposophy, three-folding,
and biodynamic agriculture were too outlandish for public adoption, even though committed followers continued to spread their
influence. Rachel Carson drew on data collected by two biodynamic
farmers on the impact of DDT when she wrote *Silent Spring*. It has
been suggested that she avoided mentioning this source in the book
because of concerns that the association with biodynamic agriculture
would damage her credibility.[30]

During the 1970s a reinvention of Anthroposophy as relevant
to socially progressive, New Age–type social movements began,
accompanied by shifts within the movement itself toward a greater
focus on developing practical applications.[31] This was apparent in
the Waldorf school movement, which grew slowly during the 1950s
and 1960s but then rapidly from the 1970s on. By the late 1980s
there were six hundred Waldorf schools worldwide. By 2022 there
were over one thousand independent Waldorf schools in sixty countries.[32] Waldorf schools attracted parents who appreciated their
emphasis on storytelling and creativity, and their tight restrictions
on the use of computers, television, and other forms of electronic
media. The schools deliberately downplayed some aspects of their
founder's thinking.[33]

Anthroposophy also emerged as an inspiration for new businesses
with an explicitly environmental agenda. In Germany in 1974, a half
century after Steiner had floated the idea, the first Anthroposophical bank was launched. In Germany, Gemeinschaft für Leinen
und Schenken (GLS; Community Bank for Loaning and Giving)
originated out of a serendipitous encounter between a Catholic
lawyer, Wilhelm Barkhoff, and an Anthroposophist attempting to
find financing for a new Waldorf school. Barkhoff became intrigued

by the idea of creating a new kind of bank to finance socially useful goods and services. GLS was eventually launched as a mutually owned cooperative bank that paid depositors no or little interest and screened lenders for values. It lent especially to Demeter-certified farms and, later, to early wind power projects.[34]

More social banks, the most important of which was Triodos in the Netherlands, were founded in the 1980s. Like GLS, Triodos and other banks such as RSF Social Finance in the United States were characterized by unusual degrees of transparency about their borrowers and businesses. They relied on deposits from people willing to accept lower interest rates in order to finance activities they approved, and lent at below-market rates. In line with Steiner's three-folding concept, they lent capital to businesses in organic food and wind energy, and played an important role in the early stages of both industries in Europe. These banks also supported schools, music venues, and other cultural institutions.[35] RSF Social Finance was launched in 1984 by Siegfried and Mark Finser, a father-and-son team of Anthroposophists, as a nongovernmental organization (NGO). Like Triodos and GLS, RSF Social Finance helped to create collaborative networks of socially influential businesses. When Philadelphia entrepreneur Judy Wicks formed the Business Alliance for Local Living Economies, intended as a network of small socially responsible businesses in 2001, RSF Social Finance offered financial support and Mark Finser joined the advisory board.[36] RSF Social Finance was to play an important role in the successful launches of the B Lab movement and the Purpose Foundation, which we will see in Chapter 10.

While GLS confined lending to Anthroposophical borrowers, Triodos broadened its portfolio over time to include other environmentally and socially responsible businesses. Mention of Steiner disappeared from the corporate website, but his influence remained evident. Like other Anthroposophical banks, it never lent solely by looking at metrics and always considered how an application was aligned with the bank's overall mission. The bank was very transparent about its loans—showing, among other things, continued

support for organic farming, Waldorf schools, and alternative medicines. By 2021, Triodos was quite large—with $25 billion in assets
under management and nearly 750,000 customers. It avoided public
listing and instead relied on depository receipts. The bank's website
explained that "if we were primarily accountable for delivering profit
to external shareholders, we could not pursue our mission to use
money exclusively for positive social, environmental and cultural
change."[37] Triodos was not a hugely profitable business, but then its
aim was not to be. The bank's financial returns have been described
by economist Rebecca Henderson as "significantly below those earned
by the large global banks in their best years, but significantly above
those earned in their worst years."[38]

There was also a new energy in the biodynamic farming movement, which had remained small and marginal since Steiner's death
but now found new relevance as concerns about the impact of the
pesticides and other chemicals used in conventional farming arose
in Europe and the United States. In France, a biodynamic organization called Nature et Progrès was created in 1964. Under the
ambitious leadership of Roland Chevriot, the organization engaged
with other environmental movements, sending observers to the fringe
meetings of the first United Nations Conference on the Environment
in Stockholm in 1972. Chevriot, who developed the first set of guide-
less for organic agriculture in France and promoted Europe-wide
cooperation on organic standards, was behind the launch of the
International Federation of Organic Agriculture Movements in 1972.
These were major steps toward establishing an organized certification and verification scheme for organic foods, which had previously
been sold on a very ad hoc basis.[39]

In Germany, where the environmental movement gained considerable traction during the 1970s, partly due to its vocal opposition to government plans to build nuclear power plants, there
was a substantial consumer base interest in purchasing organic foods.
A number of retail and wholesale businesses were created to serve
these consumers. One of the most important of these originated in
1979 in the town of Diepholz, where Ulrich Walter took over a small

organic shop that was about to close and developed a wholesale business that employed the trademark Lebensbaum, or Tree of Life. Walter was not a formal Anthroposophist, but he had extremely close relations with the movement. After finding it very difficult to secure reliable supplies of high-quality organic tea, coffee, and spices, Walter developed a wholesale business that built long-term relationships with biodynamic suppliers, including the companies in Egypt and India covered later in this chapter.[40]

Götz Rehn, who went to a Waldorf school, launched an Anthroposophical food retailer called Alnatura in 1984. It began to develop a network of organic food supermarkets and over time became a leading organic food retailer in Germany, with sales approaching $1 billion by 2020. The company remained closely committed to Anthroposophical beliefs, although many of them had transitioned to the mainstream. Its mission, according to its website, was to "think holistically," "act customer-oriented," and "be responsible."[41] Rehn declined to take his company public, saying that remaining private enabled it to treat capital as a means to "realize an idea."[42]

An innovation closely associated with the Anthroposophist movement that has also gone mainstream is community-supported agriculture. This originated in Germany and Switzerland in the 1960s when groups of farmers and people living in cities began to form cooperative partnerships to promote socially equitable and ecologically sustainable agriculture. Growers and consumers shared the risks and benefits of food production as consumers paid at the start of the growing season for a share of an anticipated harvest. Once harvesting began, they received weekly shares of vegetables in box schemes. The concept spread to the United States during the 1980s, promoted by Robyn Van En, owner of a small biodynamic farm in Massachusetts, who founded CSA North America in 1992 to support development.[43]

Some community-supported ventures evolved in other directions. In Denmark, Thomas Harrtung, a farmer, and Soren Ejlersen, a chef, experimented with forming a cooperative but found the procedures too cumbersome. They launched an organic food box company called Aarstiderne (The Seasons) in 1999. Harrtung, an active Lutheran, embraced Anthroposophy and the belief, as he later articulated it, that there was "a spiritual aspect to man and his interaction with land, sun and rain." He made a careful distinction between the followers of Steiner and other organic farmers. "Most of the organic movement has an ego-centric origin, concerned with sinful man taking over the planet and messing it up and ultimately destroying it. Bio-dynamic farming has a more meta-centric approach, about man's relationship to greater forces."[44]

Aarstiderne grew with a characteristically holistic approach. Although the firm still supplied vegetables from two original farms, it also sourced supplies from elsewhere in Denmark and internationally. It never received supplies by plane, using land travel and ships to avoid producing unnecessary carbon emissions. The promotion of community was a prominent feature of the business. The founders created school gardens to teach about plants and sustainable food.[45] In the business itself, the firm made extensive use early on of internet ordering and placed special emphasis on social networking. Customers were called "members," and there was a conversation department rather than a call center or inquiries department. Although the core farm was Demeter certified, Aarstiderne as a business was not. As Harrtung observed, "We don't want to shove it down people's throats. You should not feel that you have to buy into the whole Steiner universe just because you want a vegetable box."[46]

The business experienced ups and downs, but Aarstiderne's revenues had reached almost $120 million by 2021 and it was serving nearly twenty million meals a year. The firm was committed to strongly ecological practices across all its activities. Apart from working exclusively with biodynamic and organic farmers, it offered meal boxes that could be reused up to four times and developed strategies to minimize food waste by selling excess food in its farm shop to wholesalers, using it for fermentation and juices, donating it to the food bank, and using it as animal feed. In 2019, less than 1 percent of Aarstiderne's total food purchases went to waste.[47]

These and other Anthroposophical businesses coexisted in formal and informal networks with one another thanks to the long-established Demeter certification organization and more recent associations. In 1996, Sekem in Egypt encouraged a group of European companies, including Lebensbaum and Alnatura, to found the International Association for Partnership in Ecology and Trade, which aimed to build cooperation among farmers, manufacturers, and distributors from the North and South to improve the quality of organic products cultivated in developing countries. Partners in the association agreed to exchange information on markets and financing, to develop a code of ethics for fair trade, and to pursue scientific and cultural cooperation. A system emerged under which the partners aimed to meet four times a year to share their experiences and swap notes on best practices. Over time, other Anthroposophical companies joined the association, including Aarstiderne and Ambootia in India.[48]

There were financial ties, too. GLS and Triodos invested in Anthroposophical businesses. When an embryonic Aarstiderne business faced an unexpected cash flow problem in 2001 because people stopped ordering during the summer holidays, Triodos Bank, which had just set up a venture capital fund, took a 20 percent stake in the company in return for $2 million plus some loans, which made it possible to grow the business. The transaction included an agreed buyback five years later. In 2014, the connection with Triodos was resurrected when the newly established Triodos Organic Growth Fund took 20 percent of Aarstiderne's equity.[49]

There were also flows of private wealth. For example, in 1987 Ulrich Walter began sourcing his organic coffee from a plantation called Finca Irlanda in Mexico. Finca Irlanda was established as a Demeter-certified biodynamic venture in 1928 by a German immigrant family, making it one of the first experiments with this agricultural method. The foundation established by Walter, the Lebensbaum Foundation, opened a school for families on the plantation in 1999 and made other investments to improve the community. When Finca Irlanda got into financial difficulties in the 2010s due to a conjunction of fungal disease and a major earthquake, Walter invested in the business and became co-owner, helping to replant hundreds of thousands of coffee trees.[50] Walter also supported other biodynamic firms in Egypt and India, as we will see.

For decades Steiner's vision of spiritual-economic businesses had little impact beyond a narrow group of followers. Weleda was virtually a one-firm show. However, in the 1970s, in the context of growing environmental awareness, especially in Europe, a new interest arose in applying some of Steiner's ideas to banks and business. As memories of some of Steiner's more distasteful views faded, he was reinvented as a proto-environmentalist and an inspiration for deep responsibility in business. The founders of Anthroposophical businesses in this era saw their efforts as a means to achieve a more holistic world, one in which humans lived in harmony with nature and with the spiritual world. They offered an unassuming, but uncompromising, alternative to conventional capitalism and materialism. They were also uncompromisingly critical of shareholder capitalism, keeping their firms out of capital markets in the belief that their ecological and social purpose would inevitably be diluted if they went public. This constrained the scaling of businesses, but they sought sustainability rather than billion-dollar revenues. Anthroposophical firms were supported, too, by a semiclosed network in which banks and private investors lent financial support, while organizations such as Demeter provided other types of support, including knowledge sharing. This network extended to Anthroposophical businesses in the emerging world, where some of the worst downsides of the destruction of community and environmental degradation occurred over the last forty years. The next two sections turn to these businesses in Egypt and India.

How Ibrahim Abouleish Turned Desert into Farmland

In 1977 Ibrahim Abouleish, an Egyptian chemist and follower of Steiner, established a company called Sekem in Egypt. Against formidable odds, and with considerable difficulty, he built a biodynamic farming business that literally turned desert into farmland and, as profits grew, channeled them into educational and cultural investments to build a sustainable community. The whole endeavor provided striking evidence of the ability of a purpose-driven business to transform a local community in an impoverished and turbulent country, although it was an achievement with definite trade-offs.

When Abouleish started his business, Egypt faced long-running economic, social, and institutional challenges. In 1977, the country had a real GDP per capita in contemporary US dollars of $2,817. This was considerably higher than India in that year ($1,494), but terribly poor compared with the European countries where Anthroposophical businesses were expanding, such as Denmark ($23,360) and Germany ($20,837).[51] Egypt's low income had deep roots. The country had fared badly in the nineteenth century. A failed attempt to create a modern industrial base early in that century left it with a commodity-export-oriented economy almost entirely focused on cotton.[52] The British, who took formal control of the country in 1882, opposed attempts to create a modern industrial sector and focused instead on reinforcing the production and export of cotton.[53] Egypt became nominally independent in 1922, but British and French control over the Suez Canal, which linked the Mediterranean to the Red Sea, continued to limit the country's sovereignty. The nationalization of the Suez Canal in 1956 by the nationalist leader Gamal Abdel Nasser triggered a failed invasion by Britain, France, and Israel, followed by a prolonged period of state intervention, which decimated the significant private enterprise sector that had developed from the interwar years. Egypt did experience much-needed human capital development in the era of Nasser, but it also suffered from an inflated state bureaucracy and high levels of inefficiency.[54]

Sekem was founded some years after Nasser's successor, Anwar Sadat, had launched a new policy of *infatah*, or openness to foreign capital and market forces. Although it was mainly designed to reverse the negative features of the Nasser era, the new policy also reversed many social improvements introduced under Nasser and drove inequality. In 1977, there were massive bread riots in Egypt's cities as people took to the streets to protest the ending of food subsidies. Four years later, Sadat was assassinated by radical Islamists enraged by his signing of a peace treaty with Israel.[55]

Abouleish's journey to biodynamic farming, which took place against the backdrop of this unfolding economic and social crisis, was not straightforward. Born in the village of Mashtul, outside Cairo, in 1937 to a relatively affluent family (his father owned soap and confectionary factories), he witnessed dramatic changes in Egypt, including the overthrow of the monarchy in 1952, the coming to power of Nasser two years later, and anti-British riots leading up to the nationalization of the Suez Canal.[56] At the age of eighteen, Abouleish decided to go to university in Europe against the wishes of his parents. He ended up studying chemistry in Graz, Austria. As a student, he married Gudrun, an Austrian woman who was Catholic, although he remained a committed Muslim. Abouleish had initially planned to return to Egypt to work for his father's business, but it was expropriated by Nasser, leaving his parents without their main source of income. He decided to stay in Graz and pursue pharmaceutical research, studying philosophy in his spare time and rereading Goethe, whom he had read in Egypt.[57]

Abouleish showed some promise as a research scientist in the local pharmaceutical industry, and patented new medicines to treat osteoporosis and arteriosclerosis, but a chance encounter set him on a different course.[58] In 1972 he was invited, as an Egyptian, to give a lecture to a local audience explaining the mounting tensions between Egypt and Israel (which would result in the Yom Kippur War in the following year). After he was finished, he was approached by a member of the audience, who asked him if he knew about Anthroposophy. Martha Werth, a piano teacher, introduced him to Steiner's book *The Philosophy of Freedom*, which he began to read on a visit to her house. He later recalled that he felt that he had "grasped a tiny part of the whole world, and humans and nature were revealed to me in a new light." After reading Steiner's talks about the Old and New Testaments, he also began a quest to interpret "the Koran in a spiritually deeper way."[59]

Werth invited Abouleish to accompany her on a tour of Egypt in 1975. He saw the ancient treasures of Egyptian art and mythology in a new light, but he also saw for the first time the harsh social realities of his native country. He perceived the agricultural sector as "a catastrophe." In particular the Aswan High Dam, built in the 1960s, had disrupted the annual flooding of the Nile, replacing it with an irrigation system that spread diseases. Where lands had formerly been nourished by the seasonal flooding of the Nile, farmers were now making extensive use of fertilizers, spraying pesticides intensively on the cotton fields. There was growing evidence that farmers were poisoned in the process, while the soil was deteriorating in quality.[60]

In 1977 Abouleish decided to return to Egypt, with "a vision of a holistic project able to bring about a cultural renewal."[61] His vision was to build a community based around a biodynamic farm, with flourishing educational and cultural institutions. Although the desire to develop a biodynamic farm and fully integrated community was driven by Anthroposophical beliefs, Islam was equally important as a source of inspiration. "The Koran relates how Adam and Eve lived in paradise before satanic whispers led them to the forbidden tree and they were expelled," he later noted, "but the Koran promised to return the Garden of Eden to believers as a most beautiful reward for their devoutness—the god-fearing will live forever in gardens."[62]

After talking to officials at the Ministry of Agriculture, he purchased seventy acres of desert land from the state in Belbes, thirty-seven miles northeast of Cairo. It was an unusual choice: water supply was difficult, and there was no direct road to Cairo. He called his new community Sekem, taking the name from the hieroglyphic meaning "vitality of the sun." He began by marking out roads on his empty site and boring deep wells to locate water. A portion of the land was mapped out for a school, a medical center, and a cultural center for eurythmy and the arts. In the middle of the site there was a space for "businesses whose profits would finance the establishment and development of the cultural institutions."[63]

If Abouleish's vision was clear, so were the challenges. It is not possible to grow crops in a desert without water, and building an irrigation system proved challenging. Canals had to be built and pipes laid. A German-made irrigation machine proved ineffective in the desert soil. An initial attempt to grow shade-giving trees was disrupted when Bedouin people camped in the designated area and refused to move. Abouleish ultimately resolved the issue by using his personal contacts with none other than President Sadat, who sent soldiers to persuade them to move. (Abouleish had met Sadat at a meeting of Egyptian expatriates in the 1960s when he had impressed the future president by standing apart from the crowd and speaking in opposition to a war against Israel.)[64] Once the Bedouin had been forced off the land, Abouleish was able to plant 120,000 seedling trees. He even ended up recruiting some of the Bedouin to act as shepherds to stop goats from eating the young saplings.[65] In 1980, Abouleish again had to ask for Sadat's help when an army general decided to take over part of the Sekem farm and began bulldozing trees.[66]

After trying to use wind and solar power and finding them too expensive or ineffective, Abouleish reluctantly conceded that he would need to secure power through the state electricity board. It took him two and a half years to build a power line connected to the existing power lines, which were only five and a half miles away, but on other people's land.[67]

Once he secured water and power, he could grow something, but who would buy it? Because there was then zero domestic demand for organic crops, Abouleish sought an international market. He identified an alternative medicine company in the United States, Ohio-based Elder, which had a need for supplies of lace flower, a wild medicinal plant that grew in the desert. His knowledge of pharmacology enabled him to present himself as a plausible supplier, and he gained his first contract. The contract required him to build an essential oils extraction plant, which, given the poor skills base in Egypt, was also a major challenge. He reached out to Hassan Fathy, a pioneering Egyptian ecological architect known for his adobe-based architecture, whose book *Architecture for the Poor*, published in English in 1973, had won international acclaim. Fathy helped build the first laboratory using exclusively organic materials.[68]

Financing the business was a further challenge. Abouleish initially sought financing from an Islamic bank, which took a 40 percent equity holding. He turned to an Islamic bank because he believed it would share his principles more than a Western-style bank.[69] An ugly dispute arose, which Abouleish declined to resolve through bribery. The dispute meant that it took a considerable time to find alternative financing, which he eventually did from the state-owned National Bank of Egypt. The first flow of revenues from selling biodynamic herbs and spices began in 1981.[70] This company (later renamed Lotus) was the first business within the Sekem group.

There was considerable serendipity in the subsequent evolution of the business. In 1981, a group of German tourists visiting a nearby temple heard news of Sekem and visited. On their return to Germany, they persuaded GLS to provide a loan so Sekem could acquire forty cows, enough to provide the compost needed to fertilize the desert in a biodynamic fashion. A young German biodynamic expert, Angela Hofmann, accompanied the cows from Germany to the Sekem farm and stayed for the next three decades. GLS eventually converted its loan into a donation and became a long-term supporter of Sekem.[71] In 1983 Ulrich Walter appeared at Sekem's doors, having had no response to his written inquiries about securing a supply of organic spices and tea.[72] With the help of GLS, Lebensbaum signed a supplier relationship with Sekem. Over time, Sekem formed similar supplier relationships with other Anthroposophist businesses, including Alnatura.[73]

Abouleish ran into unexpected problems at home. He faced opposition from the Ministry of Agriculture, which believed that the composting methods in biodynamic agriculture would spread disease. It took a year to secure permission. He also struggled to build a domestic market. Abouleish worked hard to advocate the personal health benefits of organic food. "I would go on television and give interviews whenever I had a chance," he later observed, "and media people would come to our compound and advertise our lifestyle to the outside world."[74] There was a sustained campaign in the Egyptian press against organic food, noting that it was so expensive it could only serve the affluent, and accusing Sekem of only catering to Germans. At one stage the community was accused of being sun worshipers, which provoked hostility from the religious establishment. Abouleish had to convene a meeting of religious conservatives at Sekem, where he was able to convince them that his practices were in accordance with the Qur'an.[75]

Over time, the range of crops grown at Sekem increased. In 1985, the company began selling herbal tea. Three years later Abouleish and a partner from Cyprus set up a joint venture called Libra to produce and sell organically grown crops. The initiative came from the Cypriot company, which had started a vegetable-growing business in Egypt and exported the produce to Britain, and now sought an Egyptian partner. Abouleish was attracted by the opportunity to access the fresh produce business, although he was horrified by his partner's extensive use of fertilizers and pesticides.[76] The joint venture was eventually wound up, but Abouleish persisted with his dream of having an organic fresh food business. It proved costly, however, as there was a steep learning curve to growing organic vegetables, and selling vegetables grown in Egypt to Europe involved tough logistical challenges. In 1996 a new company, Hator, was launched to produce and pack fresh fruit and vegetables. Gudrun took over the management of the new venture. She trained the staff, primarily young women who packaged the vegetables, from scratch, teaching the basic hygiene needed to handle food safely.[77]

Initially, Sekem grew most of the herbs, spices, and vegetables on its own property. Abouleish found it hard to persuade local farmers of the merits of switching to biodynamic, and the spread of biodynamic methods to many small farmers was time consuming and training intensive. Over time, however, Sekem developed a network of organic supplier farms—as many as four hundred by 2020.[78] Abouleish also faced the challenge of securing organic certification, which was required if vegetables were to be sold in Europe. Initially he relied on the Swiss biodynamic certifier IMO, but this was expensive. In 1990, with the assistance of the German Demeter organization, he founded the Center of Organic Agriculture in Egypt as an independent company that could undertake certification.[79]

Cotton was Egypt's most important cash crop, but it was also subject to massive pest infestations, which promoted massive use of pesticides. The Egyptian government was interested in reducing this usage, but growing cotton on a large scale without chemicals was untested. The growing of organic cotton had been pioneered in Turkey and the United States in the late 1980s. A number of textile and clothing manufacturers had emerged that were interested in purchasing the product. They were mostly located in Germany and Switzerland, plus a handful in the United States such as Patagonia.[80]

Sekem embarked on the challenge of developing a biodynamic method for growing cotton using pheromones to control insects. In 1990, Abouleish was able to demonstrate to the Egyptian government that the yields and efficiency of organic cotton cultivation were not inferior to those of conventional methods. This made it possible for the law to be changed to facilitate abolition of the widespread practice of spraying chemical pesticides by airplane on cotton fields. In 1994, the Egyptian government started to support farmers who wanted to grow cotton organically. Abouleish created an industry association, the Egyptian Biodynamic Association, to promote the growing of biodynamic cotton. In 1996, it registered Demeter Egypt as an NGO providing training, research, and advisory services in organic and biodynamic farming. This initiative became hugely influential. By 1999, Sekem's methods had been applied to four-fifths of Egypt's cotton-growing area. Over time, pesticide use dropped by almost 90 percent in Egypt.[81]

Meanwhile, Abouleish continued to create business ventures with a focus on moving up the value chain. In 1998 he established a company called Conytex, later renamed NatureTex, which manufactured clothes from organic cotton. These were sold both under its own brands, including Cotton People Organic, and under private labels. The venture, which designed its clothing in-house, built a business that was 85 percent exports, mainly to Europe and the United States.[82]

As the business grew more complex, Abouleish was able to draw on the support of his son Helmy. Helmy was born in Austria in 1961 and lived there until his father returned to Egypt when he was sixteen. He barely spoke any Arabic when he arrived. His parents put him in the German School in Cairo, but he also began to build connections in his new country, spending a month living in a Bedouin tent in the desert. Helmy shared his father's values, including his enthusiasm for the work of Steiner. After studying business and management in Cairo, he interned at Weleda and became CEO of Sekem in 1984 after his father became ill. By the 2000s, both he and his father had become celebrities in the world of sustainability. In 2003, they were named "Outstanding Social Entrepreneurs" by the Schwab Foundation. Invitations to the World Economic Forum, World Bank conferences, and much more followed.[83]

From the start, Abouleish's core vison was less about growing organic crops as such and more about building a community. "I wanted to create a community dedicated to the holistic development of its workers and all of its stakeholders," he later recalled.[84] The use of funds from the business for educational and cultural development was central to his vision. The Sekem Development Foundation was founded in 1984 to teach about sustainable development. A nursery serving young mothers working in Sekem's factories grew into a full-scale kindergarten. A school system was started in 1987, beginning with primary education and eventually extending all the way up to adult education. The schools made a point of recruiting children from a wide range of backgrounds, including both Muslims and Christians. They moved away from the rote learning favored by the public sector and experimented with innovative pedagogies based on Steiner's principles, with courses in eurythmy, crafts, music, and dance.[85] Abouleish's investment in education was regarded as essential for the development of the whole business. Asked in an interview in 2011 about the biggest roadblock he had faced, he answered that it was the fact that people had "not developed the consciousness of the environment they live in."[86]

A special education school was started for disabled children. In 1986 Abouleish started building the Mahad, a center for adult education. In 1997, a vocational training center was founded. In 1999, the Sekem Academy was established for agricultural, pharmaceutical, and medicinal research.[87] This evolved into Heliopolis University for Sustainable Development, which taught a wide range of courses in five faculties centered on the principles of sustainable development.[88]

Ibrahim and Helmy made art central to Sekem, a commitment that was reflected in the campus's physical design. An art school was established, as were a choir and orchestra. In the design of the entire site, he alternated fields planted with grains and medicinal plants with flower beds and avenues of decorative trees.[89] In Sekem's schools, space and activities were designed to communicate the values of sustainability. Classrooms had irregular spaces with no sharp corners and a lot of daylight. The integration of art, crafts, music, and dancing worked to teach children concerns for their body and spirit and develop in them an appreciation for the full range of human flourishing. Children wore colorful aprons corresponding to emotions such as calm or energetic, teaching the psychology of color. Teachers encouraged students to produce real works in the classroom and emphasized recycling.[90] Everything was aimed, as Abouleish observed, "to teach our youth from a very young age the importance of respecting the environment they live in."[91]

Community building was institutionalized beyond the educational and health facilities. Each morning employees met in a circle and reported the plans for the day. At the end of each week, all the businesses and pedagogical institutions would meet together collectively. This arrangement was a useful device to instill norms of punctuality and planning into a workforce accustomed to neither, but in a hierarchical and collective society it also made a statement about equality and personal responsibility. Strikingly too, in a society in which interactions between different genders were constrained, men and women stood side by side in the circles holding hands.

Through arrangements such as this, one study concluded, Sekem "managed to socialize people in ways that departed from the prevailing institutional environment in Egypt."[92] In 2000 the Cooperative of Sekem Employees was created, enabling workers to discuss issues in the workplace and advocate for new amenities. This led, over time, to the opening of a pharmacy on the farm, the creation of a lending room, and the provision of free lunch every day, together with a shuttle service to take workers home.[93]

Collaboration with other Anthroposophical institutions, and sometimes other ecologically and socially responsible ventures, continued to be a dominant theme. Sekem was active in the International Association for Partnership in Ecology and Trade. GLS and Triodos provided finance, and they became formal shareholders in 2007. Oikocredit, a Dutch cooperative supporting microfinance and smaller investments in the developing world, provided funds in 2011, just as Egypt was rising up to overthrow the long-serving president Hosni Mubarak, and acquired equity in Sekem in 2015.[94] Sekem also received donations and help from individual Anthroposophists. Germany gave its young men the option to perform social service internationally as an alternative to mandatory military service, and Sekem recruited several talented young Germans as a result.[95]

Succession is always a challenge in businesses founded by visionaries. Abouleish's son Helmy was fully invested in Sekem's mission. As the tumultuous events of the Arab Spring in 2011 began to unfold, Helmy found himself in political difficulties. In 2004 he became executive director of the Industrial Modernization Center, a business development fund that was part of the Egyptian government. He believed it was essential to create industries that could offer work to the growing youth population of the country.[96] A month after the overthrow of Mubarak in February 2011, Helmy was arrested on corruption charges related to his time at the agency. His father had to step back in to run the business, and Helmy spent one hundred days in jail before being released. "I initiate much more changes in this world with Sekem," he reflected, "than if I would try again to turn the big wheels of politics."[97]

Sekem itself came under criticism during the Arab Spring. Samuel Rima, an American writer on leadership and religion who was recruited to work at Heliopolis University, reported considerable labor unrest. He observed that the heavy investments in education and health, which he praised, were combined with limited empowerment of the workers.[98] As political instability rose, Sekem found a way forward: after a long battle with the Egyptian government bureaucracy, Heliopolis University became accredited during the brief presidency of Mohamed Morsi, before his overthrow by the army in July 2013. This meant that degrees were recognized by the Egyptian Ministry of Higher Education.

Sekem suffered from the economic turbulence of the era, which included a sharp fall in the value of the Egyptian currency. Heavily indebted, partly because it had acquired more land in 2007, Sekem was hit by high interest rates. Net profits fell, a loss was recorded in 2015, and further economic problems continued to weigh on the company.[99] The continued environmental deterioration of the country as a whole was reflected in growing toxic residues in Sekem's water and air, which resulted in it not being able to certify many of its products as organic. The ratio of certified organic to total production fell from 73 percent in 2016 to 46 percent in 2019. Although Sekem had the goal of 100 percent renewable energy, by 2021 it had only reached 24 percent.[100]

When Abouleish died in 2017, Helmy was out of political trouble and the transition was smooth. He was a major figure in the Anthroposophical movement, and in 2018 he became president of Demeter International. The business had strong organizational routines and practices. The Sustainability Flower accounting framework, developed by the International Association for Partnership in Ecological Trade, reported on the company's ecological, economic, cultural, and societal performance in a detailed and transparent manner.[101]

By then three of Helmy and his wife Konstanze's daughters were active in the business, along with two of their husbands. The family, including Abouleish before he died, was resolved to find an ownership structure that would preserve the mission of Sekem. They sought,

Helmy's son-in-law Thomas observed in March 2017, "to prevent Sekem and its subsidiary institutions from being a product of profit-driven commerce, either now or in the future."[102] In 2021, the owner-ship structure of Sekem was transformed. Sekem Treuhand gGmbH was created as a nonprofit philanthropic foundation in Germany mandated to use its dividends to support "cultural and human development at Sekem and the world." The Abouleish family donated most of their shareholding in Sekem to Sekem Treuhand, which owned 59.64 percent of the holding company that oversaw the various Sekem businesses. The remaining shareholders in the holding company were the Abouleish family (3.05 percent), the Abouleish Foundation (0.5 percent), Triodos (8.44 percent), Oikocredit (10.17 percent), and GLS (18.66 percent). The Future Council was created, which held one share and 100 percent of the voting rights in Sekem Treuhand. It had "the purpose of assuring that the vision of Sekem is kept alive through a circle of committed people living and working at Sekem."[103] This was an example of the steward-ownership model, designed to guarantee a company's social mission in perpetuity, which is discussed further in Chapter 10.

By 2022, Sekem and its supply network of four hundred small-scale farms cultivated over 4,675 acres of land, most of which had been reclaimed from the desert. Sekem employed some two thousand people and had total revenues of $33 million. It had built a large domestic market for its organic products, and over two-thirds of revenues were made in the home market. There were almost three hundred students in the Sekem school and nearly two hundred in the vocational training center. Over two thousand students were enrolled in Heliopolis University.[104] An organizational structure had been put in place to guarantee the future of Sekem's mission.

Sekem offers a striking example of how a for-profit business organized on Anthroposophical principles could establish a sustainable community and counter environmental degradation in a turbulent emerging market. Sekem, as a community, had some resemblances to Bournville: pleasant and healthy working conditions were imposed rather than democratically discussed. Unlike George Cadbury,

Abouleish and his son worked with, and had the patronage of, a series of authoritarian presidents. However, there was no evidence that the family lined their pockets at the expense of others or engaged in The Body Shop–style hyperbole. The Egyptian desert was turned into organic farmland, jobs were created and small farmers supported, a steep decline in the use of chemical pesticides in cotton growing was facilitated, and thousands of students passed through the educational institutions created by the revenue of the community's various businesses. This was all achieved in a country with deep institutional voids and turbulent politics.

Ambootia and Sanjay Bansal

Sekem offers an inspiring example of what a well-connected founder committed to establishing an ethical and sustainable community can accomplish. It was far from the norm, but it was also not entirely unique. In India, Sanjay Bansal employed biodynamic agriculture to revitalize a socially and ecologically impoverished community in Darjeeling in the northwest of the country, then invested proceeds back into the community. Ambootia, however, ended up in crisis. Its rescue provides further evidence of the resilience of the Anthroposophical business network.

Tea was first grown in India in the 1820s when the East India Company introduced the plant, aiming to reduce Britain's dependence on tea from China, which was then the exclusive producer.[105] The industry evolved as a plantation-style system where millions of impoverished laborers worked in coercive conditions. The tea industry of Darjeeling, located in the foothills of the Himalayas, employed thousands of impoverished Nepalese who came to work in the plantations. The teas they picked were known as the "champagne of tea" due to their delicate floral and muscatel flavor.[106] The extensive application of chemical fertilizers after 1947 led to a sharp decline in the quality of the tea, a decline that was reinforced when the Soviet Union replaced Britain as the main market. The Soviet purchasers had low regard for the quality of tea beyond the requirement that it should appear black in color. Many tea estates uprooted their high-quality Chinery bushes, whose fine leaves produced flavorful tea, and replaced them with Assamica bush varieties, with larger leaf sizes and yields.[107]

Social conditions on the estates were horrendous. The end of colonial rule brought no change to the hierarchical and exploitative labor conditions in the industry. Estate owners presided over hundreds of thousands of impoverished Nepalese-speaking female workers who plucked tea on Darjeeling's steep slopes. While the women plucked tea, their husbands did household chores and looked after the children; alcoholism was pervasive, especially among the men. As poverty levels grew, support for the Communist Party increased, while the Nepalese-speaking Gorkha population became violent in their demands for autonomy, discouraging new investment.[108]

Bansal took over the family-owned Ambootia plantation in 1993, at a time of upheaval in the industry. He had been born on the plantation in 1961, when his father worked as the manager. His father had moved on, and Ambootia had experienced declining fortunes, to the point that the workforce was left unpaid. In 1986, a delegation of plantation workers traveled to Kolkata to implore the Bansals to acquire the tea estate and take on the liabilities. They agreed.[109] Darjeeling as a whole was then in crisis, as the collapse of the Soviet Union had eliminated its main market. Fortunately, potential new markets awaited as a new generation of European consumers, especially in Germany, were interested in paying a premium for organically produced products. Some tea growers began to convert the region to organic methods.[110] Cultural anthropologist Sarah Besky has written critically about how many plantation owners adopted over time the "language of environmental stewardship and transparency" to secure the certification needed to enhanced their earnings in international markets while providing cover for continued exploitative labor practices.[111]

Bansal, who took over the management when his father retired and his older brother died in a car accident in the same year, joined the trend. He began to convert the estate, which had 5,800 people on it, to organic practices. In contrast to most of his peers, he engaged directly and extensively with the female workers on the estate, consulting with them on the process of going organic, as well as social issues including the all-pervasive problem of alcoholism. Bansal understood that organic certification would give him an opportunity to secure a price premium, but his decision to convert to biodynamic methods in 1994 was more fundamentally influenced by his encounter with Anthroposophy as he explored the international organic movement. The tenets had immediately appealed to him, not least because he felt they resonated with views he already held as an Indian and a Hindu. "In biodynamic agriculture," he later explained, "you are aligning with the annual rhythm of energies of the cosmos, rather than working against them. . . . You revitalize the entire farm system, and you look at the farm as a living being, rather than just a production house."[112]

The conversion to biodynamic practices initially reduced Ambootia's yield by about one-quarter. Although the certification by Demeter was costly, it also gave the estate access to markets that paid much higher premiums, including high-end department stores in developed countries.[113] Ambootia was able, within a few years, to become the largest exporter of black tea from India to Germany and Japan, both premium markets. To raise margins, Bansal abandoned the long-established practice of selling tea at auction, and instead sold teas directly to retailers, who were often Anthroposophists in Europe.[114]

Ambootia was a for-profit business, but Bansal, like Abouleish, regarded profits as a means of making his community more sustainable. He set aside 4 percent of after-tax profits for social development. The company began supporting schools on the plantation, offering uniforms and scholarships. It encouraged English as the language of instruction. If pupils did well and were admitted to university, the company covered the complete cost of tuition. The investment in schools made sense economically for Ambootia, given the drift of plantation workers to the towns and the evident need to provide a reason why they should stay in the villages. But Bansal's desire to promote the long-term sustainability of the region and provide opportunities for the next generation reflected his belief in social three-folding.[115]

Bansal engaged in institution-building. In 1996 he formed the first organic agricultural association, the Indian Bio Organic Tea Association, which worked to persuade the government of the need for organic standards. After the government had an unsuccessful experience with Swiss advisers, Bansal worked with the government and eventually the first Indian organic standards were released in 2000. "Without making a big fuss about it," Bansal proudly noted, "we made the entire protocol of biodynamic standards part of the Indian organic standards. . . . These are the only standards in the whole world that include the biodynamic system of agriculture."[116] In addition, he served as chairman of the Darjeeling Tea Association between 2005 and 2011.

After a decade of running the Ambootia estate, Bansal started buying "sick" tea estates elsewhere in Darjeeling. When an estate was acquired, he visited workers in their homes or called a village meeting to explain Ambootia's principles. Typically, biodynamic methods were introduced immediately, with staff from other tea estates working to teach the new methods. In 2002, the firm also acquired its first tea estates in the state of Assam. The acquisitions were expensive, and made even more so by the three-year conversion period to biodynamic practices. At first Bansal borrowed from banks, an unusual step as debt was always avoided in the Darjeeling industry. He then sought equity investment, attracting the Dutch pension fund and the Dutch-based ethical investing cooperative Oikocredit. He also received funds, as he later observed, from "a bunch of Anthroposophical investors from Europe."[117]

Ambootia was highly leveraged when it entered a period of challenges. The region experienced severe climate change in the form of drought, and tea estates without large financial resources were vulnerable. The owners of other long-established plantations began to divest.[118] Ambootia was badly affected by a strike in 2017, which closed down the entire region for 104 days to protest a decision by the West Bengal government to introduce Bengali as a compulsory subject in schools across the state, including in Darjeeling. Financial pressures meant that not enough compost was made for the biodynamic process. In March 2020, a government-mandated lockdown in response to COVID-19 resulted in the loss of the premium first flush of tea picking. Bansal could no longer pay the wages of his workers.[119]

In June 2020, the "bunch of Anthroposophical investors" in Europe intervened. German-based Auwa, founded by Ulrich Walter, was one of the investors. Auwa had become his family office when he sold his stake in Lebensbaum to implement a smooth succession. The other investor was Dornach-based Artava. They recapitalized the parent company and effectively took ownership. Bansal and his family were removed from management control and a professional manager, Indroneel Goho, who had been hired two years earlier to strengthen financial management, was appointed chief executive. It was the end of the family's involvement in Ambootia, but not the end of the company's biodynamic commitment.[120] Goho, who had previously worked in for-profit businesses and was not an Anthroposophist, was asked to return the business to profitability, but to plough all funds back into the business for at least five years. His mandate, his new owners told him, was to find a way to "flourish as a company and as a community with 10,000 workers and 65,000 inhabitants."[121] It was going to be a challenge, as the whole Darjeeling tea industry was reeling from the effects of rising temperatures and drought, COVID-19, and political agitation. In 2021, the industry's production (6.5 million kilograms) was the lowest on record.[122] Yet the Ambootia brand remained strong, and its estates had stable markets in Europe and Japan.

Bansal's enthusiasm for buying up sick tea gardens and extending the biodynamic system was out of character for Anthroposophical business leaders, who usually take a more incremental approach, and it outran his ability to manage effectively when bad times came. Yet this should not distract from the fact that Ambootia provided a vibrant alternative to the exploitative, semifeudal conditions that were the norm in the Darjeeling tea industry. Like Sekem, it provided an alternative vision of how a for-profit business could assemble resources to renew a community rather than decimate one.

It is surprising that Steiner, who was at best an eccentric and at worst a malign thinker who died almost a century ago, should be an inspiration for some of the most deeply responsible businesses today. Yet these Anthroposophical businesses are the ultimate for-purpose businesses. Strongly held ethical and spiritual values have promoted a holistic understanding of ecological and social challenges, as in the three-folding model. These values have served as a guardrail against the kind of slippage seen in many values-driven businesses discussed in Chapter 8, especially thanks to the standards codified in the Demeter certification scheme. The entrepreneurs behind these firms chose industries—organic food, social banking, and renewable energy—with the aim of making a positive social and environmental impact. They treated their employees well (if sometimes paternalistically) and worked with other stakeholders including governments, and on occasion unpleasant ones. Building a community and investing in its cultural institutions were central to their business strategies. A determination to avoid public capital markets, combined with flows of people and capital between different Anthroposophical enterprises, provided considerable resilience. Anthroposophical businesses offer a compelling example of how for-profit businesses motivated by strong values could form a locally based but globally networked system focused entirely on the promotion of ecological and social sustainability.

Anthroposophical businesses were far from center stage in global capitalism, but their influence was greater than might be assumed from their low profiles. GLS, Triodos, and RSF Social Finance helped fund organic food and wind energy at a time when such industries received little or no public support. Lebensbaum, Alnatura, Aarstiderne, and others were significant forces behind the expansion of organic food consumption and production in Europe. Sekem and Ambootia have contributed positively to addressing the ecological and social challenges of their respective regions. They are for-profit businesses in which the pursuit of sustainability has always been the primary purpose. They see healing the soil as intimately associated with the healing of communities. They sell many of their wares to affluent, ecologically minded Western consumers, harnessing these consumers into a wide web of socially and environmentally beneficial practices. The earnings made in this values-based community have been recycled into the local community, invested heavily in cultural and educational facilities that support and enrich the lives of thousands of young people.

The Anthroposophist business model is not a recipe for rapid action. Biodynamic farming is time intensive and difficult, and there are no shortcuts to Demeter certification. The slow speed of the Anthroposophist approach, and the oddness of its underlying beliefs, might suggest that this model offers no scalable solution to the enormity of the contemporary challenges of climate change, poverty, and inequality. But Steiner's followers had a vested interest in renewed communities and a renewed planet because they felt—as believers in reincarnation—that they would in due course be beneficiaries of them. More to the point, the insight that genuine social and ecological progress would never be made simply by a new government policy or a new technology but rather needed individual transformation represented both a profound acknowledgment of the scale of the challenges awaiting humanity and an agenda to address those challenges. Mindsets had to change at the individual level, and business could not sit idly by, amassing profits and waiting for governments to find solutions. Each small step was essential to build a flourishing society.

CHAPTER 10

FROM ESG TO B CORPS

BENCHMARKING AND SCALING
VIRTUOUS PRACTICES

As the social movements of the 1970s gave way to the free-market conservativism of the 1980s, efforts to seek scalable paths to greater social responsibility in business accelerated. A new generation of entrepreneurs sought to find ways of benchmarking virtuous practices in an effort to justify including socially responsible businesses in conventional investment portfolios. These efforts were partly driven by a desire to escape overdependence on visionary individuals and to address the challenge of transition after a founder relinquished control. Although several of these initiatives sought a role for policy makers, most believed in market solutions. In this respect, they shared the assumption of the proponents of shareholder value maximization that the market knew best. But while the supporters of shareholder value maximization believed that the market would deliver optimal outcomes, proponents of the need to systematize responsible practices argued that the market could be used to correct the glaringly bad outcomes it had encouraged over recent decades.

Endeavors to systematize business responsibility were a response to the triumph of the shareholder value maximization paradigm that had swept the capitalist world. The dominance of this paradigm in the corporate world, which so many now hardly question, is actually surprising in the light of history. As we have seen, there have been many different views on the responsibilities of business over the last two centuries, but the belief that the sole purpose of business was to maximize the wealth of shareholders was certainly never widespread.

The question of whether it was the fiduciary responsibility of boards of public companies to maximize shareholder value had a complicated legal history in the United States stretching back to World War I, when Henry Ford was sued by Horace and John Dodge, two brothers who had started their own car manufacturing firm and who were also large minority shareholders in Ford's firm, after he proposed to cut his dividends in order to reinvest in the company. In the 1919 trial before the State of Michigan Supreme Court, Ford said the company was "organized to do as much good as we can, everywhere, for everybody concerned. And incidentally to make money." The judge ordered Ford Motor to pay dividends, stating that "a business corporation is organized and carried on primarily for the benefit of the stockholders."[1]

This legal decision has been regularly cited by opponents of public companies pursuing social impact at the expense of dividends. Yet the legal basis for shareholder primacy has never been conclusively demonstrated. Some legal scholars maintain that the judgment concerned the rights of a large minority shareholder, rather than shareholders in public companies as such, who never had the power to ask for dividends. In legal jargon, the judge's remarks were "mere dicta," a tangential observation that was unnecessary to reach the actual decision or "holding." A holding creates precedent in common law, not "mere dicta."[2] "United States corporate law," law scholar Lynn Stout concludes in *The Shareholder Value Myth*, "does not and never has required directors of public corporations to maximize either share price or shareholder wealth."[3]

Certainly, as we saw earlier, many large corporations in the United States after World War II took it for granted that they had a social responsibility, even if they differed on what that meant in practice. It was the very prevalence of that view that provoked a skeptical response. In 1958, an economist named Theodore Levitt published an article entitled "The Dangers of Business Responsibility" in the *Harvard Business Review*. He complained that if any business leader dared to assert "that the business of business is profits," they would "get no embossed invitations to speak at the big, prestigeful, and splashy business conferences—where social responsibility echoes as a new tyranny of fad and fancy." Levitt's reasoning was based neither on ethics nor on corporate law. Rather, he argued that managers were simply not qualified to become socially engaged. Business, he concluded, "should let the government take care of the general welfare so that business can take care of the more material aspects of welfare."[4]

A second major critique of social responsibility, and one that came to define the whole era of shareholder value maximization, came from Milton Friedman, a prominent economist and radical thinker at the University of Chicago. Friedman was a passionate advocate of free markets in a period when regulation and government intervention were the prevailing norm, and when the Cold War between the United States and the Soviet Union was being waged. In *Capitalism and Freedom* (1962), regarded as a major contribution to economic theory, he argued for, among other things, freely floating exchange rates, a volunteer army, the abolition of licensing of doctors, and a negative income tax.[5] He also attacked the theories of John Maynard Keynes, which dominated the economics profession at the time, asserting that the price level depends on the money supply and giving rise to the theory of monetarism, a restating of the quantity theory of money.[6]

In 1970 Friedman insisted, in a widely cited article in the *New York Times Magazine,* that "the social responsibility of business is to increase its profits." The responsibility of corporate executives, he argued, was to the owners of the business, who were exclusively concerned with maximizing their financial returns. It was thus incumbent on executives to "make as much money as possible while conforming to the basic rules of the society." Friedman argued that only individuals could have responsibilities, and it made no sense to say that a corporation should have responsibilities. If an individual executive engaged in spending on, say, reducing pollution more than was required by law, Friedman argued that he or she "would be spending someone else's money for a general social interest." The doctrine of social responsibility, he argued, represented an attack on a free society because it involved "the acceptance of the socialist view that political mechanisms, not market mechanisms, are the appropriate way to determine the allocation of scarce resources to alternative issues." Business leaders who talked about social responsibility, Friedman suggested, "are unwitting puppets of the intellectual forces that have been undermining the basis of a free society these past decades."[7]

Friedman laid the intellectual foundations for the major paradigm shift about the responsibility of corporations associated with the so-called Chicago school of free-market economists. In 1976, Michael Jensen and William Meckling published an article that described the shareholders in corporations as principals who hired executives as their agents. The purpose of the executives, they argued, was to maximize financial returns to the principals—an idea that came to be called agency theory. The argument rested on a distinctive view of the nature of corporations. "The private corporation or firm is simply one form of legal fiction which serves as a nexus for contracting relationships," the authors wrote. If executives decided to pursue social purpose, Jensen and Meckling argued, they imposed what they termed "agency costs" and reduced total social wealth.[8]

The reasons for the subsequent rapid diffusion of Friedman's views and agency theory are still being debated. It took place in a changed context in which the postwar era of government intervention and regulation seen in many Western countries gave way to economic liberalization, deregulation, and celebration of the benefits of the market. The spread of what came to be known as neoliberalism was both promoted and reinforced by the advent to power during the 1980s of right-wing conservatives, especially Ronald Reagan in the United States and Margaret Thatcher in Britain. In the United States, at least, the move to free-market capitalism was driven in part by wealthy right-wing benefactors who used their wealth to fund think tanks, lobbyists, and deregulation-friendly economists in order to steer intellectual and policy agendas their way.[9]

The new philosophy of shareholder value maximization achieved popularity first in English-speaking countries, which deregulated and privatized their economies first. As other countries adopted neoliberal policies, so the shareholder value paradigm followed. It was attractive to academic lawyers and economists in its simplicity and its reliance on the metric of share price. Facilitated by the importance of US capital markets, the shareholder value model spread widely even to countries with stronger stakeholder traditions, although usually with local adjustments and variations.[10]

Business schools were important too. In 1985, Jensen was persuaded to join the faculty of the Harvard Business School, where he worked until his retirement in 2000. He became highly influential, introducing a new course on agency theory called Coordination, Control, and the Management of Organizations, which was so popular that two-thirds of MBAs elected to take it.[11] Jensen used the platform offered by the School to diffuse his ideas. In "CEO Incentives," a highly influential 1990 coauthored paper in *Harvard Business Review,* he made the case for executive stock options as important devices to promote shareholder value.[12] This enabled chief executives in particular to achieve soaring rates of compensation when stock markets were rising. This method of compensation, which spread widely, was later blamed for excessive risk taking and an excessive fixation on stock prices among executives.[13]

The Harvard Business School thus became, paradoxically in view of Dean Wallace B. Donham's earlier advocacy of business responsibility, an influential disseminator of an ethically hollowed-out vision of shareholder capitalism, promoting hubris and narrow thinking in management. Many of its own well-compensated faculty grew wealthy, if ethically compromised, from consultancy fees and directorships advocating these ideas.

The shareholder maximization paradigm eventually became the new normal in management education generally, representing a major break from the past. This has only begun to change in recent years. "Virtually every MBA course," the Said Business School corporate finance expert Colin Mayer observes in *Prosperity: Better*

Business Makes the Greater Good (2018), "begins from the premise that the purpose of business is to maximize shareholder value."[14]

This is not the place to offer a full assessment of the impact of the shareholder value maximization paradigm. Suffice it to say that there was mounting evidence that it had, at best, unintended consequences. Executives were incentivized to deliver value for shareholders by being given stock options. This in turn became a driver of huge share buybacks, whose primary purpose was to drive up share prices, by US corporations. Frequently these buybacks came at the cost of innovation, and they were rarely aligned with social purpose. The desire to maximize share prices drove a short-term focus on quarterly earnings by executives and was one factor behind corporate scandals such as Enron and WorldCom.[15] Part of the reason for the unintended consequences was that, as Joseph Bower and Lynn Paine argued in a forceful article published in 2017, Friedman misunderstood the role of shareholders. Shareholders own their shares, they maintained, but they are beneficiaries of a corporation's activities rather than controlling them. Directors are fiduciaries with a duty to act in the best interest of the corporation, which might be different from doing the bidding of shareholders. Moreover, shareholders are diverse, with different time horizons and attitudes toward risk.[16]

Critics readily identified the shareholder value maximization paradigm with wider issues of inequality and abuse of corporate influence. In *American Amnesia* (2016), Jacob S. Hacker and Paul Pierson describe how big business, especially Wall Street, used lobbying to advance a strategy of free markets and minimal government intervention, resulting in mounting social crises—which in their view can only be resolved by the restoration of an active role for the state.[17] Exxon and other oil companies deliberately promoted skepticism about climate science. Such organized and willful creation of ignorance has been termed agnotology.[18] Further evidence of selfish and irresponsible corporate behavior emerged from massive leaks of electronic data from offshore centers. The Panama Papers and the Paradise Papers revealed how affluent business figures hid their wealth in secretive offshore centers, and how many of the best-known corporations in the United States and elsewhere employed offshore financial centers to minimize their tax obligations.[19]

The view that the exclusive purpose of business was maximizing shareholder value seemed especially inadequate in the face of mounting concerns about the natural environment, which grew in intensity as the scientific evidence about climate change, water shortages, extinctions, and other challenges grew ever more compelling, and concerning. Profit-focused and uncaring firms were condemned as central actors in this unfolding catastrophe. Building on the concept of the Anthropocene—the argument that human activities have resulted in a new geological age—Jason Moore's *Capitalism in the Web of Life* (2015) promotes the concept of the capitalocene, or the direct responsibility of large corporations for the carbon emissions driving climate change.[20] Rob Nixon's *Slow Violence and the Environmentalism of the Poor* (2011) describes "the vulnerability of eco-systems treated as disposable" by capitalism.[21]

By the 2000s many large corporations displayed a new embrace of social and environmental sustainability. There were headline-grabbing initiatives. The Goldman Sachs 10,000 Women project, launched in 2008, sought to provide capital, mentoring opportunities, and management education to female entrepreneurs globally. Cynics noted that the timing of the project was just as the global financial crisis was seriously tarnishing the reputation of large financial firms, but individuals were undoubtedly given new opportunities. Many companies published extensive sustainability reports, which was an improvement over promoting agnotology. There was a limited push for system-wide change, however. Even as sustainability reports proliferated, companies continued to pursue strategies that contributed to climate change, the melting of the polar ice caps, the extinction of thousands of species, and much else. At worst, much corporate environmentalism amounted to greenwashing.[22] Many large US corporations that publicly committed to fighting climate change—and other causes such as reducing wealth disparities and racial inequalities—cynically donated large funds through trade associations to bodies that explicitly sought to oppose such outcomes.[23]

The new corporate embrace of sustainability rested in part on a sleight of hand. During the 1970s, growth and large corporate size were regularly identified as environmentally damaging.[24] However, in 1987, a United Nations commission known as the Brundtland Commission embraced the concept of "sustainable development." The inclusion of economic growth in the concept of sustainable development provided an entry ticket for large corporations to claim that growing their balance sheets was not incompatible with "sustainability." By the time of the United Nations Earth Summit in Rio de Janeiro in 1992, voluntary actions by corporations to achieve sustainability, rather than government policies, had emerged as the last best hope to save the planet. Yet the vagueness of the concept of sustainability also became one of the challenges faced by those in this chapter seeking to systematize business responsibility, as we shall see.[25]

By the 2010s, the perceived drawbacks of the Friedman doctrine of shareholder value maximization and agency had become so evident that leading business organizations like the Business Roundtable and prominent business leaders such as Larry Fink began to preach the virtues of stakeholder rather than shareholder capitalism. While most of the highly remunerated hedge fund, private equity, and investment managers continue to insist that their sole responsibility is to their shareholders and to the bottom line, a growing circle of voices is pushing back and seeking to offer alternative metrics to put a price on social and environmental responsibility.

The people behind the efforts to systematize responsibility whom we will meet and follow in this chapter share the concerns of the Business Roundtable. Many of them started warning about ecological and societal problems decades before it became fashionable to do so. They believed that Friedman's argument that the only purpose of firms was to maximize financial returns to owners was an impoverished vision for entities that operated, and held their license to operate, in societies facing large challenges, and on a planet undergoing ecological degradation. In contrast to Friedman, they saw the visible hand of greater ecological and social responsibility by firms as widening individual freedoms by addressing market failures. Their aim was to move beyond admonitions and to create alternative systems and norms to Friedman and shareholder value maximization. They wanted not to just call for more sustainability and responsibility, but to create institutional contexts that would encourage firms to pursue such strategies.

Pioneering ESG Investing

The most prominent push to incentivize social responsibility in business focused on the provision of capital. At some level, the guiding premise was a simple one. If investment decisions were driven solely on the basis of the high returns, and shorn of environmental, ethical, or social considerations, there was little hope for anything beyond dividends for shareholders and high salaries for executives. However, if flows of capital could be made to favor and reward companies that embraced socially and environmentally beneficial policies, the incentive structure could tip toward responsibility and sustainability rather than against them. This simple but galvanizing insight drove some of the most prominent initiatives to create a deeply responsible business system, focusing on the provision of capital. A confusing array of terms came to be used to describe such investment: ethical investing, socially responsible investing (SRI), impact investing, and—since the 2000s—environmental, social, and governance (ESG) investing.[26] Most of these describe the same phenomenon, and all face the same challenges: How realistic is it to believe that capital could develop a conscience? And if it did, would investors receive a decent return?

Ethical investing actually has a long history that can be traced back at least to the eighteenth century, when Protestant groups in Britain and North America—particularly Quakers and Methodists—avoided investing in "sin" stocks, whether involving alcohol or slavery. "Not made by slaves" became a catchphrase for a movement boycotting products indirectly financed by the slave trade, pushing consumers to use their pocketbooks to agitate for reform.[27] Over the next two centuries these and other religious groups followed in this tradition, while more secular consciences were aroused in the United States by opposition to the Vietnam War.

In 1968, a Boston-based pension fund responded to a request by a religious client and asked the young securities analyst Alice Tepper Marlin to compile a "peace portfolio" of firms with the least involvement in supplying the war in Vietnam. It turned out to be difficult to find such information, but when she did complete the report, over six hundred other church and community groups asked for the information. The following year Tepper Marlin founded the nonprofit Council on Economic Priorities, and she served as its president for the next thirty-three years. The new organization began by publishing information on corporate involvement in supporting the Vietnam War and their environmental policies, but as later ESG investors would discover, it was no easy matter to define "good" and "bad" companies. This was seen as the council extended its reach to promoting ethical consumption, especially with its best-selling *Shopping for a Better World,* first published in 1988, which sold eight hundred thousand copies in two years and passed through multiple additions. The twenty-four top-rated consumer products companies in the 1991 edition included values-driven companies such as Aveda, Ben & Jerry's, and Tom's of Maine, although not The Body Shop, which was not ranked highly either for giving to charity or for information disclosure. However, the list of top companies also included large corporations like Avon, Colgate Palmolive, Procter & Gamble, and Quaker Oats, which were listed for disparate criteria, including reducing waste and emissions, employing solar energy, the provision of parental leave, and number of female vice presidents.[28]

New experiments in social investing were launched in the 1970s. In 1971 two United Methodist ministers launched the Pax World Fund, the first broadly diversified and publicly available mutual fund to use ethical as well as financial screens in its investment decisions. It screened out war-related investments but also sought out companies in industries deemed life-enhancing such as food, housing, and health care. A decade later, the fund's assets had only reached $11 million. The same slow growth could be found in ethical funds established by conventional investment firms such as Dreyfus's Third Century Fund and Calvert Investment's Calvert Social Investment Fund.[29]

It was during the 1980s that a number of women who broke into the all-male investment world in Boston became instrumental in scaling ethical investment beyond the niche. Joan Bavaria, a dropout from a college of art and the divorced mother of two when she secured a job as a secretary at the Bank of Boston, was the single most important figure in this movement. She was, unusually, promoted quickly to investment manager, a position where she encountered wealthy female clients who expressed concerns that their money should be used in a positive way. Her interest in responsible investing developed incrementally, shaped by the questions raised by some of her clients.[30] It is likely that her unconventional early career in a still very male-dominated industry, and her training as an artist, encouraged a willingness to experiment and to look beyond returns at social impact.

Bavaria moved in 1975 to Franklin Management and married its founder. At Franklin, she came across more clients who wanted to invest in firms doing positive rather than negative things for society. She began to screen out companies in her portfolios that had negative environmental impacts, sold alcohol or tobacco, or invested in apartheid-era South Africa. A separate subsidiary was formed inside the investment house in 1982 and spun off as Franklin Research and Development Corporation (FRDC), a cooperative owned by its employees. As a majority woman-owned firm, FRDC was unlike any other private investment firm at the time. By 1988 it had $162 million ($350 million in 2021 dollars) in assets under management.[31] It was renamed Trillium Asset Management in 1999 and remained an independent company until it was acquired by Australia's Perpetual Limited in 2020, eight years after Bavaria's death.

Bavaria did a lot more than invest. Unlike previous socially responsible investors, she met with management teams to discuss ways that their companies could improve their practices and used proxy filings to voice FRDC's viewpoint. This became a hallmark of the company's strategy.[32] Her aim was not so much to transform capitalism as to incrementally make individual firms more responsible, one at a time. At a more systematic and potentially more scalable level, Bavaria also sought to formally measure and rank the social responsibility performance of companies in which she invested. FRDC used a combination of traditional financial analysis, research by nonprofits, and interviews with managers to rank companies that showed promising financial upsides and passed their screens for evaluating investments on seven issues. The seven issues were sensitivity to the environmental impact of the company's operations; quality and breadth of the company's employee relations; citizenship in the local and world communities; involvement in South Africa; efficient and safe use of energy, including no involvement with nuclear power; product and service quality; and social usefulness.[33]

FRDC published its ratings and invested in companies that it believed would deliver attractive financial and social returns in the long term. Bavaria saw no tension between the two types of returns. She believed that strong environmental and social policies would increase profitability. This assumption became an enduring belief behind ESG investing. It was the key to success in attracting funds, as investors were offered good financial returns in exchange for doing good. However, the approach provided a range of challenges and potential drawbacks. For one thing, financial performance was much easier to measure than performance on social and environmental impacts. As managers sought to deliver strong financial returns to their clients, there was an in-built tendency to prioritize financial returns over ill-defined social returns.

These challenges were less apparent in the earlier stages of FRDC, not least because Bavaria was personally engaged with the managements of firms in which she invested. She was able to grow her assets by serving a small but significant demographic wanting to do good with their money. Two-thirds of FRDC's investors were high-net-worth individuals, and the remainder were churches and small foundations.[34] As we saw in Chapter 8, Bavaria dropped The Body Shop from her portfolio when revelations surfaced about its suboptimal social performance.

Bavaria's solution to the challenge of benchmarking effective social and environmental responsibility was to build a community that would develop and share metrics. She moved early to build relationships with other like-minded investment houses, including Pax World and Calvert. By 1985 this group had evolved into a nonprofit trade association named the Social Investment Forum (later US SIF), which built a network of investors dedicated to socially and environmentally responsible investing. It began to develop a set of principles for corporate conduct on the environment, inspired by the Sullivan Principles, a code of conduct established by Bishop Leon Sullivan, who sat on the board of General Motors, to guide investment in South Africa.[35] In March 1989 a huge oil spill in Alaskan waters from the tanker *Exxon Valdez* served as a catalyst for elevating these efforts. The spill energized the discussions about how to improve the environmental practices of big business.[36] SIF wrote the Valdez Principles (subsequently renamed the Ceres Principles) to catalyze the release of standardized information on environmental performance, designed to operate along the lines of the Financial Accounting Standards Board in the United States.[37]

Bavaria formed the nonprofit Ceres (Coalition for Environmentally Responsible Economies) to manage the Ceres Principles. While SIF focused solely on investors, Ceres sought to gather investors, environmental organizations, and public interest groups to persuade companies to adopt and practice the Ceres Principles. Signatories paid an upfront fee and an annual administrative fee for the cost of monitoring and verification of compliance. Ceres began as a fragile affair, lacking its own budget and operating out of the FRDC office. During the first two years only twenty companies became signatories, including Aveda and Ben & Jerry's. In 1993 Sunoco, an oil refiner, became the first Fortune 500 company to endorse the Ceres Principles. It remained the only oil company signatory as of 2022.[38]

In 1996 Bavaria recruited Bob Massie, an Episcopal priest, Democratic politician, and social justice campaigner, as president of Ceres. Massie got straight to work developing a set of environmental and social reporting standards. The following year, he launched the Global Reporting Initiative (GRI) in alliance with Allen White of the Tellus Institute in Boston, which provided consulting services to Ceres. In 2000 GRI launched its first set of guidelines, which provided the first global framework for sustainability reporting. Following John Elkington's development of the triple bottom line concept, of which, as we saw earlier, The Body Shop was an early adopter, GRI enabled companies to report the economic, social, and environmental impact of their activities. The guidelines provided a set of reporting principles and a recommended reporting format and content. They were modified on a regular basis.[39] A growing number of stakeholders, including large companies, labor, nongovernmental organizations (NGOs), and investors, became engaged in the process of testing, feedback, and consultation. This process was seen as crucial to creating a community of stakeholders invested in GRI.[40]

In 2002, Ceres spun GRI off as an independent entity and, in recognition that European companies were more receptive to the concepts of SRI than their American counterparts, it was organized as a nonprofit based in the Netherlands. By 2008, over 1,500 companies around the world had adopted its reporting standard, although less than 20 percent of the companies were based in the United States, and most were larger publicly traded companies. The foundational idea was that GRI offered a voluntary and more inclusive alternative to government regulation that would serve the goals of all the stakeholders.[41] The downsides of this approach became evident over time. There was limited quality control over the voluntary and selective disclosure of information. The multistakeholder approach lacked an overarching framework of what constituted sustainability, or rather it was assumed than any mention of economic, social, and environmental impact provided proof of such sustainability.[42]

Bavaria was a remarkable creator and promoter of organizations designed to systematize and measure corporate responsibility. Strikingly, she was only one of a cohort of women who laid the basis for ESG investing. A Massachusetts activist who protested the Vietnam War in her high school years, Amy Domini had an unconventional start to her career: she dropped out of a teaching training college and eventually took a job as a photocopy clerk at Tucker Anthony, a stock brokerage firm where her grandfather worked. After rising to become the secretary to the secretary of the CEO, she asked to be trained as a broker and became, in 1975, the only female stockbroker at the firm.[43]

In 1978, Domini faced an ethical dilemma. A research analyst at Tucker Anthony recommended she and her colleagues buy the stock of a military contractor. According to the analyst, the firm, which employed former government officials, was slated to win a big government contract after engaging in lobbying efforts. After writing down a list of clients to call, Domini paused. Years later, she remembered thinking to herself, "Amy, how far have you fallen? How far had I fallen that I might consider calling people I was fond of and urging them to make an investment in a killing machine, a company that had essentially bought its way, or bribed its way, into a contract?"[44]

She decided not to call her clients. Instead, she began to pursue what she called "ethical investing." Although she was unable to find a comprehensive source of information about corporate social and environmental activities, she conducted her own research on the ethical impacts of various companies and developed ideas about how one could go about investing responsibly. Like Bavaria, Domini had clients who wanted their money used in a more responsible fashion.[45]

After she signed up to teach a course on ethical investing at an adult education institution, an editor got in touch with her to ask whether she would be interested in writing a book on the subject. *Ethical Investing,* which she wrote with the assistance of her then-husband Peter Kinder, came out in 1984. The book was dedicated to Bavaria—Domini would go on to work at FRDC between 1985 and 1987—and shared most of her beliefs. The preface outlined three assumptions. First, that "every investment" had an "ethical dimension." Second, that "ethical standards" had to be applied to "potential investments." Third, that "investors who apply their ethical criteria to investments are more successful than those that do not."[46] As in Bavaria's case, this third point was an assumption that rested more on hope than on evidence.

As an active Episcopalian, Domini was guided by her faith and religious beliefs. While accepting an honorary degree at Yale Divinity School in 2007, she articulated these beliefs. "For me," she told the assembled audience, "finance and capitalism are not exempt from God's will." She added that she "found that when I let my 'Jesus time' out of the Sunday morning box and into my career, I became a powerful force for good."[47] Domini saw ethical investing as a way of promoting universal human dignity. She noted in one interview, "The goal of socially responsible investing had, for me, morphed into being a way to use finance to ensure human dignity."[48]

While working at Loring, Wolcott & Coolidge, a financial planning house, after 1987, Domini began to feel that "a research product that was designed for all of us who had more or less the same standards in place could be of value to the entire industry."[49] This led to a decision to open her own ethical investing firm. Along with Kinder and researcher Steven Lydenberg, she cofounded KLD Research & Analytics. At first, the firm operated in the back of Domini and Kinder's home.[50] As Lydenberg later observed, KLD's vision was to "mainstream social investing, to provide enough data for the traditional investment community to make good decisions."[51]

In 1990, KLD launched the Domini 400 Social Index (DSI), a portfolio of companies identified as socially responsible using proprietary screening criteria. The DSI included approximately 257 companies from the Standard & Poor's 500 Index, 100 other large- and mid-capitalization companies selected to diversify the sector representation in the DSI, and 40 smaller companies that were chosen for "superior social responsibility records." Companies had to demonstrate potential for strong financial performance to be included. The DSI had five primary screens: any company engaged in military contracting, alcohol and tobacco, gambling, nuclear power, or South

Africa was excluded. In addition, there were five secondary screens: environmental performance, product quality and attitude toward consumers, corporate citizenship, employee relations, and support for women and minorities. The secondary screens were not purely exclusionary and involved "qualitative evaluations of what a company is doing to make society better and to preserve the environment."[52] KLD also encouraged shareholder activism through proxy voting, which became a tactic Domini employed throughout her career.[53] KLD provided an aggregate score for each company. Critics noted the screens were quite subjective—and they changed over time—while the informational value of aggregating disparate factors into a single number was not obvious.[54]

KLD garnered limited interest when it first attempted to license the index to large mutual fund companies.[55] To earn revenue, Domini established her own mutual fund in 1991, called the Domini Social Equity Fund, launched with a $600,000 investment from the retirement savings of an affluent colleague. Initial growth was slow, but the Domini Fund significantly outperformed the S&P 500 between 1995 and 1999. This was less proof that social responsibility pays, however, than a reflection of the fact that the screening criteria led to a portfolio of technology stocks that boomed at that time. After the dot-com crash in 2000, the Domini Fund fell sharply for three years, although on average during the first fourteen years of its existence the index tracked closely with the S&P 500.[56]

Screening decisions lacked transparency and resulted in unlikely firms being included in both the Domini Fund and the DSI. The former included major holdings of Coca-Cola and PepsiCo, whose contribution to the growth of obesity in the United States and elsewhere was much discussed, as well as Enron and WorldCom before they collapsed in accounting scandals. The inclusion of McDonald's in the DSI also attracted criticism. In 2003, the environmentalist and entrepreneur Paul Hawken waged a crusade against Domini for calling McDonald's fast-food business—"a company whose mission harms children and its workers," in Hawken's words—socially responsible. He pondered whether SRI was best seen as "a way for upper-class people to launder their money." Domini responded by arguing that McDonald's had made progress in reducing its solid waste output, promoting racial and gender diversity among middle- and upper-management positions, and being responsive to other social and environmental concerns. It therefore fell into the category of one of her "better" companies.[57] This pragmatic acceptance of imperfection was central to Domini's approach, as well as Bavaria's.

Women were prominent figures in the spread of SRI as it diffused internationally. In 1988 Tessa Tennant, who interned with Bavaria at FRDC, established Jupiter Ecology Fund, one of Britain's first environmental funds. She went on to cofound the Carbon Disclosure Project in 2002, which encouraged thousands of companies to disclose their carbon emissions, although critics noted that the quality of disclosure was uneven.[58] In Japan, Mizue Tsukushi, who had converted to Catholicism as a child and met Tennant at the Kyoto climate change conference in 1997, established the Good Bankers in 1998. In the following year she partnered with Nikko, the country's third-largest brokerage fund, to launch Asia's first SRI fund, the Nikko Eco Fund. It attracted an extraordinary 23 billion yen ($200 million) of funds in ten days, and 100 billion ($880 million) within four months, primarily from individual women and young people rather than traditional investors. But the momentum was subsequently lost because of stock market turbulence caused by the end of the dot-com boom. Eco funds fell out of favor, and it proved hard to regain momentum. The Nikko Eco Fund's net assets stood at 6.7 billion yen ($56.7 million) in March 2022.[59]

In 1995 the Swiss banker Reto Ringger, a rare man among the early pioneers, launched Sustainable Asset Management, which was built on the premise that more environmentally responsible firms were also likely to be more valuable over time. He partnered with Dow Jones, the American financial firm, to launch the Dow Jones Sustainability Index in 1999, and secured funding from Swiss Re, a leading reinsurance company, which was concerned about the growing risks caused by climate change and other environmental damage. A family of indexes was created over time.[60]

The involvement of conventional firms such as Nikko and Swiss Re in these indexes signaled the mainstreaming of SRI. New terms entered the vocabulary. The most important originated with the Global Compact initiative launched in 2000 by Kofi Annan, then secretary general of the United Nations. In 2004, he invited a group of large financial institutions to consider how to better integrate environmental, social, and corporate governance factors into asset management and other financial products and services. The resulting report, entitled *Who Cares Wins,* mainstreamed the language of ESG, which edged out the term SRI.[61] Corporations were invited to voluntarily align their strategies with the ESG goals of the Global Compact, an approach that—critics complained—provided ample opportunities for greenwashing and few incentives for meaningful change.[62]

Whatever the challenges, ESG investing grew to a size that was unimaginable when Bavaria started her journey. According to one Organisation for Economic Co-operation and Development report in 2020, the total assets under management that "incorporates some element of ESG review and decision-making" had reached $11 trillion in the United States and $17 trillion in Europe.[63] As the experience of the Nikko Eco Fund indicated, there was considerable caution in Japan about the category, and one estimate suggested that the country's sustainable investing assets were only around $474 billion in 2016. There was then a sudden surge to reach $2.8 trillion in 2020, which represented 24 percent of total managed assets in the country. The equivalent share in the United States was 33 percent.[64]

While the scale of ESG investing was clear, its impact was more debatable. It was no longer a form of activist investing, as it had been in the early days of Bavaria, and the extent to which it really encouraged managements to be more socially and environmentally responsible was unclear. The screening methodologies and ratings came under constant criticism, including for a lack of transparency. Reporting was erratic and inconsistent, and focused on activities rather than outcomes.[65]

Part of the problem was the bundling of diffuse components in the single concept of ESG. Hard metrics existed for environmental factors such as carbon emissions and waste generation, but plausible measurement of the S in the ESG equation seriously lagged. Many Western multinationals have supply chains in Asia and elsewhere riddled with human rights abuses, including forced and child labor, gender inequality, and repression of bargaining rights. These "social" impacts were largely ignored in ESG reporting. It was not until 2021 that GRI's Universal Standards asked companies to report if they allowed workers throughout their value chains to engage in collective bargaining.[66] Overall, the social impact of outsourcing decisions, whether on domestic employment or national security, was seldom mentioned in ESG reports.

ESG metrics often measured incremental changes, such as increased ethnic diversity at the board level or decreased water usage, but seldom graded firms on the extent to which they were working in countries whose governments committed serious human rights abuses and where the rule of law was weak. Although ratings are frequently lauded as providing warnings to management about potential risks, they are as a result notably inadequate at forewarning of major political risks. The exodus of several hundred leading Western companies from Russia after the invasion of Ukraine in February 2022 was a reminder of how many firms profited from a country whose government invaded neighbors, poisoned opponents, and repressed democracy. The ESG ratings of firms such as BP and Shell, Danone and Unilever, Henkel and Carlsberg, and others had been unaffected by their substantial investments in Russia. If they had been, they might have found themselves less exposed when a major geopolitical crisis struck. Meanwhile, the war itself raised serious issues regarding the boundaries of ESG investing. While the defense industry has traditionally not been included in the category of "sustainable," the conflict in Ukraine resulted in calls for armaments to be classified as sustainable, which would allow ESG investors to invest in defense companies who supported sovereign states against aggressive neighbors.[67]

Financial metrics were the most straightforward of all. "Any organization facing a conflict between its financial performance (most obviously performance affecting share price and dividends) and its social or environmental performance," one early critical study observed in 2002, "is bound to give preference to the financial in all but the most extreme cases."[68] Two decades later a study of "dual-purpose companies"—firms that pursued financial and social goals simultaneously—observed that financial demands were prioritized when trade-offs were apparent, and proposed that this tendency increased in countries in which there was a high acceptance of market liberalism and limited government intervention.[69] The portfolios of ESG funds were often disturbingly similar to those of conventional funds, reflecting the need to generate competitive financial returns. Meanwhile, a study of the use of ESG performance metrics for CEO compensation concluded that they were more likely to serve as a booster to executive pay than to serve broad stakeholder interests, in part because such metrics reflected only a narrow subset of stakeholders.[70]

A network of academics and management consultants emerged with the primary mission of showing that ESG investing was profitable investing. They encouraged win-win outcomes as an article of faith. A large number of metastudies were made on the relationship between ESG investing and financial performance, but a positive correlation between doing good and superior financial performance proved elusive.[71] In 2016, a widely cited study by Mozaffar Khan, George Serafeim, and Aaron Yoon appeared to demonstrate a substantial correlation between corporate sustainability and higher stock performance.[72] However subsequent research questioned the statistical methodology of this research and found no evidence that corporate sustainability measures could predict stock returns.[73]

The challenge of showing that doing good pays was made even more difficult by a proliferating number of metrics seeking to define what good was. GRI reporting was joined by the Carbon Disclosure Project, the Sustainability Accounting Standards Board, and other metrics. The seventeen Sustainable Development Goals launched by the United Nations in 2015 included broad economic, environmental, and social ambitions, with no consideration of the contradictions between them. The seventeen goals were in turn divided into 169 targets measured by 232 indicators.[74] In the last resort, ESG data was so varied and inconsistent that it was not a useful exercise to try to correlate it with anything.[75]

Bavaria's belief—shared by other pioneers of ESG investing—that companies could be incentivized to be more responsible by investors appeared to be a productive way of systematizing responsibility and reducing its dependence on visionary individuals. The combination of investment and shareholder activism has certainly raised the profile of environmental and social issues in corporate boardrooms. Yet as ESG investing scaled and became one financial product among many, the pressures to earn competitive financial returns resulted in responsibility being codified so broadly that the term lost meaning. At best, the scale of ESG funds has worked to expand management's attention from a narrow and short-term focus on maximizing shareholder value and alerted them to environmental and social risks they would not have identified on their own. And it mobilized investors to think more about the impact of where they are putting their money. At worst, ESG metrics amount to little more than the investment community's equivalent of fake news. Big business was provided with the credentials to claim it was an increasingly responsible guardian of a sustainable world, when in many cases it was not.[76] For critics like Cambridge University's Diane Coyle, who is skeptical that the business community is likely to police itself, absent government intervention, ESG reporting "reflects a vacuum in political leadership. To reach a zero-carbon economy," she reflects, "the state cannot count on businesses to voluntarily pare back profits."[77] "ESG," a cover of the *Economist* in July 2022 pessimistically proclaimed, "Three letters that won't save the planet."[78]

A more productive path for ESG investing might have been to make the explicit argument that lower financial returns were more often than not likely to be the short-term cost of pursuing major social and environmental responsibility. Anthroposophical social banks explicitly offered depositors lower interest rates for this very reason. This would have given investors an option to provide subsidized capital to support projects that a rational capital market would not, but that would benefit the environment and society as a whole. Such a strategy may not have attracted trillions of dollars, but at least the momentum to obfuscate the meaning of responsibility and sustainability could have been averted. More conceptually, the bundling together of E, S, and G was a misstep, as it assembled in one concept too many disparate factors measured in different ways. As it is, the jury remains out on whether ESG has the potential to make a real impact beyond attracting trillions of dollars of investor funds. For that to happen, data will have to be improved, benchmarks standardized, and ratings made more transparent. It remains to be seen whether that is still on offer, or whether the whole sector has become so irretrievably blighted by hype that it is an asset bubble in danger of doing more harm than good.

B Corporations: Remaking Capitalism?

A different approach to systematizing business responsibility began in 2006 with the foundation of a nonprofit organization called the B Lab (the B stands for beneficial), which sought to create a new type of company—B Corporations (or B Corps)—whose governance structure mandated them to consider performance based not only on finances but on the company's contribution to society and the natural environment. Like ESG investing, the rapid growth of B Corps attracted considerable attention among management academics, though less so beyond academia.[79] They were hailed by the Cornell (now University of Cambridge) management professor Christopher Marquis—in the words of the subtitle of his 2020 book *Better Business* on the subject—as "remaking capitalism."[80]

The three founders of the B Corp movement—Jay Coen Gilbert, Bart Houlahan, and Andrew Kassoy—met as students at Stanford University in the late 1980s. Coen Gilbert went on to cofound a basketball apparel brand called AND1 in 1993. He recruited

Houlahan, then working at an investment bank, as chief financial officer and subsequently president, and Kassoy was an early investor in the company. Within twelve years AND1 had reached $250 million in sales. It also developed a distinctive employee-centric culture and gave away 5 percent of its profits to charity annually. Growing competition led to the decision to take a private equity investor. Eventually AND1 was sold to American Sporting Goods, a large manufacturer of sporting footwear, in 2005. The firm's experiments in social responsibility were quickly discarded, and the brand was taken down-market, following the pattern of high-profile values-driven companies acquired by conventional firms explored in Chapter 8.[81]

As they watched the fate of AND1, Coen Gilbert, Houlahan, and Kassoy decided not to establish another such firm, but instead to create a new system in an effort to introduce normative institutional changes to capitalism. They focused on the alleged fiduciary duty of boards to maximize shareholder value. As we have seen, whether this was supported by corporate law is contested, but the triumph of the views of Milton Friedman and of agency theory did strengthen the widespread impression that there was a legal precedent for shareholder primacy and that there were legal problems centered, particularly, on the sale of companies. In 1986 the Supreme Court of Delaware, a state where many US companies are incorporated, issued an opinion in the case of the cosmetics company Revlon stating that firms were obliged to sell to the highest bidder. It was this ruling that Coen Gilbert, Houlahan, and Kassoy felt left them no choice but to sell AND1 to the highest bidder.[82] The three men came up with the idea of developing new corporate statutes for deliberately socially and environmentally responsible firms, combined with a certification system to assess their performance on these metrics. It was an explicit recognition that individual firms, however noble, needed an alternative system if they were to survive and not be swallowed up in due course by conventional behemoths interested in cool brands but not their associated values.[83]

The three men launched B Lab, the overarching organizational structure for the venture, in 2006. The founders were careful to position the initiative within existing networks of social businesses. They invited Mark Finser of RSF Social Finance to join the board. Finser had heard Coen Gilbert, Houlahan, and Kassoy pitching their ideas to potential investors, and thought it was "like Steiner downloading some organic threefold ideas." RSF provided funding, and promoted membership, once the new venture was underway.[84] Coen Gilbert, Houlahan, and Kassoy wrote a Declaration of Interdependence, which began, "We envision a global economy that uses business as a force for good." They envisaged that the new B Corps would be "purpose driven" and create "benefit for all stakeholders, not just shareholders."[85]

The corporate statutes that Coen Gilbert, Houlahan, and Kassoy developed for B Corps extended the concept of fiduciary responsibility to include environmental and social responsibility. They wanted this embedded in corporate law, so B Lab developed a model for a benefit corporation law, which they needed to get passed in every state in the United States because corporate law is governed at the state level. In 2010, Maryland became the first state to pass such legislation. The model public benefit law expanded the fiduciary duty of directors to multiple stakeholders, mandated firms to pursue a positive impact on society and the environment, and required the publication of reports on the societal impact of the firm. B Corps that were incorporated in states that passed such benefit legislation were required to become "benefit corporations" after they were certified.[86] By 2022, thirty-seven states had passed legislation recognizing benefit corporations.[87]

Within a year of its launch, B Lab also developed a certification standard for B Corps called B Impact Assessment, which evaluated a company's ESG performance.[88] Unlike certifications that applied to specific products or buildings, B Corp certification evaluated a business in its entirety. By the end of 2007, eighty-two B Corps were certified.[89]

To be certified, a company has to meet three requirements. It needs to score 80 points or higher (out of a possible 200) on the B Impact Assessment. It has to meet a legal requirement to consider all stakeholders (not just shareholders) when making decisions by adopting a corporate structure such as a B Corp. And it has to publish its B Impact Assessment score report summary. Nonprofits were not eligible to become certified B Corps, but other types of corporations, including cooperatives and limited liability companies, were. To complete the certification process, B Corps were required to pay a fee (scaled according to a company's annual revenue) and to sign the B Corp Declaration of Interdependence. The length of certification was initially two years, increased to three years in 2018, after which time the B Corp would need to complete another B Impact Assessment.[90] Certifications could, and did, lapse. Certification provided one-half of B Lab's revenues; the remainder came from philanthropic capital raised from foundations, corporations, government agencies, and individuals.[91]

The B Impact Assessments were rigorous, but even they had their limitations. It was impossible to deduce the impact of the firm from the various scores. Companies reported their own data rather than being audited by an independent organization. Once certified, however, every B Corp faces a 10 percent chance of being randomly chosen to undergo an on-site validation of their score.[92] Kassoy was quoted as saying that the overall goal was to "make good easy." The model spotlights "good companies" but does not address companies harming the environment or society.[93]

By the early 2020s, the B Corp movement was gaining attention, from management scholars such as Marquis and from the occasional European politician. In 2021 Ed Miliband, a former leader of the Labour Party in Britain, hailed B Corps as a model for reformed company law.[94] Yet the vast majority of the 5,000 certified B Corps in seventy-nine countries (as of May 2022) remain quite small businesses, and around one-half have revenues of less than $1 million. Many of the firms that have received certification were already well-established supporters of deep responsibility. This included companies featured earlier in this book. Trillium Asset Management became a certified B Corp in 2008. RSF Social Finance was organized as a nonprofit and therefore could not be certified, but in 2009 its wholly owned affiliate RSF Capital Management was certified. Patagonia became a B Corp in 2012, on the first day it was allowed under California law. Natura became a B Corp in 2014. Triodos Bank became a certified B Corp in April 2015, on the day when the B Corp movement launched in Europe. The certification process primarily encouraged already socially minded firms to further refine and develop their existing policies.[95] Anecdotal evidence suggests that certification did attract motivated younger employees eager to work for a firm that was addressing the world's ills rather than making them worse. However, a study of the organizational impact of B Corp certification found little evidence that social and environmental mission became more integrated with financial mission, and suggested that management tended to be more interested in legitimacy and reputation building when it chose B Corp status.[96]

Publicly traded companies tiptoed into the B Corps movement. After a flurry of initial public offerings in recent years, the number reached thirty at the start of 2022, ten of which were in the United States. These included the online insurer Lemonade; Vital Farms, the largest pasture-raised egg brand in the United States; and Warby Parker, a prescription glasses retailer. Elsewhere, publicly quoted B Corps included Natura in Brazil, the Australian financial services company Liberty Financial, Taiwan's financial service provider O-Bank, Spain's green energy supplier Holaluz, and Chile's Concha y Toro, one of the largest wine producers in the world.[97] The sudden growth of publicly traded B Corps was a noteworthy development, but the absolute numbers remained tiny as of yet.

A handful of B Corps were affiliates of large conventional multinationals. Swiss-based Nestlé, US-based Procter & Gamble, and Japan-based Kikkoman had at least one B certified subsidiary. Britain's Unilever and France's Danone had more. In 2012 Ben & Jerry's, owned by Unilever for over a decade, became a certified B Corp. Subsequently, Unilever made multiple purchases of small personal care and other companies that were certified B Corps, including Seventh Generation (US), Pukka Herbs (UK) and Mãe Terra (Brazil). By 2022 Unilever had nine subsidiaries with B certification, including five in the United States, two in Britain, and one each in Brazil and Australia.[98]

The food and beverage company Danone became even more engaged than Unilever. By 2022 Danone had twenty-three certified B Corps among its businesses, covering 50 percent of its total sales. The company had a track record in social responsibility. In 1972 the founder, Antoine Riboud, had shocked the French employers' association when he gave a speech saying business had a responsibility to assist social progress beyond "the factory gate or the office door." In 2020, Danone became the first listed company to become an Entreprise à Mission, a legal framework enabled by French legislation in the previous year that created a governance structure to oversee the progress of environmental and societal goals. This status was embedded in the company's Articles of Association. In 2021, when Danone's share price fell sharply because of the impact of COVID-19, US-based activist investor Artisan Partners led a campaign to persuade the board to remove the then chief executive, Emmanuel Faber, on the grounds that he was too focused on ESG and not paying sufficient attention to the interests of shareholders. It appeared that the firm's Entreprise à Mission status might constrain a radical revision of its previous social commitments, yet the incident did expose a more general problem facing B Corps.[99]

The Danone story was a reminder that power remained with the investors, who could change their minds. "In the worst case," Harvard Business School professor Rebecca Henderson observes in *Reimaging Capitalism in a World on Fire*, "ruthless investors can take control of the company by voting in a new board, give only lip-service to the creation of public benefit, and simply recreate a conventional firm."[100]

The founders of B Corps had little initial interest in expanding beyond the United States. But in 2012 four Latin American social entrepreneurs—María Emilia Correa, Juan Pablo Larenas, Gonzalo

Muñoz, and Pedro Tarak—traveled to New York with a proposal to take B Corps to their region. The meeting began stiffly, until Tarak asked each person to share how they were feeling and what their motivations were for being present at the meeting. As Correa later recalled, "I remember Jay [Coen Gilbert] and Andrew [Kassoy] looking like, 'What? Feelings?'" She continued, "And it was really beautiful, because we starting saying what motivated us. . . . In a couple of hours, we were the best friends ever."[101]

It was agreed that the B Impact Assessment and B Lab's other resources would be translated into Spanish and Portuguese, but the Latin Americans envisaged a bolder plan. They wanted, as Larenas later recalled, "to build a community which would change the rules of the game."[102] The ambition was to influence many different stakeholders, not only entrepreneurs, but also consumers, investors, academics, and policy makers. Engagement with policy makers was deemed essential because, as Correa put it, "public policies set the rules of the game for those engaged in society and the market."[103]

In March 2012, Sistema B launched foundations in Chile, Argentina, and Colombia. The name "Sistema" emphasized the systematic nature of the problem the founders sought to address. TriCiclos, a Chilean recycling company that Correa and Muñoz had jointly founded, was certified as the first B Corp, or Empresa B, as they were known in the region. Within the first four years of its operations, Sistema B certified over 230 Latin American B Corps, with over $3 billion in annual turnover.[104] As in the United States, the companies that signed up for certification had for the most part long-established reputations for social and ecological responsibility. An example was the Colombian-based restaurant company Crêpes & Waffles, which became a certified B Corp in 2016. Founded by two university students—Beatriz Fernández and Eduardo Macias—in 1980, the company grew as a prominent restaurant chain in Colombia and opened branches in neighboring countries and Spain. It became noteworthy for its progressive social policies, hiring women who often had minimal professional experience and offering private health insurance and housing loans. If employees experienced domestic violence, it offered to transfer them to other restaurant branches to allow them to leave their abusive partners.[105]

If the certification of firms such as Crêpes & Waffles could be seen as "making the good easy," the explicit commitment to system-wide impact was more ambitious. A system of low-cost workshops called B Multipliers was created to train people to spread the word about Sistema B. Participants included not only people from the business world but also teachers and students. By 2020 some two thousand people had been trained, making it possible for Sistema B to spread to other countries in the region.[106] Frustrated that universities in the region declined to include information about B Corps in their curricula, Sistema B launched the nonprofit organization Academia B, based in the United States, as a way of connecting teachers, researchers, and students to the broader B Corp movement. Academia B focused on producing educational tools because, as Correa noted, professors found that "most cases and books do not focus on Latin America" and they "largely deal with traditional companies and conventional issues."[107] Progress with policy makers was limited, although by 2021 three more countries—Ecuador, Peru, and Colombia—had passed benefit corporation legislation.[108]

Sistema B also took the initiative to expand the movement globally. It helped start B Lab Europe and launch B Lab Portugal and B Lab Lusophone Africa.[109] There were some initial tensions between Sistema B and the American founders, who thought the Latin Americans should focus on certification rather than engaging multiple stakeholders. The upshot was a reorganization of the entire movement in 2020. B Lab US became a local organization, and B Lab Global, now led by Larenas, was created to act as a truly global organization to pursue system-wide change. Larenas found that there were ten different mission statements for the seven organizations that made up B Lab Global, so his first priority was to develop a common vision. B Lab Global articulated a new statement of the kinds of change it sought: behavioral change, structural change (changing the rules of the game), and cultural change (shifting the narrative about business and societal expectations).[110] It was a bold vision aimed at achieving fundamental transformation of the prevailing economic system. Networks of B Corps in the same industry began to form. An example is the B Beauty Coalition, formed in 2022 and composed, initially, of thirty companies. The Body Shop and Weleda are among its members. The coalition aims to share information and research on how best to improve environmental and social impacts across the industry. Ingredient sourcing, packaging, and logistics were the starting focus.[111]

By May 2022, the five thousand B Corps collectively employed around four hundred thousand workers. Over half of B Corps were outside the United States and Canada, concentrated in Europe, Australia, and Latin America. Latin America alone had eight hundred certified B Corps, and the movement attracted a growing number of large-scale businesses. In 2021, Colombia's Juan Valdez Café became the first coffee chain in the world to become a certified B Corp. Owned by the National Federation of Coffee Growers, mostly small and medium producers, Juan Valdez Café buys its coffee from 540,000 suppliers in Colombia and operates a chain of coffee shops in that country and globally.[112]

In contrast, the movement had only a modest impact in Africa and Asia: there were still only 35 certified B Corps in mainland China (the first was in 2016) and a further 18 in Hong Kong and Macau, 34 in Taiwan, 20 in South Korea, 19 in Singapore, 12 in Japan, and 7 in India.[113] The relevance of B Corps in these countries was often little understood. In Japan, for example, there were long-established traditions about societal responsibility, making the cost in money and time of seeking B Lab certification, which had to be completed in English, seem redundant.[114] Certification had the potential to improve a company's reputation, which might yield advantages in countries with weak institutional structures and low levels of trust, but this would only be effective if consumers and others were aware of the B Corp movement.

Overall, the B Corp movement represents a significant new major endeavor to systematize deeply responsible business. Extending fiduciary responsibility to include social and environmental responsibility, and rigorous certification, reduced dependence on visionary founders. For critics of the system of market capitalism as a whole, though, B Corps represented little more than a Band-Aid. Anand Giridharadas, in his polemical book *Winners Take All: The Elite Charade of Changing the World,* has little but disdain for the movement. "A new breed of community-minded so-called B Corporations has been born," he commented tartly in 2018, "reflecting a faith that more enlightened corporate self-interest—rather than, say, public regulation—is the surest guarantor of the public welfare."[115] This is too harsh, not least because the movement does seek to influence public policy, for the better. Individual B Corps include a roll call of some of the most socially and ecologically responsible businesses in the world. Yet the movement is not immune to the problem of leadership transitions, and it remains far too small to change the world.

Focolare Spirituality and the Economy of Communion

The founders of ESG investing and the B Corp movement sought to build a system of deep responsibility based on institutions and metrics rather than virtue and spirituality. This opened up the potential for scaling, but it also removed certain guardrails against backsliding, hype, or worse. Anthroposophy offered an example of an informal system in which philosophical beliefs provided underlying guardrails. The Economy of Communion, created by an Italian social reformer in Brazil in 1991 and inspired by the beliefs and practices of the Roman Catholic Church, provides an example of a more formal effort to build a business community centered on the principles of charity, community, and redistribution.

Once again, there were historical antecedents. Catholic social teaching, led by papal encyclicals, had produced an accumulated body of recommendations for business practice since the nineteenth century. Pope Leo XIII's *Rerum Novarum,* issued in 1891, affirmed the rights of workers to receive wages that enabled them to live and sustain a family and to have trade unions. Subsequent encyclicals followed, including *Quadragesimo Anno* in 1931, which criticized unrestrained capitalism and insisted that fair wages be paid to workers; *Mater et Magistra* in 1961, which maintained that charity and not self-interest should drive economic decisions; and *Laborem Exercens* in 1981, calling for fair wages, benefits, and the right of association. In 1991, countering the doctrine of shareholder supremacy that had by now firmly taken hold in the United States and was rapidly spreading to Europe and elsewhere, Pope John Paul II's *Centesimus Annus* provided an explicit statement on the social purpose of business: "The purpose of a business firm is not simply to make a profit, but is to be found in its very existence as a community of persons who in various ways are endeavoring to satisfy their basic needs and who form a particular group at the service of the whole of society."[116]

It was this teaching that provided the motivation for Chiara Lubich to form the Economy of Communion at Araceli near São Paolo, Brazil, in 1991. Lubich sought to bring together entrepreneurs, workers, consumers, and other stakeholders to promote a new approach to business based on communion, charity, and reciprocity.

The endeavor was born out of the Focolare (meaning "hearth" in Italian) spiritual movement, which originated when Lubich and a group of friends ministered to the sick and wounded in Trent in wartime Italy. The imagery of the hearth was meant to convey intimacy and warmth. After the war ended, the local bishop gave his approval for the Focolare Movement to expand to other parts of Italy.[117] Focolare spread mostly by word of mouth. Its activities spanned politics, culture, publishing, and social services and religious formation. It encouraged spiritually infused economic practices such as the sharing of possessions. The movement was officially approved by the Catholic Church in 1962 and given the formal name Work of Mary. By 2022, it claimed that it had more than two million members in 182 countries. Organizationally, Focolore operated on three levels: there were individual houses located in major cities, consisting of five to eight people who had made a lifelong commitment to communal living; model towns; and a global center located near Rome.[118]

The Focolare Movement became particularly popular in Brazil. It was on a visit to São Paolo that Lubich observed the huge chasm between areas of great wealth and run-down shanty towns called favelas (slums). Galvanized by Pope John Paul II's *Centesimus Annus*, Lubich met with members of local communities to discuss how to alleviate poverty. From these conversations, the idea emerged of creating a new economic model to be called the Economy of Communion that would address this challenge.[119]

The central aim of the Economy of Communion was to use business as a mechanism to increase equality. People belonging to the Focolare Movement were invited to establish businesses, which would generate the resources needed to relieve poverty. Profits were to be divided three ways: one-third would be distributed to the poor; one-third reinvested in the business; and one-third used to create the infrastructure needed to promote a culture of giving, including houses and model towns. The businesses were privately owned, but the ownership of equity by people who shared Focolare ideals was encouraged, as there needed to be agreement to forgo dividends.[120]

Economy of Communion businesses were generally based in dedicated business parks in Focolare towns, providing jobs for these communities, as well as opportunities for collaboration between firms.[121] The first park, Sparaco, built near São Paolo in 1993, was funded by a new public limited company called ESPRI, which had 3,300 shareholders, mostly Focolare members in Brazil. ESPRI bought land and developed infrastructure and then rented out the properties to Economy of Communion businesses. Other parks followed in Italy, Argentina, Croatia, and Belgium.[122] Lubich was determined, like Steiner and the founders of Sistema B, to build an intellectual foundation for her movement. "It must become a scientific theory with the input of competent economists capable of outlining both theory and practice," she wrote in 2001, "comparing it with other economic systems, and giving rise not only to degree theses, but to schools from which many can learn."[123]

A decade later over 860 businesses, mostly small in size and primarily in Europe and Latin America, were part of the Economy of Communion.[124] Lubich died in 2008, but the movement continued to grow after her death. A number of investigations showed that

these were genuinely purposeful endeavors. This was not a movement of greenwashers.[125] Yet scaling proved a challenge, both because
much depended on an embrace of Focolare's distinct tenets based
on universal brotherhood and because of more practical challenges.
In Italy and Brazil, two countries where Focolare was particularly
active, many small businesses avoided paying taxes, which were
nominally very high. As tax evasion was unthinkable for a member
of the Economy of Communion, it is likely that many small firms
were reluctant to join the movement out of concern that they
would be rendered uncompetitive.[126] The informality of the Focolare
Movement, based on the idea of the intimate "hearth," also did
not translate smoothly into business practice. Over two-thirds of
Economy of Communion businesses surveyed for a study published
in 2004, thirteen years after the movement started, had yet to share
any profits.[127]

Lubich developed a market solution to social problems, but the
market did not naturally lend itself to redistribution, reciprocity,
and gifting.[128] Lubich sought to redefine the market as a place where
profits were not seen as an end to themselves but as a way to share
resources. The Economy of Communion was not a utopian exercise.
It collaborated with more secular proponents of business responsibility: there were close ties between the Economy of Communion and
Sistema B in Brazil, for instance.[129] A form of stakeholder capitalism
infused with spiritual values, it helped many people living in poverty
and offered a glimpse of how an alternative business system could be
built around sharing rather than the personal accumulation of wealth,
and love rather than greed.

Steward-Owned Companies

Individual firms committed to ecological and social responsibility
could find support through membership in the B Corp movement
or the Economy of Communion, but a change of ownership or a gen-
erational shift could spell the end of social commitments and send
a firm down another, profit-maximizing path. A solution to this

dilemma was steward ownership. Although a variety of legal structures exist under this broad umbrella, as will be shown below, the common underlying idea is of a company being "self-owned" and managed by stewards who have exclusive voting rights, but no economic rights in the company. The position is passed on to a next generation of stewards chosen for their skills and values. In such firms, profits are reinvested, spent in philanthropy, and sometimes used to reward investors, who hold no voting rights. Shareholders and investors can never dictate decisions and strategy in such a firm. In contrast to the mantra of Milton Friedman, the responsibility and purpose of a steward-owned company was not to maximize profits for its owners but to produce socially useful goods and services and to support society more generally. As voting rights can never be sold, the structure is permanent. A firm owned under these arrangements can never "go public" and abandon its purpose.

Although interest in steward ownership has risen sharply in recent years, the concept is not new. Robert Bosch concluded as far back as the early twentieth century that for his firm to remain committed to social responsibility, its ownership had to be reorganized in such a fashion that the social mission could not be changed. In Bosch's case, his heirs created such an organizational structure. The ten steward-owners of Robert Bosch Industrietreuhand control Robert Bosch Stiftung, which reinvests its dividends and supports extensive philanthropy. The arrangement has resulted in a successful, highly innovative, and deeply philanthropic business enterprise.

There are other historical examples of different forms of steward ownership, mostly in Europe. In 1888, the ownership of the German optical companies Carl Zeiss and Schott was placed in the Carl-Zeiss-Stiftung, a foundation whose constitution prohibited the sale of shares. The foundation supported these highly innovative companies noted for their social responsibility to employees, their contributions to their hometown of Jena, and their scientific research.[130]

In Britain, the John Lewis Partnership, founded in 1929 and now one of that country's largest retailers, employing around seventy-eight thousand people in 2022, was another example of steward ownership. In 1929 John Spedan Lewis, the son of the founder of the business, established the trust and partnership, which enabled him to control the business while distributing profits to employees. Thirty years later he gave his remaining shares to the trust, and the partnership became wholly owned by employees, who were termed "partners." Lewis explicitly sought to provide an alternative structure, believing that capitalism, as he wrote in 1948, was "so perverted and distorted as to produce the disastrously excessive inequalities that in our modern world are so gravely endangering the stability of society."[131] The partnership functioned as a democracy, with an elaborate system of checks and balances, and offered exceptional conditions for employees, including final-salary pensions and perks ranging from holiday homes to memberships in clubs.[132]

A more recent case of steward ownership is the internet pioneer Mozilla, which is ultimately owned by the nonprofit Mozilla Foundation. The foundation operates on the basis of ten principles. These include the following: "The internet is a global public resource that must remain open and accessible"; "Free and open source software promotes the development of the internet as a public resource"; and "Magnifying the public benefit aspects of the internet is an important goal, worthy of time, attention and commitment."[133]

Getting a steward-ownership organization right is no easy task. There are inherent tensions inside such organizations when it comes to who actually should make decisions. The original Carl-Zeiss-Stiftung was headed by a *Stiftungskommissar,* who was often linked to the ministry of higher education of the state government, leading to political interference in the running of the company. The tension became acute when a Nazi was appointed to the post in 1933 and, after initial resistance by managers, Jewish workers were removed from the company. Later, forced labor was used. It was only after the end of World War II that managers were able to extract themselves from the politicians.[134] At the John Lewis Partnership, there were tensions because although there was a considerable amount of participation by partners, senior management was not very accountable.[135] The company's retail sales were very adversely impacted by the COVID-19 pandemic, leading to store closures and redundancies, and prompting diversifications into real estate and financial services in endeavors to increase revenues.[136] Yet in the big picture each of these examples was successful in the marketplace over the long term, was noticeably innovative, and received plaudits for the treatment of employees and wider social contributions.

Steward-owned companies lack a common organization, but this has begun to change. In 2015 Achim and Adrian Hensen, identical twins, and Armin Steuernagel and Alexander Kühl, who met while studying economics at Oxford University, founded the Purpose Foundation in Hamburg, Germany, as a network to foster steward ownership. All four men were in their thirties.[137] They knew about Zeiss and Bosch, but Anthroposophy appears to have been a strong influence, if not a wholly dominant one. Steuernagel attended a Waldorf school, and at age sixteen he founded a mail-order company called Waldorfshop, which sold products used in Waldorf education.[138] "Purpose does not see itself as an anthroposophical institution," Kühl explained in 2020, "but its founders have anthroposophy at the back of their minds. Steiner says that just like intellectual property after a period of time (30–50 years) ownership of a company should become public."[139] Purpose was one of the partner institutions of the World Goetheanum Association, formed in Dornach in 2018 as part of a movement that "seeks, promotes and implements a new, comprehensive view of the human being." Fellow partners included familiar Anthroposophical companies such as the parent company of Ambootia, Demeter, GLS, RSF Social Finance, Sekem, and Weleda. Helmy Abouleish was a member of the association committee of the association.[140]

Purpose sought to generate know-how about steward ownership; provide hands-on support with legal, governance, and other matters; and assist with financing. Two funds were established that invest exclusively in steward-owned companies, Purpose Ventures and Purpose Evergreen Capital. By 2022, Purpose claimed to have assisted one hundred companies in moving toward steward ownership and to have provided $286 million in capital. It had advised companies in Australia, Brazil, Colombia, and Indonesia, although most of its work was in Europe.[141]

Like the founders of the B Corp movement, the founders of Purpose sought to secure changes in corporate law to facilitate their mission. In Germany it was organized, as in the case of Sekem Treuhand, as a gGmbH, a nonprofit whose purpose was to serve the common good. They also lobbied for a new legal corporate form—stewardship—which they termed *GmbH mit gebundenem Vermögen*, GmbH-gebV (company with tied assets).[142] This remained a contested idea, but it did receive support from members of the German coalition government formed in December 2021.[143] There was, as yet, little legislative interest in this idea beyond Germany.

In 2017 Purpose opened a branch in Berkeley, California, led by Camille Canon. As in the early stages of the B Corp movement, RSF Social Finance provided financial support and collaborated on projects in the United States.[144] US corporate laws facilitate some forms of employee ownership, but are less amenable to steward-ownership structures than European laws, but the Purpose Foundation discovered that an obscure section of trust law could be used to achieve the same end. Although trusts normally have human beneficiaries, it turned out that it was possible to create a "perpetual-purpose trust" to fulfill the same purpose. The foundation began by helping retiring owners of responsible businesses to transfer their ownership shares to perpetual-purpose trusts rather than selling their company to a firm that might abandon their policies.

The first case was the Oregon-based Organically Grown Company, the largest organic produce distributor in the Pacific Northwest, which was originally established as a nonprofit farmer cooperative and later became an employee-owned business. As the founders approached retirement, they became concerned that the company was an attractive take-over target and that the strong social policies they had pursued would be lost. In 2018, employing funds lent by Purpose Evergreen Capital and RSF Social Finance, shareholders were brought out and ownership passed to a perpetual-purpose trust. The new Sustainable Food and Agriculture Perpetual Purpose Trust was established in perpetuity. Its purpose was to "support the efforts of independent, values-aligned organizations that advance sustainable agriculture practices and food systems." Power was shared between three bodies. First, the corporate trustee was responsible for the prudent management of the trust. Second, the Trust Protection Committee served the role of steward and included employees, investors, and key customers. Finally, the trust enforcer was in charge of making sure the purposes of the trust were being pursued.[145] The company also became a B Corp in the same year.

The roles played by the Purpose Foundation, RSF Finance, and the B Lab in the Organically Grown Company's shift to a perpetual-purpose trust serve as an important reminder that the various strategies to systematize deeply responsible businesses have not proceeded in isolation. There is extensive collaboration and a real momentum to build alternative systems that could support and sustain the many individual entrepreneurs and business leaders who sought to make a positive social and environmental impact.

The momentum behind the stewardship concept was emphasized in 2022 when Yvon Chouinard, his wife, Malinda, and their children, Claire and Fletcher, transferred ownership of Patagonia, a certified B Corp since 2012 and whose sales had reached $1 billion per annum, to a specially designed trust and a nonprofit organization. The family irrevocably transferred Patagonia's voting stock, equivalent to 2 percent of the overall shares, to the Patagonia Purpose Trust, designed to preserve the company's values in perpetuity. The remaining 98 percent of Patagonia's shares were donated to the nonprofit Holdfast Collective, which would be the recipient of Patagonia's dividends after reinvestment in the business and is mandated to use the funds to combat climate change, although how policy decisions were to be made remains to be seen. "Earth is now our only shareholder," Chouinard declared in an open letter announcing the change.[146]

Collectively the thousands of B Corps, the firms in the Economy of Communion, and the firms organized under steward-owners represented an alternative, more ecologically and socially positive world than the narrow vision of capitalism offered by Friedman and his followers.

Most of the initiatives reviewed in this chapter remain a work in progress, even as environmental decay and social injustice proceed at pace. ESG investing has strong momentum in global financial markets, and it has raised the profile of environmental and societal impact in corporate boardrooms. But it rests on a bevy of metrics supplied on a voluntary basis that provide a path to greenwashing as much as to flourishing. Sistema B's recognition of the need to embrace other stakeholders, including policy makers, offers a promising demonstration of how business can act as a catalyst for positive change. Yet the B Corp movement, as fast growing as it is, is a niche in the business world as a whole. The steward-ownership movement offers the prospect of a radical reinvention of the laws of ownership to create corporate structures capable of building value for all stakeholders, but it is still in its infancy.

There is much to be pessimistic about in the third decade of the twenty-first century. Ecological devastation, social decay, wars, and refugees are everywhere apparent, even as the world of business is awash with exaggerated claims of being sustainable and responsible, supported by confusing or downright misleading metrics. But it is also possible to discern pathways to a future when deeply responsible business could become the norm. These alternative business systems are not threats to freedom, in Friedman's characterization, but rather enablers of greater freedom through their willingness to address market failures. It is clear, given the long history of endeavors to create such businesses, that considerable obstacles will have to be overcome to change the role of business in society. New ways of thinking, new structures, and new incentives will have to be developed alongside new forms of business enterprise. I hope this book can take its place as one of the forces inspiring and suggesting such a change.

CONCLUSION

BUSINESS AND A BETTER FUTURE

Contemporary denunciations of capitalism as a system always incompatible with social purpose are deeply ahistorical. Adam Smith, the allegorical founder of capitalism, believed that markets would only deliver socially productive outcomes if participants were guided by ethical considerations. As we delved into the history of deep responsibility, we saw many examples of business leaders across time and space who combined making profits and pursuing positive social impact. German business in the late nineteenth century may have been paternalistic, but many of these companies invested considerable resources in caring for employees, as did some of their British and American counterparts, like George Cadbury and Edward Filene. J. N. Tata and Shibusawa Eiichi embraced ethical behavior and positive social impact as central to their businesses. In the 1920s, the dean of the Harvard Business School, Wallace Donham, implored American business leaders to follow a form of stakeholder capitalism. By the postwar decades the concept of corporate social responsibility was so mainstream in American big business that Theodore Levitt and Milton Friedman were provoked to rail against it. The era of shareholder primacy ushered in by Friedman, William Meckling, and Michael Jensen in the 1970s is more of an aberration than a norm in the long history of capitalism. Unfortunately, that does not make it any less persistent.

History shows that capitalism has always featured a diversity of business types. Each generation has seen some profoundly irresponsible business leaders and their companies—whether deliberate fraudsters, despoilers of the natural environment, or unscrupulous

342

opportunists. These firms have coexisted with what can be described as "regular" companies—the great majority of firms—that make profits lawfully and honestly. Most of them probably undertook at least small acts of charity, for example to sick employees or their local communities. This category includes the many who adopted the mantra of shareholder value maximization in more recent years. This commitment to lawful business practices does not mean that the individual actions of these firms have not collectively yielded negative ecological and social outcomes. The externalization of ecological and social costs, fully sanctified by laws and accounting conventions, lies at the heart of today's environmental and social problems, which is one reason why many look to government and regulation to solve the problems.

A third and much smaller cohort of business leaders, the ones examined in this book, pursued profit alongside deep social purpose. They didn't aim to reserve a small share of their profits for good causes or to bolster their corporate images with vacuous announcements that they had a "purpose." Rather, they perceived their roles as being to radically improve their societies, whether by confronting inequality, nation-building in an equitable fashion, or campaigning for policy changes. Although these deeply responsible business leaders were never typical of their times, they were not marginal figures either. They created substantial businesses, many of which remain active today, and contributed positively to their communities and societies beyond their firms. This is not a book about eccentrics or utopians.

The stories told here provide rich and nuanced evidence of what a deeply responsible business leader has looked like at different times. I have identified three consistent practices across different time periods and cultures that are reflected in the leaders profiled in these pages.

The first shared practice is that they created and sold products and services that were genuinely socially useful. George Cadbury wanted to avoid anything to do with war and to provide a desirable alternative to alcohol in the form of drinking chocolate. Edward

Filene saw virtue in mass retail because he believed low prices (and good wages) were an important means of reducing inequality. Kasturbhai Lalbhai followed his Jain beliefs and avoided any industry that harmed life—even microorganisms. He believed that independent India needed its own chemicals industry, and he structured his business so as to reduce rural unemployment. Anthroposophical businesses, whether Aarstiderne in Denmark or Sekem in Egypt, focused on environmental and social sustainability and saw the construction of flourishing communities as their reason for existing.

The underlying and essential insight is that all businesses are not created equal—something that environmental, social, and governance (ESG) investing in its most expansive form sometimes neglects as it seeks profitable returns. "Sinful" industries are partly in the eye of the beholder—not everyone shares Cadbury's and Lalbhai's view that alcohol deserves to be on the blacklist—but it is inconceivable for businesses engaged in some industries, such as gambling, tobacco, and junk food, to ever be regarded as responsible. There are many less clear-cut cases, such as developers of violent computer games for children and marketers of cosmetics to preteen girls, whose leaders would benefit from greater reflection on their social impact. The manufacturing of armaments has typically not been considered as an ESG investment, but should this be the case when those armaments are used to defend a sovereign nation such as Ukraine under unjustified attack from an autocracy? The boundaries of what industry is responsible and what is not are hard to define, and their determination rests on value judgments. Still, all business leaders need to ask themselves whether their products and services help or harm their societies.

A second practice shared by all deeply responsible business leaders is that they interact with other stakeholders with respect and humility. This involves a recognition that firms are social institutions that exist within a society and not apart from it. From this insight flows a sense of responsibility toward employees, suppliers, customers, and the natural environment. A belief in the primacy of shareholders is not socially responsible. That said, the stories told here show that a socially productive stakeholder approach is neither easy nor straightforward. Strategies to provide benefits to employees—from better wages to subsidized housing and health care—can be seen as self-interested and are often rife with paternalism. There are other complications, too. Filene encountered resistance from workers who did not want to be stakeholders—at least not on his terms. A firm has many stakeholders, and this raises the question of whether some should take a priority over others. Lalbhai prioritized supporting India's struggle for independence, building his country's industrial capacity, and creating the cultural and educational infrastructure of Ahmedabad over the wages and rights of his workers. The pros and cons of particular choices can be debated, but what is undoubtable is that choosing how to prioritize between stakeholders raises complex ethical and economic issues, which make it a more difficult terrain than simply pursuing shareholder primacy.

Many of the business leaders profiled in this book expressed humility when dealing with other stakeholders, recognizing that solving societal problems must be a collective endeavor. Some acknowledged that, whatever their own contribution and achievements, government policies were essential for shifting the rules of the game. Cadbury, Filene, Lalbhai, Sanjay Bansal, the founders of Sistema B, and others exercised corporate political responsibility when they lobbied governments for more socially and ecologically sustainable policies and regulations. This was the opposite of the corporate political irresponsibility that runs rampant in capitals around the world today, where companies lobby for policies favorable to them.

The third practice of deeply responsible businesses is to believe in the importance of community and to hold that business has a role to play in contributing to its vitality. Affecting a single city might be less glamorous than "reimagining" capitalism, but it can greatly enhance the lives of generations of people. Examples include the work of Cadbury and Lalbhai in Bournville and Ahmedabad, respectively; Shibusawa's garden city of Denenchofu; An Wang's renewal of Lowell; the business parks in Focolare towns; and the extraordinary Sekem community created by Ibrahim and Helmy Abouleish.

The provision of employment is only one aspect of community-building. Investments in educational and cultural facilities made these communities better places to live. In some cases, including Bournville, Denenchofu, and Ahmedabad, great attention was given to green spaces and the physical design of the site. As we bear witness to the decimation of communities today, we can find solace in the fact that history shows how deeply responsible business leaders can be agents of community renewal with long-lasting consequences.

The stories in this book are all anchored in time and place, but many of the aspirations of the business leaders profiled are being replicated by a new generation of entrepreneurs today who are active in the B Corp movement and ESG investing. Combining profit and social purpose is possible and worthwhile, and it is not necessary to be a saint to pursue this path. There have been plenty of warts and trade-offs on display. Paternalism and ego-driven behavior were common. Filene's character seems to have undermined his plans to share power and wealth with his employees, and Robert Bosch may have despised the Nazis and shielded Jews, but he was a major supplier to the German war machine. Shibusawa believed in social purpose and the common good, but he also had a major blind spot when it came to Japanese militarism in Asia. Donham was too cautious, or perhaps he lacked the courage, to secure most of his desired curricular changes. Anita Roddick's desire to tell a good story and grow her business quickly led her to turn hype into hyperbole and to acquiesce to business practices she claimed to abjure.

But imperfections should not blind us to these entrepreneurs' genuine pursuit of social purpose and their real achievements. Friedman argued that to believe businesses should pursue social responsibility represented a threat to free societies, primarily because it subverted market mechanisms. It was an argument developed in the context of the perceived threat from Soviet-style socialism, which has long since passed, to be replaced by other threats ranging from environmental catastrophe to posttruth societies and new forms of geopolitical rivalries. The shareholder value maximization paradigm limits freedoms rather than protecting them. Providing consumers with socially useful goods and services, offering employees generous bene-fits, building communities, creating cultural and educational infra-structures, seeking to reverse environmental degradation—these are acts that offer individuals freedoms that market mechanisms fail to provide. The visible hands of deeply responsible leaders were cre-ators of new freedoms rather than harbingers of coercive socialism.

The Enduring Values of Deeply Responsible Business Leaders

The business leaders featured in this book shared common charac-teristics despite the different contexts in which they operated. They were guided by strongly held values that shaped how they viewed the world and their careers, companies, and public lives. While they were not without flaws, they were virtuous, and the principles of honesty and fairness guided their actions. Many were also guided by their spiritual beliefs. They perceived that there was more to life than making money and accumulating possessions. They did not conceive of firms as self-contained boxes remote from the societies in which they were based. Nor did they dismiss bad ecological and social impacts as externalities. Their profit and loss accounts, broadly construed, included ecological and societal returns as well as finan-cial ones.

The paths to these values and beliefs were varied and were some-times shaped by religion. The formally religious in this book included Cadbury, Tata, Lalbhai, George Romney, Tom Chappell, the Abou-leishes, Bansal, and Chiara Lubich. The diversity of their faiths—Quaker, Zoroastrian, Jain, Mormon, Episcopalian, Muslim, Hindu, and Catholic—demonstrates that faith and its attendant values, rather than any particular religion, was key. Others embraced a more philo-sophical or abstract system of beliefs, whether Confucian, Anthro-posophist, or something else. Donham spent his Saturday afternoons with the philosopher Alfred North Whitehead. Others, including Robert Owen, Bosch, Roddick, Joan Bavaria, Yvon Chouinard, and the founders of the B Corp movement, came to their views of the in-terconnectedness of life intuitively or through their life experiences.

However it arose, this belief in our fundamental interconnectedness was an important motivator for deep responsibility. It encouraged efforts to find solutions in collaboration with others, as well as experimentation with radical new ways of doing things. And it promoted genuine moral commitments.

Their values encouraged these deeply responsible entrepreneurs to see financial profits as a means to an end, not the end itself. The end was to build a business whose resources and innovations contributed to building a more flourishing future society. Once growth and profits become ends in themselves, as Chouinard of Patagonia and others noted, a business ceases to be socially responsible. Most of the business leaders seen here built substantial businesses, but scaling businesses without losing values is a perilous endeavor, as the case of Roddick, among others, demonstrated. Intergenerational family businesses, like those of Lalbhai and Tata in India, emerged as particularly robust in retaining social values even as they scaled.

Practical wisdom turned values into concrete actions. This involved a careful calibration between beliefs that should be personally held and ones that should guide business practice. Cadbury knew better than to impose his pacifist views on his employees during World War I, but his commitment to alleviating poverty and challenging inequality led him to build a model village and lobby for old-age pensions. Shibusawa was able to influence hundreds of companies by carefully managing his obligations to each and ceding the spotlight to others. Lalbhai was deeply committed to India's freedom and development as an independent nation, and he deliberately chose not to exploit his ties to benefit his company or his family. It was often an absence of practical wisdom that turned noble ideas into failures. Filene was unable to convince his own employees of his vision for industrial democracy. William Norris misjudged the complexities of making computerized education an effective tool to improve the learning trajectories of inner-city children, not least by misunderstanding the full potential of the PLATO software system. The businesses of Wang and Bansal eventually suffered due to poor decisions in the face of changing circumstances.

348

Donham believed that if he could insert ethical values into the curriculum of the Harvard Business School's MBA program, then the next generation of professional managers would exercise "increased responsibility," but this belief probably rested on a flawed understanding of what could be taught, and what could not be taught, at a business school. Neither his students nor most of his faculty showed much interest in learning new values, even at a time when Franklin D. Roosevelt's New Deal was transforming American society. Donham's own institution drew from a preselected population of men in their late twenties and faculty who wanted to make money rather than think philosophically. The same is true of most business schools today. Fundamental ethical values, sometimes described using the amorphous phrase "moral compass," are generally formed early in life, frequently within families or in early schooling. This was precisely the insight, a century ago, of Rudolf Steiner, the founder of the Waldorf school movement. There is much work to be done in K–12 school systems in many parts of the world today to move away from narrow specialization and testing of technical skills toward more holistic pedagogies resting on strong ethical foundations.

Yet business schools do have an important role in teaching practical wisdom. Although courses on social enterprise, business and society, and business and the environment are proliferating in management education, they are still often built around core courses in finance, strategy, and other topics, which still largely reflect the assumptions of the shareholder value paradigm. Going forward, ecological and social responsibility needs to be integrated into every course, rather than being treated as worthy add-ons. Business schools diffused the shareholder value paradigm, and they now need to research and teach more productive ways of motivating business enterprises. This will not be an easy transition to achieve given that the fixed assets of business schools are tenured faculty prone to hold theories and assumptions in vogue in the past when they were building their own careers. It will require pressure from a new generation of students more attuned by the ecological and social crises of their era to question and dispute the narrow vision of shareholder value maximization. Meanwhile, Donham's belief that exposure to history and philosophy can help train the mind and hone the decision-making ability of future business leaders remains a compelling insight because of the potential to provide students with far more context with which to make decisions. By showing the transformative social impacts of responsible businesses, and counterexamples of irresponsible businesses, history provides students today with the opportunity to avoid pitfalls and learn from compelling role models of the past.

Making Deeply Responsible Business the Norm

If the evidence in this book belies the contention that social purpose and capitalism are incompatible, the fact remains that deeply responsible businesses have never been the norm. Good role models have never attracted enough emulators regardless of time period and geography. The most straightforward reason for this is that deeply responsible business practices are financially expensive. The internalization of ecological and social costs that are conventionally and legally treated as externalities is costly in time and resources, and it puts deeply responsible businesses at a competitive disadvantage compared with conventional firms.

That said, there are commercial benefits of having a reputation for ethical and responsible conduct, although these are hard to measure. The virtuous practices of companies like Patagonia, Sekem, and Natura attract customers to the brand, enabling them to buy some virtue along with the product. In many instances, though, consumer willingness to pay for social and ecological responsibility remains limited even as, for example, relentlessly pessimistic reports mount up about climate change and other environmental challenges. Welfare spending and housing have increased the loyalty of the workforces, whether they were factory workers in Bournville and Stuttgart or organic farmers in Egypt, and improved their engagement and personal sense of pride. More generally, employees are more likely to work with passion for a firm whose values they support and believe in, leading to more commitment and creativity.

Still, decades of research on ESG investing has failed to come up with robust evidence that more responsible firms will constantly deliver better financial returns than conventional firms. Bavaria, Amy Domini, and other pioneers of ESG investing were almost certainly overoptimistic in this respect, but the bundling of quite disparate factors under the umbrella description of "ESG" has not been helpful in trying to measure results, financial or otherwise. If the rewards of deep responsibility were higher profits, market forces and herd behavior would have encouraged many other firms to follow suit. But even if it may be wishful thinking to imagine that environmentally and socially responsible practices would lead to higher financial returns, these guiding values may prevent companies from falling prey to a form of short-termism that seeks to drive dividends and share prices at the expense of the long-term health of the firm, let alone society.

Having a reputation for deep responsibility could sometimes be a double-edged sword. Cadbury won his libel case against the newspaper that accused him of supporting slavery in Portuguese-colonized Africa, but he received only derisory damages because it was expected that his firm would behave with the highest morality. When Control Data Corporation experienced difficult conditions, Norris's social programs were used to push him out of the company. Roddick's high-profile campaigning and ambitious claims about The Body Shop's social contributions set her up to be taken down by an investigative journalist. If one benchmarks a company against high moral standards, it is easy to find flaws.

The wave of globalization that has accompanied liberalization and deregulation since the 1980s has been a fair-weather friend to deep responsibility. It has been particularly successful at diffusing globally the rhetoric of sustainability and responsibility legitimized by certification schemes, sustainability reports, and ESG investing. This has raised awareness of environmental and other challenges, but it has also provided corporations everywhere the tools to alleviate the consciences of investors and consumers while continuing to put profits ahead of social purpose. Meanwhile, the spread of greenwashing and other forms of exaggerated corporate rhetoric has made it harder to identify good companies and thus to earn any real reputational premium. The practical consequences of globalization have served to raise barriers to responsibility. Large corporations have become unanchored from specific communities and even nations in new ways. It has become easier to downsize and offshore operations, and to pass revenues through tax-avoiding offshore financial centers. Corporate decisions are made in response to global capital flows, driven by financial institutions such as pension funds, and based on the advice of management consultants. Unfettered global capitalism in the era of shareholder primacy was much better designed to achieve efficiencies in capital allocation than the flourishing of human society.

Context matters greatly. We have seen that the reputational rewards of being seen as socially responsible appear greater in countries with weaker institutional frameworks and more visible manifestations of corruption in government and business. Shibusawa built his business in Japan at a time when the country was undergoing transformational institutional and social change. Ethical standards in business were low, which enhanced the reputations of his *gappon* companies, although not to the extent of converting the competing zaibatsu such as Mitsubishi to their practices. In India, Lalbhai's company and those of Tata, Ardeshir Godrej, and Jamnalal Bajaj held robust reputations that attracted talent and customers, generation after generation. Their model of responsibility did not become the norm, but they were influential and respected members of the business community in India. Sekem in Egypt and Natura in Brazil stood out for their probity and responsibility. In developed markets, the reputational advantage of being a good company was still present, but likely to be less potent.

One of the issues we have returned to throughout the book is the sustainability of deeply responsible businesses after the founder leaves or dies. Cadbury is a classic case. The firm continued under family control after George Cadbury died, and it retained many of the values he promoted for decades, but as family ownership was diluted, there was a dilution of values, leading eventually to the hostile takeover by Kraft. This story was repeated in other cases. After Edward Filene left his business, the welfare benefits that he and his brother Lincoln developed continued, but not the more visionary plans to democratize the ownership of the company. Shibusawa's principles of *gapponshugi* proved hard to maintain after his death because his influence was so personal and he held little equity in the companies he founded, which could have been passed on to like-minded followers. And even the most socially responsible chief executives of public companies, such as Romney and Norris, quickly saw their initiatives dissipate when they left the firm. Similarly, many of the "values-driven" companies formed in the last decades of the twentieth century succumbed to conventional companies once their founders allowed outside equity into the firm. Ben & Jerry's is a rare case of a company that retained its own independent board capable of protecting its values and ability to make autonomous decisions. Unilever conspicuously avoided such arrangements in subsequent acquisitions.

The fact that deep responsibility was costly meant, as people from Cadbury to Chouinard observed, that it was particularly difficult to combine responsibility with the structures and constraints of a public company. Whatever the exact status of fiduciary duty in different legal systems, as a broad generalization most shareholders, whether individual or institutional, buy equity to secure income rather than to save the world. Being quoted on the public capital markets became the kiss of death for deep responsibility.

It was closely held firms that offered the best prospects of sustaining the values and cultures of their founders. Family businesses, such as those in India, are important in this respect, as values can be transmitted between generations, although critics might observe that if the social responsibility of dynastic families rested on acquiring considerable wealth in unequal societies, it is not evident that social purpose was always being served. We have also seen alternative arrangements beyond the use of family to preserve values. Owen and Filene came to the conclusion that cooperative ownership was the best way to achieve and preserve deep responsibility. Anthroposophists offered another model: they kept the ownership of a firm such as Weleda in the hands of paid-up followers, and provided new capital and management when a firm such as Ambootia stumbled.

It is the historical difficulties of sustaining deep responsibility that make the recent attempts to build responsible systems capable of supporting and financing individual firms so potentially important. The B Corp movement is promising in this regard. Changing the statutes of a company to mandate a fiduciary duty to society and the environment as well as shareholders relieves some of its dependence on a visionary founder. Managements can change, but the fiduciary duty will remain. While the original strategy of "making the good easy" held limited prospect of achieving radical change, the vision of the founders of Sistema B offered a bolder path. They rightly identified that a business was just one component of a system that needed a major reset if it was to reduce harm and create social benefits. They recognized, in their engagement with policy makers, educators, and others, that individual businesses could be a catalyst to change public opinion about the expected behavior of firms. B Lab Global is now a global organization composed of thousands of small and medium-sized businesses that (mostly) seek a better world. It is possible, just possible, that the timing may finally be right for such an endeavor to succeed, given the severity of the ecological and social problems that are facing the world, and the multiple shockwaves caused by the fallout from the COVID-19 pandemic and the Russian invasion of Ukraine.

The steward-ownership model has the potential to offer an even more robust solution to the challenge of sustainability. While family businesses, cooperatives, and B Corps could all, in theory, be turned into conventional businesses, ownership by a trust committed in perpetuity to social responsibility offers a permanent path forward. The examples of the Carl-Zeiss-Stiftung, the John Lewis Partnership, and Bosch suggest that it is possible to build world-class businesses characterized by long-term vision, innovation, and deep commitment to philanthropy. In this regard, the recent adoption of forms of steward ownership by Sekem and Patagonia suggest a promising path forward. Only time will tell.

Deep Responsibility Cannot Save the World—but It Can Certainly Help

A final theme running through this book has been whether deep responsibility is truly beneficial for society, and if it is, how can we measure and evaluate the contribution? At the most basic level, I have documented the positive social impacts of a handful of exemplary business leaders. They did not build businesses in socially destructive industries—although Cadbury secured cocoa supplies from the quasi-slave labor employed in São Tomé, while Bosch's company played an important role in the German military machine in both world wars. They did not routinely bribe or corrupt government officials or anyone else. They facilitated social progress, usually ahead of the willingness of governments to do so.

Cadbury and Filene were bold crusaders against the scourge of inequality in their times, and they used their firms as laboratories to experiment with alternative policies. Their employees were treated fairly and equitably and were offered opportunities to live better lives than most of their peers. Romney followed in this tradition by pioneering profit-sharing in the automobile industry. Norris and Wang used the wealth created by the new computer industry resources to provide jobs for people in disadvantaged communities. Shibusawa and Lalbhai developed new industries—and the jobs that went with them—in their countries. Ibrahim and Helmy Abouleish created an agricultural community out of a desert and helped wean the Egyptian cotton industry off its dependence on polluting chemicals. Roddick challenged gender stereotypes and excessive packaging in the beauty industry and pushed buyers to be more aware of the social and environmental consequences of their purchases.

These practices were all highly innovative, and they demonstrated the positive social impact that a business can exercise, should it choose to do so. Even when outcomes were not especially successful or permanent, the intent was often bold. An example is Romney's campaign for smaller cars that were less wasteful at a time of rampant consumerism in the United States. It was not ultimately successful, but had it been, the environmental impact of the automobile industry would have been significantly reduced.

There were blemishes too. I have taken the position that juxta-posing positive and negative impacts is a more effective way to high-light moral dilemmas and trade-offs than attempting to reach an overall assessment of each person. There seem to be no robust cri-teria to assess whether Bosch's sheltering of anti-Nazi resistance leaders and Jews in Nazi Germany in the 1930s was more or less socially positive than his firm's major contribution to the Nazi war effort. This is an extreme case, but there were plenty of others with gray areas. Roddick's ability to challenge gender stereotypes and highlight the treatment of workers in Africa and Latin America rested on the brand value that she had created in part by exaggerating her claims to virtue. Cadbury's many good deeds rested on a business that secured its raw cocoa for a time from workers laboring under slave conditions. Bavaria and Domini may have oversold the promise of ESG and left open the door for companies to misrepresent their actions and motives.

A further complication in assessing the overall impact of the deeply responsible business leaders in this book is that some of their biggest contributions and greatest legacies came from their activi-ties beyond the borders of their own firms. This book began with Cadbury's campaigning for social reforms, including old-age pen-sions and the creation of the Bournville Village Trust, now one of the largest nonprofit housing trusts in Britain. In chapter after chapter there were further examples. The credit unions that Filene promoted became one of the more important financial innovations in twentieth-century America; they improved the opportunities of millions of people. Bosch gave huge gifts to promote education and to support the city of Stuttgart while providing in his will for such philanthropic giving to be institutionalized permanently. Both Tata and Shibusawa promoted education in their respective countries: Tata was especially influential in the field of scientific education, while Shibusawa supported both commercial and women's education. As the "father of capitalism" in Japan, Shibusawa also created and left behind a number of institutional frameworks for businesses to operate in, including the Tokyo Bankers Association and the Tokyo Chamber of Commerce. Lalbhai was one of the most important industrialists to support Mohandas Gandhi's independence campaign, and he created a number of influential cultural and educational institutions in the city of Ahmedabad. Wang was a valued benefactor to educational, medical, and artistic institutions in the city of Boston. Roddick believed business leaders were remembered for their engagement with civil society rather than their actual businesses. In her case, this was surely true. Collectively their societal contributions beyond the boundaries of their firms were huge, and these need to be included in any measure of the impact of deep responsibility.

Going forward, do we simply need more deeply responsible business leaders of their ilk to solve the grand challenges of today? The answer is no. Individual business leaders, however virtuous, have never been sufficient to rewrite the rules of the marketplace to promote the level of responsibility needed for major ecological and social change. It is highly implausible to imagine that the chief executives of large public corporations will radically change strategies in favor of making more socially productive impacts if doing so is likely to adversely affect their bottom lines. This is not because they are inherently ethically flawed people but rather because they are trapped in a world of investment analysts, activist investors, and pension funds in need of returns for aging populations. Still, this is not to say that the leaders of large public companies should settle for bland rhetorical statements about sustainability, inclusivity, and other fashionable sound bites. They must push as hard as they can against the constraints of the prevailing shareholder value paradigm, in the interests of their own corporations as well as society.

Against this background, public policy has a fundamental role to play in setting the rules of the game in ways that would, to adapt

Joseph Schumpeter's famous phrase, enable the creative element of capitalism to flourish while minimizing its destructive component. Only governments have the power to design tax systems that can enable more equitable wealth distribution or discourage corporate tax evasion. Only governments can impose the carbon taxes required to reduce greenhouse gas emissions and protect private data from being exploited without permission for commercial gain. Governments, not business, possess the legitimacy to make legal, fiscal, and other changes that would shift the incentives for public companies to act with greater ecological and social responsibility. The policy and legal context has to change if more responsible public companies are to flourish. Whether many governments have the competence to act, or hold people's trust, is another matter.

The responsibility of business leaders is not to stand in the way of socially and ecologically productive policies—something they have often proved skilled at doing. They should follow, rather, the examples of Cadbury, Filene, Romney, and others seen here who passionately—and selflessly—advocate for the improvement of society, often ahead of government policies. Business leaders who have built their businesses on virtuous principles will have the moral authority, and often the intellectual and technical resources, to improve public policies.

Although government action is necessary to solve some of the grand challenges we face—the climate crisis and massive wealth inequalities most obviously—individual business leaders have crucial and decisive roles to play. For one thing, they can decide not to distort policy-making by spending huge sums of money lobbying for special interests. They can abstain from deliberately causing ecological and social damage to people and the planet. Then there's the active element of acting for the common good, like the leaders covered in this book. They can serve as catalysts, sources of innovative solutions to intractable problems, and dynamic if humble partners with policy makers, nongovernmental organizations, citizens' groups, and others engaged in pursuing a flourishing society and natural environment.

One reason I wrote this book was to create a primer, to tell the stories not of heroes but of real people who never forgot that their actions had consequences—and that they could also make profits by choosing good actions with good consequences. The good deeds of each of the entrepreneurs profiled here can have multiplier effects if other entrepreneurs join them. When one acts boldly, others may follow. Individual action matters. My wish is that the business leaders reading this book will be inspired by their examples and want to find ways to make profits while making their communities and their world more flourishing places for all of their citizens.

NOTES

Introduction

1. Thomas Piketty, *Capital in the Twenty-First Century* (Cambridge, MA: Belknap Press of Harvard University Press, 2014).

2. Wallace B. Donham, "Address," *Bulletin of the Harvard Business School Alumni Association* 3, no. 6 (July 1, 1927): 195–196.

3. Wallace B. Donham, "The Social Significance of Business," *Bulletin of the Harvard Business School Alumni Association* 4, no. 3 (February 1, 1928): 100.

4. See, for example, Dominic Barton, "Capitalism for the Long Term," *Harvard Business Review* 13, no. 1 (2013): 80–88.

5. Larry Fink, annual letter to CEOs, January 16, 2018.

6. Business Roundtable, "Business Roundtable Redefines the Purpose of a Corporation to Promote 'an Economy That Serves All Americans,'" August 19, 2019, https://www .businessroundtable.org/business-roundtable-redefines-the-purpose-of-a-corporation-to -promote-an-economy-that-serves-all-americans.

7. Jacob S. Hacker and Paul Pierson, *American Amnesia: How the War on Government Led Us to Forget What Made America Prosper* (New York: Simon and Schuster, 2016); Jason W. Moore, *Capitalism in the Web of Life: Ecology and the Accumulation of Capital* (New York: Verso, 2015); Rob Nixon, *Slow Violence and the Environmentalism of the Poor* (Cambridge, MA: Harvard University Press, 2011); Naomi Klein, *This Changes Everything: Capitalism vs. the Climate* (New York: Simon and Schuster, 2014); Shoshana Zuboff, *The Age of Surveillance Capitalism: The Fight for a Human Future at the New Frontier of Power* (New York: PublicAffairs, 2019).

8. Nicole Aschoff, *The New Prophets of Capital* (Brooklyn, NY: Verso, 2015); Anand Giridharadas, *Winners Take All: The Elite Charade of Changing the World* (New York: Knopf Doubleday, 2018).

9. Dominic Barton, Dezsö Horváth, and Matthias Kipping, eds., *Re-imagining Capitalism: Building a Responsible Long-Term Model* (Oxford: Oxford University Press, 2016).

10. Rebecca Henderson, *Reimagining Capitalism in a World on Fire* (New York: Public-Affairs, 2020).

11. John R. Ehrenfeld, *The Right Way to Flourish* (New York: Routledge, 2020), 16.

12. Alasdair MacIntyre, *After Virtue: A Study in Moral Theory* (Notre Dame, IN: University of Notre Dame Press, 2007); David Dawson and Craig Bartholomew, "Virtues, Managers and Business People: Finding a Place for MacIntyre in a Business Context," *Journal of Business Ethics* 48, no. 2 (2003): 127–138.

13. Ikujiro Nonaka and Hirotaka Takeuchi, *The Wise Company: How Companies Create Continuous Innovation* (Oxford: Oxford University Press, 2019), 22–24.

14. Milton Friedman, "A Friedman Doctrine—The Social Responsibility of Business Is to Increase Its Profits," *New York Times Magazine,* September 13, 1970, https://www.nytimes.com/1970/09/13/archives/a-friedman-doctrine-the-social-responsibility-of-business-is-to.html.

15. This definition is similar to that of Luk Bouckaert and Laszlo Zsolnai in "Spirituality and Business," in *Handbook of Spirituality and Business,* ed. Bouckaert and Zsolnai (New York: Palgrave Macmillan, 2011), 4–5. See also Peter Pruzan, "Spirituality as a Firm Basis for Corporate Social Responsibility," in *The Oxford Handbook of Corporate Social Responsibility,* ed. Andrew Crane et al. (Oxford: Oxford University Press, 2008), 552–559.

16. Samuel D. Rima, *Spiritual Capital: A Moral Core for Social and Economic Justice* (Burlington, VT: Gower, 2013), 168–170.

17. Colin Mayer, *Prosperity: Better Business Makes the Greater Good* (Oxford: Oxford University Press, 2018), chap. 3.

18. For example, see James Davis, *Medieval Market Morality: Life, Law and Ethics in the English Marketplace, 1200–1500* (Cambridge: Cambridge University Press, 2012).

19. Jacob Soll, *The Reckoning: Financial Accountability and the Rise and Fall of Nations* (New York: Basic Books, 2014), 21.

20. Cerian Charlotte Griffiths, "Prosecuting Fraud in the Metropolis, 1760–1820" (PhD diss., University of Liverpool, 2017).

21. Amartya Sen, "Does Business Economics Make Economic Sense?," *Business Ethics Quarterly* 3, no. 1 (1993): 45–54.

22. Adam Smith, *An Inquiry into the Nature and Causes of the Wealth of Nations,* ed. R. H. Campbell, A. S. Skinner, and W. B. Todd, vol. 2 of *The Glasgow Edition of the Works and Correspondence of Adam Smith* (Indianapolis: Liberty Fund, 1981), 456.

23. Eric Schliesser, *Adam Smith: Systematic Philosophy and Public Thinker* (Oxford: Oxford University Press, 2017), 252; Smith, *Wealth of Nations,* 96.

24. Emma Rothschild, "Adam Smith and the Invisible Hand," *American Economic Review* 84, no. 2 (1994): 319–322.

25. Adam Smith, *The Theory of Moral Sentiments,* ed. D. D. Raphael and A. L. Macfie, vol. 1 of *The Glasgow Edition of the Works and Correspondence of Adam Smith* (Indianapolis: Liberty Fund, 1982), 184–185.

26. David Daiches Raphael, *The Impartial Spectator: Adam Smith's Moral Philosophy* (Oxford: Oxford University Press, 2007); Patricia H. Werhane, *Adam Smith and His Legacy for Modern Capitalism* (Oxford: Oxford University Press, 1991); Russ Roberts, *How Adam Smith Can Change Your Life: An Unexpected Guide to Human Nature and Happiness* (New York: Portfolio/Penguin, 2014).

27. Isabelle Szmigin and Robert Ruth, "Shared Value and the Impartial Spectator Test," *Journal of Business Ethics* 114, no. 1 (2013): 171–182.

28. Deirdre McCloskey, "Adam Smith, the Last of the Former Virtue Ethicists," *Journal of Political Economy* 40, no. 1 (2008): 43–71.

29. Carnegie Corporation of New York, Charter, Constitution and Bylaws, Article II; Olivier Zunz, *Philanthropy in America: A History* (Princeton, NJ: Princeton University Press, 2012), 22–24.

30. Gabriel Abend, *The Moral Background: An Inquiry into the History of Business Ethics* (Princeton, NJ: Princeton University Press, 2014).

31. Mairi Maclean et al., "Management Learning in Historical Perspective: Rediscovering Rowntree and the British Interwar Management Movement," *Academy of Management Learning and Education* 19, no. 1 (2020): 2, 10; Benjamin Seebohm Rowntree, *The Human Factor in Business: Experiments in Industrial Democracy* (London: Longmans, 1921).

32. Oliver Sheldon, *The Philosophy of Management* (London: Pitman, 1923), 75, 76, 99.

33. Jeremy Moon, *Corporate Social Responsibility: A Very Short Introduction* (Oxford: Oxford University Press, 2014), 3; Archie B. Carroll et al., *Corporate Responsibility: The American Experience* (New York: Cambridge University Press, 2012), 212; Howard R. Bowen, *The Social Responsibilities of the Businessman* (Iowa City: University of Iowa Press, 1953).

1. The Value of Human Dignity

1. Indrajit Ray, "Identifying the Woes of the Cotton Textile Industry in Bengal: Tales of the Nineteenth Century," *Economic History Review* 62, no. 4 (November 2009): 857–892.

2. Ian Douglas, Rob Hodgson, and Nigel Lawson, "Industry, Environment and Health through 200 Years in Manchester," *Ecological Economics* 41, no. 2 (2002): 240–241.

3. Friedrich Engels, *The Condition of the Working-Class in England in 1844*, trans. Florence Kelley Wischnewetzky (London: G. Allen and Unwin 1892), 53.

4. Jeremy Moon, *Corporate Social Responsibility: A Very Short Introduction* (Oxford: Oxford University Press, 2014), 8–9.

5. Neil McKendrick, "Josiah Wedgwood and Factory Discipline," *Historical Journal* 4, no. 1 (1961): 30–55.

6. Ophélie Siméon, *Robert Owen's Experiment at New Lanark: From Paternalism to Socialism* (Cham, Switzerland: Palgrave Macmillan, 2017), 1, 4, 57.

7. Siméon, *Robert Owen's Experiment*, 20, 80, 95, 102, 122.

8. Jack Reynolds, *The Great Paternalist: Titus Salt and the Growth of Nineteenth-Century Bradford* (New York: St. Martin's Press, 1983); Mary B. Rose, *The Gregs of Quarry Bank Mill: The Rise and Decline of a Family Firm, 1750–1914* (New York: Cambridge University Press, 1986); Siméon, *Robert Owen's Experiment*, 109.

9. Siméon, *Robert Owen's Experiment*, 66, 74, 88–91, 98, 123.

10. Siméon, *Robert Owen's Experiment*, 110–114.

11. See the classic article by E. P. Thompson, "Time, Work-Discipline, and Industrial Capitalism," *Past and Present* 38 (1967): 56–97.

12. Mary B. Rose, *Firms, Networks and Business Values: The British and American Cotton Industries since 1750* (New York: Cambridge University Press, 2000), 121.

13. John F. Wilson, *British Business History, 1720–1994* (Manchester: Manchester University Press, 1995), 34–35.

14. Siméon, *Robert Owen's Experiment*, 48, 50, 52–53, 59, 63, 78–79, 111–112, 119.

15. John F. Wilson, *British Business History*, 132; Siméon, *Robert Owen's Experiment*, 121, 132, 161; David Sunderland, *Social Capital, Trust and the Industrial Revolution* (New York: Routledge, 2007), 200.

16. Siméon, *Robert Owen's Experiment*, 160.

17. Rose, *Firms, Networks*, 125.

18. John F. Wilson, Anthony Webster, and Rachael Vorberg-Rugh, *Building Co-operation: A Business History of the Co-operative Group, 1863–2013* (Oxford: Oxford University Press, 2013), chaps. 2–4.

19. Robert Fitzgerald, *British Labour Management and Industrial Welfare, 1846–1939* (London: Croom Helm, 1988); Howard F. Gospel, *Markets, Firms and the Management of Labour in Modern Britain* (Cambridge: Cambridge University Press, 1992).

20. Charles Wilson, *The History of Unilever: A Study in Economic Growth and Social Change*, 2 vols. (London: Cassell, 1954), 1:297–312, 2:271–297.

21. David J. Jeremy, "The Enlightened Paternalist in Action: William Hesketh Lever at Port Sunlight before 1914," *Business History* 33, no. 1 (1991): 58–81; John Griffiths, "'Give My Regards to Uncle Billy . . .': The Rites and Rituals of Company Life at Lever Brothers, c.1900–c.1990," *Business History* 37, no. 4 (1995): 25–45.

22. John F. Wilson, Webster, and Vorberg-Rugh, *Building Co-operation*, 119–120.

23. Larry H. Ingle, *First among Friends: George Fox and the Creation of Quakerism* (Oxford: Oxford University Press, 1994).

24. For short histories of these firms, see Mike King, *Quakernomics: An Ethical Capitalism* (New York: Anthem Press, 2014), pt. 11. The title of this section is gratefully adopted from this book.

25. Richard Turnbull, *Quaker Capitalism: Lessons for Today* (Oxford: Centre for Enterprise, Markets and Ethics, 2014), 18, https://theceme.org/wp-content/uploads/2015/07/Quaker-Capitalism.pdf.

26. Maurice Kirby, "Quakerism, Entrepreneurship and the Family Firm in North-East England," in *Entrepreneurship, Networks and Modern Business,* ed. Jonathan Brown and Mary B. Rose (Manchester: Manchester University Press, 1993), 106–107.

27. Nicole Woolsey Biggart and Rick Delbridge, "Systems of Exchange," *Academy of Management Review* 29, no. 1 (2004): 40.

28. Leslie Hannah, "The Moral Economy of Business: A Historical Perspective on Ethics and Efficiency," in *Civil Histories: Essays Presented to Sir Keith Thomas,* ed. Peter Burke, Brian Harrison, and Paul Slack (Oxford: Oxford University Press, 2000), 296.

29. Turnbull, *Quaker Capitalism*.

30. Mark Freeman, "Quakers, Business, and Philanthropy," in *The Oxford Handbook of Quaker Studies,* ed. Stephen W. Angell and Pink Dandelion (Oxford: Oxford University Press, 2013), 422.

31. Ann Prior and Maurice Kirby, "The Society of Friends and Business Culture, 1700–1830," in *Religion, Business and Wealth in Modern Britain,* ed. David J. Jeremy (New York: Routledge, 1998), 117–129.

32. Esther Sahle, *Quakers in the British Atlantic World, c.1660–1800* (Woodbridge, UK: Boydell, 2021).

33. James Walvin, *The Quakers: Money and Morals* (London: John Murray, 1997), 124.

34. Elizabeth Cazden, "Quakers, Slavery, Anti-slavery, and Race," in Angell and Dandelion, *Oxford Handbook of Quaker Studies,* 347–362.

35. "About Quakers," Friends General Conference, accessed March 27, 2020, https://www.fgcquaker.org/discover/faqs-about-quakers#Anything?.

36. Kate Peters, *Print Culture and the Early Quakers* (New York: Cambridge University Press, 2005), 2.

37. Biggart and Delbridge, "Systems of Exchange," 40.

38. King, *Quakernomics*, 38–40.

39. Maurice W. Kirby, "The Failure of a Quaker Business Dynasty: The Peases of Darlington, 1830–1902," in *Business and Religion in Britain,* ed. David J. Jeremy (Aldershot, UK: Gower, 1988), 149–151.

40. T. A. B. Corley, "How Quakers Coped with Business Success: Quaker Industrialists 1860–1914," in Jeremy, *Business and Religion in Britain,* 175–176.

41. King, *Quakernomics,* 97–100.

42. Corley, "How Quakers Coped," 171–184.

43. Nicholas Burton and Matthew Sinnicks, "Quaker Business Ethics as MacIntyrean Tradition," *Journal of Business Ethics* 176 (2022): 507–518.

44. Colin Mayer, *Prosperity: Better Business Makes the Greater Good* (Oxford: Oxford University Press, 2018), 107.

45. Iolo A. Williams, *The Firm of Cadbury* (London: Constable, 1931).

46. Diane Wordsworth, *The Life of Richard Cadbury* (Philadelphia: Pen and Sword History, 2020).

47. A. G. Gardiner, *Life of George Cadbury* (London: Cassell and Company, 1923), 12–22.

48. Walvin, *Quakers,* 158–160.

49. Chris Smith, John Child, and Michael Rowlinson, *Reshaping Work: The Cadbury Experience* (Cambridge: Cambridge University Press, 1990), 51–52.

50. William G. Clarence-Smith, "Chocolate Consumption from the Sixteenth Century to the Great Chocolate Boom," in *The Economics of Chocolate,* ed. Mara P. Squicciarini and Johan Swinnen (Oxford: Oxford University Press, 2016), 43–70.

51. Robert Fitzgerald, *Rowntree and the Marketing Revolution* (Cambridge: Cambridge University Press, 1995), 54–57.

52. Basil G. Murray, "Cadbury, George," in *Dictionary of Business Biography,* ed. David Jeremy, vol. 1 (London: Butterworths, 1984), 547–553; Fitzgerald, *Rowntree,* 75–89.

53. Peter Miskell, "Cavity Protection or Cosmetic Perfection? Innovation and Marketing of Toothpaste Brands in the United States and Western Europe, 1955–1985," *Business History Review* 78, no. 1 (2004): 33–34; Ina Zweiniger-Bargielowska, *Managing the Body: Beauty, Health, and Fitness in Britain, 1880–1939* (New York: Oxford University Press, 2010); Sarah B. Campbell, "Waists, Health and History: Obesity in Nineteenth Century Britain" (PhD diss., Oxford University, 2014).

54. Samira Kawash, *Candy: A Century of Panic and Pleasure* (New York: Faber and Faber, 2013), 330–331.

55. Stefania Moramarco and Loreto Nemi, "Nutritional and Health Effects of Chocolate," in Squicciarini and Swinnen, *Economics of Chocolate,* 134–156.

56. Gardiner, *Life,* 39–58.

57. Williams, *Firm of Cadbury,* 162.

58. Murray, "Cadbury, George."

59. John Bromhead, "George Cadbury's Contribution to Sport," *The Sports Historian* 20, no. 1 (2000): 97–117.

60. T. A. B. Corley, "Changing Quaker Attitudes to Wealth, 1690–1950," in *Religion, Business and Wealth in Modern Britain,* ed. David J. Jeremy (London: Routledge, 1998), 142.

61. Walvin, *Quakers,* 187.

62. Gardiner, *Life,* 118.

63. Gardiner, *Life,* 120.

64. Michael Rowlinson and John Hassard, "The Invention of Corporate Culture: A History of the Histories of Cadbury," *Human Relations* 46, no. 3 (1993): 311.

65. Michael Harrison, "William Alexander Harvey (1874–1951): Bournville and After," accessed July 4, 2020, http://www-etsav.upc.es/personals/iphs2004/pdf/082_p.pdf; Monica Penick and Christopher Long, eds., *The Rise of Everyday Design: The Arts and Crafts Movement in Britain and America* (New Haven, CT: Yale University Press, 2019).

66. Roger Homan, "Quakers and Visual Culture," in Angell and Dandelion, *Oxford Handbook of Quaker Studies,* 499.

67. William Alexander Harvey, *The Model Village and Its Cottages: Bournville* (London: B. T. Batsford, 1906), 10–11.

68. David J. Jeremy, *Capitalists and Christians: Business Leaders and the Churches in Britain* (Oxford: Clarendon Press, 1990), 144; Charles Delheim, "The Creation of a Company Culture: Cadburys, 1861–1931," *American Historical Review* 92, no. 1 (1987): 20; Andrew Reekes, *Two Titans, One City: Joseph Chamberlain and George Cadbury* (Alcester, UK: West Midlands History, 2017), 41.

69. Gardiner, *Life,* 97.
70. Murray, "Cadbury, George," 551.
71. Williams, *Firm of Cadbury,* 157.
72. Fitzgerald, *Rowntree,* 197, 227.
73. Rowlinson and Hassard, "Invention of Corporate Culture."
74. Rowlinson and Hassard, "Invention of Corporate Culture," 312–313.
75. Brian Lewis, *"So Clean": Lord Leverhulme, Soap and Civilization* (Manchester: Manchester University Press, 2008), 160–163.
76. Jules Marchal, *Lord Leverhulme's Ghosts: Colonial Exploitation in the Congo* (London: Verso, 2008), 4.
77. Marchal, *Lord Leverhulme's Ghosts,* 13–22.
78. Alice Gregory, "Can an Artists' Collective in Africa Repair a Colonial Legacy?," *New Yorker,* July 18, 2022.
79. "Statement Re: Labour on the Cocoa Plantations in Portuguese West Africa," attached to George Cadbury to Sir Edward Grey, October 19, 1906, File 4739/35394, FO 367/18, UK National Archives (hereafter NA).
80. "Statement Re: Labour."
81. George Cadbury to Sir Edward Grey, October 19, 1906, File 4739/35394, FO 367/18, NA.
82. George Cadbury to Sir Edward Grey, November 7, 1906, File 37619, FO 367/18, NA.
83. Jeremy, *Capitalists and Christians,* 146.
84. Henry Woodd Nevinson, "The Slave-Trade of Today: Conclusion: The Islands of Doom," *Harper's,* February 1906; Henry W. Nevinson, *A Modern Slavery* (London: Harper and Brothers, 1906).
85. Jeremy, *Capitalists and Christians,* 148–150.
86. Jeremy, *Capitalists and Christians,* 151.
87. Jeremy, *Capitalists and Christians,* 151–152.
88. Foreign Office to Secretary of the Board of Trade, September 18, 1914, File 49319/4, CO 3233/670, NA.
89. Gardiner, *Life,* 250–251.
90. Polly Hill, *The Migrant Cocoa-Farmers of Southern Ghana: A Study in Rural Capitalism* (Cambridge: Cambridge University Press, 1963).
91. Gardiner, *Life,* 120.
92. Mayer, *Prosperity,* 86–87; Smith, Child, and Rowlinson, *Reshaping Work,* 78–95.
93. Laura F. Spira, *The Cadbury Committee: A History* (Oxford: Oxford University Press, 2013).
94. Freeman, "Quakers, Business, and Philanthropy," 423–435.
95. Gardiner, *Life,* 120.
96. Thomas C. Kennedy, *British Quakerism, 1860–1920: The Transformation of a Religious Community* (Oxford: Oxford University Press, 2001), 171.
97. Kennedy, *British Quakerism,* 171–191.
98. Ambrose Mong, *Guns and Gospels: Imperialism and Evangelism in China* (Cambridge: James Clarke, 2016), chap. 6.
99. Gardiner, *Life,* 136–138.
100. Gardiner, *Life,* 128–130.
101. Gardiner, *Life,* 132–134.
102. Bromhead, "George Cadbury's Contribution," 106.
103. John Cooper, *The British Welfare Revolution, 1906–13* (London: Bloomsbury Academic, 2017), 38.

104. Reekes, *Two Titans, One City,* 59; Cooper, *British Welfare Revolution,* 68.

105. Murray, "Cadbury, George," 553.

106. Gardiner, *Life,* 220–221.

107. Gardiner, *Life,* 239–241.

108. Murray, "Cadbury, George," 553.

109. Sally Harris, *Out of Control: British Foreign Policy and the Union of Democratic Control 1914–1918* (Hull: University of Hull Press, 1996), 159.

110. Gardiner, *Life,* 299–306.

111. Olivier Zunz, *Philanthropy in America: A History* (Princeton, NJ: Princeton University Press, 2012), 296; Charles Harvey et al., "Andrew Carnegie and the Foundations of Contemporary Entrepreneurial Philanthropy," *Business History* 53, no. 3 (2011): 425–450.

112. "Snacking Made Right," Mondelez International, accessed December 25, 2021, https://www.mondelezinternational.com/Snacking-Made-Right.

113. Dominic Casciani, "Is This the Nicest Place to Live in Britain?," BBC News, July 9, 2003, http://news.bbc.co.uk/2/hi/uk_news/3056286.stm.

2. Redistribution of Power

1. Edward A. Filene, *The Way Out: A Business-Man Looks at the World* (London: George Routledge and Sons, 1925), 23.

2. Filene, *The Way Out,* 143.

3. Stanley L. Engerman and Robert E. Gallman, eds., *The Cambridge Economic History of the United States,* vol. 2, *The Long Nineteenth Century* (New York: Cambridge University Press, 2008); Eric Foner and Lisa McGurr, eds., *American History Now* (Philadelphia: Temple University Press, 2011).

4. The classic account of the growth of big business in the nineteenth century is Alfred D. Chandler, *The Visible Hand* (Cambridge, MA: Harvard University Press, 1977). For a more recent account, see Walter A. Friedman, *American Business History: A Very Short Introduction* (Oxford: Oxford University Press, 2020).

5. Jacob A. Riis, *How the Other Half Lives: Studies among the Tenements of New York* (New York: Charles Scribner's Sons, 1890).

6. Clayne Pope, "Inequality in the Nineteenth Century," in Engerman and Gallman, *Cambridge Economic History,* 109–142.

7. Mark Twain and Charles Dudley Warner, *The Gilded Age: A Tale of Today* (New York: Trident Press, 1964).

8. Richard R. John, "Who Were the Gilders? And Other Seldom-Asked Questions about Business, Technology, and Political Economy in the United States, 1877–1900," *Journal of the Gilded Age and Progressive Era* 8, no. 4 (2009): 474–480.

9. Lou Galambos, *The Public Image of Big Business in America, 1880–1940: A Quantitative Study in Social Change* (Baltimore: John Hopkins University Press, 1975); George H. Douglas, "Muckrakers," in *The Oxford Encyclopedia of American Political and Legal History,* ed. Donald T. Critchlow and Philip R. VanderMeer (Oxford: Oxford University Press, 2013).

10. David Brian Robertson, "Labor's Role in Politics," in Critchlow and VanderMeer, *Oxford Encyclopedia;* David Brian Robertson, *Capital, Labor, and State: The Battle for American Labor Markets from the Civil War to the New Deal* (Lanham, MD: Rowman and Littlefield, 2000).

11. Nelson Lichtenstein, *State of the Union: A Century of American Labor* (Princeton, NJ: Princeton University Press, 2012); Archie B. Carroll et al., *Corporate Responsibility: The American Experience* (Cambridge: Cambridge University Press, 2012).

12. Morrell Heald, *The Social Responsibilities of Business* (New Brunswick, NJ: Transaction Publishers, 1988), 35.

13. Gene Clanton, "Populist Party," in *The Oxford Companion to United States History*, ed. Paul S. Boyer (Oxford: Oxford University Press, 2001).

14. Robert M. Crunden, *Ministers of Reform: The Progressives' Achievement in American Civilization, 1889–1920* (New York: Basic Books, 1982); David Brian Robertson, "The Progressive Era," in *The Oxford Handbook of U.S. Social Policy*, ed. Daniel Béland, Kimberly J. Morgan, and Christopher Howard (Oxford: Oxford University Press, 2014).

15. Heald, *Social Responsibilities of Business*, 3–5; Robert F. Dazell, *Enterprising Elite: The Boston Associates and the World They Made* (New York: Norton, 1993); Kenneth Lipartito, "The Utopian Corporation," in *Constructing Corporate America: History, Politics, Culture*, ed. Kenneth Lipartito and David B. Sicilia (New York: Oxford University Press, 2004), 94–119.

16. Carroll et al., *Corporate Responsibility*, 80–81; Janice L. Reiff and Susan E. Hirsch, "Pullman and Its Public Image: Image and Aim in Making and Interpreting History," *Public Historian* 11, no. 4 (1989): 94–112.

17. Mort Rosenblum, *Chocolate: A Bittersweet Saga of Dark and Light* (New York: North Point Press, 2005), chap. 5.

18. Joël Glenn Brenner, *The Emperors of Chocolate: Inside the Secret World of Hershey and Mars* (New York: Random House, 1999), 89.

19. Vicki Howard, *From Main Street to Mall: The Rise and Fall of the American Department Stores* (Philadelphia: University of Pennsylvania Press, 2015), 16–24.

20. Laura Phillips Sawyer, *American Fair Trade: Proprietary Capitalism, Corporatism, and the "New Competition," 1890–1940* (New York: Cambridge University Press, 2018), chap. 2.

21. Meg Jacobs, *Pocketbook Politics: Economic Citizenship in Twentieth-Century America* (Princeton, NJ: Princeton University Press, 2005), chap. 1; Sawyer, *American Fair Trade*.

22. Howard, *From Main Street*, 30–49.

23. William Leach, *Land of Desire: Merchants, Power, and the Rise of a New American Culture* (New York: Pantheon Books, 1993), 118.

24. Ralph M. Hower, *History of Macy's of New York* (Cambridge, MA: Harvard University Press, 1943), 207, 305, 382–389; Leach, *Land of Desire*, 119.

25. Leach, *Land of Desire*, 118–122.

26. Edward A. Filene, *Successful Living in This Machine Age* (New York: Simon and Schuster, 1931), 73–74.

27. Edward A. Filene, "George Washington and Financial Liberty: Address before the California Credit Union League, Sacramento, February 22, 1936," in *Speaking of Change: A Selection of Speeches and Articles by Edward A. Filene* (New York: Former Associates of Edward A. Filene, 1939), 158.

28. George E. Berkley, *The Filenes* (Boston: International Pocket Library, 1998), 31; Marcus Bacher, "Edward Albert Filene," Immigrant Entrepreneurship, March 19, 2014, https://www.immigrantentrepreneurship.org/entries/edward-albert-filene.

29. Berkley, *Filenes*, 21–26.

30. Edward A. Filene, *Successful Living*, 73–74.

31. Berkley, *Filenes*, 31.

32. Saul Engelbourg, "Edward A. Filene: Merchant, Civil Leader, and Jew," *American Jewish Historical Quarterly* 66, no. 1 (1976): 107; Lillian Schoedler, "E.A.," *The Bridge* 3, no. 4 (June 1938): 5; Berkley, *Filenes*, 37.

33. Sargent Kennedy, "Wm. Filene's Sons Co.: A Study of the Filene Cooperative Association" (MBA thesis, Harvard Business School, 1937), CL476.5, vol. 1, Baker Library

Special Collections, Harvard Business School, p. 2; Schoedler, "E.A.," 5; memorandum dated October 18, 1909, Box 62, Kirstein Collection, Baker Library Special Collections, Harvard Business School.

34. Regina Lee Blaszczyk, "The Rise and Fall of European Fashion at Filene's in Boston," in *European Fashion: The Creation of a Global Industry,* ed. Regina Lee Blaszczyk and Véronique Pouillard (Manchester: Manchester University Press, 2018), 172–177.

35. Jacobs, *Pocketbook Politics,* 19.

36. Sargent Kennedy, "Interviews at Wm. Filene's Sons," summer 1936, CL476.5, vol. 2, Baker Library Special Collections, Harvard Business School, K30.

37. Berkley, *Filenes,* 121–122.

38. Berkley, *Filenes,* 52; Edward A. Filene, *Morals in Business* (Berkeley: University of California Press, 1935), 24–27.

39. Edward A. Filene, "Morals in Business: A Weinstock Lecture at the University of California, Berkeley, Cal., February 7, 1934," in *Speaking of Change,* 180.

40. Edward A. Filene, *The Consumer's Dollar* (New York: John Day, 1934), 25.

41. Berkley, *Filenes,* 123–126, 164–167; Bacher, "Edward Albert Filene."

42. This is the central argument of Jacobs, *Pocketbook Politics.*

43. Edward A. Filene, *Consumer's Dollar,* 5; Edward A. Filene, *Morals in Business,* 44; Edward A. Filene, *Successful Living,* 31–34.

44. Jacobs, *Pocketbook Politics,* 49–50; Berkley, *Filenes,* 170.

45. Berkley, *Filenes,* 17–18.

46. A. Lincoln Filene, *A Merchant's Horizon* (Boston: Houghton Mifflin, 1924), 50.

47. Filene, *Merchant's Horizon,* 51.

48. Berkley, *Filenes,* 91.

49. Edward A. Filene, *Way Out,* 114.

50. Kennedy, "Wm. Filene's Sons Co.," 10; Andrea Tone, *The Business of Benevolence: Industrial Paternalism in Progressive America* (Ithaca, NY: Cornell University Press, 2018), 209; Kim McQuaid, "An American Owenite: Edward A. Filene and the Parameters of Industrial Reform, 1890–1937," *American Journal of Economics and Sociology* 35, no. 1 (1976): 78.

51. Mary La Dame, *The Filene Store: A Study of Employees' Relation to Management in a Retail Store* (New York: Russell Sage Foundation, 1930), 88–89.

52. Engelbourg, "Edward A. Filene," 107.

53. Berkley, *Filenes,* 76, 108–109, 160–161.

54. Engelbourg, "Edward A. Filene," 109.

55. Berkley, *Filenes,* 174–175.

56. Kennedy, "Wm. Filene's Sons Co.," 35.

57. "The Merchant Who Subsidized Truth," *Milwaukee Journal,* October 21, 1949; Engelbourg, "Edward A. Filene," 112.

58. Berkley, *Filenes,* 224–225, 231.

59. George W. Coleman, "Memorial Service: In Memory of Mr. Edward A. Filene," Ford Hall, Boston, Massachusetts, October 7, 1937, Box 3, Twentieth Century Fund Records, New York Public Library; Berkley, *Filenes,* 64–65.

60. Berkley, *Filenes,* 70–71, 74–75.

61. Berkley, *Filenes,* 160–170.

62. "Lincoln Filene, Merchant, Dead," *New York Times,* August 28, 1957.

63. "Founders' Biographies," Lincoln and Therese Filene Foundation, accessed April 30, 2020, https://www.filenefoundation.org/lincoln-therese/; "Our Mission," American Arbitration Association, accessed April 30, 2020, https://www.adr.org/mission.

64. Engelbourg, "Edward A. Filene," 110.

65. Berkley, *Filenes*, 224–225.

66. Berkley, *Filenes*, 226–227.

67. Berkley, *Filenes*, 229–233.

68. Berkley, *Filenes*, 236–237; Engelbourg, "Edward A. Filene," 113.

69. Berkley, *Filenes*, 238–241.

70. Engelbourg, "Edward A. Filene," 111.

71. "Federated Department Stores, History," FundingUniverse, accessed December 25, 2021, http://www.fundinguniverse.com/company-histories/federated-department-stores-inc-history.

72. David Meyers, Beverly Meyers, and Elise Meyers Walker, *Look to Lazarus: The Big Store* (Mount Pleasant, SC: Arcadia Publishing, 2011), 147–148; Michael J. Lisicky, *Abraham and Straus: It's Worth a Trip from Anywhere* (Mount Pleasant, SC: Arcadia Publishing, 2017), 47.

73. Coleman, "Memorial Service"; Berkley, *Filenes, 67*; Lincoln Steffens, *The Autobiography of Lincoln Steffens, Abridged* (New York: Harcourt, Brace, 1937), 368.

74. Berkley, *Filenes,* 80.

75. Berkley, *Filenes,* 80–81.

76. Thomas K. McCraw, *Prophets of Regulation* (Cambridge, MA: Harvard University Press, 1984), 82.

77. Berkley, *Filenes,* 80–83.

78. Sawyer, *American Fair Trade,* 110–127; Berkley, *Filenes,* 83–86.

79. Richard Heath, "Woodbourne and the Boston 1915 Movement," Jamaica Plain Historical Society, February 23, 1998, https://www.jphs.org/20th-century/woodbourne-and-the-boston-1915-movement.html.

80. Heath, "Woodbourne."

81. Heath, "Woodbourne"; "Woodbourne Homeowner Handbook: A Guide to the History and Care of Houses in the Woodbourne Neighborhood of Boston," City of Boston, January 1999, https://www.cityofboston.gov/images_documents/Woodbourne_Homeowner_Handbook_tcm3-21079.pdf.

82. Heath, "Woodbourne"; McQuaid, "American Owenite," 80.

83. Timothy W. Guinnane, "A Failed Institutional Transplant: Raiffeisen's Credit Cooperatives in Ireland, 1894–1914," *Explorations in Economic History* 31, no. 1 (1994): 38–61.

84. J. Carroll Moody and Gilbert C. Fite, *The Credit Union Movement: Origins and Development 1850–1970* (Lincoln: University of Nebraska Press, 1971), 28–30.

85. Bacher, "Edward Albert Filene."

86. Moody and Fite, *Credit Union Movement,* 44–45, 50–52, 70–71.

87. Draft entry for William Filene in *The National Cyclopedia of American Biography,* April 1, 1962, Box 3, Century Foundation Records, New York Public Library; Berkley, *Filenes,* 8–16; Bacher, "Edward Albert Filene."

88. Edward A. Filene, *Speaking of Change,* 320–321; Berkley, *Filenes,* 76.

89. Moody and Fite, *Credit Union Movement,* 46–47; Berkley, *Filenes,* 103.

90. Engelbourg, "Edward A. Filene," 118.

91. Oscar Handlin, "American Views of the Jew at the Opening of the Twentieth Century," *Publications of the American Jewish Historical Society* 40, no. 4 (1951): 323–344.

92. Moody and Fite, *Credit Union Movement,* 70–71.

93. Moody and Fite, *Credit Union Movement,* 46–47; Berkley, *Filenes,* 103.

94. Moody and Fite, *Credit Union Movement,* 46.

95. Moody and Fite, *Credit Union Movement,* 78–80.

96. Moody and Fite, *Credit Union Movement,* 81–83.

97. Moody and Fite, *Credit Union Movement,* 126.

98. Moody and Fite, *Credit Union Movement,* chap. 5.

99. Moody and Fite, *Credit Union Movement,* 156–168.

100. Moody and Fite, *Credit Union Movement,* chap. 8.

101. Moody and Fite, *Credit Union Movement,* 208.

102. Edward A. Filene, *Speaking of Change,* 182, 188–189.

103. Adolf A. Berle, *Leaning against the Dawn: An Appreciation of the Twentieth Century Fund and Its Fifty Years of Adventure in Seeking to Influence American Development Toward a More Effectively Just Civilization, 1919–1969* (New York City: Twentieth Century Fund, 1969), 19–24.

104. Moody and Fite, *Credit Union Movement,* 79–80.

105. Edward A. Filene, *Consumer's Dollar,* 8.

106. "Merchant Who Subsidized Truth."

107. David Welch, *Propaganda and German Cinema, 1933–1945* (Oxford: Clarendon Press, 1983); Peter Kenez, *Cinema and Soviet Society: From the Revolution to the Death of Stalin* (London: I. B. Tauris, 2001).

108. Edward A. Filene, *Way Out,* 144; Robert Lacey, *Ford: The Men and the Machine* (New York: Random House, 1986), 29, 205.

109. Victoria de Grazia, *Irresistible Empire: America's Advance through Twentieth-Century Europe* (Cambridge, MA: Belknap Press of Harvard University Press, 2005), 175; Engelbourg, "Edward A. Filene," 120–122.

110. Engelbourg, "Edward A. Filene," 120–122.

111. Schoedler, "E.A.," 13; McQuaid, "American Owenite," 81; "History," International Chamber of Commerce, accessed April 30, 2020, https://iccwbo.org/about-us/who-we-are/history/.

112. James W. Cortada, *IBM: The Rise and Fall and Reinvention of a Global Icon* (Cambridge, MA: MIT Press, 2019), 113–116; Geoffrey Jones, Grace Ballor, and Adrian Brown, "Thomas J. Watson, IBM and Nazi Germany" (Harvard Business School Case 9-807-133, revised January 13, 2021); Thomas Doherty, *Hollywood and Hitler, 1933–1939* (New York: Columbia University Press, 2013).

113. Michael J. Sproule, *Propaganda and Democracy: The American Experience of Media and Mass Persuasion* (New York: Cambridge University Press, 1997), 129–131; Eileen Gambrill, *Propaganda in the Helping Professions* (Oxford: Oxford University Press, 2012), 109.

114. Sproule, *Propaganda and Democracy,* 143–145, 150–152, 156; Martin Manning and Herbert Romerstein, "Institute for Propaganda Analysis (IPA)," in *Historical Dictionary of American Propaganda* (Westport, CT: Greenwood Press, 2004), 140.

115. "A Plan for Cooperative Distribution in the United States," February 9, 1933, Century Foundation Records, New York Public Library. This memorandum was unsigned but appears to have been written by Filene. The ideas were further formulated in "The Edward A. Filene Plan for the Organization of a Chain of Cooperative Department Stores," April 29, 1935, Century Foundation Records, New York Public Library.

116. "Edward A. Filene, 77, Dies in Paris," *New York Times,* September 26, 1937; Berkley, *Filenes,* 256.

117. *Managers Manual for Co-operative Stores,* 2nd ed. (Boston: Edward A. Filene Good Will Fund, 1945); *Consumer Cooperative Leadership* (Boston: Edward A. Filene Good Will Fund, 1942).

118. Bacher, "Edward Albert Filene"; "Edward A. Filene, 77"; "Merchant Who Subsidized Truth."

119. Coleman, "Memorial Service."

120. Steffens, *Autobiography of Lincoln Steffens,* 369.

121. Thomas Piketty, *Capital in the Twenty-First Century* (Cambridge, MA: Belknap Press of Harvard University Press, 2014), 292.

3. Promoting Choice and Facing Dictatorship

1. Alfred D. Chandler, *Scale and Scope* (Cambridge, MA: Harvard University Press, 1990), 23, 394.

2. Harm G. Schröter, "Continuity and Change: German Multinationals since 1850," in *The Rise of Multinationals in Continental Europe,* ed. Geoffrey Jones and Harm G. Schröter (Aldershot, UK: Edward Elgar, 1993), 29.

3. Jeffrey Fear, "German Capitalism," in *Creating Modern Capitalism,* ed. Thomas K. McCraw (Cambridge, MA: Harvard University Press, 1997), 151; Sibylle Lehmann-Hasemeyer and Jochen Streb, "Does Social Security Crowd Out Private Savings? The Case of Bismarck's System of Social Insurance," *European Review of Economic History* 22 (2017): 303.

4. "Bismarck's Reichstag Speech on the Law for Workers' Compensation (March 15, 1884)," German History in Documents and Images, accessed May 26, 2021, https://ghdi.ghi-dc.org/sub_document.cfm?document_id=1809.

5. Marcel van Meerhaeghe, "Bismarck and the Social Question," *Journal of Economic Studies* 33, no. 4 (2006): 284–301; Fear, "German Capitalism," 152.

6. Thilo Kuntz, "German Corporate Law in the 20th Century," in *Research Handbook on the History of Corporate and Company Law,* ed. Harwell Wells (Cheltenham, UK: Edward Elgar, 2018), 222.

7. Schröter, "Continuity and Change," 30–31.

8. Gerald D. Feldman, "German Business between War and Revolution: The Origins of the Stinner-Liegen Agreement," in *Entstehung und Wandel der Mordernen Gesellschaft,* ed. Gerhard A. Ritter (Berlin: De Gruyter, 1970), 315.

9. Susanne Hilger, "Welfare Policy in German Big Business after the First World War: Vereinigte Stahlwerke AG, 1926–33," *Business History* 40, no. 1 (1998): 52.

10. Erik de Gier, *Capitalist Workingman's Paradises Revisited* (Amsterdam: Amsterdam University Press, 2016), 115–116.

11. Eugene C. McCreary, "Social Welfare and Business: The Krupp Welfare Program, 1860–1914," *Business History Review* 42, no. 1 (1968): 100.

12. McCreary, "Social Welfare and Business," 100.

13. McCreary, "Social Welfare and Business," 101–105.

14. McCreary, "Social Welfare and Business," 99.

15. De Gier, *Capitalist Workingman's Paradises Revisited,* 113–114.

16. De Gier, *Capitalist Workingman's Paradises Revisited,* 105–106, 120–124.

17. Cedric Bolz, "From 'Garden City Precursors' to 'Cemeteries for the Living': Contemporary Discourse on Krupp Housing and 'Besucherpolitik' in Wilhelmine Germany," *Urban History* 37, no. 1 (2010): 108–109; "Margarethenhöhe," Ruhr Museum, accessed June 29, 2022, https://ruhrmuseum.de/standorte/in-essen/margarethenhoehe.

18. Bolz, "From 'Garden City Precursors,'" 91–92.

19. McCreary, "Social Welfare and Business," 108–110.

20. Wilfried Feldenkirchen, *Siemens: From Workshop to Global Player* (Munich: Piper, 2000), 78.

21. Feldenkirchen, *Siemens,* 111.

22. Feldenkirchen, *Siemens,* 112–119; Jürgen Kocka, *Unternehmensverwaltung und Angestelltenschaft am Biespiel Siemens 1847–1914* (Stuttgart: Ernst Klett Verlag, 1969), 82–93.

23. Feldenkirchen, *Siemens,* 114; Heidrun Homburg, "Scientific Management and Personnel Policy in the Modern German Enterprise, 1918–1939: The Case of Siemens," in

Managerial Strategies and Industrial Relations, ed. Howard F. Gospel and Craig R. Littler (London: Heinemann Educational Books, 1983), 142–143.

24. Kuntz, "German Corporate Law," 214.

25. Dieter Krüger, *Das Stinnes-Legien-Abkommen 1918–1924: Voraussetzungen, Entstehung, Umsetzung und Bedeutung* (Berlin: Duncker and Humblot, 2018); Feldman, "German Business."

26. Feldenkirchen, *Siemens,* 150–152.

27. Feldenkirchen, *Siemens,* 153.

28. Quoted in Karl H. P. Bienek, *Strassen in Siemensstadt: Ihre Herkunft, Bedeutung, Geschichte, und Bauwerk* (Berlin: ERS Verlag, 1991), 8.

29. De Gier, *Capitalist Workingman's Paradises Revisited,* 119–120.

30. Homburg, "Scientific Management," 143.

31. Peter Theiner, *Robert Bosch: An Entrepreneur in the Age of Extremes* (Munich: C. H. Beck, 2019), 16.

32. Theiner, *Robert Bosch,* 17.

33. Theiner, *Robert Bosch,* 27, 35.

34. Robert Jütte, "The Healing Power of Nature," in "Robert Bosch: His Life and Work," *Journal of Bosch History,* Supplement 1 (n.d.): 52–55, https://d-nb.info/105599288X /34.

35. Theiner, *Robert Bosch,* 35.

36. Theiner, *Robert Bosch,* 31. The Knights of Labor collapsed in 1886 after becoming embroiled in a national general strike in support of the eight-hour day.

37. De Gier, *Capitalist Workingman's Paradises Revisited,* 119–120.

38. Theiner, *Robert Bosch,* 40–44.

39. Dieter Schmitt, "The Spark of Genius," in "Robert Bosch: His Life and Work," 32–34.

40. Quoted in Christine Siegel, "'Associates,' Not Wage Earners," in "Robert Bosch: His Life and Work," 42.

41. Toni Pierenkemper, "Robert Bosch, der Industrielle: Zum Typus des deutschen Unternehmers in der Hochindustrialisierung," *Kultur & Technik* 11 (1987): 5–18.

42. Theiner, *Robert Bosch,* 44; Siegel, "'Associates,'" 45.

43. Theodor Heuss, *Robert Bosch: His Life and Achievements* (New York: Henry Holt, 1994), 380; Theiner, *Robert Bosch,* 68.

44. Heuss, *Robert Bosch,* 58–60, 158.

45. Heuss, *Robert Bosch,* 191; Theiner, *Robert Bosch,* 80–81.

46. Joachim Rogall, "Liberal Politics and Social Responsibility," in "Robert Bosch: His Life and Work," 56.

47. Theiner, *Robert Bosch,* 79–80.

48. Jürgen Mulert, "Erfolgsbeteiligung und Vermögensbildung der Arbeitnehmer bei der Firma Robert Bosch Zwischen 1886 und 1945," *Zeitschrift für Unternehmensgeschichte* 30 (1985): 5.

49. Heuss, *Robert Bosch,* 384–385, 391.

50. Heuss, *Robert Bosch,* 190; Theiner, *Robert Bosch,* 68.

51. Theiner, *Robert Bosch,* 81–84.

52. Theiner, *Robert Bosch,* 102.

53. Theiner, *Robert Bosch,* 190–192; "From Vermögensverwaltung Bosch to Robert Bosch Stiftung," Bosch, accessed January 27, 2022, https://www.bosch.com/stories/origin -robert-bosch-stiftung.

54. Theiner, *Robert Bosch,* 197–198.

55. Theiner, *Robert Bosch,* 243.

56. Theiner, *Robert Bosch*, 188–189; Mira Wilkins, *The History of Foreign Investment in the United States, 1914–1945* (Cambridge, MA: Harvard University Press, 2004), 116.

57. Theiner, *Robert Bosch*, 187.

58. Christine Siegel, "The Years That Changed Everything," in "Robert Bosch: His Life and Work," 38–41.

59. Robert Bosch, *The Prevention of Future Crises in the World Economic System* (London: Constable, 1937), 10.

60. Heuss, *Robert Bosch*, 156.

61. Quoted in "Apart from the Alleviation of All Kinds of Hardship," Bosch, accessed June 21, 2021, https://www.bosch.com/stories/robert-bosch-education-and-healthcare/.

62. Theiner, *Robert Bosch*, 104, 117.

63. Quoted in Sabine Lutz, "Education and Healthcare," in "Robert Bosch: His Life and Work," 49–50.

64. Theiner, *Robert Bosch*, 112–113; Lutz, "Education and Healthcare," 49–50.

65. Theiner, *Robert Bosch*, 121, 125, 199.

66. Theiner, *Robert Bosch*, 301.

67. Jütte, "Healing Power of Nature"; Theiner, *Robert Bosch*, 303.

68. Theiner, *Robert Bosch*, 200–202.

69. Martyn Bond, *Hitler's Cosmopolitan Bastard: Count Richard Coudenhove-Kalergi and His Vision of Europe* (Montreal: McGill–Queen's University Press, 2021), 138.

70. Rogall, "Liberal Politics," 56–59.

71. Theiner, *Robert Bosch*, 213–219.

72. Bond, *Hitler's Cosmopolitan Bastard*.

73. Theiner, *Robert Bosch*, 239.

74. Ralf Banken, "Introduction: The Room for Manoeuvre for Firms in the Third Reich," *Business History* 62, no. 3 (2020): 377.

75. Lothar Gall et al., *The Deutsche Bank, 1870–1995* (London: Weidenfeld and Nicolson, 1995), 283.

76. Harold James, *The Deutsche Bank and the Nazi Economic War against the Jews* (Cambridge: Cambridge University Press, 2001).

77. Geoffrey Jones and Christina Lubinski, "Managing Political Risk in Global Business: Beiersdorf 1914–1990," *Enterprise and Society* 13, no. 1 (2012): 11; Alfred Reckendrees, *Beiersdorf: The Company behind the Brands Nivea, Tesa, Hansaplast & Co* (Munich: Verlag C. H. Beck, 2018).

78. Hans Mommsen, *Alternatives to Hitler: German Resistance under the Third Reich* (London: I. B. Tauris, 2003), 36.

79. On IG Farben, see Peter Hayes, "The European Strategies of IG Farben, 1925–45," in *Quest for Economic Empire: European Strategies of German Big Business in the Twentieth Century*, ed. Volker R. Berghahn (Providence, RI: Berghahn Books, 1996), 55–64.

80. Stanley Goldman, "A Fuhrer of Industry: Krupp before, during, and after Nuremberg," *Loyola of Los Angeles International and Comparative Law Review* 39 (2017): 187–208, http://digitalcommons.lmu.edu/ilr/vol39/iss1/9.

81. Peter Hayes, *From Cooperation to Complicity: Degussa in the Third Reich* (New York: Cambridge University Press, 2004).

82. Patricia Posner, *The Pharmacist of Auschwitz: The Untold Story of Victor Capesius* (London: Crux, 2017), 61–70.

83. Gerald D. Feldman, *Allianz and the German Insurance Business, 1933–1945* (Cambridge: Cambridge University Press, 2001); Karen Bartlett, *Architects of Death: The Family Who Engineered the Holocaust* (London: Biteback Publishing, 2018).

84. Banken, "Introduction," 385.

85. Johannes Bähr, "Between Values Orientation and Economic Logic: Bosch in the Third Reich," *Business History* 62, no. 3 (2020): 442.

86. Bähr, "Between Values Orientation," 442.

87. Bähr, "Between Values Orientation," 443–445.

88. Bähr, "Between Values Orientation," 447; Theiner, *Robert Bosch*, 286.

89. Bähr, "Between Values Orientation," 445.

90. Theiner, *Robert Bosch*, 320.

91. Bähr, "Between Values Orientation," 446–447; Angela Martin, *Ich sah den Namen Bosch* (Berlin: Metropol, 2002).

92. "Robert Bosch, Industrialist, Dies in Berlin," *New York Herald Tribune*, March 13, 1942.

93. David de Jong, *Nazi Billionaires: The Dark History of Germany's Wealthiest Dynasties* (Boston: Mariner, 2022).

94. Jonathan Kolieb, "Through the Looking-Glass: Nuremberg's Confusing Legacy on Corporate Accountability under International Law," *American University International Law Review* 32, no. 2 (2015): 569–604, http://digitalcommons.wcl.american.edu/auilr/vol32/iss2/5.

95. Kuntz, "German Corporate Law," 222–223.

96. "Reconstruction 1946–1959," Bosch, accessed January 23, 2022, https://www.bosch .com/stories/1946-1959-new-beginning-and-reconstruction/.

97. Theiner, *Robert Bosch*, 401.

98. Purpose Foundation, *Steward Ownership: Rethinking Ownership in the 21st Century* (Basel: Purpose Foundation, n.d.), 46–49.

99. Bosch, *Shifting Paradigms: Annual Report 2020* (Stuttgart: Bosch, 2021).

100. Colin Mayer, *Prosperity: Better Business Makes the Greater Good* (Oxford: Oxford University Press, 2018), 162.

4. The Challenge of Latecomer States

1. This chapter follows standard Japanese name usage. Shibusawa was the family name, and Eiichi his given name.

2. Geoffrey Jones, "The Great Divergence and the Great Convergence," in *The Routledge Companion to the Makers of Global Business*, ed. Teresa da Silva Lopes, Christina Lubinski, and Heidi J. S. Tworek (New York: Routledge, 2020), 578–592.

3. Ronald Findlay and Kevin H. O'Rourke, "Commodity Market Integration, 1500–2000," in *Globalization in Historical Perspective*, ed. Michael D. Bordo, Alan M. Taylor, and Jeffrey G. Williamson (Chicago: University of Chicago Press, 2003), 35–43.

4. "Maddison Project Database 2020," University of Groningen, accessed January 29, 2022, https://www.rug.nl/ggdc/historicaldevelopment/maddison/releases/maddison-project -database-2020. This latest version of the Maddison database uses a standard measure of 2011 international dollars, which are a hypothetical unit of currency that has the same purchasing power parity that the US dollar had in the United States in 2011.

5. Jeffrey G. Williamson, "Five Centuries of Latin American Income Inequality," *Revista de Historia Economica—Journal of Iberian and Latin American Economic History* 28, no. 2 (2010): 227–252.

6. Paul Bairoch, "International Industrialization Levels from 1750 to 1980," *Journal of European Economic History* 11, no. 1 (1982): 269–333.

7. The huge literature on the history of India and the role of the East India Company can be approached in Barbara D. Metcalf and Thomas R. Metcalf, *A Concise History of Modern India* (Cambridge: Cambridge University Press, 2006); and Jeffrey Craig, *Modern India: A Very Short Introduction* (Oxford: Oxford University Press, 2017).

8. David Clingingsmith and Jeffrey G. Williamson, "De-industrialization in 18th and 19th Century India: Mughal Decline, Climate Shocks and British Industrial Ascent," *Explorations in Economic History* 45, no. 3 (July 2008): 209–234.

9. Tirthankar Roy, *The Economic History of India, 1857–1947* (New Delhi: Oxford University Press, 2000), chap. 7.

10. Roy, *Economic History,* 310–311; R. Govinda and K. Biswal, "Mapping Literacy in India: Who Are the Illiterates and Where Do We Find Them?," background paper prepared for the Education for All Global Monitoring Report 2006, *Literacy for Life,* United Nations Educational, Scientific and Cultural Organization, April 20, 2005, https://unesdoc.unesco.org /ark:/48223/pf0000146016.

11. Carl A. Trocki, *Opium, Empire and the Global Political Economy: A Study of the Asian Opium Trade, 1750–1950* (London: Routledge, 1999), 86.

12. Bas van Leeuwen and Jieli van Leeuwen-Li, "Education since 1820," in *How Was Life? Global Well-Being since 1820,* ed. Jan Luiten van Zanden et al. (Paris: OECD, 2014), 87–100.

13. Stanley L. Engerman, Elisa V. Mariscal, and Kenneth L. Sokoloff, "The Evolution of Schooling in the Americas, 1800–1925," in *Human Capital and Institutions: A Long-Run View,* ed. David Eltis, Frank D. Lewis, and Kenneth L. Sokoloff (Cambridge: Cambridge University Press, 2009), 93–142.

14. Maria Ines Barbero, "Business Groups in Nineteenth and Twentieth Century Argentina," in *The Impact of Globalization on Argentina and Chile,* ed. Geoffrey Jones and Andrea Lluch (Northampton, MA: Edward Elgar, 2015), 8–14; Geoffrey Jones and Andrea Lluch, "Ernesto Tornquist: Making a Fortune on the Pampas" (Harvard Business School Case 9-807-155, rev. April 14, 2020).

15. Cynthia Sanborn, "Philanthropy in Latin America: Historical Traditions and Current Trends," in *Philanthropy and Social Change in Latin America,* ed. Cynthia Sanborn and Felipe Portocarrero (Cambridge, MA: Harvard University Press, 2005), 5–6.

16. Sundar Pushpa, *Business and Community: The Story of Corporate Social Responsibility in India* (New Delhi: Sage, 2013), 37–40.

17. Dwijendra Tripathi, *The Oxford History of Indian Business* (Oxford: Oxford University Press, 2004), 119–120.

18. Tirthankar Roy, *A Business History of India* (Cambridge: Cambridge University Press, 2018), 109; Ashok V. Desai, "The Parsis: Entrepreneurial Success," in *The Oxford India Anthology of Business History,* ed. Medha M. Kudaisya (New Delhi: Oxford University Press, 2011), 122–130.

19. Christine Dobbin, *Asian Entrepreneurial Minorities: Conjoint Communities in the Making of the World Economy, 1570–1940* (Richmond, UK: Curzon, 1996), 97.

20. Pushpa, *Business and Community,* 87, 96, 99.

21. Roy, *Business History of India,* 111.

22. Mircea Raianu, *Tata: The Global Corporation That Built Indian Capitalism* (Cambridge, MA: Harvard University Press, 2021), 20–29.

23. Tripathi, *Oxford History of Indian Business,* 149.

24. Tripathi, *Oxford History of Indian Business,* 151.

25. Raianu, *Tata,* 29–30; Skip Worden, "The Role of Religious and Nationalist Ethics in Strategic Leadership: The Case of J. N. Tata," *Journal of Business Ethics* 47, no. 2 (2003): 155.

26. Tripathi, *Oxford History of Indian Business,* 161.

27. Quoted in Gareth Austin, Carlos Dávila, and Geoffrey Jones, "The Alternative Business History: Business in Emerging Markets," *Business History Review* 91, no. 3 (Fall 2017): 563.

28. "People First," Tata Group, accessed May 3, 2020, https://www.tata.com/newsroom/people-first-labour-welfare.

29. Worden, "Role of Religious and Nationalist Ethics," 153–154, 157–160.

30. Mircea Raianu, "The Incorporation of India: The Tata Business Firm between Empire and Nation, ca. 1860–1970," *Enterprise and Society* 19, no. 4 (2018): 817.

31. Quoted in Pushpa, *Business and Community,* 105–106.

32. Pushpa, *Business and Community,* 105.

33. Worden, "Role of Religious and Nationalist Ethics," 155–157.

34. Pushpa, *Business and Community,* 106.

35. Kikkawa Takeo, "Introduction," in *Ethical Capitalism: Shibusawa Eiichi and Business Leadership in Global Perspective,* ed. Patrick Fridenson and Kikkawa Takeo (Toronto: University of Toronto Press, 2017), 9.

36. Raianu, *Tata,* 25–26; Chih-lung Lin, "Japanese Shipping in India and the British Resistance, 1891–1918," *International History Review* 32, no. 2 (2010): 308; Shibusawa Masahide, "Shibusawa Eiichi and India," in *Japan-India Dialogue: Public Symposium Report* (Tokyo: International House of Japan and Japan Foundation, 2012), 9–10, https://www.i-house.or.jp/programs/wp-content/uploads/2011/12/symposium_report.pdf.

37. Andrew Gordon, *A Modern History of Japan* (New York: Oxford University Press, 2014), 1–21.

38. Gordon, *Modern History of Japan,* 22–34.

39. Gordon, *Modern History of Japan,* 51.

40. Shimada Masakazu, *The Entrepreneur Who Built Modern Japan: Shibusawa Eiichi* (Tokyo: Japan Publishing Industry Foundation for Culture, 2017), 2–14.

41. Shimada, *Entrepreneur Who Built Modern Japan,* 19.

42. John Sagers, "Shibusawa Eiichi, Dai Ichi Bank, and the Spirit of Japanese Capitalism, 1860–1930," *Shashi: The Journal of Japanese Business and Company History* 3, no. 1 (2014): 4.

43. Gordon, *Modern History of Japan,* 57–59, 61–71.

44. Gordon, *Modern History of Japan,* 70–72.

45. Johannes Hirschmeier and Tsunehiko Yui, *The Development of Japanese Business, 1600–1980* (London: George Allen and Unwin, 1981), 142.

46. William D. Wray, *Mitsubishi and the N.Y.K., 1870–1914* (Cambridge, MA: Harvard University Press, 1984).

47. Shimada Masakazu, "Tensions between the Open Market Model and the Closed Zaibatsu Model," in Fridenson and Kikkawa, *Ethical Capitalism,* 29.

48. John H. Sagers, *Confucian Capitalism: Shibusawa Eiichi, Business Ethics, and Economic Development in Meiji Japan* (London: Palgrave Macmillan, 2018), 96.

49. Shimada, *Entrepreneur Who Built Modern Japan,* 35.

50. Kimura Masato, "Shibusawa Eiichi's View of Business Morality in Global Society," in Fridenson and Kikkawa, *Ethical Capitalism,* 126–127.

51. Sagers, *Confucian Capitalism,* 75.

52. Shibusawa Masahide, *The Private Diplomacy of Shibusawa Eiichi: Visionary Entrepreneur and Transnationalist of Modern Japan* (Folkestone, UK: Renaissance Books, 2018), 68.

53. Takao Tsuchiya, "Pioneers of Modern Japan: V: Shibusawa Eiichi," *Japan Quarterly* 12, no. 1 (January 1965): 107.

54. Shimada, "Tensions between the Open Market Model," 21–23.

55. Sagers, *Confucian Capitalism,* 91.

56. Kazuo Sugiyama, "Business Finance in Japanese Business History," *Japanese Yearbook on Business History* 1 (1985): 27.

57. Rie Sugiyama, "Shibusawa Eiichi's Strategies towards Local Business and Social Welfare" (unpublished manuscript, 2020).

58. Sagers, *Confucian Capitalism,* 93.
59. Shibusawa, *Private Diplomacy,* 132–133.
60. Ken Tadashi Oshima, "Denenchōfu: Building the Garden City in Japan," *Journal of the Society of Architectural Historians* 55, no. 2 (1996): 150.
61. "Chronology of the Life of Shibusawa Eiichi," Shibusawa Eiichi Memorial Foundation, accessed March 21, 2021, https://www.shibusawa.or.jp/english/eiichi/chronology.html.
62. Shibusawa, *Private Diplomacy,* 73–86, 223–224.
63. The real GDP per capita of the United States, Britain, and Germany in 1931 was $9,931, $8,190, and $5,821, respectively. All three had fallen because of the onset of the Great Depression. The equivalent figures for China and India were $1,105 and $1,133, respectively. "Maddison Project Database 2020."
64. Nicholas F. Gier, "Whitehead, Confucius, and the Aesthetics of Virtue," *Asian Philosophy* 14, no. 2 (2004): 171–190.
65. Sagers, *Confucian Capitalism,* 192.
66. Sagers, *Confucian Capitalism,* 9.
67. Tanaka Kazuhiro, "Harmony between Morality and Economy," in Fridenson and Kikkawa, *Ethical Capitalism,* 41–43.
68. Tanaka, "Harmony between Morality and Economy," 48.
69. Sugiyama, "Shibusawa Eiichi's Strategies."
70. Shimada, *Entrepreneur Who Built Modern Japan,* 126–161; Sugiyama, "Shibusawa Eiichi's Strategies."
71. Kimura, "Shibusawa Eiichi's View," 123.
72. Fridenson and Kikkawa, *Ethical Capitalism.*
73. Sagers, *Confucian Capitalism,* 192.
74. Janet Hunter and Geoffrey Jones, "Ethical Business, Corruption and Economic Development in Comparative Perspective," in *Business, Ethics and Institutions,* ed. Asli M. Colpan and Geoffrey Jones (New York: Routledge, 2020), 230–234.
75. Sagers, *Confucian Capitalism,* 7.
76. Sagers, *Confucian Capitalism,* 173.
77. Shimada, *Entrepreneur Who Built Modern Japan,* 142–149.
78. Sugiyama, "Shibusawa Eiichi's Strategies."
79. Sagers, "Shibusawa Eiichi," 5.
80. Kikkawa Takeo, "The Crisis of Capitalism and the Gapponshugi of Shibusawa Eiichi," in Fridenson and Kikkawa, *Ethical Capitalism,* 179.
81. Shimada, *Entrepreneur Who Built Modern Japan,* 131–139.
82. Shimada, *Entrepreneur Who Built Modern Japan,* 127–131.
83. *A Life of Jinzo Naruse,* 2nd ed. (Tokyo: Japanese Women's University, 2002), https://www5.jwu.ac.jp/st/grp/naruse150/pdf/naruse_english.pdf.
84. Kimura, "Shibusawa Eiichi's View," 123.
85. Sagers, *Confucian Capitalism,* 202–203.
86. Sagers, *Confucian Capitalism,* 203–205.
87. Alexis Dudden, *Japan's Colonization of Korea: Discourse and Power* (Honolulu: University of Hawai'i Press, 2005).
88. Quoted in Geoffrey Jones, Gabriel Ellsworth, and Ryo Takahasi, "From Farm Boy to Financier: Eiichi Shibusawa and the Creation of Modern Japan" (Harvard Business School Case 9-321-043, rev. July 20, 2021), 14.
89. Sagers, *Confucian Capitalism,* 162.
90. Sagers, "Shibusawa Eiichi."
91. Shibusawa, *Private Diplomacy,* 284–294.

92. Raianu, "Incorporation of India," 822.

93. Roy, *Business History of India,* 171, 244.

94. "Our History," Mizuho Financial Group, accessed February 1, 2022, https://www .mizuhogroup.com/who-we-are/history.

95. Geoffrey Jones and Rei Morimoto, "Is the Business World Finally Ready for the Wisdom of Shibusawa?," Working Knowledge, Harvard Business School, November 5, 2021, https://hbswk.hbs.edu/item/is-the-business-world-finally-ready-for-the-wisdom-of -shibusawa.

96. Reiji Yoshida, "Japan Announces New ¥10,000, ¥5,000 and ¥1,000 Bank Notes as Reiwa Era Looms," *Japan Times,* April 9, 2019.

5. Educating Future Leaders

1. Wallace B. Donham, "Address," *Bulletin of the Harvard Business School Alumni Association* 3, no. 6 (July 1, 1927): 195–196.

2. Robert R. Locke, *The End of the Practical Man: Entrepreneurship and Higher Education in Germany, France, and Great Britain, 1880–1940* (Greenwich, CT: JAI Press, 1984); Rolv Petter Amdam, "Business Education," in *The Oxford History Handbook of Business History,* ed. Geoffrey Jones and Jonathan Zeitlin (Oxford: Oxford University Press, 2008), 584–586.

3. Rakesh Khurana, *From Higher Aims to Hired Hands: The Social Transformation of American Business Schools and the Unfulfilled Promise of Management as a Profession* (Princeton, NJ: Princeton University Press, 2007), 88–89.

4. Steven A. Sass, *The Pragmatic Imagination: A History of the Wharton School, 1881– 1981* (Philadelphia: University of Pennsylvania Press, 1982), chaps. 1 and 2.

5. Wayne G. Broehl, *Tuck & Tucker: The Origin of the Graduate Business School* (Hanover, NH: University Press of New England, 1999), 35–43.

6. Khurana, *From Higher Aims,* 105–111.

7. Amdam, "Business Education," 584.

8. Khurana, *From Higher Aims,* 111, 133–134. For the class of 2021, 57 percent entered consultancy and financial services, and 97 percent all forms of business. A further 3 percent entered government or nonprofits.

9. Steven Conn, *Nothing Succeeds like Failure: The Sad History of American Business Schools* (Ithaca, NY: Cornell University Press, 2019), 57–59.

10. Broehl, *Tuck & Tucker,* 36.

11. Jeffrey L. Cruikshank, *A Delicate Experiment: The Harvard Business School, 1908– 1945* (Boston: Harvard Business School Press, 1987), 35.

12. Khurana, *From Higher Aims,* 115; Earl J. Hamilton, "Edwin Francis Gay," *American Economic Review* 37, no. 3 (1947): 410–413.

13. Gabriel Abend, *The Moral Background: An Inquiry into the History of Business Ethics* (Princeton, NJ: Princeton University Press, 2014), 180–181.

14. Abend, *Moral Background,* 193.

15. Abend, *Moral Background,* 185. The remaining principles were integrity, pursuit of knowledge, continuity of service, continuity of operation, performance of contracts in letter and in spirit, truthfulness, elimination of waste, avoidance of unfair competition, impartial arbitration, lawful cooperation, and acting in ways that inspire public confidence and so make restrictive legislation unnecessary.

16. Gabriel Abend, "The Origins of Business Ethics in American Universities, 1902– 1936," *Business Ethics Quarterly* 23, no. 2 (2013): 178–181.

17. Abend, "Origins of Business Ethics," 183.

18. The speech was published two years later as Roswell C. McCrea, "The Curriculum of a School of Commerce," in *Proceedings of the Second Pan American Scientific Congress: Section IV, Pt. 1* (Washington, DC: Government Printing Office, 1917), 280.

19. Sass, *Pragmatic Imagination,* 167–173.

20. Khurana, *From Higher Aims,* 92–96; Robert Kanigel, *The One Best Way: Frederick Winslow Taylor and the Enigma of Efficiency* (New York: Viking Books, 1997); Hugo Münsterberg, *Psychology and Industrial Efficiency* (Boston: Houghton Mifflin, 1913).

21. Khurana, *From Higher Aims,* 145–146.

22. Khurana, *From Higher Aims,* 119–121.

23. Thorstein Veblen, *The Higher Learning in America* (Stanford, CA: Academic Reprints, 1954), 203; Ellen S. O'Connor, "The Politics of Management Thought: A Case Study of the Harvard Business School and the Human Relations School," *Academy of Management Review* 24, no. 1 (1999): 121.

24. Khurana, *From Higher Aims,* 97.

25. Abend, "Origins of Business Ethics," 178–181.

26. Cruikshank, *Delicate Experiment,* 94–95; David A. Garvin, "Making the Case," *Harvard Magazine,* September–October 2003, https://harvardmagazine.com/2003/09/making-the-case-html; Frederik Ohles et al., "Donham, Wallace Brett," in *Biographical Dictionary of Modern American Educators* (Westport, CT: Greenwood Press, 1978), 89–90.

27. Marc A. VanOverbeke, *The Standardization of American Schooling: Linking Secondary and Higher Education, 1870–1910* (New York: Palgrave Macmillan, 2008), 107–108.

28. Cruikshank, *Delicate Experiment,* 94–95; Ohles et al., "Donham, Wallace Brett," 89–90.

29. Cruikshank, *Delicate Experiment,* 94–95; Ohles et al., "Donham, Wallace Brett," 89–90.

30. Garvin, "Making the Case"; Ohles et al., "Donham, Wallace Brett," 89–90.

31. Ohles et al., "Donham, Wallace Brett," 89–90; Cruikshank, *Delicate Experiment,* 94.

32. Cruikshank, *Delicate Experiment,* 94–95.

33. Graduate School of Business Administration, Harvard University, *Corporation Finance ("Business 25"): Official Report of the Lectures in Full in 1908–1909* (Boston: President and Fellows of Harvard College, 1909), 189–206.

34. Cruikshank, *Delicate Experiment,* 95.

35. O'Connor, "Politics of Management Thought," 121.

36. Cruikshank, *Delicate Experiment,* 95–109; Colleen Walsh, "From Law School to Business School—Evolution of the Case Method," *Harvard Gazette,* April 3, 2008, https://news.harvard.edu/gazette/story/2008/04/from-law-school-to-business-school-evolution-of-the-case-method/; Edmond F. Wright to Charles E. Olson, May 27, 1930, Dean's Office Correspondence Files (Wallace B. Donham, Dean), HBS Archives, Baker Library, Harvard Business School; "Ex-Dean W. Donham of Busy School Dies in Cambridge Home," *Harbus News,* November 30, 1954, https://www.thecrimson.com/article/1954/11/30/ex-dean-w-donham-of-busy-school/.

37. Mie Augier and James G. March, *The Roots, Rituals, and Rhetorics of Change: North American Business Schools after the Second World War* (Stanford, CA: Stanford University Press, 2011), 152–153.

38. Cruikshank, *Delicate Experiment,* 135.

39. Todd Bridgman, Stephen Cummings, and Colm McLaughlin, "Restating the Case: How Revisiting the Development of the Case Method Can Help Us Think Differently about the Future of the Business School," *Academy of Management Learning and Education* 15, no. 4 (2016): 728–729, 734; Cruikshank, *Delicate Experiment,* 94–95.

40. Bridgman, Cummings, and McLaughlin, "Restating the Case," 728–729, 734; Cruikshank, *Delicate Experiment*, 95.

41. Stephen Cummings et al., *A New History of Management* (Cambridge: Cambridge University Press, 2017), 161.

42. O'Connor, "Politics of Management Thought," 122.

43. Cruikshank, *Delicate Experiment*, 168.

44. Wallace Donham, "Business Management as a Profession: The Professional Side of Business Training," speech given at the Bureau of Personnel Administration, February 25, 1926, Dean's Office Correspondence Files (Wallace B. Donham, Dean), HBS Archives, Baker Library, Harvard Business School.

45. Wallace B. Donham, "The Social Significance of Business," *Bulletin of the Harvard Business School Alumni Association* 4, no. 3 (February 1, 1928), 100–105, 116–118.

46. Cruikshank, *Delicate Experiment*, 168; Hani Morgan, "Carl Frederick Taeusch (1889–1951)," in *Dictionary of Modern American Philosophers*, ed. John R. Shook (New York: Bloomsbury, 2005), 2373–2374; Wallace Donham to C. Sidney Shepard, May 27, 1927, Dean's Office Correspondence Files (Wallace B. Donham, Dean), HBS Archives, Baker Library, Harvard Business School.

47. Wallace Donham to Henry Allen Moe, secretary, John Simon Guggenheim Memorial Foundation, January 5, 1927, Dean's Office Correspondence Files (Wallace B. Donham, Dean), HBS Archives, Baker Library, Harvard Business School.

48. Abend, "Origins of Business Ethics," 178–179.

49. Wallace Donham to Ralph E. Heilman, October 22, 1928, Dean's Office Correspondence Files (Wallace B. Donham, Dean), HBS Archives, Baker Library, Harvard Business School.

50. Official Register of Harvard University, Graduate School of Business Administration, vol. 25, no. 12 (March 24, 1928), 40, Baker Library Special Collections, Harvard Business School.

51. "Dr. Carl Taeusch, Ex-Professor, 72: Author, Teacher of Public Administration Is Dead," *New York Times*, September 23, 1961; Morgan, "Carl Frederick Taeusch"; C. F. Taeusch, "Should the Doctor Testify?," *International Journal of Ethics* 38, no. 4 (1928): 401–415; Carl F. Taeusch, "Business Ethics," *International Journal of Ethics* 42, no. 1 (1931): 273–288.

52. Carl F. Taeusch, *Policy and Ethics in Business* (New York: McGraw-Hill, 1931), vii–ix, 197–201.

53. A. D. Henderson to Wallace Donham, March 28, 1933, Dean's Office Correspondence Files (Wallace B. Donham, Dean), HBS Archives, Baker Library, Harvard Business School.

54. Wallace Donham to A. D. Henderson, March 30, 1933, Dean's Office Correspondence Files (Wallace B. Donham, Dean), HBS Archives, Baker Library, Harvard Business School.

55. Cruikshank, *Delicate Experiment*, 168.

56. Official Register of Harvard University, Graduate School of Business Administration, vol. 32, no. 6 (March 2, 1935), 75.

57. "Dr. Carl Taeusch, Ex-Professor"; Morgan, "Carl Frederick Taeusch."

58. O'Connor, "Politics of Management Thought," 121.

59. Donham, "Social Significance of Business," 122.

60. Wallace Donham to A. Lawrence Lowell, November 4, 1924, Dean's Office Correspondence Files (Wallace B. Donham, Dean), HBS Archives, Baker Library, Harvard Business School.

61. Thomas K. McCraw, Nancy F. Koehn, and H. V. Nelles, "Business History," in *The Intellectual Venture Capitalist: John H. McArthur and the Work of the Harvard Business*

School, 1980–1995, ed. Thomas K. McCraw and Jeffrey L. Cruikshank (Boston: Harvard Business School Press, 1999), 246.

62. Robert Fredona and Sophus A. Reinert, "The Harvard Research Center in Entrepreneurial History and the Daimonic Entrepreneur," *History of Political Economy* 49, no. 2 (2017): 273; "Norman Scott Brien Gras, 1884–1956," *Business History Review* 30, no. 4 (1956): 357–360; McCraw, Koehn, and Nelles, "Business History," 246–247.

63. N. S. B. Gras and Henrietta M. Larson, *Casebook in American Business History* (New York: Irvington Publishers, 1939). On Larson's career, see Mary Yeager, "Mavericks and Mavens of Business History: Miriam Beard and Henrietta Larson," *Enterprise and Society* 2, no. 4 (2001): 687–768.

64. Henrietta Larson, "Brush-Up Lecture," Business History Course Notes, December 1953, Henrietta Larson Papers, Baker Library Special Collections.

65. N. S. B. Gras, *Business and Capitalism: An Introduction to Business History* (1939; repr., Washington, DC: Beard Books, 2003), 227.

66. Gras, *Business and Capitalism,* 227–237.

67. Victor Lowe, *Alfred North Whitehead: The Man and His Work,* vol. 1 (Baltimore: Johns Hopkins University Press, 1985), 33, 44–48, 84–85, 224, 316–317; Ronald Desmet and Andrew David Irvine, "Alfred North Whitehead," in *The Stanford Encyclopedia of Philosophy,* ed. Edward N. Zalta, Fall 2018, https://plato.stanford.edu/archives/fall2018/entries /whitehead.

68. George Louis Kline, *Alfred North Whitehead: Essays on His Philosophy* (Lanham, MD: University Press of America, 1989), 10.

69. John Edwin Smith, *The Spirit of American Philosophy* (Albany: State University of New York Press, 1983), 163; Victor Lowe, *Alfred North Whitehead: The Man and His Work,* vol. 2 (Baltimore: Johns Hopkins University Press, 1990), 157–158; Bridgman, Cummings, and McLaughlin, "Restating the Case," 731.

70. Alfred North Whitehead, *Science and the Modern World* (Cambridge: Cambridge University Press, 2011), 64.

71. Lowe, *Alfred North Whitehead,* 2:183.

72. Alfred North Whitehead, *Religion in the Making* (Cambridge: Cambridge University Press, 2011), 26.

73. Whitehead, *Religion in the Making,* 8, 26.

74. Alfred North Whitehead, *The Aims of Education* (New York: Free Press, 1929), 2.

75. Lowe, *Alfred North Whitehead,* 2:46.

76. Franz Riffert, "Whitehead's Cyclic Theory of Learning and Contemporary Empirical Educational Research," in *Alfred North Whitehead on Learning and Education: Theory and Application,* ed. Franz Riffert (Cambridge: Cambridge Scholars Press, 2005), 89–99.

77. Wallace Donham, "Business and Religion," *Bulletin of the Harvard Business School Alumni* Association, 2, no. 4 (May 6, 1926): 121, 123.

78. Wallace Donham to Right Reverend Logan H. Roots, January 2, 1936, Dean's Office Correspondence Files (Wallace B. Donham, Dean), HBS Archives, Baker Library, Harvard Business School.

79. Donham, "Social Significance of Business," 103.

80. Wallace B. Donham, *Education for Responsible Living* (Cambridge, MA: Harvard University Press, 1944), 115.

81. Wallace Brett Donham, "Why Experiment? The Case System in College Teaching of Social Science," *Journal of General Education* 3, no. 2 (1949): 151.

82. Donham, "Why Experiment?," 145–156; Brian Hendley, "In Search of the Elusive Whitehead: A Cautionary Tale," *Process Studies* 31, no. 2 (2002): 57; Cruikshank, *Delicate Experiment,* 155.

83. For example, see Wallace Donham to A. D. Henderson, March 30, 1933; Wallace Donham to Hon. Charles Francis Adams, January 21, 1931; and speech to the Sunday Breakfast Club, meeting no. 2, March 26, 1933, all in Dean's Office Correspondence Files (Wallace B. Donham, Dean), HBS Archives, Baker Library, Harvard Business School; and Wallace B. Donham, *Business Adrift* (New York: Whittlesey House, 1931).

84. Hendley, "In Search of the Elusive Whitehead," 57–58.

85. Whitehead, *Aims of Education*, 101.

86. Lowe, *Alfred North Whitehead*, 2:165.

87. Tor Hernes, "Alfred North Whitehead (1861–1947)," in *The Oxford Handbook of Process Philosophy and Organization Studies*, ed. Jenny Helin et al. (Oxford: Oxford University Press, 2014), 257.

88. Desmet and Irvine, "Alfred North Whitehead."

89. Donham, *Education for Responsible Living*, 119.

90. Lou Galambos, *The Public Image of Big Business in America, 1880–1940: A Quantitative Study in Social Change* (Baltimore: John Hopkins University Press, 1975), chap. 7; Christian Olaf Christiansen, *Progressive Business: An Intellectual History of the Role of Business in American Society* (Oxford: Oxford University Press, 2015), 59–60.

91. Wallace B. Donham, "Can American Business Meet the Present Emergency?," *Harvard Business Review* 9, no. 3 (April 1931).

92. Wallace Donham to Hon. Charles Francis Adams, Secretary of the Navy, January 21, 1931, Office of the Dean (Donham) Records, 1919–1942, Baker Library Special Collections.

93. Christiansen, *Progressive Business*, 60.

94. Arthur Meier Schlesinger, *The Coming of the New Deal, 1933–1935*, vol. 2 (Boston: Houghton Mifflin, 2003), 501.

95. Khurana, *From Higher Aims*, 184–186, 190–191.

96. Donham, *Business Adrift*.

97. Alfred North Whitehead, "On Foresight," in Donham, *Business Adrift*, xxvii.

98. Donham, *Business Adrift*, vii.

99. Whitehead, "Introduction. On Foresight," in Donham, *Business Adrift*, xxv, xxviii.

100. Donham, *Business Adrift*, 9, 154.

101. Cruikshank, *Delicate Experiment*, 198.

102. American Association of Collegiate Schools of Business, "Proceedings of the Eighteenth Annual Meeting (April 22–25, 1936)," AACSB Folder, Baker Library Special Collections, 120–121.

103. O'Connor, "Politics of Management Thought," 122–124; Khurana, *From Higher Aims*, 221–222.

104. Michel Anteby and Rakesh Khurana, "The Human Relations Movement: Harvard Business School and the Hawthorne Experiments (1924–1933)," Harvard Business School, Baker Library Historical Collections, accessed September 14, 2018, https://www.library.hbs.edu/hc/hawthorne/intro.html.

105. Khurana, *From Higher Aims*, 222.

106. O'Connor, "Politics of Management Thought," 122.

107. W. B. Donham to James B. Conant, February 5, 1937, Office of the Dean (Donham) Records, 1919–1942, Baker Library Special Collections.

108. Frank Ayres to Thomas S. Shepperd, president, Ulen and Company, March 31, 1933, Industrial Life Control Folder, Baker Library Special Collections.

109. "Use of Pictures in a School of Business Administration," *Bulletin of the Business Historical Society* 6, no. 2 (March 1932): 5–9.

110. Philip Cabot to James B. Conant, December 3, 1934, Philip Cabot Papers, Baker Library Special Collections.

111. Cabot to Conant, December 3, 1934; "Philip Cabot," *Bulletin of the Business Historical Society* 16, no. 3 (June 1942): 64–66, http://www.jstor.org/stable/3110946.

112. Cabot to Conant, December 3, 1934.

113. "Business and Industrial Leaders Attend Special Harvard Classes," January 18, 1936, special dispatch to the *Sun,* Philip Cabot Papers, Baker Library Special Collections.

114. Business Executives' Discussion Group, 1936–1937, April meeting 1937; and Business Executives' Discussion Group, 1937–38, December 1937, both in Philip Cabot Papers, Baker Library Special Collections.

115. "Programs for Meetings of Prof. Cabot's Business Executives' Discussion Group, 1934–35, and 1935–36, 1936–37, and 1937–38"; and "Week End 8th + 9th Feb [1936]: The Social Problems of an Industrial Civilization," both in Philip Cabot Papers, Baker Library Special Collections.

116. Philip Cabot to Rogers Flather, February 12, 1940, Philip Cabot Papers, Baker Library Special Collections.

117. Philip Cabot to Frank Abrams, December 2, 1939, Philip Cabot Papers, Baker Library Special Collections.

118. Philip Cabot to President Franklin D. Roosevelt, May 8, 1941, Philip Cabot Papers, Baker Library Special Collections.

119. "Philip Cabot."

120. Khurana, *From Higher Aims,* 190–191.

121. Wallace Donham, *Business Looks at the Unforeseen* (New York: Whittlesey House, 1932), 59–61.

122. Donham, *Business Looks,* 13.

123. Donham, *Business Looks,* 70.

124. Wallace Donham, memorandum to the faculty, October 3, 1934, Office of the Dean (Donham) Records, 1919–1942, Baker Library Special Collections.

125. Khurana, *From Higher Aims,* 190–191.

126. James B. Conant to Wallace Donham, October 25, 1934, Office of the Dean (Donham) Records, 1919–1942, Baker Library Special Collections.

127. Peter Tufano, "Training Leaders to Win Wars and Forge Peace: Lessons from History," *Business History Review* 94, no. 4 (2020): 821–833; Cruikshank, *Delicate Experiment,* 216–276.

128. Donham, *Education for Responsible Living.*

129. Serge Elisséeff, "Wallace Brett Donham (1877–1954)," *Harvard Journal of Asiatic Studies* 18, no. 1/2 (1955): vii–ix.

130. Andrew Jack, "Social Purpose: How Business Schools around the World Measure Up," *Financial Times,* October 20, 2019; Seb Murry, "Pursuit of Social Purpose Sends Business Schools Back to Their Roots," *Financial Times,* January 16, 2022.

131. Hugh Mercer Curtler, "Can Virtue Be Taught?," *Humanitas* 7, no. 1 (1994): 43–50.

132. Donald K. David, "Business Responsibilities in an Uncertain World," *Harvard Business Review* 27, no. 3 (1949): 1; Bert Spector, "'Business Responsibilities in a Divided World': The Cold War Roots of the Corporate Social Responsibility Movement," *Enterprise and Society* 9, no. 2 (2018): 314–366.

133. Lynn Sharp Paine and Thomas R. Piper, "Ethics, Organizations, and Business Schools," in McCraw and Cruikshank, *Intellectual Venture Capitalist,* 226. The study cited was Robert A. Gordon and James E. Howell, *Higher Education for Business* (New York: Columbia University Press, 1959), 111.

134. John S. Rosenberg, "Harvard Business School's Bold Agenda," *Harvard Magazine,* January 12, 2022.

6. Building a Nation, Addressing Disparities

1. These figures are drawn from "Life Expectancy (from Birth) in India from 1800 to 2020," Statista, June 2019, https://www.statista.com/statistics/1041383/life-expectancy-india -all-time/; "Life Expectancy (from Birth) in Japan, from 1860 to 2020," Statista, June 2019, https://www.statista.com/statistics/1041369/life-expectancy-japan-all-time/; and "Life Expectancy (from Birth) in the United States, from 1860 to 2020," Statista, August 2019, https://www .statista.com/statistics/1040079/life-expectancy-united-states-all-time/. See also Jeffrey Craig, *Modern India: A Very Short Introduction* (Oxford: Oxford University Press, 2017), 52.

2. Craig, *Modern India*, 27–28; Barbara D. Metcalf and Thomas R. Metcalf, *A Concise History of Modern India* (New York: Cambridge University Press, 2006), 155–166.

3. Metcalf and Metcalf, *Concise History of Modern India*, 169–175.

4. Metcalf and Metcalf, *Concise History of Modern India*, 181–185, 189–193.

5. Jaydeep Balakrishnan, Ayesha Malhotra, and Loren Falkenberg, "Multilevel Corporate Responsibility: A Comparison of Gandhi's Trusteeship with Stakeholder and Stewardship Frameworks," *Journal of Business Ethics* 141, no. 1 (2017): 133–150; Cam Caldwell et al., "Ethical Stewardship—Implications for Leadership and Trust," *Journal of Business Ethics* 78, nos. 1–2 (2008): 153–164.

6. Sundar Pushpa, *Business and Community: The Story of Corporate Social Responsibility on India* (New Delhi: Sage, 2013), 41.

7. Makrand Mehta, "Gandhi and Ahmedabad, 1915–20," *Economic and Political Weekly*, January 22, 2005, 296.

8. Christopher Key Chapple, "Jainism and Ecology," Yale Forum on Religion and Ecology, accessed June 12, 2021, https://fore.yale.edu/World-Religions/Jainism/Overview -Essay.

9. Jaithirth Rao, *Economist Gandhi: The Roots and the Relevance of the Political Economy of the Mahatma* (Gurugram, India: Penguin Portfolio, 2021); Jaithirth Rao and Shishir K. Jha, "A Less Acknowledged Source of Gandhi's Ideas of Trusteeship," *Perspectives* 53, no. 37 (2018): 36–41.

10. Geoffrey Carnall, *Gandhi's Interpreter: A Life of Horace Alexander* (Edinburgh: Edinburgh University Press, 2010); Marjorie Sykes, *An Indian Tapestry: Quaker Threads in the History of India, Pakistan and Bangladesh* (York, UK: Sessions Book Trust, 1997); Nicola Christine Jolly, "A Critical Investigation of the Breadth of Mahatma Gandhi's Religious Pluralism through an Examination of His Engagements with Atheists, Quakers and Inter-religious Marriage" (PhD diss., University of Birmingham, 2013), 120, 161–209.

11. Mircea Raianu, *Tata: The Global Corporation That Built Indian Capitalism* (Cambridge, MA: Harvard University Press, 2021), 175.

12. Medha Kudaisya, "'The Promise of Partnership': Indian Business, the State, and the Bombay Plan of 1944," *Business History Review* 88, no. 1 (2014): 104.

13. Tirthankar Roy, *A Business History of India* (Cambridge: Cambridge University Press, 2018), 147.

14. Thomas A. Timburg, *The Marwaris, from Traders to Industrialist* (New Delhi: Vikas, 1978); Timberg, *The Marwaris: From Jagat Seth to the Birlas* (New Delhi: Allen Lane, 2014); Tirthankar Roy, "Diaspora: Marwari," *Oxford Handbook Topics in History*, October 2015, https://www.oxfordhandbooks.com/view/10.1093/oxfordhb/9780199935369.001.0001 /oxfordhb-9780199935369-e-22.

15. Medha M. Kudaisya, *The Life and Times of G. D. Birla* (New Delhi: Oxford University Press, 2003), 43–44; Roy, *Business History of India*, 95–98; Dwijendra Tripathi, *The Oxford History of Indian Business* (Oxford: Oxford University Press, 2004), 166–170.

16. Kudaisya, *Life and Times of G. D. Birla*, 39.

17. Kudaisya, *Life and Times of G. D. Birla,* 188–196.

18. Pushpa, *Business and Community,* 148.

19. Roy, "Diaspora: Marwari," 11.

20. Medha Malik Kudaisya, "G. D. Birla, Big Business and India's Partition," *South Asia: Journal of South Asian Studies* 18 (1995): 194.

21. Quoted in Bidyat Chakrabarty, *Corporate Social Responsibility in India* (London: Routledge, 2012), 69.

22. Kudaisya, *Life and Times of G. D. Birla,* 162.

23. Kudaisya, "G. D. Birla," 194–195.

24. Pushpa, *Business and Community,* 147–149.

25. B. R. Nanda, *In Gandhi's Footsteps: The Life and Times of Jamnalal Bajaj* (New Delhi: Oxford University Press, 1990).

26. Nanda, *In Gandhi's Footsteps,* 20–21; "About Us," Shiksha Mandal, accessed February 24, 2022, https://www.shikshamandal.org/main/about-us/.

27. Pushpa, *Business and Community,* 52–53; Geoffrey Jones, Prabakar "PK" Kothandaraman, and Kerry Herman, "Jamnalal Bajaj, Mahatma Gandhi, and the Struggle for Indian Independence" (Harvard Business School Case 9-807-028, rev. October 14, 2020).

28. Olivier Zunz, *Philanthropy in America: A History* (Princeton, NJ: Princeton University Press, 2012), 296; Charles Harvey et al., "Andrew Carnegie and the Foundations of Contemporary Entrepreneurial Philanthropy," *Business History* 53, no. 3 (2011): 425–450.

29. Gita Piramal, *Business Legends* (New Delhi: Penguin, 1998), 309.

30. Siddhartha Raychaudhuri, "Colonialism, Indigenous Elites and the Transformation of Cities in the Non-Western World: Ahmedabad (Western India), 1890–1947," *Modern Asian Studies* 35, no. 3 (2001): 679–680.

31. Roy, *Business History of India,* 112–113; Tripathi, *Oxford History of Indian Business,* 95–96, 98, 105, 106, 115.

32. Tripathi, *Oxford History of Indian Business,* 114–115.

33. Dwijendra Tripathi, *The Dynamics of a Tradition: Kasturbhai Lalbhai and His Entrepreneurship* (New Delhi: Manohar, 1981), 46.

34. Tripathi, *Dynamics of a Tradition,* 50, 53.

35. Tripathi, *Dynamics of a Tradition,* 47–50.

36. Tripathi, *Dynamics of a Tradition,* 57.

37. Piramal, *Business Legends,* 306–307.

38. Quoted in Peter Church, *Profiles in Enterprise: Inspiring Stories of Indian Business Leaders* (New Delhi: Roli, 2015), 220.

39. Piramal, *Business Legends,* 412–413.

40. Piramal, *Business Legends,* 424.

41. Tripathi, *Dynamics of a Tradition,* 58.

42. Piramal, *Business Legends,* 304.

43. Tripathi, *Dynamics of a Tradition,* 61–64.

44. Tripathi, *Dynamics of a Tradition,* 64–66.

45. Tripathi, *Oxford History of Indian Business,* 190–191.

46. Mallika Sarabhai, interview by V. G. Narayanan, Ahmedabad, India, December 15, 2016, Creating Emerging Markets Oral History Collection, Baker Library Special Collections, Harvard Business School. She is the granddaughter of Ambalal Sarabhai.

47. Tripathi, *Dynamics of a Tradition,* 66–70.

48. Tripathi, *Oxford History of Indian Business,* 191.

49. Tripathi, *Dynamics of a Tradition,* 159–160.

50. Tripathi, *Dynamics of a Tradition,* 46–47, 151–154, 164–165. On the managing agency system, see Tripathi, *Oxford History of Indian Business,* 112–113.

51. Tripathi, *Dynamics of a Tradition,* 79–85.

52. Piramal, *Business Legends.*

53. Atul Shah and Aidan Rankin, *Jainism and Ethical Finance* (New York: Routledge, 2018), 200–207.

54. Tripathi, *Dynamics of a Tradition.*

55. Shah and Rankin, *Jainism and Ethical Finance,* 108–128, 149.

56. Shah and Rankin, *Jainism and Ethical Finance,* 25–26.

57. Tripathi, *Dynamics of a Tradition,* 89.

58. Tripathi, *Dynamics of a Tradition,* 173.

59. Pushpa, *Business and Community,* 154.

60. Tripathi, *Dynamics of a Tradition,* 175–179; Piramal, *Business Legends,* 332–333.

61. Piramal, *Business Legends,* 325–326.

62. Kudaisya, *Life and Times of G. D. Birla,* 112–117.

63. Piramal, *Business Legends,* 302–303; Tripathi, *Dynamics of a Tradition,* 179–180.

64. Tripathi, *Dynamics of a Tradition,* 181.

65. Kudaisya, "'Promise of Partnership.'"

66. Raychaudhuri, "Colonialism, Indigenous Elites," 689–690.

67. Tripathi, *Dynamics of a Tradition.*

68. Tripathi, *Dynamics of a Tradition,* 192–193; Raychaudhuri, "Colonialism, Indigenous Elites," 714; Nina Jacob, "A Comparative Study of Creative versus Non-creative Organizations" (PhD diss., Gujarat University, 1990), chap. 6, https://shodhganga.inflibnet.ac.in/bitstream/10603/48470/13/13_chapter%206.pdf.

69. Howard Spodek, *Ahmedabad: Shock City of Twentieth-Century India* (Bloomington: Indiana University Press, 2011), 125.

70. Tripathi, *Dynamics of a Tradition,* 193–194.

71. Tripathi, *Dynamics of a Tradition,* 199–200.

72. Claude Markovits, *Merchants, Traders, Entrepreneurs: Indian Business in the Colonial Era* (London: Palgrave Macmillan, 2008), 88, 90, Kudaisya, "G. D. Birla," 204.

73. Spodek, *Ahmedabad,* 126.

74. Kudaisya, "G. D. Birla," 210–212.

75. Tripathi, *Dynamics of a Tradition,* 104.

76. Kudaisya, "'Promise of Partnership,'" 128–131; Kudaisya, *Life and Times of G. D. Birla,* 303–330.

77. Roy, *Business History of India,* 153–202.

78. Tripathi, *Dynamics of a Tradition,* 99.

79. Sanjay Lalbhai, interview by Sudev J. Sheth, Ahmedabad, India, February 6, 2019, Creating Emerging Markets Oral History Collection, Baker Library Special Collections.

80. Tripathi, *Dynamics of a Tradition,* 108–109, 112–113.

81. Tripathi, *Dynamics of a Tradition,* 114–116.

82. Tripathi, *Dynamics of a Tradition,* 95.

83. Tripathi, *Dynamics of a Tradition,* 99–100; Piramal, *Business Legends,* 396–397.

84. Atul homepage, accessed February 25, 2022, https://www.atul.co.in/; "Atul Ltd Growing Business with Social Purpose since Independence," *Business World,* January 6, 2021.

85. Piramal, *Business Legends,* 398–400.

86. Tripathi, *Dynamics of a Tradition,* 118–127.

87. Tripathi, *Dynamics of a Tradition,* 130–146.

88. "Siddharth Kasturbhai Lalbhai's Atul Entering 70th Year of Operations," ANI, February 2, 2021, https://www.aninews.in/news/business/business/siddharth-kasturbhai-lalbhais-atul-entering-70th-year-of-operations20210202152204/.

89. Tripathi, *Dynamics of a Tradition,* 149–150.

90. Dwijendra Tripathi and Jyoti Jumani, *The Oxford History of Contemporary Indian Business* (New Delhi: Oxford University Press, 2013), 28.

91. Lalbhai, interview by Sheth.

92. Geoffrey Jones and Rachael Comunale, "Oral History and the Business History of Emerging Markets," *Enterprise and Society* 20, no. 1 (March 2019): 25.

93. Lalbhai, interview by Sheth.

94. Tripathi, *Dynamics of a Tradition,* 166–168.

95. Pushpa, *Business and Community,* 178.

96. Tripathi, *Dynamics of a Tradition,* 187–188.

97. Tripathi, *Dynamics of a Tradition,* 189.

98. Robert S. Anderson, *Nucleus and Nation: Scientists, International Networks, and Power in India* (Chicago: University of Chicago Press, 2010), 280–283.

99. Anderson, *Nucleus and Nation,* 283.

100. Tripathi, *Dynamics of a Tradition,* 195–196; Anderson, *Nucleus and Nation,* 286–287.

101. Rolv Petter Amdam, "The Internationalization of Executive Education," in *The Routledge Companion to the Makers of Global Business,* ed. Teresa da Silva Lopes, Christina Lubinski, and Heidi J. S. Tworek (New York: Routledge, 2020), 131–132. The Harvard Business School's overall international strategy in the postwar period is discussed in Rolv Petter Amdam and Gabriel R.G. Benito, "Opening the Black Box of International Strategy Formulation: How Harvard Business School Became a Multinational Enterprise," *Academy of Management Learning and Education* 21, no. 2 (2022): 167–187.

102. Tripathi and Jamani, *Oxford History of Contemporary Indian Business,* 207–208.

103. Anderson, *Nucleus and Nation,* 285.

104. Ad Hoc Committee on HBS International Activities to Acting Dean George Baker, memo, April 13, 1962, Box 1, Arch E67.41.A, Baker Library Special Collections, Harvard Business School (hereafter Arch E67.41.A). This report cites early reports.

105. File Annual Reports—India 1963–66, Box 1, Arch E67.41.A.

106. Piramal, *Business Legends,* 424.

107. First Annual Report Submitted to Douglas Ensminger (Ford Foundation), December 31, 1963, Box 1, Arch E67.41.A.

108. Piramal, *Business Legends,* 424.

109. For example, Minutes of the Sixth Meeting of the Building Committee of the Institute, April 27–28, 1964, Box 2, File Buildings, 1962–63, Arch E67.41.A.

110. Third Annual Report to Douglas Ensminger (Ford Foundation), December 31, 1965, Box 1, Arch E67.41.A.

111. Appendix E to 17th Board of Governors Meetings, March 26, 1966, Box 12, File 1st Board of Governors Meetings, Arch E67.41.A.

112. Allan Cohen, "Harvard's Role at the Indian Institute of Management: Some Recommendations," confidential memorandum, in Allan Cohen to Professor Harry L. Hansen, September 8, 1964, File Choudry, D. Kamila, 1964–64, Box 2, Arch E67.41.A; Chitra Unnithan, "Vikram Sarabhai's Love Affair Gave Birth to IIM-A, Book Says," *Times of India,* January 8, 2014, https://timesofindia.indiatimes.com/india/Vikram-Sarabhais-love-affair-gave-birth-to-IIM-A-book-says/articleshow/28534030.cms.

113. Anderson, *Nucleus and Nation,* 285.

114. John B. Fox to Professor Harry L. Hansen, February 27, 1963, File Ford Foundation in India, Box 4, Arch E67.41.A.

115. Tripathi, *Dynamics of a Tradition,* 189–190.

116. Jamari Darden et al., "'We Were Just Doing What Needed to Be Done,'" Harvard Business School, March 1, 2018, https://www.alumni.hbs.edu/stories/Pages/story-bulletin.aspx?num=6567.

117. Cheng Gao et al., "Overcoming Institutional Voids: A Reputation-Based View of Long-Run Survival," *Strategic Management Journal* 38, no. 11 (2017): 2147–2167.

118. Atul Foundation, *Annual Report 2020–21* (Gujarat, India: Atul Foundation, 2021), https://www.atul.co.in/Atul-Foundation/Atul%20Foundation%202020-21.pdf.

119. Tripathi, *Oxford History of Indian Business,* 302.

7. Modest Consumerism, Urban Blight, Tech Solutions, and the Quest to Improve Society

1. The phrase "Greed is good" was spoken by the financier Gordon Gekko, played by Michael Douglas, in the 1987 movie *Wall Street,* directed by Oliver Stone.

2. Hilary Herbold, "Never a Level Playing Field: Blacks and the GI Bill," *Journal of Blacks in Higher Education* 6 (1994–1995): 104–108; Suzanne Mettler, *Soldiers to Citizens: The G.I. Bill and the Making of the Greatest Generation* (New York: Oxford University Press, 2007).

3. Lizabeth Cohen, *A Consumers' Republic: The Politics of Mass Consumption in Postwar America* (New York: Vintage Books, 2008), 124.

4. Archie B. Carroll et al., *Corporate Responsibility: The American Experience* (Cambridge: Cambridge University Press, 2012), 189.

5. Olivier Zunz, *Philanthropy in America: A History* (Princeton, NJ: Princeton University Press, 2012), 139; Morrell Heald, *The Social Responsibilities of Business* (New Brunswick, NJ: Transaction Publishers, 1988), 205.

6. John K. Galbraith, *American Capitalism: The Concept of Countervailing Power* (Boston: Houghton Mifflin, 1962), 86; Christian Olaf Christiansen, *Progressive Business: An Intellectual History of the Role of Business in American Society* (Oxford: Oxford University Press, 2015), 115–122. When Galbraith was writing, around one-third of American workers were unionized. In 2022, the figure was only 6 percent.

7. Francis X. Sutton et al., *The American Business Creed* (New York: Shocken Books, 1962), 34; Christiansen, *Progressive Business,* 85–90.

8. Rami Kaplan, "Who Has Been Regulating Whom, Business or Society? The Mid-20th-Century Institutionalization of 'Corporate Responsibility' in the USA," *Socio-economic Review* 13, no. 1 (2017): 127. See also Christy Ford Chapin, "The Politics of Corporate Social Responsibility in American Health Care and Home Loans," *Business History Review* 90, no. 4 (2016): 647–670.

9. Nicolas J. Duquette, "Founders' Fortunes and Philanthropy: A History of the U.S. Charitable-Contribution Deduction," *Business History Review* 93, no. 3 (2019): 568–570.

10. Carroll et al., *Corporate Responsibility,* 217–219.

11. Carroll et al., *Corporate Responsibility,* 246–248, 250–251.

12. "Walter Haas Jr., Ex-Ceo of Levi's, Dead at 79," *Women's Wear Daily,* September 22, 1995, 12; Walter A. Haas Jr., "The True Blue Gospel of Levi's," *Business and Society Review* 67 (Fall 1988): 45–47.

13. Jeffrey L. Cruikshank and David B. Sicilia, *The Engine That Could: 75 Years of Values-Driven Change at Cummins Engine Company* (Boston: Harvard Business School Press, 1997), 179–181.

14. Eric Pace, "J. Irwin Miller, 95, Patron of Modern Architecture, Dies," *New York Times*, August 19, 2004; Nancy Kriplen, *J. Irwin Miller: The Shaping of an American Town* (Bloomington: Indiana University Press, 2019).

15. Cruikshank and Sicilia, *Engine That Could*, 237–239.

16. Kriplen, *J. Irwin Miller*, 99.

17. T. J. Watson Jr., *A Business and Its Beliefs* (New York: McGraw-Hill, 1963).

18. James W. Cortada, *IBM: The Rise and Fall and Reinvention of a Global Icon* (Cambridge, MA: MIT Press, 2019), 235–238, 249–251.

19. Carroll et al., *Corporate Responsibility*, 249.

20. Howard R. Bowen, *The Social Responsibilities of the Businessman* (Iowa City: University of Iowa Press, 1953), 6–7.

21. Aurélien Acquier, Jean-Pascal Gond, and Jean Pasquero, "Rediscovering Howard R. Bowen's Legacy: The Unachieved Agenda and Continuing Relevance of Social Responsibilities of the Businessman," *Business and Society* 50, no. 4 (2011): 607–646.

22. Acquier, Gond, and Pasquero, "Rediscovering Howard R. Bowen's Legacy," 611.

23. Jeremy Moon, *Corporate Social Responsibility: A Very Short Introduction* (Oxford: Oxford University Press, 2014), 49; Carroll et al., *Corporate Responsibility*, 212–214.

24. Bowen, *Social Responsibilities*, 40.

25. Acquier, Gond, and Pasquero, "Rediscovering Howard R. Bowen's Legacy," 623–625.

26. Bowen, *Social Responsibilities*, 6–7.

27. Howard R. Bowen, *The Business Enterprise as a Subject for Research* (New York: Social Science Research Council, May 1955), 61.

28. Quoted in Acquier, Gond, and Pasquero, "Rediscovering Howard R. Bowen's Legacy," 637.

29. Gary Cross, *An All-Consuming Century: Why Commercialism Won in Modern America* (New York: Columbia University Press, 2000), 111.

30. Cohen, *Consumers' Republic*.

31. Thorstein Veblen, *The Theory of the Leisure Class* (New York: Macmillan, 1912); Charles Camic, *Veblen: The Making of an Economist Who Unmade Economics* (Cambridge, MA: Harvard University Press, 2020).

32. On the turbulent history of Consumer Research and its successor Consumer Union, see Charles F. McGovern, *Sold American: Consumption and Citizenship, 1890–1945* (Chapel Hill: University of North Carolina Press, 2006).

33. Cross, *All-Consuming Century*, chap. 4.

34. Cross, *All-Consuming Century*, 129.

35. John Kenneth Galbraith, *The Affluent Society* (New York: Houghton Mifflin, 1958), 129.

36. Galbraith, *Affluent Society*, 262.

37. Charlotte Curtis, "The Affluent Society, 1983," *New York Times*, November 22, 1983.

38. Vance Packard, *The Status Seekers* (New York: David McKay, 1959); Daniel Horowitz, *Vance Packard and American Social Criticism* (Chapel Hill: University of North Carolina Press, 1994), 110–121.

39. Cohen, *Consumers' Republic*, 212, 298; Cross, *All-Consuming Century*, 147.

40. Cohen, *Consumers' Republic*, 332.

41. Vance Packard, *The Waste Makers* (New York: David McKay, 1960), 11.

42. Packard, *Waste Makers*, 7.

43. Susan Strasser, *Waste and Want: A Social History of Trash* (New York: Holt, 1999), 277.

44. T. George Harris, *Romney's Way: A Man and an Idea* (Englewood Cliffs: Prentice-Hall, 1968), 42–46.

45. Charles K. Hyde, *Storied Independent Automakers: Nash, Hudson, and American Motors* (Detroit: Wayne State University Press, 2009), 170.

46. George W. Romney to Senator David I. Walsh, January 2, 1940, Box 1, George Romney Papers, Bentley Historical Library, University of Michigan; Hyde, *Storied Independent Automakers*, 171.

47. Tom Mahoney, *The Story of George Romney: Builder, Salesman, Crusader* (New York: Harper and Brothers, 1960), 99; Harris, *Romney's Way*, 92–94.

48. "The Book of Mosiah: Chapter 23," Church of Jesus Christ of Latter-Day Saints, accessed June 7, 2022, https://www.churchofjesuschrist.org/study/scriptures/bofm/mosiah/23?lang=eng.

49. In 2020, reporters revealed that the Mormon Church had one of the world's largest investment funds. Ian Lovett and Rachael Levy, "The Mormon Church Amassed $100 Billion. It Was the Best-Kept Secret in the Investment World," *Wall Street Journal*, February 8, 2020.

50. "Why So Many Good Business Leaders Are Mormons," *Economist*, May 4, 2012; Robert O'Brien Marriott, *The J. Willard Marriott Story* (Salt Lake City: Deseret, 1977); Lee Roderick, *True Wealth: The Vision and Genius of Innovator James LeVoy Sorenson* (Los Angeles: Probitas Press, 2017).

51. Matthew R. Miles and Jason M. Adkins, "Mormon Mobilization in Contemporary U.S. Politics," *Oxford Research Encyclopedia of Politics*, February 25, 2019, https://oxfordre.com/politics/view/10.1093/acrefore/9780190228637.001.0001/acrefore-9780190228637-e-871.

52. "Organizational Structure of the Church," Church of Jesus Christ of Latter-Day Saints, accessed June 16, 2020, https://newsroom.churchofjesuschrist.org/topic/organizational-structure-of-the-church.

53. Matthew Bowman, "Mormonism's Surprisingly Deep Affinity for Progressive Politics," *New Republic*, November 21, 2011; Benjamin Wallace-Wells, "George Romney for President, 1968," *New York Magazine*, May 18, 2012.

54. Harris, *Romney's Way*, 108; Hyde, *Storied Independent Automakers*, 172.

55. Harris, *Romney's Way*, 109–111.

56. Harris, *Romney's Way*, 109–111.

57. Harris, *Romney's Way*, 115–117; Mahoney, *George Romney*, 122–123.

58. George W. Romney to Gaskell W. Romney, July 12, 1948, Box 2, Romney Papers, Bentley Historical Library; Hyde, *Storied Independent Automakers*, 172–173.

59. Harris, *Romney's Way*, 140–143.

60. Hyde, *Storied Independent Automakers*, 169, 177.

61. Hyde, *Storied Independent Automakers*, 174.

62. Hyde, *Storied Independent Automakers*, 169.

63. "Hudson Motors," Detroit Historical Society, accessed June 7, 2022, https://detroithistorical.org/learn/encyclopedia-of-detroit/hudson-motors.

64. Hyde, *Storied Independent Automakers*, 86–87.

65. Hyde, *Storied Independent Automakers*, 185.

66. Hyde, *Storied Independent Automakers*, 173.

67. Cross, *All-Consuming Century*, 151.

68. The company offered a 108-inch wheelbase Rambler between 1956 and 1957. George Romney, *The Tobé Lectures in Retail Distribution at the Harvard Business School: Third Series (1958–1959)* (Cambridge, MA: Harvard Graduate School of Business Administration, 1959), 28–30; Mahoney, *George Romney*, 158–159, 200; Hyde, *Storied Independent Automakers*, 184, 187.

69. George W. Romney, verbatim transcript of address at Rambler dealer announcement meeting, Oakland, California, September 21, 1961, Box 10, Romney Papers, Bentley Historical Library.

70. Harris, *Romney's Way*, 144–145, 184–186; Hyde, *Storied Independent Automakers*, 179, 184, 187; Patrick Foster, *American Motors Corporation: The Rise and Fall of America's Last Independent Automaker* (Minneapolis: Quarto Publishing Group, 2013), 39.

71. Romney, *Tobé Lectures*, 30; Mahoney, *George Romney*, 158–159, 200.

72. Hyde, *Storied Independent Automakers*, 184.

73. Romney, *Tobé Lectures*, 31.

74. Romney, *Tobé Lectures*, 31; Mahoney, *George Romney*, 19, 21–23, 43.

75. Harris, *Romney's Way*, 155.

76. Harris, *Romney's Way*, 154.

77. George W. Romney, address at annual dinner of Region 4, American Association of Motor Vehicle Administrators, Hotel Utah, Salt Lake City, Utah, June 17, 1941, George Romney Papers, Harold B. Lee Library, Brigham Young University.

78. Harris, *Romney's Way*, 154, 159.

79. George W. Romney, verbatim transcript of address at Rambler dealer announcement meeting, Oakland, California, September 21, 1961, Box 10, Romney Papers, Bentley Historical Library.

80. American Motors Corporation and the United Automobile Workers, "Union-American Motors Statement," *New York Times*, August 27, 1961.

81. George W. Romney, "The National Significance of American Motors' Progress-Sharing Labor Contract," script of television broadcast, NBC-TV, October 1, 1961; George W. Romney, verbatim transcript of address at Rambler dealer announcement meeting, Oakland, California, September 21, 1961, Box 10, Romney Papers, Bentley Historical Library.

82. "Profit Sharing in Detroit," *New York Times*, August 28, 1961.

83. George W. Romney, speech before the Conference of Christians and Jews, Los Angeles, California, May 20, 1959, Box 11, Romney Papers, Bentley Historical Library. The quotation from Alfred North Whitehead was taken from his introduction to Wallace B. Donham's book *Business Adrift* (New York: Whittlesey House, 1931), xxix.

84. Hyde, *Storied Independent Automakers*, 187–188.

85. Stephen Hess and David S. Broder, "George Romney: The Michigan Missionary," *The Progressive*, November 1967.

86. Hyde, *Storied Independent Automakers*, 185–186; American Motors Corporation, Annual Report, 1958, 1959, and 1960, retrieved from ProQuest Historical Annual Reports, July 3, 2019.

87. George W. Romney, "Basic, Balanced Excellence: Rambler," transcript of address to Rambler dealers at 1961 announcement meeting, Dallas, Texas, September 1, 1960, Box 9, Romney Papers, Bentley Historical Library.

88. George W. Romney, verbatim transcript of address at Rambler dealer announcement meeting, Oakland, California, September 21, 1961, Box 10, Romney Papers, Bentley Historical Library.

89. Cross, *All-Consuming Century*, 176.

90. Andrea Holt, *Thinking Small: The Long, Strange Trip of the Volkswagen Beetle* (New York: Random House, 2012).

91. Hyde, *Storied Independent Automakers*, 185, 190; Foster, *American Motors Corporation*, 65.

92. Hyde, *Storied Independent Automakers*, 187.

93. Hyde, *Storied Independent Automakers*, 25–26; Harris, *Romney's Way*, 165.

94. Selig S. Harrison, "Romney and the Republicans," *New Republic*, March 5, 1962.

95. Mahoney, *George Romney,* 226.

96. Harris, *Romney's Way,* 213–215; Mahoney, *George Romney,* 239–247.

97. Romney, personal statement, Bloomfield Hills, Michigan, February 10, 1962, Romney Papers, Harold B. Lee Library.

98. Hyde, *Storied Independent Automakers,* 193.

99. Clark R. Mollenhoff, *George Romney: Mormon in Politics* (New York: Meredith Press, 1968), 188–189, 223–224, 251.

100. American Motors Corporation, Annual Report, 1963, 1964, 1965, 1966, retrieved from ProQuest Historical Annual Reports, July 3, 2019.

101. Hyde, *Storied Independent Automakers,* 199; David R. Jones, "American Motors Is Seeking to End Profit-Sharing Plan," *New York Times,* October 8, 1964; David R. Jones, "American Motors Lists Profit Plan," *New York Times,* October 17, 1964.

102. Melissa Locker, "RIP Herbie: A Very Brief Timeline of the VW Beetle," *Fast Company,* July 10, 2019.

103. Hyde, *Storied Independent Automakers,* chaps. 8 and 9.

104. Lizabeth Cohen, *Saving America's Cities: Ed Logue and the Struggle to Renew Urban America in the Suburban Age* (New York: Farrar, Straus and Giroux, 2019), 53–58, 61, 111, 127–131, 136–138, 157–159, 203–205.

105. Nikole Hannah-Jones, "What Is Owed," *New York Times Magazine,* June 30, 2020.

106. James Patterson, *Grand Expectations: The United States, 1945–1974* (New York: Oxford University Press, 1996), 72–74. Three additional communities were built: Willingboro Township, New Jersey, started in 1958 and originally known as Levittown; Levittown, Puerto Rico, started in 1963; and Bowie, Maryland, started in 1964.

107. Cohen, *Saving America's Cities,* 158, 210, 339.

108. Allison Shertzer and Randall P. Walsh, "Racial Sorting and the Emergence of Segregation in American Cities," *Review of Economics and Statistics* 101, no. 3 (2019): 415–427.

109. Leah Platt Boustan, "Was Postwar Suburbanization 'White Flight'? Evidence from the Black Migration," *Quarterly Journal of Economics* 125, no. 1 (2010): 417–443.

110. Patterson, *Grand Expectations,* 75.

111. In 2022, New York Levittown's population was 72.3 percent white, 15.3 Hispanic, 8.5 percent Asian, and 1.4 percent African American.

112. Mollenhoff, *George Romney,* 196–198, 203–204, 271–272.

113. Edward J. Blum and Paul Harvey, "How (George) Romney Championed Civil Rights and Challenged His Church," *Atlantic,* August 13, 2012.

114. Chris Bonastia, "Hedging His Bets: Why Nixon Killed HUD's Desegregation Efforts," *Social Science History* 28, no. 1 (Spring 2004): 19–52; Nikole Hannah-Jones, "Living Apart: How the Government Betrayed a Landmark Civil Rights Law," ProPublica, June 25, 2015, https://www.propublica.org/article/living-apart-how-the-government-betrayed-a-landmark-civil-rights-law; Mehrsa Baradaran, "The Real Roots of 'Black Capitalism,'" *New York Times,* March 31, 2019.

115. Heald, *Social Responsibilities of Business,* 222–223, 228; Brian W. Rapp, *Managing Local Government for Improved Performance: A Practical Approach* (Boulder, CO: Westview Press, 1977), 292–293; Joan Cook, "Lemuel Ricketts Boulware, 95; Headed Labor Relations for G.E.," *New York Times,* November 8, 1990.

116. Cohen, *Saving America's Cities,* 126, 212.

117. Tom McCraw, *American Business since 1920: How It Worked* (Wheeling, IL: Harlan Davidson, 2009), 214.

118. David Hart, "From 'Ward of the State' to 'Revolutionary without a Movement': The Political Development of William C. Norris and Control Data Corporation, 1957–1986," *Enterprise and Society* 6, no. 2 (2005): 197–223.

119. Tom Nicholas and Laura Gaie Singleton, "Control Data Corporation and the Urban Crisis" (Harvard Business School Case 808-096, November 2007, rev. January 2020), 5–6.

120. James C. Worthy, *William C. Norris: Portrait of a Maverick* (Cambridge, MA: Ballinger, 1987), 16–18.

121. Nicholas and Singleton, "Control Data Corporation," 7–9.

122. Hart, "'Ward of the State,'" 217.

123. William Norris, "Social Problems and Control Data," memo, April 15, 1968, quoted in Nicholas and Singleton, "Control Data Corporation," 23.

124. Worthy, *William C. Norris,* 151–156.

125. Elisabeth Van Meer, "PLATO: From Computer-Based Education to Corporate Social Responsibility," *Iterations* 2, no. 1 (2003): 2–5.

126. Brian Dear, *The Friendly Orange Glow: The Untold Story of the PLATO System and the Dawn of Cyberculture* (New York: Pantheon, 2017), 435–437.

127. Quoted in Meer, "PLATO," 7.

128. Quoted in Meer, "PLATO," 6.

129. Worthy, *William C. Norris,* 144–147, 160–163.

130. Alfred D. Chandler, *Inventing the Electronic Century* (New York: Free Press, 2001), 135–139; McCraw, *American Business,* 214–216; Peter Judge, "IT Pioneer William Norris Dies at 95," CNET, August 23, 2006, https://www.cnet.com/tech/tech-industry/it-pioneer-william-norris-dies-at-95/.

131. Don Clark and Stephen Miller, "Super Computer: Tech Guru Tackled Social Ills, Too," *Wall Street Journal,* August 26, 2006.

132. Meer, "PLATO," 13. Plato remains in business as a computer-based education company.

133. Dear, *Friendly Orange Glow,* 493–494.

134. Paul E. Ceruzzi, *A History of Modern Computing* (Cambridge, MA: MIT Press, 1998), 255.

135. J. A. N. Lee, "An Wang," IEEE Computer Society, accessed February 28, 2022, https://history.computer.org/pioneers/wang.html.

136. David Wessel, "Calculated Change," *Wall Street Journal,* November 6, 1984.

137. Charles C. Kenney, *Riding the Runaway Horse: The Rise and Decline of Wang Laboratories* (Boston: Little, Brown, 1992).

138. "Wang Lab's Run for a Second Billion," *Business Week,* May 17, 1982.

139. An Wang, *Lessons: An Autobiography* (Reading, MA: Addison-Wesley, 1986), 4, 19, 76.

140. Wang, *Lessons,* 225.

141. Wang, *Lessons,* 228.

142. Kenney, *Riding the Runaway Horse,* 106–107.

143. Wang, *Lessons,* 230.

144. Kenney, *Riding the Runaway Horse,* 107–108.

145. Kenney, *Riding the Runaway Horse,* 106.

146. Editorial, "Wang Does It Again," *Sunday Sun* (Lowell, MA), March 22, 1981.

147. Fox Butterfield, "Chinese Immigrant Emerges as Boston's Best Benefactor," *New York Times,* May 5, 1984.

148. Transcript of speech in 1985, File 014103595_VT_0007_01, Wang Laboratories Collection, Baker Library Historical Collections, Harvard Business School.

149. Dennis Hevesi, "An Wang, 70, Is Dead of Cancer; Inventor and Maker of Computers," *New York Times,* March 25, 1990.

150. Lee, "An Wang."

151. Anna Lee Saxenian, *Regional Advantage: Culture and Competition in Silicon Valley and Route 128* (Cambridge, MA: Harvard University Press, 1994).

152. Lee, "An Wang."

153. Lee, "An Wang."

8. The Rise of Values-Driven Businesses

1. Russell Duncan, "The Summer of Love and Protest: Transatlantic Counterculture in the 1960s," in *The Transatlantic Sixties: Europe and the United States in the Counterculture Decade,* ed. Grzegorz Kosc et al. (Bielefeld, Germany: Transcript Verlag, 2013), 144–173.

2. Warren J. Belasco, *Appetite for Change: How the Counterculture Took on the Food Industry* (Ithaca, NY: Cornell University Press, 2007).

3. Duncan, "Summer of Love," 160–163.

4. History.com editors, "The Beatles Arrive in New York," History.com, last updated February 4, 2022, https://www.history.com/this-day-in-history/beatles-arrive-in-new-york.

5. Martin Klimke and Joachim Scharloth, "1968 in Europe: An Introduction," in *1968 in Europe: A History of Protests and Activism, 1956–1977,* ed. Martin Klimke and Joachim Scharloth (London: Palgrave Macmillan, 2008), 3; Holger Nehring, "Great Britain," in Klimke and Scharloth, *1968 in Europe,* 126–127.

6. Ingrid Gilcher-Holtey, "France," in Klimke and Scharloth, *1968 in Europe,* 111–124.

7. Ramachandra Guha, *Environmentalism: A Global History* (New York: Longman, 2000), 4.

8. Geoffrey Jones, *Profits and Sustainability: A History of Green Entrepreneurship* (Oxford: Oxford University Press, 2017), 55–57; Graham Vernon Jacks and Robert Orr Whyte, *The Rape of the Earth: A World Survey of Soil Erosion* (London: Faber and Faber, 1939), 210; William Vogt, *Road to Survival* (New York: William Sloane Associates, 1948), 34–37; Spencer R. Weart, *The Discovery of Global Warming* (Cambridge, MA: Harvard University Press, 2008).

9. Howard R. Bowen, *The Social Responsibilities of the Businessman* (Iowa City: University of Iowa Press, 1953), 227.

10. Rachel Carson, *Silent Spring* (Boston: Houghton Mifflin, 1962).

11. F. F. M. Clark, "Pesticides and the UK's Silent Spring, 1963–1964: Poison in the Garden of England," *Notes and Records of the Royal Society of London* 71, no. 3 (2017): 297–327.

12. Geoffrey Jones and Christina Lubinski, "Making 'Green Giants': Environment Sustainability in the German Chemical Industry, 1950s–1980s," *Business History* 56, no. 4 (2014): 623–649; Rex Weyler, *Greenpeace: How a Group of Ecologists, Journalists, and Visionaries Changed the World* (Vancouver, BC: Raincoast Books, 2004); Adam Rome, *The Genius of Earth Day: How a 1970 Teach-In Unexpectedly Made the First Green Generation* (New York: Hill and Wang, 2013).

13. Christopher Rootes, "The Environment Movement," in Klimke and Scharloth, *1968 in Europe,* 295–305.

14. Angel Kwolek-Folland, *Incorporating Women: A Brief History of Women and Business in the United States* (New York: Twayne, 1998).

15. Betty Friedan, *The Feminine Mystique* (New York: Norton, 1963).

16. Stephanie Coontz, *A Strange Stirring: The "Feminine Mystique" and American Women at the Dawn of the 1960s* (New York: Basic Books, 2011), 101–106, 149–150.

17. Carolyn G. Heilbrun, *Education of a Woman: The Life of Gloria Steinem* (New York: Dial Press, 1995).

18. Bonnie G. Smith, ed., *Global Feminisms since 1945* (New York: Routledge, 2000).

19. Elizabeth Meehan, "British Feminism from the 1960s to the 1980s," in *British Feminism in the Twentieth Century,* ed. Harold L. Smith (Amherst: University of Massachusetts Press, 1990), 193–194.

20. Ben Cohen and Mal Warwick, *Values-Driven Business: How to Change the World, Make Money, and Have Fun* (San Francisco: Berrett-Koehler, 2006). The term became widely used in management publications. For example, Jennefer Witter, "The Benefits of a Value-Driven Business," *Forbes,* May 16, 2019.

21. Jones, *Profits and Sustainability,* 118–121.

22. Wesley D. Sine and Brandon H. Lee, "Tilting at Windmills? The Environmental Movement and the Emergence of the US Wind Energy Sector," *Administrative Science Quarterly* 54, no. 1 (2009): 123–155; Ion Bogdan Vasi, *Winds of Change: The Environmental Movement and the Global Development of the Wind Energy Industry* (Oxford: Oxford University Press, 2011).

23. Jones, *Profits and Sustainability,* 326–329.

24. Jones, *Profits and Sustainability,* 24–31.

25. Joe Dobrow, *Natural Prophets: From Health to Whole Foods: How the Pioneers of the Industry Changed the Way We Eat and Reshaped American Business* (New York: Rodale Press, 2014), 34–38.

26. Dobrow, *Natural Prophets,* 61–66.

27. Belasco, *Appetite for Change,* 99.

28. John Mackey and Raj Sisodia, *Conscious Capitalism: Liberating the Heroic Spirit of Business* (Boston: Harvard Business Review Press, 2013), 2–4.

29. Mackey and Sisodia, *Conscious Capitalism,* 8–9.

30. Dobrow, *Natural Prophets,* 180–190.

31. Belasco, *Appetite for Change,* 98; Dobrow, *Natural Prophets,* 38; William Shurtleff and Akiko Aoyagi, comps., *History of Erewhon—Natural Foods Pioneer in the United States (1966–2011)* (Soyinfo Center, April 18, 2006), https://www.soyinfocenter.com/pdf/Erewhon.pdf.

32. Belasco, *Appetite for Change,* 98.

33. Jones, *Profits and Sustainability,* 97–98, 368–370.

34. Mario Moya, "Hain Celestial Settles Class Action for Mislabeling Organic Cosmetics," *Moya Law,* January 25, 2016, https://moyalawfirm.com/hain-celestial-settles-class-action-for-mislabeling-organic-cosmetics/.

35. Dobrow, *Natural Prophets,* 243–244.

36. Julie Guthman, *Agrarian Dreams: The Paradox of Organic Farming in California* (Berkeley: University of California Press, 2004), 30–31.

37. "Behind the Barcodes: End Human Suffering behind Our Food," Oxfam, accessed June 8, 2022, https://www.oxfamamerica.org/explore/issues/humanitarian-response-and-leaders/hunger-and-famine/behind-the-barcodes/.

38. Ben Cohen and Jerry Greenfield, *Ben & Jerry's Double-Dip: Lead with Your Values and Make Money, Too* (New York: Simon and Schuster, 1997), 23.

39. Cohen and Greenfield, *Ben & Jerry's,* 30.

40. Cohen and Greenfield, *Ben & Jerry's,* 52–53.

41. Brad Edmondson, *Ice Cream Social: The Struggle for the Soul of Ben & Jerry's* (San Francisco: Berrett-Koehler, 2014), 59–60.

42. Edmondson, *Ice Cream Social,* 69–95.

43. Edmondson, *Ice Cream Social,* 115–156.

44. Amy Raphael, "Britain's Coolest Organic Couple," *Guardian,* April 18, 2004; Craig Sams and Josephine Fairley, *The Story of Green & Black's* (London: Random House Business, 2009).

45. Susie Khamis, "A Case Study in Compromise: The Green & Black's Brand of Ethical Chocolate," *Australasian Journal of Popular Culture* 1, no. 1 (2011): 21–22.

46. Sams and Fairley, *Story of Green & Black's*, 55.

47. Sams and Fairley, *Story of Green & Black's*, 61.

48. Sams and Fairley, *Story of Green & Black's*, 80–98.

49. Khamis, "Case Study in Compromise," 23.

50. Khamis, "Case Study in Compromise," 21–22, 24–27.

51. Another example in clothing was Eileen Fischer, who started a women's fashion design and retail business in New York in 1984.

52. Yvon Chouinard and Vincent Stanley, *The Responsible Company: What We've Learned from Patagonia's First 40 Years* (Ventura, CA: Patagonia Books, 2012); Geoffrey Jones, *Varieties of Green Business: Industries, Nations and Time* (Northampton, MA: Edward Elgar, 2018), 230–231, 236.

53. Chouinard and Stanley, *Responsible Company*, 49–54; Jones, *Varieties of Green Business*, 236; Nick Paumgarten, "Patagonia's Philosopher-King," *New Yorker*, September 12, 2016.

54. Paumgarten, "Patagonia's Philosopher-King."

55. Yvon Chouinard, "Why Food," Patagonia Provisions, April 23, 2020, https://www.patagoniaprovisions.com/pages/why-food-essay.

56. "Our Story," Regenerative Organic Certified, accessed June 8, 2022, https://regenorganic.org/#storytime.

57. Catherine Morin, "Patagonia's Customer Base and the Rise of an Environmental Ethos," CRM.org, June 24, 2020, https://crm.org/articles/patagonias-customer-base-and-the-rise-of-an-environmental-ethos.

58. "Facts and Figures about Materials, Waste and Recycling," United States Environmental Protection Agency, accessed June 8, 2022, https://www.epa.gov/facts-and-figures-about-materials-waste-and-recycling.

59. Jones, *Profits and Sustainability*, 58.

60. Geoffrey Jones, *Beauty Imagined: A History of the Global Beauty Industry* (Oxford: Oxford University Press, 2010), 49–50, 62–63.

61. Helena Rubinstein, *Beauty in the Making* (New York: published by the author, 1915), 34–35, https://www.cosmeticsandskin.com/booklets/rubinstein-making.php.

62. Helena Rubinstein, *My Life for Beauty* (New York: Simon and Schuster, 1966), 127.

63. Geoffrey Jones and Kathy Choi, "Helena Rubinstein: Making Up the Modern Woman" (Harvard Business School Case 9-317-116, rev. December 2020).

64. Timothy Burke, *Lifebuoy Men, Lux Women: Commodification, Consumption, and Cleanliness in Modern Zimbabwe* (Durham, NC: Duke University Press, 1996), 17–34.

65. Juliet E. K. Walker, *The History of Black Business in America: Capitalism, Race, Entrepreneurship* (New York: Twayne, 1998), 208–211.

66. Catherine Davenport, "Skin Deep: African American Women and the Building of Beauty Culture in South Carolina" (master's thesis, University of South Carolina, 2017); A'Lelia Bundles, *On Her Own Ground: The Life and Times of Madam C. J. Walker* (New York: Simon and Schuster, 2001).

67. Walker, *History of Black Business*, 183–187.

68. Poro College, *Poro Hair and Beauty Culture* (Saint Louis: Poro College, 1922), 8.

69. "Who Was One of Madam C. J. Walker's Most Important Role Models?," Freeman Institute, accessed June 8, 2022, https://freemaninstitute.com/poro.htm.

70. Katina Manko, *Ding Dong! Avon Calling! The Women and Men of Avon Products Incorporated* (New York: Oxford University Press, 2021), chap. 1.

71. "Here and There with Nannette," *Oakland Tribune*, May 27, 1923, https://www
.newspapers.com/clip/71942422/oakland-tribune.

72. Elizabeth Arden, *The Quest of the Beautiful* (New York: Elizabeth Arden, 1928), 5.

73. Richard S. Tedlow, *Giants of Enterprise: Seven Business Innovators and the Empires They Built* (New York: HarperCollins, 2001), 474n1. The quotation is from 1950.

74. Lee Israel, *Estée Lauder: Beyond the Magic* (New York: Macmillan, 1985); Lee Israel, *Can You Ever Forgive Me?* (New York: Simon and Schuster, 2008).

75. Kathy Peiss, *Hope in a Jar* (New York: Henry Holt, 1998), 260.

76. Naomi Wolf, *The Beauty Myth: How Images of Beauty Are Used against Women* (New York: W. Morrow, 1991).

77. Wolf, *Beauty Myth,* 12, 17.

78. Clare Coulson, "Mary Quant, Fashion and the Fight for Female Empowerment," *The Glossary,* July 18, 2019, https://theglossarymagazine.com/arts-culture/mary-quant-female
-empowerment-60s-fashion/.

79. Margaret Allen, *Selling Dreams: Inside the Beauty Industry* (New York: Simon and Schuster, 1981), 79–81.

80. Tom Chappell, *The Soul of a Business* (New York: Bantam Books, 1993), xiii, 1–7.

81. Chappell, *Soul of a Business,* 32.

82. Jones, *Beauty Imagined,* 283, 285–286.

83. Horst M. Rechelbacher, *Minding Your Business: Profits That Restore the Planet* (San Rafael, CA: Earth Aware, 2008), xiii.

84. Geoffrey Jones and Ricardo Reisen de Pinho, "Natura: Global Business Made in Brazil" (Harvard Business School Case 9-807-029, rev. October 20, 2012); Tania Casada and Rosa Maria Fischer, "Natura-Ekos: From the Forest to Cajamar" (Social Enterprise Knowledge Network, case study SKE016, July 29, 2003).

85. Christopher A. Bartlett, Kenton Elderkin, and Krista McQuade, "The Body Shop International" (Harvard Business School Case 9-392-032, rev. July 13, 1995), 1.

86. Bo Burlingham, "This Woman Changed Business Forever (1990 Profile)," *Inc.,* accessed February 19, 2021, https://www.inc.com/magazine/19900601/5201.html.

87. Body Shop, *Annual Report and Accounts* (Body Shop, 1993).

88. Philip Elmer-Dewitt and Elizabeth Lea, "Anita the Agitator," *Time,* January 25, 1993.

89. Bartlett, Elderkin, and McQuade, "Body Shop International."

90. Peter Marshall, "PSONA Films—Anita Roddick—My Story," YouTube, March 15, 2016, video, 30:30, https://www.youtube.com/watch?v=Dpq4SyNbUbY.

91. Anita Roddick, *Body and Soul: Profits with Principles—the Amazing Success Story of Anita Roddick and The Body Shop* (New York: Crown Trade Paperbacks, 1994), 7; Bartlett, Elderkin, and McQuade, "Body Shop International," 2.

92. Roddick, *Body and Soul,* 68–71.

93. Roddick, *Body and Soul,* 73–76.

94. Jon Entine, "Shattered Image: Is The Body Shop Too Good to Be True?," *Business Ethics,* September/October 1994, 23–28.

95. Jon Entine, "A Social and Environmental Audit of The Body Shop: Anita Roddick and the Question of Character" (unpublished manuscript, July 1996, rev. July 2003), https://studylib.net/doc/8037457/a-social-and-environmental-audit-of-the-body-shop.

96. Jon Entine, "The Myth of the Green Queen," *National Post* (Canada), September 21, 2007. Jenny Weng, "Body Time, Longtime Berkeley Skin Care Company, Closes after 5 Decades," *Daily Californian,* April 26, 2018, confirms the pioneering nature of the Berkeley store but says the sale of the name happened in 1992.

97. Marjorie Kelly to editorial advisory board members, September 13, 1994, copy supplied in email from Jon Entine to Susannah Deily-Swearingen, February 26, 2021.

98. Roddick, *Body and Soul*, 86.

99. Kevin McKague, David Wheeler, and Rivan K. Haub, "The Body Shop International" (teaching case, Schulich School of Business, York University, n.d. [assumed 2002/2003]); Sam Greenhill, "How a £4,000 Body Shop Loan Made £146 Million," This Is Money, June 26, 2010, https://www.thisismoney.co.uk/money/news/article-1696860/How-a-4000-Body-Shop-loan-made-146m.html.

100. "Gordon Roddick: My First Million," *Financial Times,* October 30, 2009.

101. Bartlett, Elderkin, and McQuade, "Body Shop International."

102. Marshall, "PSONA Films."

103. Anita Roddick, *Anita Roddick: The Mind of a Leader: Legends* (Astromax Entertainment, 2014), Audible audiobook, 54 mins., https://www.audible.com/pd/Anita-Roddick-The-Mind-of-a-Leader-Legends-Audiobook/B00JWVZ6DY. This interview was conducted in 2006.

104. Quoted in Jones, *Profits and Sustainability,* 367.

105. Roddick, *Mind of a Leader.*

106. Bartlett, Elderkin, and McQuade, "Body Shop International," 3n1.

107. Roddick, *Body and Soul,* 109.

108. Bartlett, Elderkin, and McQuade, "Body Shop International," 7.

109. Roddick, *Body and Soul,* 9.

110. Roddick, *Body and Soul,* 15.

111. Anita Roddick, interview by Antony Clare, *In the Psychiatrist's Chair,* BBC 4, broadcast August 1, 2015, https://podtail.com/en/podcast/in-the-psychiatrist-s-chair/anita-roddick/.

112. Stuart Elliott, "The Body Shop's Campaign Offers Reality, Not Miracles," *New York Times,* August 26, 1997.

113. Letter by Anita Roddick, in Body Shop, *Annual Report and Accounts* (Body Shop, 1998), 20.

114. Elliot, "Body Shop's Campaign."

115. Sharon Haywood, "Remembering Ruby," Anybody, June 21, 2009, http://www.any-body.org/anybody_vent/2009/6/21/remembering-ruby.html.

116. Roddick, *Body and Soul,* 13.

117. Roddick, *Mind of a Leader.*

118. Bartlett, Elderkin, and McQuade, "Body Shop International," 6–7.

119. Roddick, *Mind of a Leader.*

120. McKague, Wheeler, and Haub, "Body Shop International," 9.

121. Jon Entine, "The Stranger-Than-Truth Story of The Body Shop," in *Killed: Great Journalism Too Hot to Print,* ed. David Wallis (New York: Nation Books, 2004), 186–187.

122. Entine, "Social and Environmental Audit."

123. Roddick, *Body and Soul,* 167–171; Bartlett, Elderkin, and McQuade, "Body Shop International," 9; McKague, Wheeler, and Haub, "Body Shop International," 6.

124. Entine, "Shattered Image."

125. Roddick, *Body and Soul,* 171–172.

126. Entine, "Shattered Image."

127. Kelly to editorial advisory board members, September 13, 1994.

128. Richard W. Stevenson, "Market Place: Body Shop's Green Image Is Attacked," *New York Times,* September 2, 1994.

129. "Body Shop Again Criticized," *New York Times,* September 23, 1994.

130. "The Soapworks Story," Soapworks, accessed February 20, 2021, https://madeingb.com/2020/08/26/soapworks-limited/.

131. Bartlett, Elderkin, and McQuade, "Body Shop International," 10.

132. Marshall, "PSONA Films."

133. Body Shop, *Annual Report* (Body Shop, 1994), 15.

134. Bartlett, Elderkin, and McQuade, "Body Shop International," 10. The Body Shop retained ownership until it was acquired by L'Oréal in 2006. Four years later the Soapworks management bought control.

135. McKague, Wheeler, and Haub, "Body Shop International."

136. Roddick, *Body and Soul,* 23.

137. "Body Shop Officially Opens Its Stake," *Windpower Monthly,* November 1, 1994.

138. Jones, *Profits and Sustainability,* 178.

139. Sharon M. Livesey and Kate Kearins, "Transparent and Caring Corporations? A Study of Sustainability Reports by The Body Shop and Royal Dutch/Shell," *Organization and Environment* 15, no. 3 (September 2002): 238–239.

140. McKague, Wheeler, and Haub, "Body Shop International."

141. Robert G. Eccles and Birgit Spiesshofer, "Integrated Reporting for Re-imagined Capitalism" (Harvard Business School Working Paper No. 16-032, 2015).

142. Jon Entine, "The Body Shop: Truth & Consequences," *Drug and Cosmetics Industry* 156, no. 2 (1995): 54–60.

143. Entine, "Shattered Image."

144. Quoted in Entine, "Myth."

145. Rodolphe Balz, interview by Loubna Bouamane, April 13, 2011. On Balz, see Yasmine Ryan, "Setting a Standard for Organic Cosmetics," *New York Times,* June 3, 2010.

146. Roddick, *Mind of a Leader.*

147. Roddick, *Body and Soul,* 17.

148. Roddick, *Mind of a Leader.*

149. Bartlett, Elderkin, and McQuade, "Body Shop International," 8; Anita Roddick, *Business as Unusual* (London: Thorsons, 2000), 173.

150. McKague, Wheeler, and Haub, "Body Shop International," exhibit D.

151. Letter by Roddick, 2.

152. Ken Saro-Wiwa, *Silence Would Be Treason: Last Writings of Ken Saro-Wiwa,* ed. Ide Corley, Helen Fallon, and Laurence Cox (Dakar, Senegal: Daraja Press, 2013), 136. I would like to thank Jeff Strabone for this reference.

153. Roddick, *Business as Unusual,* 168.

154. Roddick, *Business as Unusual,* 174.

155. Roddick, *Business as Unusual,* 174–175; "The Body Shop," Children on the Edge, accessed February 21, 2021, https://www.childrenontheedge.org/thebodyshop.html.

156. Anita Roddick, "Take It Personally," in *Take It Personally: How to Make Conscious Choices to Change the World,* ed. Anita Roddick (Berkeley, CA: Conari Press, 2001), 12.

157. Roddick, "Take It Personally," 14.

158. McKague, Wheeler, and Haub, "Body Shop International."

159. Roddick, *Mind of a Leader.*

160. Roddick, *Business as Unusual,* 254.

161. McKague, Wheeler, and Haub, "Body Shop International," 13–15; Entine, "Myth."

162. "The Body Shop International PLC History," FundingUniverse, accessed June 8, 2022, http://www.fundinguniverse.com/company-histories/the-body-shop-international-plc-history/.

163. Suzanne Kapner, "Body Shop's Founders Give Up Control," *New York Times,* February 13, 2002; Elizabeth Rigby and Adam Jones, "L'Oréal to Take Over Body Shop," *Financial Times,* March 17, 2006.

164. Rigby and Jones, "L'Oréal."

165. Claudia Cahalane, "Interview: Anita Roddick, Body Shop Founder," *Guardian,* November 3, 2006.

166. Cahil Milmo, "Body Shop's Popularity Plunges after L'Oréal Sale," *Independent,* April 1, 2009.

167. Jones, *Profits and Sustainability,* 368–375.

168. Cecilia Kang, "Here Comes the Full Amazon-ification of Whole Foods," *New York Times,* February 28, 2022.

169. Brad Edmonson, *Ice Cream Social* (San Francisco: Berrett-Koehler, 2008), chaps. 12 and 13.

170. Judith Evans and Harriet Agnew, "Unilever Faces Lawsuit over Ben & Jerry's Israel Move," *Financial Times,* March 3, 2022.

171. Rebecca Cooney, "Analysis: A Turbulent End to The Body Shop Foundation," Third Sector, July 13, 2017, https://www.thirdsector.co.uk/analysis-turbulent-end-body-shop-foundation/governance/article/1438950.

172. Terry Slavin, "'The Spirit of Anita Roddick Is Strong with Us': Why Natura Bought The Body Shop," Reuters Events, October 26, 2017, https://www.reutersevents.com/sustainability/spirit-anita-roddick-strong-us-why-natura-bought-body-shop.

173. Oliver Balch, "Denying Climate Change Is Evil," *Guardian,* May 10, 2019.

9. Social Three-Folding

1. Saskia Sassen, *The Global City: New York, London, Tokyo* (Princeton, NJ: Princeton University Press, 2001).

2. Raghuram Rajan, *The Third Pillar: How Markets and the State Leave the Community Behind* (New York: Penguin, 2019), 172–173, 175–182.

3. Rajan, *Third Pillar.*

4. Gary Lachman, *Rudolf Steiner: An Introduction to His Life and Work* (New York: Penguin, 2007).

5. Wouter Hanegraaff, *Western Esotericism: A Guide for the Perplexed* (New York: Bloomsbury, 2013), 40–41.

6. Gary Lachman, *The Secret Teachers of the Western World* (New York: Penguin Random House, 2015), 397.

7. Lachman, *Rudolf Steiner.*

8. Peter Staudenmaier, "Race and Redemption: Racial and Ethnic Evolution in Rudolf Steiner's Anthroposophy," *Nova Religio* 11, no. 3 (2008): 9.

9. Dan McKanan, *Eco-Alchemy: Anthroposophy and the History and Future of Environmentalism* (Oakland: University of California Press, 2018), 197.

10. Peter Staudenmaier, *Between Occultism and Nazism: Anthroposophy and the Politics of Race in the Fascist Era* (Leiden: Brill, 2014), chap. 2.

11. McKanan, *Eco-Alchemy,* 122–123; Stephen E. Usher, "The Threefold Social Organism: An Introduction," Rudolf Steiner Web, accessed January 17, 2021, https://www.rudolfsteinerweb.com/Threefold_Social_Order.php/.

12. C. Otto Scharmer, "Ten Economic Insights of Rudolf Steiner," *Kosmos,* Winter 2019; Usher, "Threefold Social Organism."

13. Carole M. Cusack, "'And the Building Becomes Man': Meaning and Aesthetics in Rudolf Steiner's Goetheanum," in *Handbook of New Religious and Cultural Production,* ed. Carole M. Cusack and Alex Norman (Leiden: Brill, 2012), 173–191.

14. Geoffrey Jones, *Profits and Sustainability: A History of Green Entrepreneurship* (Oxford: Oxford University Press, 2017), 33.

15. Henry Barnes, "Rudolf Steiner & the History of Waldorf Education," Waldorf Education, accessed January 2, 2019, https://www.waldorfeducation.org/waldorf-education/rudolf-steiner-the-history-of-waldorf-education.

16. Gunter Vogt, *Entstehung und Entwicklung des ökologischen Landbaus im deutschprachigen Raum* (Bad Dürkheim, Germany: Stiftung Ökologie und Landhau, 2000), 197–199.

17. Uwe Werner, *Das Unternehmen Weleda, 1921–1945* (Berlin: BMW, 2014), 54–56.

18. Vogt, *Entstehung und Entwicklung*, 98, 116, 126.

19. Alex Norman, "Cosmic Flavour, Spiritual Nutrition: The Biodynamic Agricultural Method and the Legacy of Rudolf Steiner's Anthroposophy in Viticulture," in Cusack and Norman, *Handbook of New Religious*, 214–218.

20. Peter Selg, *Dr. Oskar Schmiedel, 1887–1959: Der erste anthroposophische Pharmazeut und Weleda-Director: Eine Dokumentation* (Arlesheim, Germany: Ita Wegman Institut, 2010), 101–102.

21. Geoffrey Ahern, *The Sun at Midnight: The Rudolf Steiner Movement and the Western Esoteric Tradition* (Wellingborough, UK: The Aquarian Press, 1984), 35–37.

22. Staudenmaier, *Between Occultism and Nazism,* chaps. 3 and 4.

23. McKanan, *Eco-Alchemy*, 33–34.

24. McKanah, *Eco-Alchemy*, 35; Ahern, *Sun at Midnight*, 37–46.

25. "Weleda Today," Weleda, accessed July 17, 2020, https://www.weleda.com/about-us/our-heritage/welda-today#:~:text=Weleda%20consists%20of%2019%20majority,employs%20approximately%202%2C000%20people%20worldwide.

26. Gunter Vogt, "The Origins of Organic Farming," in *Organic Farming: An International History,* ed. William Lockeretz (Trowbridge, UK: Cromwell Press, 2007), 19–22.

27. John Paull, "Biodynamic Agriculture: The Journey from Koberwitz to the World, 1924–1938," *Journal of Organic Systems* 6 (2011): 27–41.

28. Karen Priestman, "Illusion of Coexistence: The Waldorf Schools in the Third Reich, 1933–1941" (PhD diss., University of Laurier, 2009).

29. Robin Jackson, "The Birth of the Worldwide Camphill Movement in the North of Scotland: The Challenging Vision of Dr Karl König," *Northern Scotland* 10, no. 2 (November 2019): 157–187.

30. McKanan, *Eco-Alchemy*, 66–69.

31. McKanan, *Eco-Alchemy*, 72–119.

32. "Our History," Rudolf Steiner School, accessed January 31, 2022, https://steiner.edu/history/.

33. Jennifer Sapio, "Waldorf Schools Are Inherently Racist Cults," Medium, June 13, 2020, https://medium.com/age-of-awareness/waldorf-schools-are-inherently-racist-cults-91193d1fbef6; Chris Cook, "Why Are Steiner Schools So Controversial?," BBC World News, August 4, 2014, https://www.bbc.com/news/education-28646118.

34. Caspar Dohmen, *Good Bank: Das Modell der GLS Bank* (Freiburg, Germany: Orange Press, 2011), 38–39.

35. Geoffrey Jones, *Varieties of Green Business: Industries, Nations and Time* (Northampton, MA: Edward Elgar, 2018), 97–100; Frank Jan de Graaf, "Triodos Bank—Mission-Driven Success Pays Off: From Dutch Enfant Terrible to European Business Leader," in *Banking with Integrity: The Winners of the Financial Crisis?,* ed. Heiko Spitzeck, Michael Pirson, and Claus Diersmeier (London: Palgrave Macmillan, 2012), 161.

36. "About Us," RSF Social Finance, accessed July 30, 2020, https://rsfsocialfinance.org/our-story/; McKanan, *Eco-Alchemy*, 130–141; Judy Wicks, *Good Morning, Beautiful Business: The Unexpected Journey of an Activist Entrepreneur and Local Economy Pioneer* (White River Junction, VT: Chelsea Green, 2013), 201–221.

37. "Our Organisational Structure," Triodos Bank, accessed July 23, 2020, https://www.triodos.com/governance#organisational-structure.

38. Rebecca Henderson, *Reimagining Capitalism in a World on Fire* (New York: Public-Affairs, 2020), 146.

39. Claude Aubert, interview by Loubna Bouamane, January 12, 2012.

40. Lebensbaum homepage, accessed April 14, 2021, https://www.lebensbaum.com; Benjamin Brockhaus, "Geistige Grundlagen einer transformativen Unternehmensführung: Auszüge aus den Interviewtranskripten," 2018, https://jimdo-storage.global.ssl.fastly.net/file /d927eb47-2fff-4fc3-85da-5916f689f7e9/Interviewtranskripte2017.pdf.

41. Alnatura homepage, accessed July 19, 2020, https://www.alnatura.de/de-de/ueber-uns/.

42. Götz Rehn, "Anthroposophie und die Wirtschaft," interview by *Süddeutsche Zeitung,* January 17, 2011.

43. McKanan, *Eco-Alchemy,* 141–151.

44. Thomas Harrtung, interview by Geoffrey Jones, Barritskov, Denmark, May 22, 2013.

45. "Søren Ejlersen, Co-founder of Aarstiderne," *Regeneration Podcast,* June 4, 2020, https://www.amazon.com/14-S%C3%B8ren-Ejlersen-Co-founder-Aarstiderne/dp/B08KMFL631.

46. Harrtung, interview by Jones.

47. "Aarstiderne Case Study," Triodos Investment Management, March 18, 2019, https://www.triodos-im.com/articles/projects/aarstiderne-2019.

48. Johanna Mair and Christian Seelos, "The Sekem Initiative: A Holistic Vision to Develop People," in *The New Social Entrepreneurship: What Awaits Social Entrepreneurial Ventures?,* ed. Francesco Perrini (Northampton, MA: Edward Elgar, 2006), 218; Helmy Abouleish, interview by Geoffrey Jones, Cairo, Egypt and Boston, August 22, 2022, Creating Emerging Markets Oral History Collection, Baker Library Special Collections, Harvard Business School.

49. Harrtung, interview by Jones.

50. "Neues von der Finca Irlanda," Lebensbaum, March 31, 2019, https://www.le bensbaum.com/de/journal/neues-von-der-finca-irlanda.

51. "Maddison Project Database 2020," University of Groningen, accessed January 8, 2022, https://www.rug.nl/ggdc/historicaldevelopment/maddison/releases/maddison-project -database-2020.

52. Ulas Karakoc, Sevket Pamuk, and Laura Panza, "Industrialization in Egypt and Turkey, 1870–2010," in *The Spread of Modern Industry to the Periphery since 1871,* ed. Kevin H. O'Rourke and Jeffrey G. Williamson (Oxford: Oxford University Press, 2017), 146.

53. Robert Mabro and Samir Radwan, *The Industrialization of Egypt, 1939–1973* (Oxford: Clarendon Press, 1976), 26.

54. Henry J. Bruton, "Egypt's Development in the Seventies," *Economic Development and Cultural Change* 31, no. 4 (1983): 679–704.

55. Anthony McDermott, *Egypt from Nasser to Mubarak: A Flawed Revolution* (New York: Croom Helm, 1988), 53–54.

56. Ibrahim Abouleish, *Sekem: A Sustainable Community in the Egyptian Desert* (Edinburgh: Floris Books, 2005), 28.

57. Abouleish, *Sekem,* 45–47.

58. Abouleish, *Sekem,* 50.

59. Abouleish, *Sekem,* 51–53.

60. Abouleish, *Sekem,* 59.

61. Abouleish, *Sekem,* 63.

62. Ibrahim Abouleish and Helmy Abouleish, "Garden in the Desert: Sekem Makes Comprehensive Sustainable Development a Reality in Egypt," *Innovations: Technology, Governance, Globalization* 3, no. 3 (2008): 32.

63. Abouleish, *Sekem,* 74.

64. Abouleish, *Sekem,* 48–49.

65. Abouleish, *Sekem,* 77–82.

66. Abouleish, *Sekem,* 101.

67. Abouleish, *Sekem,* 84–85.

68. Abouleish, *Sekem,* 87–88; Ibrahim Abouleish, interview by Loubna Bouamane, October 5, 2011.

69. Abouleish, *Sekem,* 88.

70. Abouleish, *Sekem,* 89–91.

71. Pamela Varley and Christian Seelos, "Transforming Desert Land and Human Potential: Egypt's 'SEKEM' Initiative Reaches a Crossroads" (Harvard Kennedy School Working Paper KS 1266, May 13, 2018).

72. Lebensbaum homepage, accessed April 14, 2021, https://www.lebensbaum.com.

73. Abouleish, *Sekem,* 125.

74. Abouleish, *Sekem,* 99; Abouleish, interview by Bouamane.

75. Abouleish and Abouleish, "Garden in the Desert," 37–40.

76. Abouleish and Abouleish, "Garden in the Desert," 33.

77. Abouleish and Abouleish, "Garden in the Desert," 34.

78. Varley and Seelos, "Transforming Desert Land."

79. Abouleish, *Sekem,* 134–135.

80. P. Ton, *Organic Cotton: An Opportunity for Trade* (Geneva: International Trade Centre UNCTAD/WTO, 2007).

81. Mair and Seelos, "Sekem Initiative," 213–214; "SEKEM at the 'Organic Cotton Round Table' in Hamburg," Sekem, December 27, 2016, https://www.sekem.com/en/sekem -at-the-organic-cotton-round-table-in-hamburg; Abouleish, interview by Jones.

82. Sekem, *Annual Report, 2019* (Cairo: Sekem, 2020), https://www.ecospire.com/listing /naturetex-for-clothes-sekem-group/.

83. Varley and Seelos, "Transforming Desert Land."

84. Abouleish, interview by Bouamane.

85. "Education Is More Than Learning," Sekem, accessed June 9, 2022, https://www .sekem.com/en/cultural-life/education-schools.

86. Abouleish, interview by Bouamane.

87. Abouleish, *Sekem,* 167–168, 180–181, 184.

88. "Heliopolis University for Sustainable Development," Sekem, accessed June 9, 2022, https://www.sekem.com/en/cultural-lef/Heliopolis-university.

89. Abouleish, *Sekem,* 192–194.

90. Laila M. Khdeir and Gehan A. Nagy, "Examining the Impacts of Integrating Sustainability Values into Creating Spaces for Children," paper presented at the First International Conference: Towards a Better Quality of Life, November 23–26, 2017, 1–11.

91. Abouleish, interview by Bouamane.

92. Tomislav Rimac, Johanna Mair, and Julie Battilana, "Social Entrepreneurs, Socialization Processes, and Social Change: The Case of SEKEM," in *Using a Positive Lens to Explore Social Change and Organizations,* ed. Karen Golden-Biddle and Jane E. Dutton (New York: Routledge, 2012), 72.

93. Varley and Seelos, "Transforming Desert Land."

94. "About Loans for Cows and Other Stories," Sekem, February 15, 2017, https://www .sekem.com/en/about-loans-for-cows-and-other-stories.

95. Mair and Seelos, "Sekem Initiative," 220.

96. Abouleish and Abouleish, "Garden in the Desert," 46–48.

97. "Helmy Abouleish: Life Is Great," Sekem, December 28, 2016, https://www.sekem .com/en/helmy-abouleish-life-is-great.

98. Samuel D. Rima, *Spiritual Capital: A Moral Core for Social and Economic Justice* (Farnham, UK: Gower, 2013), 232.

99. Varley and Seelos, "Transforming Desert Land," 14.

100. Sekem, *Annual Report, 2021* (Cairo: Sekem, 2022).

101. Gianluca Vitale et al., "Integrated Management Approach towards Sustainability: An Egyptian Business Case Study," *Sustainability* 11, no. 5 (2019): 1–26.

102. Petra Gessner, "Deutsch-ägyptische Nachfolgelösung," *Wir Magazin,* March 10, 2017.

103. Sekem, *Annual Report, 2020* (Cairo: Sekem, 2021), 9.

104. Sekem, *Annual Report, 2019;* Rima, *Spiritual Capital,* 233–234.

105. Dwijendra Tripathi, *The Oxford History of Indian Business* (Oxford: Oxford University Press, 2004), 66–67.

106. Sarah Besky, *The Darjeeling Distinction: Labor and Justice on Fair-Trade Tea Plantations in India* (Berkeley: University of California Press, 2013), 51–58.

107. Jeff Koehler, *Darjeeling: A History of the World's Greatest Tea* (New York: Bloomsbury, 2015), 145.

108. Koehler, *Darjeeling,* 161.

109. Sanjay Bansal, interview by Geoffrey Jones, Kolkata, India, April 27, 2016, Creating Emerging Markets Oral History Collection, Baker Library Special Collections, Harvard Business School.

110. A. Kurian and K. V. Peter, *Commercial Crops Technology* (Delhi: New India Publishing Agency, 2007), 436.

111. Besky, *Darjeeling Distinction,* 115.

112. Bansal, interview by Jones.

113. Koehler, *Darjeeling,* 145.

114. Bansal, interview by Jones.

115. Bansal, interview by Jones.

116. Bansal, interview by Jones.

117. Bansal, interview by Jones.

118. Pramod Giri, "Veteran Bengal Planter Gifts His Stake in Iconic Makaibari Tea Estate to Workers," *Hindustan Times,* March 30, 2018.

119. Vivek Chhetri, "Tea Exporter in Distress: Parent Company Virtually Collapsing under the Burden of Dues," *Telegraph India Online,* July 13, 2020, https://www.telegraphindia.com/west-bengal/tea-exporter-of-darjeeling-in-distress/cid/1786193; Indroneel Goho, interview by Geoffrey Jones, Zoom, April 9, 2021.

120. Sambit Saha, "Foreign Investors to Take Management Control of Darjeeling Organic Tea Estates," *Telegraph India Online,* March 16, 2021, https://www.telegraphindia.com/business/foreign-investors-to-take-management-control-of-darjeeling-organic-tea-estates/cid/1797059; Goho, interview by Jones.

121. Goho, interview by Jones.

122. Chintu Das, "Darjeeling Tea Production Hits a New Low in 2021," Krishi Jagran, January 4, 2022, https://krishijagran.com/agriculture-world/darjeeling-tea-production-hits-a-new-low-in-2021/.

10. From ESG to B Corps

1. Archie B. Carroll et al., *Corporate Responsibility: The American Experience* (New York: Cambridge University Press, 2012), 143.

2. Lynn Stout, *The Shareholder Value Myth* (San Francisco: Berrett-Koehler, 2012), 26–27.

3. Stout, *Shareholder Value Myth*, 3.

4. Theodore Levitt, "The Dangers of Social Responsibility," *Harvard Business Review* 36, no. 5 (1958): 41–50.

5. Milton Friedman, *Capitalism and Freedom* (Chicago: University of Chicago Press, 1962).

6. Milton Friedman, *Studies in the Quantity Theory of Money* (Chicago: University of Chicago Press, 1956).

7. Milton Friedman, "A Friedman Doctrine—the Social Responsibility of Business Is to Increase Its Profits," *New York Times Magazine,* September 13, 1970, https://www.nytimes.com/1970/09/13/archives/a-friedman-doctrine-the-social-responsibility-of-business-is-to.html.

8. Michael C. Jensen and William H. Meckling, "Theory of the Firm: Managerial Behavior, Agency Costs, and Ownership Structure," *Journal of Financial Economics* 3, no. 4 (1976): 311.

9. Kurt Andersen, *Evil Geniuses: The Unmaking of America: A Recent History* (New York: Random House, 2020); Robert Reich, *The System: Who Rigged It, How We Fix It* (New York: Knopf, 2020).

10. William Lazonick and Mary O'Sullivan, "Maximizing Shareholder Value: A New Ideology for Corporate Governance," *Economy and Society* 29, no. 1 (2000): 13–35; Lazaros Goutas and Christel Lane, "The Translation of Shareholder Value in the German Business System: A Comparative Study of DaimlerChrysler and Volkswagen AG," *Competition and Change* 13, no. 4 (2009): 327–346.

11. Duff McDonald, *The Golden Passport: Harvard Business School, the Limits of Capitalism, and the Moral Failure of the MBA Elite* (New York: Harper Business, 2017), 365–378; Michael C. Jensen et al., "Organizations and Markets," in *The Intellectual Venture Capitalist: John H. McArthur and the Work of the Harvard Business School, 1980–1995,* ed. Thomas K. McCraw and Jeffrey L. Cruikshank (Boston: Harvard Business School Press, 1999), 166–182.

12. Michael C. Jensen and Kevin J. Murphy, "CEO Incentives: It's Not How Much You Pay, but How," *Harvard Business Review,* May–June 1990, https://hbr.org/1990/05/ceo-incentives-its-not-how-much-you-pay-but-how.

13. Brian J. Hall and Kevin J. Murphy, "The Trouble with Stock Options," *Journal of Economic Perspectives* 17, no. 3 (2003): 49–70.

14. Colin Mayer, *Prosperity: Better Business Makes the Greater Good* (Oxford: Oxford University Press, 2018), 2.

15. William Lazonick and Jang-Sup Shin, *Predatory Value Extraction: How the Looting of the Business Corporation Became the U.S. Norm and How Sustainable Prosperity Can Be Restored* (New York: Oxford University Press, 2020); Clifton Clarke and Hershey H. Friedman, "'Maximizing Shareholder Value': A Theory Run Amok," *i-manager's Journal on Management* 10, no. 4 (2016): 45–60.

16. Joseph L. Bower and Lynn S. Paine, "The Error at the Heart of Corporate Leadership," *Harvard Business Review,* May–June 2017, https://hbr.org/2017/05/the-error-at-the-heart-of-corporate-leadership.

17. Jacob S. Hacker and Paul Pierson, *American Amnesia: How the War on Government Led Us to Forget What Made America Prosper* (New York: Simon and Schuster, 2016).

18. Naomi Oreskes and Erik M. Conway, *Merchants of Doubt* (New York: Bloomsbury, 2010); Geoffrey Supran and Naomi Oreskes, "Assessing ExxonMobil's Climate Change Communications (1977–2014)," *Environmental Research Letters* 12, no. 8 (2017): 084019.

19. "Paradise Papers: Everything You Need to Know about the Leak," BBC World News, November 10, 2017, https://www.bbc.com/news/world-41880153.

20. Jason W. Moore, *Capitalism in the Web of Life: Ecology and the Accumulation of Capital* (New York: Verso, 2015).

21. Rob Nixon, *Slow Violence and the Environmentalism of the Poor* (Cambridge, MA: Harvard University Press, 2011).

22. Frances Brown, *After Greenwashing: Symbolic Corporate Environmentalism and Society* (Cambridge: Cambridge University Press, 2014).

23. "Conflicted Consequences," Center for Political Accountability, July 21, 2020, https://politicalaccountability.net/hifi/files/Conflicted-Consequences.pdf.

24. Ernst F. Schumacher, *Small Is Beautiful: Economics as if People Mattered* (London: Blond and Briggs, 1973); Donella H. Meadows et al., *The Limits to Growth: A Report for the Club of Rome's Project on the Predicament of Mankind* (New York: Universe Books, 1972).

25. Ann-Kristin Bergquist, "Business and Sustainability," in *The Routledge Companion to the Makers of Global Business,* ed. Teresa da Silva Lopes, Christina Lubinski, and Heidi J. S. Tworek (New York: Routledge, 2020), 556; Ann-Kristin Bergquist et al., "Understanding and Overcoming Roadblocks to Environmental Sustainability: Past Roads and Future Prospects," *Business History Review* 93, no. 1 (2019): 127–148.

26. Joakim Sanberg et al., "The Heterogeneity of Socially Responsible Investment," *Journal of Business Ethics* 87 (2009): 519–533.

27. Bronwen Everill, *Not Made by Slaves: Ethical Capitalism in the Age of Abolition* (Cambridge, MA: Harvard University Press, 2020).

28. Emily Barman, *Caring Capitalism* (Cambridge: Cambridge University Press, 2016), 101; Alice Tepper Marlin, acceptance speech for the Right Livelihood Award, December 12, 1990; Alice Tepper Marlin et al., *Shopping for a Better World: A Quick and Easy Guide to Socially Responsible Supermarket Shopping* (New York: Council on Economic Priorities, 1991), 80–94.

29. Geoffrey Jones, *Profits and Sustainability: A History of Green Entrepreneurship* (Oxford: Oxford University Press, 2017), 281–282.

30. Geoffrey Jones and Seema Amble, "Joan Bavaria and Multi-dimensional Capitalism" (Harvard Business School Case 9-317-028, rev. December 4, 2018).

31. Jones and Amble, "Joan Bavaria."

32. Ceres, "Joan Bavaria Tribute," Vimeo, May 27, 2009, video, 5:59, https//vimeo.com /4868373.

33. Anne Delehunt, "Franklin Research and Development Corporation" (Harvard Business School Case 9-390-027, 1989), 6.

34. Jones and Amble, "Joan Bavaria."

35. Jessica A. Levy, "Black Power in the Boardroom: Corporate America, the Sullivan Principles, and the Anti-Apartheid Struggle," *Enterprise and Society* 21, no. 1 (2020): 170–209.

36. Stephen Davis, Jon Lukomnik, and David Pitt-Watson, *The New Capitalists: How Citizen Investors Are Reshaping the Corporate Agenda* (Cambridge, MA: Harvard Business School Press, 2013), 160.

37. Jones and Amble, "Joan Bavaria," 9–10.

38. Joan Bavaria, "Ceres and the Valdez Principles," in *The Social Investment Almanac: A Comprehensive Guide to Socially Responsible Investing,* ed. Peter D. Kinder, Steven D. Lydenberg, and Amy L. Domini (New York: Henry Holt, 1992), 138–142; "Safety and Environmental Responsibilities," Sunoco, accessed June 10, 2022, https://sunocoyonkers.com /sunoco/sunoco-safety-and-environmental-responsibilities.

39. "Our Mission and History," Global Reporting Initiative, accessed March 11, 2022, https://www.globalreporting.org/about-gri/mission-history/.

40. Halina Szejnwald Brown, Martin de Jong, and Teodorina Lessidenska, "The Rise of the Global Reporting Initiative: A Case of Institutional Entrepreneurship," *Environmental Politics* 18, no. 2 (2009): 184–185.

41. Brown, de Jong, and Lessidenska, "Rise of the Global Reporting Initiative," 193.

42. Markus J. Milne and Rob Gray, "W(h)ither Ecology? The Triple Bottom Line, the Global Reporting Initiative, and Corporate Sustainability Reporting," *Journal of Business Ethics* 118 (2013): 13–29.

43. Amy Domini, "Northfield Mt. Hermon Commencement," May 28, 2008, https://amydomini.com/northfield-mt-hermon-commencement-2/; Amy Domini, "Reflections from a Career Investor," 3BL Media, April 21, 2015, https://www.3blmedia.com/News/Reflections-Career-Investor-Amy-Domini; Marc Gunther, *Faith and Fortune: The Quiet Revolution to Reform American Business* (New York: Crown Business, 2004), 221.

44. Gunther, *Faith and Fortune*, 216–217.

45. Gunther, *Faith and Fortune*, 217; Domini, "Northfield Mt. Hermon Commencement."

46. Amy Domini with Peter Kinder, *Ethical Investing* (Boston: Addison-Wesley, 1984), xi.

47. Amy Domini, "Acceptance of Honorary Degree at Yale Divinity School," October 10, 2007, https://amydomini.com/acceptance-of-honorary-degree-at-yale-divinity-school/.

48. Gunther, *Faith and Fortune*, 223.

49. Sandra Waddock, *The Difference Makers: How Social and Institutional Entrepreneurs Created the Corporate Responsibility Movement* (Abingdon, UK: Routledge, 2017), 92.

50. Amy Domini, "Biography," accessed January 23, 2020, https://amydomini.com/insights/biography/; "Standard RFI," Domini Social Investments, accessed January 28, 2020, https://www.domini.com/sites/default/files/_files/Standard_RFI_Presentation.pdf; Waddock, *Difference Makers*, 92, 97.

51. Waddock, *Difference Makers*, 96.

52. Lloyd Kurtz, Steven D. Lydenberg, and Peter D. Kinder, "The Domini Social Index: A New Benchmark for Social Investors," in Kinder, Lydenberg, and Domini, *Social Investment Almanac*, 287–322.

53. Sheri J. Caplan, *Petticoats and Pinstripes: Portraits of Women in Wall Street's History* (Santa Barbara, CA: Praeger, 2013), 174–175.

54. J. (Hans) van Oosterhout and Pursey P. M. A. R. Heugens, "Much Ado about Nothing: A Conceptual Critique of Corporate Social Responsibility," in *The Oxford Handbook of Corporate Social Responsibility*, ed. Andrew Crane et al. (Oxford: Oxford University Press, 2008), 205–209.

55. Waddock, *Difference Makers*, 98.

56. Gunther, *Faith and Fortune*, 226.

57. Gunther, *Faith and Fortune*, 229–231; Ellie Winninghoff, "Green Capitalism," *Salon,* December 9, 2004, https://www.salon.com/2004/12/08/sri/.

58. "Remembering Tessa Tennant, Giant of Green Finance," *Economist,* August 5, 2018; Daniel C. Matisoff, Douglas S. Noonan, and John J. O'Brien, "Convergence in Environmental Reporting: Assessing the Carbon Disclosure Project," *Business Strategy and the Environment* 22, no. 5 (2013): 285–305.

59. "Nikko Eco Fund" (in Japanese), accessed March 15, 2022, https://www.nikkoam.com/fund/detail/252263; Mizue Tsukushi, "Women's Finance Initiative Activities Japanese Economy: SRI's Growth Potential in Japan," *Japan Spotlight,* May/June 2010.

60. Alois Flatz, Lena Serck-Hanssen, and Erica Tucker-Bassin, "The Dow Jones Sustainability Group Index," in *Sustainable Banking: The Greening of Finance,* ed. Jan Jaap Bouma, Marcel Jeuken, and Leon Klinkers (Sheffield, UK: Greenleaf Publishing, 2001), 222–233.

61. The Global Compact, *Who Cares Wins: Connecting Financial Markets to a Changing World* (United Nations Department of Public Information, December 2004),

https://d306pr3pise04h.cloudfront.net/docs/issues_doc%2FFinancial_markets%2Fwho
_cares_who_wins.pdf.

62. Malte Rohwer-Kahlmann, "UN Global Compact: Is Big Business Saving the World?,"
DW, September 21, 2017, https://www.dw.com/en/un-global-compact-is-big-business-saving
-the-world/a-40614516.

63. Riccardo Boffo and Robert Patalano, *ESG Investing: Practices, Progress and Challenges* (Paris: OECD, 2020), https://www.oecd.org/finance/ESG-Investing-Practices-Progress
-Challenges.pdf, 15.

64. JPX Sustainable Finance Platform Development Working Group, *First Report* (February 25, 2022), https://www.jpx.co.jp/news/0090/nlsgeu0000065amd-att/JPXSFPlatform
DevelopmentWGFirstReport.pdf.

65. George Serafeim, "ESG: Hyperboles and Reality" (Harvard Business School Working
Paper 22-031, 2021).

66. Ping Manongdo, "Firms Can No Longer Shirk from Reporting on the S in ESG,"
Eco-business, March 18, 2022.

67. Harriet Agnew, Adrienne Klasa, and Simon Mundy, "How ESG Investing Came to
a Reckoning," *Financial Times,* June 6, 2022, https://www.ft.com/content/5ec1dfcf-eea3-42af
-aea2-19d739ef8a55.

68. Rob Gray and Markus Milne, "Sustainability Reporting: Who's Kidding Whom?,"
Chartered Accountants Journal of New Zealand 81, no. 6 (2002): 66.

69. Julie Battilana et al., "Beyond Shareholder Value Maximization: Accounting for Financial / Social Trade-Offs in Dual-Purpose Companies," *Academy of Management Review*
47, no. 2 (2022): 237–258.

70. Lucian A. Bebchuk and Roberto Tarrarita, "The Perils and Questionable Promise
of ESG-Based Compensation," *Journal of Corporation Law* (forthcoming).

71. Joshua D. Margolis and James P. Walsh, "Misery Loves Companies: Rethinking So-
cial Initiatives by Business," *Administrative Science Quarterly* 48, no. 2 (2003): 268–305;
Miriam von Wallis and Christian Klein, "Ethical Requirement and Financial Interest: A
Literature Review on Socially Responsible Investing," *Business Research* 8 (2015): 71–83;
Andrew Lynn, "Why 'Doing Well by Doing Good' Went Wrong: Getting beyond 'Good
Ethics Pays' Claims in Managerial Thinking," *Academy of Management Review* 46, no. 3 (2021):
512–533.

72. Mozaffar Khan, George Serafeim, and Aaron Yoon, "Corporate Sustainability: First
Evidence of Materiality," *Accounting Review* 91, no. 6 (2016): 1697–1724.

73. Luca Berchicci and Andrew A. King, "Corporate Sustainability: A Model Uncer-
tainty Analysis of Materiality," *Journal of Financial Reporting* (forthcoming).

74. Diane Coyle, "The Revolution Will Not Be Privatized," *Foreign Affairs,* January /
February 2022, https://www.foreignaffairs.com/articles/world/2021-12-14/revolution-will-not
-be-privatized.

75. Sakis Kotsantonis and George Serafeim, "Four Things No One Will Tell You about
ESG Data," *Journal of Applied Corporate Finance* 31, no. 2 (2019): 50–58.

76. Bergquist, "Business and Sustainability," 552–556.

77. Coyle, "Revolution Will Not Be Privatized."

78. *Economist,* July 23–29, 2022.

79. Suntae Kim et al., "Why Companies Are Becoming B Corporations," *Harvard
Business Review,* June 17, 2016, https://hbr.org/2016/06/why-companies-are-becoming-b
-corporations.

80. Christopher Marquis, *Better Business: How the B Corp Movement Is Remaking
Capitalism* (New Haven, CT: Yale University Press, 2020), ix.

81. Marquis, *Better Business,* 47–52.

82. Marquis, *Better Business,* 85–86.

83. Marquis, *Better Business,* 56–57.

84. Dan McKanan, *Eco-Alchemy: Anthroposophy and the History and Future of Environmentalism* (Oakland: University of California Press, 2018), 140; Marquis, *Better Business,* 150.

85. Marquis, *Better Business,* 60.

86. Marquis, *Better Business,* 87–94.

87. "State by State Status of Legislation," B Lab US and Canada, accessed January 24, 2022, https://benefitcorp.net/policymakers/state-by-state-status.

88. Marquis, *Better Business,* 67–68.

89. "How Did the B Corp Movement Start?," Certified B Corporation, accessed March 4, 2020, https://bcorporation.net/faq-item/how-did-b-corp-movement-start.

90. Ryan Honeyman and Tiffany Jana, *The B Corp Handbook: How You Can Use Business as a Force for Good,* 2nd ed. (Oakland, CA: Berrett-Koehler, 2019), chap. 1; Mary Margaret Frank, Elena Loutskina, and Gerry Yemen, "A Community for Change: B Lab and Certified B Corps" (Technical Note F-1878, Darden Business Publishing, University of Virginia, August 27, 2019), 2.

91. "Funders & Finances," B Lab, accessed March 16, 2020, https://bcorporation.net/about-b-lab/funders-and-finances.

92. Alex Buerkle, Kylee Chang, and Max Storto, *Just Good Business: An Investor's Guide to B Corps* (Yale Center for Business and the Environment, Patagonia, and Caprock, March 2018), https://cbey.yale.edu/sites/default/files/Just%20Good%20Business_An%20Investor%27s%20Guide%20to%20B%20Corps_March%202018.pdf.

93. Anand Giridharadas, *Winners Take All: The Elite Charade of Changing the World* (New York: Knopf Doubleday, 2018), 250.

94. Ed Miliband, *Go Big: How to Fix Our World* (London: Bodley Head, 2021).

95. Judy Wicks, *Good Morning, Beautiful Business: The Unexpected Journey of an Activist Entrepreneur and Local Economy Pioneer* (White River Junction, VT: Chelsea, 2013), 240.

96. Edward M. Gamble, Simon C. Parker, and Peter W. Monroe, "Measuring the Integration of Social and Environmental Missions in Hybrid Organizations," *Journal of Business Ethics* 167, no. 2 (2020): 271–284.

97. List of Public B Corps and Benefit Corps and Other Certified Subsidiaries, supplied to the author by Marcel Fukayama, head of Global Policy at B Lab Global, January 25, 2022.

98. List of Public B Corps and Benefit Corps.

99. John Tagliabue, "Antoine Ribaud, Builder of French Food Giant, Dies at 83," *New York Times,* May 7, 2002; Christopher Marquis, "CEO Compensation Was Out of Control. How Emmanuel Faber Was Changing the Game in Governance and Employee Equity," *Forbes,* August 16, 2021.

100. Rebecca Henderson, *Reimagining Capitalism in a World on Fire* (New York: PublicAffairs, 2020), 154.

101. María Emilia Correa, interview by Emily Grandjean, May 1, 2020.

102. Juan Pablo Larenas, interview by Geoffrey Jones, Zoom, March 11, 2021.

103. María Emilia Correa, interview by Andrea Lluch, Boston, May 8, 2019, Creating Emerging Markets Oral History Collection, Baker Library Special Collections, Harvard Business School.

104. Pedro Tarak, interview by Andrea Lluch, Buenos Aires, Argentina, July 19, 2018, Creating Emerging Markets Oral History Collection, Baker Library Special Collections, Harvard Business School; "Sistema B: Historical Report, 2011–2015," Sistema B, accessed March 20, 2020, http://www.sistemab.org/wp-content/uploads/2016/08/Memoria-SB-2015_INGLES.pdf.

105. Beatriz Fernández, interview by Andrea Lluch, Bogotá, Colombia, May 16, 2018, Creating Emerging Markets Oral History Collection, Baker Library Special Collections.

106. Marquis, *Better Business*, 172.

107. "About Us," Academia B, accessed March 18, 2020, http://academiab.org/en/what-is-academia-b/; Correa, interview by Lluch.

108. Larenas, interview by Jones.

109. "Sistema B: Historical Report, 2011–2015."

110. Larenas, interview by Jones.

111. "Introducing 'B Beauty,'" press release, January 10, 2022, https://www.bcorpbeauty.org/wp-content/uploads/2022/04/B-Corp-Beauty-Coalition.Press-Release.FINAL_.pdf.

112. "Colombia's Juan Valdez Café Becomes B Corp Certified," *Global Coffee Report*, April 16, 2021.

113. Marcel Fukayama to Geoffrey Jones, email, April 12, 2022; B Lab homepage, accessed June 10, 2022, https://www.bcorporation.net.

114. Naoki Ishii, Ishii Zouen Landscape (a certified B Corporation), interview by Akiko Saito, June 30, 2021. Ishii pointed out the long-established concept of *sanpo-yoshi* (good for the seller, good for the buyer, and good for society). Geoffrey Jones, "B Corps: Can It Remake Capitalism in Japan?," *Keizaikei (Kanto Gakuin Journal of Economics and Management)* 284 (November 2021): 8–10.

115. Giridharadas, *Winners Take All*, 6.

116. Andrew V. Abela, "Profit and More: Catholic Social Teaching and the Purpose of the Firm," *Journal of Business Ethics* 31, no. 2 (2001): 107–116.

117. "Culture of Giving," Economy of Communion, accessed April 7, 2020, https://www.edc-online.org/en/chi-siamo-it/cultura-del-dare.html; "About Us," Focolare Movement, accessed March 26, 2020, https://www.focolare.org/en/chi-siamo/#aboutus; Meghan Dorney, "'Love One Another': The Focolare Movement and Its Mission," *Boston Pilot*, November 7, 2003, https://www.thebostonpilot.com/articleprint.asp?id=1318.

118. Lorna Gold, *The Sharing Economy: Solidarity Networks Transforming Globalization* (Burlington, VT: Ashgate, 2004), 49–61; Lorna Gold, *New Financial Horizons: The Emergence of an Economy of Communion* (Hyde Park, NY: New City Press, 2010), 39–49; "About Us," Focolare Movement.

119. Amy Uelmen and Thomas Masters, "Economy of Communion," in *Encyclopedia of Catholic Social Thought, Social Science, and Social Policy,* vol. 3, ed. Michael L. Coulter, Richard S. Myers, and Joseph A. Varacalli (Lanham, MD: Scarecrow Press, 2012), 86.

120. Gold, *Sharing Economy*, 87–89.

121. Gold, *Sharing Economy*, 90.

122. Gold, *New Financial Horizons*, 115.

123. Chiara Lubich, "Some Aspects of the *Economy of Communion*," Focolare Movement, April 5, 2001, https://eocnorthamerica.files.wordpress.com/2015/11/chi_20010405_en.pdf.

124. "Economy of Communion," Focolare Movement, accessed March 26, 2020, https://www.focolare.org/usa/professional-life/economy-of-communion/.

125. Gold, *New Financial Horizons*, 171; Todd Hartch, *The Rebirth of Latin American Christianity* (Oxford: Oxford University Press, 2014), 163; "About Us," Mundell & Associates, accessed April 22, 2020, https://mundellassociates.com/company/; "Social Mission," Mundell & Associates, accessed April 22, 2020, https://mundellassociates.com/company/social-mission/.

126. Gold, *Sharing Economy*, 134–137.

127. Gold, *Sharing Economy*, 173–174.

128. Luigino Bruni and Amelia J. Uelmen, "Religious Values and Corporate Decision Making: The Economy of Communion Project," *Fordham Journal of Corporate and Financial Law* 11 (2012): 645–680.

129. María Emilia Correa to Geoffrey Jones, email, January 20, 2021.

130. Werner Plumpe, *Eine Vision, zwei Unternehmen: 125 Jahre Carl-Zeiss-Stiftung* (Munich: Verlag C. H. Beck, 2014).

131. John Spedan Lewis, *Partnership for All* (London: Kerr-Cros, 1948), 100.

132. Purpose Foundation, *Steward-Ownership: Rethinking Ownership in the 21st Century* (Basel: Purpose Foundation, n.d.), https://www.purpose-us.com/writing/steward-ownership, 52–56.

133. "The Mozilla Manifesto," Mozilla, accessed June 13, 2022, https://www.mozilla.org /en-US/about/manifesto/.

134. Plumpe, *Eine Vision, zwei Unternehmen,* 84, 147, 192–193, 214.

135. Graeme Salaman and John Storey, *A Better Way of Doing Business? Lessons from the John Lewis Partnership* (Oxford: Oxford University Press, 2016); Bernard Paranque and Hugh Willmott, "Cooperatives—Saviours or Gravediggers of Capitalism? Critical Performativity and the John Lewis Partnership," *Organization* 21, no. 5 (2014): 604–625.

136. Jonathan Eley, "John Lewis to Restore Full-Year Bonus for Staff after Sales Rebound," *Financial Times,* March 10, 2022, https://www.ft.com/content/f84185e5-e1e9-4c8b -909b-dacd13410070.

137. Peter Brors, "Diese vier Unternehmer wollen das Verantwortungseigentum fördern," *Handelsblatt,* November 21, 2019, https://www.handelsblatt.com/unternehmen/mittelstand /familienunternehmer/purpose-stiftung-diese-vier-unternehmer-wollen-das-verantwortung seigentum-foerdern/25253058.html?ticket=ST-5346632-p6JaOV1ru7f5e2FN9qhX-ap1.

138. "Über Uns," Waldorfshop, accessed January 24, 2022, https://www.waldorfshop.eu /ueber-uns.

139. Christopher Houghton Budd, "Die Rolle der Korporationen: Wie sollen wir Unternehmen im 21. Jahrhundert verstehen?," EC Report, Goetheanum Yearly Economics Conference paper, February 2020, https://economics.goetheanum.org/fileadmin/economics/Topic _Reports/2020_Topic_Report_Die_Rolle_der_Korporationen__de_.pdf.

140. "Partners of the World Goetheanum Association," World Goetheanum Association, accessed February 4, 2022, https://worldgoetheanum.org/en/partner/partner.

141. Purpose Foundation homepage, accessed February 4, 2022, https://purpose-economy .org/en/.

142. Jakob Willeke, "Unternehmen, die sich selbst gehören," *Oekologie und Landbau,* January 2022.

143. Corinna Budras, "Die Koalition plant eine Rechtsreform-Revolution," *Frankfurter Allgemeine,* November 30, 2021.

144. Purpose Foundation and RSF Social Finance, *State of Alternative Ownership in the US: Emerging Trends in Steward-Ownership and Alternative Financing, Learning Journey Report 2019* (Purpose Foundation and RSF Social Finance, n.d.), https://2lm7za162459 1zimq52rpjbg19lk-wpengine.netdna-ssl.com/wp-content/uploads/2019/10/LearningJourney Report_Oct2019.pdf.

145. Susan N. Gary, "The Oregon Stewardship Trust: A New Type of Purpose Trust That Enables Steward-Ownership of a Business," *University of Cincinnati Law Review* 83, no. 3 (2019): 707–733.

146. Yvon Chouinard, "Earth Is Now Our Only Shareholder," open letter, https://www .patagonia.com/ownership/; David Gelles, "Billionaire No More: Patagonia Founder Gives Away the Company," *New York Times,* September 14, 2022.

ACKNOWLEDGMENTS

Against the background of ecological degradation, vast wealth inequalities between and within countries, and gross racial and other injustices, the world is awash with calls for business to be more responsible and to have a purpose. Mysterious acronyms abound. Tens of billions of dollars are engaged in environmental, social, and governance investing in global capital markets. Leading companies undertake Global Reporting Initiative reporting. Corporations announce they are aligned with the seventeen Sustainable Development Goals proposed by the United Nations. This book is motivated by the belief that ours is not the first generation to talk about the social purpose of business, and that there is much to be learned from the past to help us think about what is happening today and inform our journey to a better future.

The history of socially responsible business, and the tensions between profit and purpose, can be approached in many ways. Each has its own validity. In the spirit of the Harvard Business School, where I have taught for over two decades, I chose to focus on the stories of individual business leaders and to weave their stories into global history over the past two hundred years. Experiments in social responsibility have not been confined to any time period or particular country.

The business leaders in this book are not presented as exemplars and heroes, but rather as human beings with a variety of frailties who found themselves in often challenging circumstances and who perceived that business could make their societies and the planet better rather than worse. I hope that their stories can inform current debates about what business purpose and responsibility really means, and what it can and cannot achieve. An important takeaway is that, although pursuing social purpose is far superior to acting irresponsibly, there are also plentiful trade-offs and gray areas.

This book has been several years in the making, and during two of those years COVID-19 made everything more difficult than usual. So my progress depended even more than usual on the help and forbearance of others. I would like to thank Emily Grandjean, my research associate during the first years of the project, for her hard work and enthusiasm. I also received valuable research support over the years from Daniela Beyersdorfer, Loubna Bouamane, Susannah Deily-Swearingen, Mona Rahmani, Akiko Saito, Nobuo Sato, Malini Sen, and Enlan Wang. Many people helped by making connections, interviewing, sharing ideas, and reading drafts. I would like to thank in particular Seema Amble, Grace Ballor, Ann-Kristin Bergquist, Alberto Castro, Asli Colpan, Teresa da Silva Lopes, Walter Friedman, Valeria Giacomin, Charles Harvey, Ai Hisano, Andrea Lluch, Mairi Maclean, Rei Morimoto, Sabine Pitteloud, Sofia Salgado, Laura Phillips Sawyer, Sudev Sheth, Alvaro Ferreira Silva, Rie Sugiyama, Emilie Takayama, Richard Tedlow, Chimnay Tumbe, and Mira Wilkins. I also thank two anonymous readers of my manuscript for their valuable comments. Multiple cohorts of MBA students taking my course Entrepreneurship and Global Capitalism obliged me to think hard about the responsibility of business to the world. My former MBA student Irene Kwok inspired me to redesign the whole project. At Baker Library, Laura Linard and Rachel Wise were wonderful. Sanjay Bansal, María Emilia Correa, Marcel Fukayama, Indroneel Goho, Thomas Harrtung, Juan Pablo Larenas, Greg Marsh, and Rob Prichard were among the entrepreneurs and institution builders who gave freely of their time. Jeff Strabone worked his editorial magic on my text, and as did Joy de Menil as the manuscript passed through Harvard University Press. The research for this book was generously funded by the Division of Research and Faculty Development at the Harvard Business School, to which I am extremely grateful.

Finally, I thank Dylan and Rattana for their endurance.

INDEX

Aarstiderne, 279, 280, 299, 344
Abouleish, Helmy, 289, 290, 291, 294, 338, 345
Abouleish, Ibrahim, 281–294; biodynamic farming by, 13, 265, 281–294, 299–300 (*see also* Sekem); community integration goals of, 282, 284, 289–290, 345; Egyptian context for, 282–284, 291–292; personal history of, 283–284; spirituality influencing, 283, 284, 286–287, 347; succession following, 291–293
advertising and marketing: anti-organic food, 287; automobile industry, 201–202; beauty industry, 238, 240, 243, 249, 254, 256; big business's false, 48; Cadbury's stance on, 28, 41; consumerism and misleading, 194–195; Nazi influence on, 92; values-driven businesses' approach to, 234, 243
agency theory, 12, 218, 304–305, 324
agnotology, 306, 307
agriculture: biodynamic (*see* biodynamic farming); community-supported, 278; Norris's involvement in, 208, 212; organic market for, 228–231, 233–234, 236–237, 243 (*see also* biodynamic farming); regenerative, 237; Shibusawa's family in, 109; values-driven businesses in food and, 227–235, 236–237, 243–244
Ahmedabad, 159, 163–164, 166, 169–172, 178–181, 182, 183, 184, 346, 357
Ahmedabad Education Society, 172–173, 178, 183
Ahmedabad Millowners Association, 169–170, 178, 181

alcohol: Cadbury's rules against, 32, 41; chocolate drinks vs., 28, 343; ESG investing avoiding stock in, 309, 316, 344; Indian views of, 162, 168, 294, 295; Mormon views of, 196; Quaker views of, 24, 26, 28, 309; US prohibition of, 194; Wedgwood's limitations on, 10
Alexander, Horace, 159–160
Alnatura, 278, 280, 286, 299
AMA (Automobile Manufacturers Association), 197, 199, 200
Ambedkar, B. R., 161, 182
Ambootia, 294–300; biodynamic farming, 265, 280, 294–300; community integration goals of, 294, 295–296, 298–299; crisis and rescue of, 294, 296–297; employees of, 294–299; financing of, 296, 298, 354; Indian tea industry context for, 294–295, 298–299; in industry associations, 280, 296; steward-ownership model and, 338
American Cyanamid, 175–176
American Fair Trade League, 51, 62
American Federation of Labor, 48, 137
American Motors Corporation (AMC), 187, 193, 198–203, 204, 355
Anandji Kalyanji Trust, 159, 164, 165, 172
AND1, 323–324
Anthroposophy: banks based on, 275–276, 322–323, 354; biodynamic farming and, 13, 267, 272–275, 277–281, 283–284, 292, 294, 295, 298–300; business and, 275–281; Steiner's philosophy on, 13, 267–268, 271–274, 283, 299–300, 338; steward-ownership model influenced by, 338

43–44; deep responsibility reflecting, 347; Filene's, 56; Lalbhai's, 168, 182–183; Shibusawa's respect for, 117, 119–120; traits of, 5, 9, 117

Volkswagen, 202, 204–205

voting rights: industrialization and, 17–18; shareholder proxy voting, 317; steward's, 336; women's, 18, 67, 224–225

wages: Body Shop's, 250, 251, 252; Bosch paying high, 84; Cadbury paying high, 29; Catholic call for fair, 332–333; executive, 305–306, 321; Filene's stance on, 56, 70; Gilded Age levels of, 51; Indian, 169, 175; industrialization and, 17; minimum, 56, 74; for sick days, 22, 29, 76; UK social responsibility experiments paying reasonable, 17; for vacation days, 51, 84; values-driven businesses' payment of, 231, 233

Waldorf educational system, 271, 274, 275, 278, 338, 349

Walker, Madam C. J., 239–240

Walter, Ulrich, 277–278, 280–281, 286, 298

Walz, Hans, 86, 87, 93–94, 97

Wanamaker, 50, 52

Wang, An: community investment by, 214–215, 216–217, 218, 345, 355; overview of leadership of, 12, 187; philanthropy of, 213, 218, 357; social issues addressed by, 212–218

waste avoidance: biodynamic farming approach to, 279; Body Shop, 253–254; environmental social activism on, 223; ESG investing reflecting, 310, 318, 320; Filene's, 55; Lalbhai's, 167, 168; US postwar business stance on, 187, 193, 194, 195, 201, 217; values-driven businesses' goals of, 237–238

wealth: Filene's efforts to redistribute, 55–56, 61, 62–66, 70–71, 186, 344, 346; Gilded Age concentration of, 46, 53; historical changes in, 9; Indian business leaders' pursuit of, 182; inequality of (see income inequality); latecomer states' business leader focus on, 99, 102–107,

112; Shibusawa's views of, 117–118; UK social responsibility experiments for fairer distribution of, 20

Wegman, Ita, 271, 273

Weimar Republic, 74, 75, 79, 86, 96

Weleda, 272, 273, 281, 289, 331, 338, 354

Werth, Martha, 283–284

Wharton School, 130, 133, 149, 153

Whitehead, Alfred North: Donham and, 11, 131, 142–148, 150, 154–156, 185, 347; Romney quoting, 201; Steiner and, 269

Whole Foods Market, 229–230, 231, 244, 260, 261

women: beauty industry and, 238–241, 249–250, 254, 355; in biodynamic farming, 287, 290, 295–296; Cadbury's rules on married women not working, 32–33; ESG investing and, 307, 310–323; feminist movement, 224–226, 227, 240–241, 249–250; Filene's employment of, 54; Gilded Age wages for, 51; Indian efforts for rights of, 162, 170, 176–177, 225; Shibusawa's advocacy for education of, 120–121, 357; US postwar business employment of, 190; values-driven businesses and, 232, 238–241, 249–250, 254, 259; voting rights for, 18, 67, 224–225

Woodbrooke (Birmingham, UK), 39, 40, 160

workers compensation and accident insurance, 73, 76, 106

World War I: Bosch affected by, 85–86, 89, 90–91, 97; Cadbury's stance on, 42, 44, 348; environmental activism dissipated by, 223; Germany and, 74, 269, 270; India in, 158, 160, 164, 169; Japan in, 122; outbreak of, 74; Steiner's philosophy and, 269, 270; US entry into, 49

World War II: business school changes with, 151–152, 153, 154; Japan in, 123; Lalbhai's ethics during, 168; Nazi regime in (see Nazi regime); outbreak of, 95; US businesses and, 185–186, 197, 213; US entry into, 153

Zoroastrianism, 104, 106, 124, 268, 347